Satire:
Modern Essays
in Criticism

Edited by
RONALD PAULSON
The Johns Hopkins University

Satire:
Modern Essays
in Criticism

PRENTICE-HALL, INC. *Englewood Cliffs, New Jersey*

Prentice-Hall English Literature Series
MAYNARD MACK, *Editor*

Library of Congress Catalog Card Number: 70–124339

P 13-791236-6
C 13-791244-7

Printed in the United States of America

Current Printing (last number):
10 9 8 7 6 5 4 3 2 1

Prentice-Hall International, Inc., *London*
Prentice-Hall of Australia, Pty. Ltd., *Sydney*
Prentice-Hall of Canada, Ltd., *Toronto*
Prentice-Hall of India Private Limited, *New Delhi*
Prentice-Hall of Japan, Inc., *Tokyo*

Contents

v

Introduction

Quintilian said of the Romans, "Satura totra nostra est"—*satura* is wholly our invention. We can say with almost as great assurance that the criticism of satire is our invention. Discussion of satire before the twentieth century was to a large extent confined to its etymology, its social function (general or particular ridicule), and the motives of the satirist (good or ill nature). The only fruitful theorizers about the nature of the satiric form or experience were the practitioners themselves, most often in their apologias. Dryden, Pope, Byron, and Shaw were essentially defenders of their own practice and character. Literary critics devoted themselves to the more general species comedy, and by the mid-eighteenth century when systematic attention might have been paid to ridicule, comedy's satiric aspect, it had become a poor cousin not much talked of. It remained so until the twentieth century. Only in the last few decades has a poetics of satire been attempted and to a large extent worked out.

Clearly, comedy and satire shade off into one another, and it is by no means unreasonable to subsume satire under the larger, happier, and more philosophically viable term "comedy." In the great mass of literary and philosophical theories of comedy that converge on the twentieth century, satire is often incidentally illuminated. Some theories of comedy are almost what we might now call theories of satire. The two most all-embracing physiological and psychological (affective) theories of the comic are superiority (triumph) and release (liberty). These correspond to two equally basic satiric effects: the insider's ridicule of the outsider, and his explosion of freedom as he breaks out of (or discomfits) a stultifying, over-codified society. A third category, oscillation or attitude-mixing, can, as a satiric method, work either for triumph or release. Even the incongruity theories that grew up in the eighteenth century to explain the nonsatiric sources of laughter have produced a series of comic dualities (that is, the idea entertained vs. the sensuously discernible object, or the ideal vs. the actual), which, with a small shift of emphasis, become superiority theories: when one side becomes normative, the other is ridiculed.[1] There is only one kind of laughter that per se cannot become satiric. That is the laughter of sympathy—all laughter *with* as opposed to *at* an object. As soon as the laughter turns at something or somebody, it is approaching the satiric range.

Henri Bergson's essay *Laughter* (1900), which opened the new century, makes the source of laughter the apprehension of a mechanical encrustation on the vital or natural. Without writing on satire himself, he exerted a large influence on the people who later did. For, as he makes clear, his theory is a social one. The ideal is elasticity, adaptability, the *élan vital*, and so the laughable is the inelastic or rigid. To take one of his own well-known, excruciatingly unfunny jokes: Cassini the astronomer has invited a lady to see an eclipse of the moon. Arriving too late, the lady says, "M. de Cassini, I know, will have the goodness to begin it all over again, to please me."[2] According to Bergson, nature is here disguised or mechanized. The lady thinks that Cassini has faked the eclipse, and such a fake is a disguise of nature, a rigid encrustation on it, and this is comic. But there are other possible interpretations of this joke: the society lady who expects all nature, the whole solar system, to be at her beck and call, is contrasted with the solar system itself, nature, and ideas of cosmic *élan vital*. Since it is only a brief joke, almost abstract in its simplicity, Arthur Koestler is probably right that the comic effect results from sheer incongruity.[3] But I think it is evident that the joke contains at least the germ of a satiric situation. Bergson's theory of comedy leads in fact to the analysis of Quixotic behavior—a man acting according to a rigid code that is at odds with the complexity of his own nature and of the world.

Freud's comments on tendentious wit also cast light on satire, as do the insights of Ramon Fernandez, James Feibleman, and many other theorists of comedy.[4] Nevertheless, I have included in this collection only essays that talk about something called "satire." The step from talking about comedy to talking about satire was not an unimportant one and tells us something about our times. For the criticism of satire in the twentieth century is a phenomenon parallel to the writing of satire, which after more than a century of stagnation suddenly came to life with the disillusionment with western society that culminated in the First World War. A second wave of satires, following the Second World War, bore yet a more somber message. If this was an "age of satire" in all forms from novel and drama through stand-up comedians, it was partly because the existentialist view of life, which best fitted the circumstances, seemed to be more accurately reflected in satire than in any other literary mode.

Ronald Knox's essay of 1927, "Satire and Humor," was an important first step because it answered the essayists on comedy, speaking out for the importance and universality of satire as against humor, and ending with a call for the writing of satire. The first apologia for the contemporary satirist, it served as a stimulus to the young Evelyn Waugh and other emergent satirists, and at the same time laid down the assumptions of moral responsibility and artistic control upon which David Worcester built his *Art of Satire* (1940), the first serious book-length rehabilitation of satire.

Looking back on the 1920s, Wyndham Lewis (with W. H. Auden, one of the few practicing satirists to write on satire) gave a much broader interpretation of satire's importance. What he meant by "satire" was not too different from T. E. Hulme's "classicism"; its value, aesthetic not moral, is as a critical, ironic, coolly surgical instrument which is contrasted to the Romantic poet's beautician-work on experience. If we apply Lewis' definition, a kind of satiric climate can be discerned in the works of the post-Flaubertians from Joyce and Eliot to Lewis himself. The Victorian sensibility is, explicitly or implicitly, the butt of a satiric way of regarding experience.

Eliot's immensely influential poetry of the 1920s was in a broad sense satiric, and the analytic criticism which derived from his essays and throve on his poetry was an ideal instrument for dealing with irony, ambiguity, and tension in literary works. Eliot's Prufrock and Tiresias were not different in kind from the feigned speakers of many of Swift's and Pope's satires; the allusive method of Eliot was very similar to that of Dryden and Pope in their major satires. The crux of satiric defenses had always been the much-abused character of the satirist himself. Now the rhetorical and fictive quality of satire was stressed by Worcester and Maynard Mack, who argued that it is not an angry man cursing his enemy, but a very cool artist playing, when necessary, at being angry, manipulating his masks and his audience, modulating from high burlesque to low and from contemporary allusions to classical. Distance, control, and strategy are what raise satire above mere quarrelsomeness. Satire's reliance on rhetoric allowed analytic techniques of the New Criticism to be applied which would never have pertained usefully to comedy. One result was a great many excellent analyses of the satiric operation of particular authors and their works, which might be collected with profit in another volume the size of the present one.

The New Criticism also tended to judge poetry by the criterion of organic unity, and so the writers on satire in the 1940s and 1950s attempted to distinguish "satire" as a form from "satiric"—a general tone. The beginnings of this development, however, were in anthropology and classical philology, with exploration of the magic powers of the satirist and the meaning of *satura*—the term designating Roman formal verse satire. With the impact of Fraser's *Golden Bough* and F. M. Cornford's *Origin of Attic Comedy*, the form of the fertility ritual affected theories of all the major genres. If the ritual combat (agon) between the Old Year and the New, Summer and Winter, Rainfull and Drought, the Old King and the New, is divided into segments, a series of actions can be formulated. The death of the old—the element of sacrifice—is the chosen province of tragedy; the victory of the new (becoming associated with the true) is the focus of comedy; and the exorcising of the old, sterile, and false (process rather than, an in the other two cases, drama) is that of satire. From these insights followed F. N. Robinson's study of the satirist as magician, the exorcist of sterility, and satire's derivation from the primitive curse. (Jessie Weston's *From Ritual to Romance* and once again Eliot's *Waste Land*, drew literary attention to this aspect of satire.) The equivalent of Robinson's essay among the classicists was G. L. Hendrickson's study of the Roman form *satura*, which corresponded in interesting ways to the satiric part of the fertility ritual. Drawing on both sources, Mary Claire Randolph described the formal characteristics of *satura* as an $A-B$ structure, with A representing the presentation of the evil or folly and B the indication of an ideal or norm against which A is judged. As she found, satire, in spite of its apparently casual organization, has a strong unity of subject and theme, dependent on redundancies of images, allusions, and locutions. Most satire is formally conservative, following the general structural lines of Horace and Juvenal. It offered, in fact, as simple and obvious a case of unity as a New Critic could wish for.

These points were established and perhaps over-established. The emphasis on satire's controlled artistry elicited a counter-attack in the late 1950s and the 1960s—in Robert C. Elliott's exploration of the unsettling effects that remain in even the most sophisticated literary satire, and also in Edward W. Rosenheim's argument that satire was after all only an attack on discernible historic particulars. The most influential of these modifications was Northrop Frye's *Anatomy of Criticism*, in which the *A–B* structure of satire was extended into a "myth" of a false society combating and overwhelming a true society. Frye called the whole satiric experience, which covers almost as large an area as Wyndham Lewis' "satire," the "Mythos of Winter," and made this a species and subsection of "mythic" truth about experience in general.

All of these approaches returned the center of satiric study from the structural integrity of the particular literary work to the poet, his audience, his historical context, and general extrinsic truths. What emerges, I believe, are two strains of satire studies, sometimes joined. One is concerned more with the similarities between all satires and the other with their dissimilarities. The first treats the myths, the conventions, the schemata that lie under and even shape all satire. Thus Frye and Alvin Kernan would argue that no matter what the historic particular—a Domitian, a Walpole, or a Castlereagh—the satiric "world" or "scene" is the same, crowded and chaotic with the same symbols of decay and corruption. On the other hand there are studies of the devices, the rhetorical tricks and subterfuges, the particular symbols and displacements, which the satirist has developed over the centuries to meet specific challenges as well as society's growing distrust. Censorship, sentimentality, and apathy are among the roadblocks the satirist has overcome by the development of the apologia, irony, various personae, and elaborate fictions like that of the satirist satirized. These studies are moving in the direction of a history of the satiric mode in the same sense that Sir Kenneth Clark's *The Nude* and *Landscape into Art* are histories of the genres of the nude and landscape in painting.

A new, yet more immediate interest in satire has evolved in the last few years. 1945–55 was, inspite of great advances in satire writing and criticism, the heyday of tragedy as a prestige genre. In the aftermath of a terrible war against an evil enemy, writers tried to make their experience tragic, critics examined tragedies and the criticism of tragedy, course in tragedy were a popular part of the college curriculum, and tragedy was understood (as at other times in history) to be the highest genre to which a writer might aspire. But as the New Critical analyses of past tragedies (especially late Shakespearean and Jacobean and the increasing popular Euripidean) revealed the complex mixture of evil and good in the hero, and American intellectuals discovered what they took to be shocking depths of depravity in our own actions in recent wars and also in our fabled past, the satiric aspect of tragedy began to assume more prominence than the heroic. (O. J. Campbell had drawn attention to this aspect of tragedy in the late 1930s). Against such absolutes of human potentiality as the War, the Final Solution, the Bomb, and the bland American optimism of the 1950s, satire seemed the only appropriate point of view. Artists invented a long series of paradigms of the absurd, of which the sick joke, Lenny Bruce's routines, Joseph Heller's *Catch-22*, Thomas Pynchon's *V*, and William Burroughs' *Naked Lunch*, were specimens. The satiric tone, moreover, was found useful in discursive as well as imaginative writing to break down the pompous and tragic assumptions about (depending on one's politics) the stature of man or of society. Satire habitually turns tragic heroes into a Dr. Strangelove or a General Jack D. Ripper; the heroic quest becomes an obsession with technology and patriotism to the exclusion of all else.

The last decade, a time when it was hard to imagine anyone designating a highest genre, has seen experience through the eyes of the lowliest genre, which from Horace onward has deprecated its prosiness and lack of pretension to anything but the "truth." Moreover, whatever efficacy genres as such retained for some schools of criticism, they now appeared more compellingly as examples of conventions restricting the artistic imagination. It was not uncommon for critics to point at the sad effects of a writer trying to impose Aristotelian or Shakespearean conventions of tragedy on contemporary experience. According to the culture heroes of these years—Herbert Marcuse, Norman O. Brown, R. D. Laing, Marshall McLuhan—it was a time when conventions and other hidden persuaders were so thick and pervasive, so often unnoticed and dumbly accepted, that analytic instruments of all kinds, with satire the sharpest, were engaged to cut through them. The satirist's subversive quality, at least as he appears to society, became as important as the "power" of his satire.

Frye's *Anatomy of Criticism* is one of the cultural documents of our time at least partly because its characterization of the satiric world view in the "Mythos of Winter" sums up one general view of contemporary society in the 1960s shared by Marcuse and Laing, as well as by Heller and Pynchon. But Frye also makes clear that it is a mythical structure with no more or less validity than the myths of spring and autumn, and from his *Anatomy* we must infer a picture of the human mind as a clutter of unnoticed and uncriticized but restrictive conventions for ordering experience (hobbyhorses in E. H. Gombrich's sense).[5] Ironically but appropriately, satire, the tool for cutting and dissecting, also raises this problem for the literary historian with unique clarity. At least as late as the seventeenth and eighteenth centuries, and in many cases up to the present, satire was a real genre, regarded as such by writers, and with particular conventions. Moreover, it was one that infiltrated other forms of writing that often had less clear generic conventions. One direction criticism has taken, with satire as a prime specimen, is to broach the whole problem of the relationship of the artist's conscious or articulated meanings to those that slip in through various back doors by the conventions of the genre in which he writes, or are generated unawares by the very process of articulation. It might be illuminating to point out to a writer like Pynchon, whose whole exposure is of mechanical patterns of thought and action that have replaced feeling, that his own structures and assumptions are conventionally satiric.

Satire criticism, one must feel in closing this volume, is very much in *medias res*. Satire continues to serve as a test case for methodological experiments of the New Criticism's revisionist heirs, as well as of critics drawing upon the disciplines of anthropology, sociology, and philosophy. Past satire, as a way of looking at the world or as a system of formal structures, as a poet adapting himself to circumstances or playing an eternal refrain, represents an important part of the total aesthetic experience that must be explored and understood if we are to understand ourselves. And contemporary satire (unlike contemporary tragedy) is very much alive. As a way of expressing our experience it continues to grow and change in the hands of its practitioners, and to participate in our age we shall have to come to terms with its particularities.

Baltimore, Md.   R.P.

NOTES

1 The incongruity theory was developed in the eighteenth century as a reaction against the extreme statement of the superiority theory propounded by Thomas Hobbes; Lord Kames and James Beattie were its main theoreticians, and incongruity has been the basis of comic theory for later thinkers reaching from Kant and Schopenhauer to Arthur Koestler. For an excellent account of the theory's development, see Stuart Tave, *The Amiable Humorist* (Chicago: 1960).

2 Bergson, *Laughter*, in *Comedy*, ed. Wylie Sypher (New York: Doubleday Anchor Books, 1956), p. 89.

3 Koestler, *Insight and Outlook* (New York: Macmillan, 1949), p 418.

4 Freud, *Der Witz und seine Beziehung zum Unbewussten* (Vienna: 1905) and "Der Humor," Imago, XIV (1928); Fernandez, *Molière* (Paris: 1929); Feibleman, *In Praise of Comedy* (New York: 1939).

5 See Gombrich, "Meditations on a Hobby Horse or the Roots of Artistic Form," in *Meditations on a Hobby Horse and other Essays on the Theory of Art* (London, 1963), 1–11.

Satire:
   Modern Essays
      in Criticism

FRED NORRIS ROBINSON

Satirists and Enchanters in Early Irish Literature

It would appear from various references in Elizabethan writers that the feature of Irish literature which most impressed Englishmen of the time was the supposed power of Irish poets to work destruction with their verse. Sidney, at the end of his Defense of Poesy, in his parting curse upon the disdainer of the art, will not wish him "the ass's ears of Midas, nor to be driven by a Poet's verses, as Bubonax was, to hang himself, nor to be rhymed to death, as is said to be done in Ireland."[1] Again, in Reginald Scot's Discovery of Witchcraft, it is said that Irishmen, speaking of their witches, "will not stick to affirm that they can rhyme either man or beast to death."[2] And a number of writers refer to the destruction of rats by means of such potent verses. In the Epilogue to Ben Jonson's Poetaster,[3] the author declares that he will

> Rhyme them to death, as they do Irish rats,
> In drumming tunes;

and Rosalind, in As You Like It, humorously compares Orlando's rhymes to those which had released her soul from a lower existence and helped it to achieve its transmigration. "I was never so berhymed," she declares, "since Pythagoras' time, that I was an Irish rat, which I can hardly remember."[4]

From *Studies in the History of Religions Presented to Crawford Howell Toy*, ed. D. G. Lyon and G. F. Moore (New York, 1912), pp. 95–130. Reprinted by permission of The Macmillan Company.

1

The story of the destruction or expulsion of rats or mice is told of a number of Irishmen in different periods. In fact Eugene O'Curry, who made a report on the subject in 1855, for the Royal Irish Academy,[5] remarks that he once tried to perform the feat himself, but failed, perhaps because his words were too hard for the vermin to understand! The most famous early instance, probably, is that of the poet Senchan, who lived in the seventh century. According to the Proceedings of the Great Bardic Institution (Imtheacht na Tromdhaimhe),[6] a tale of the Middle Irish period, an egg which had been saved for Senchan's meal was eaten up by the "nimble race," namely, the mice. "That was not proper for them," said Senchan; "nevertheless there is not a king or chief, be he ever so great, but these mice would wish to leave the traces of their own teeth in his food; and in that they err, for food should not be used by any person after (the print of) their teeth; and I will satirize them." Then follow stanzas in which Senchan threatens the mice with death, and they beg him to accept compensation instead. As a result of his verses, ten mice fell dead in his presence; whereupon he said to them: "It is not you that I ought to have satirized, but the party whose duty it is to suppress you, namely, the tribe of cats." And then he pronounced a satire on Irusan, the chief, lord, and Brehon of all the cats. But the victim this time took the attack less meekly. Irusan came—"blunt-mouthed, rapacious, panting, determined, jagged-eared, broad-breasted, prominent-jointed, sharp and smooth-clawed, split-nosed, sharp and rough-toothed, thick-mouthed, nimble, powerful, deep-flanked, terror-striking, angry, extremely vindictive, quick, purring, glare-eyed,"—in this guise he came and carried off Senchan on his back; and the poet, after trying flattery without avail, was barely saved by St. Kieran, who killed Irusan as he passed his cell.

Exploits like these doubtless appealed to the English as being particularly appropriate to poets of the "wild Irish," whose extraordinary character and customs were a favorite topic with British writers from Giraldus Cambrensis down to Edmund Spenser.[7] And the story of Senchan itself is old enough to have been known in England before the days of Elizabeth.

The Middle Irish account of the "Great Bardic Company" will be discussed again later. But it is already clear from the passages quoted that "satire," or the Irish term which is so translated, is not employed in the ordinary English sense of the word. The poet's victims, whether rats and cats, as in the tale of Senchan, or men, as in many

stories to be mentioned later, are not destroyed by the natural operation of literary art. The verses used are magic spells, and the whole
procedure belongs in the realm of sorcery. This was recognized by
Reginald Scot, who classed the Irish rat-spells with other performances
of witches or "eye-biters"; and by Sir William Temple, who associated
the Irish practice in question with the magic runes of the ancient
Teutons.[8] The use of incantations to accomplish supernatural ends,
whether of good or evil, is so familiar the world over that this obvious
interpretation of the Irish story needs no defence or illustration; and
one might at first be disposed to dismiss the whole matter with the
suggestion that "satire" is not a suitable translation of the Irish term
for such verses as those of Senchan. There is manifestly a "long and
large difference" between these talismanic spells, often half-meaning-
less in content, and the highly acute and intellectual form of poetry
which has been chiefly known in Europe by the name of satire. It
seems like an unjustifiable looseness in language to use the same word
for such dissimilar things. But as soon as one begins to examine the
so-called satirical material in Irish literature, one finds difficulties in
dispensing with the name. In the first place, the Irish language itself
employs the same words (most commonly *aer* and its derivatives)[9] for
the rat-spells of Senchan and for the stricter satire of a later age.
Furthermore, the persons described as pronouncing satires, even of the
old destructive sort, were by no means always mere enchanters, but in
many cases poets of high station, either in history or in saga. And
finally, the subjects of their maleficent verse—often, for example, the
inhospitality or other vices of chieftains—are such as might form suitable themes of genuine satire; and the purpose of the poets is frequently described as being to produce ridicule and shame. In short, it
seems impossible in old Celtic literature to draw a line between what is
strictly satire and what is not; and one ends by realizing that, for the
ancient Celts themselves, the distinction did not exist. Just as their
poets were not clearly separable from druids and medicine-men, but
often combined in one person the functions of all three,[10] so they
freely mingled natural and supernatural processes in the practice of
their arts. Destructive spells and poems of slander or abuse were all
thought of together as the work, and it sometimes seems almost the
chief work, of the tribal man of letters. And the retention of one term
for all these products, at least while speaking of a literature where
such conditions prevailed, is certainly defensible, and may be positively
instructive in emphasizing the continuity of literary development.

Of course it is not to be supposed that Irish literature is peculiar in the respects that have been described. The combination of the functions of poet and magician is characteristic of early stages of civilization and appears in many parts of the world. Among various peoples, too, the satirical office of the poet has been given special prominence; and where this is the case, in simple states of society, a certain amount of sorcery may always be suspected in the poet's work. But in the literature of the *Kulturvölker* evidence is not always preserved of the lower civilization that went before, and the relation between sorcery and satire is by no means everywhere apparent. In Greek and Latin, for example, there are comparatively few traces of the magician-poet, though the use of incantations was common enough in ancient classical civilization and the terms ἐπαοιδή and *carmen* have a well-recognized magic association.[11] The familiar story of Archilochus, whose iambics led to the death of Lycambes and his daughters, shows, to be sure, the destructive power of satire. But it is hardly a case in point, unless it be assumed that an original story of magical destruction has been rationalized into an account of death from shame; and there is no necessity for such an assumption.[12] In general, the satire of the Greeks and Romans cannot be easily traced back beyond a fairly sophisticated age;[13] and the satire of modern Europe, it may be added, is in large measure classical and literary in origin.

Better parallels to the Irish situation are furnished by the popular poetry of ancient Arabia. There, according to an opinion which has found favour with Arabic scholars, the common name of the poet, *Shā'ir*, meant originally "the knowing one, the one possessed of supernatural knowledge."[14] There, as in Ireland, the satirical function of the order is very conspicuous. Men give the poets rich gifts to escape disfavor, or place them under restraint and punishment as dangerous persons. In one instance, it is said, the Calif Al-Mansur abandoned marriage with a noble woman of the Taghlib for fear of the effects of a satire which Djarir had pronounced against her. A large number of the old Arabic satires have been preserved, and with regard to them, as with regard to the Irish poems, it is hard to say how far they are real lampoons and how far incantations.[15] The supernatural element, so far as the present writer has observed, is less emphasized in the Arabic than in the Irish, and there is more real satire, more genuine mockery or criticism, in the Arabic verses. The Arabs had perhaps advanced a step farther than the Irish from the stage of the magician-poet.[16] But, on the whole, the similarity between the two literatures in the matters under discussion is most striking and instructive.

Among the peoples of central and northern Europe it can hardly be doubted that conditions like those of the Irish once prevailed, though evidence on the subject is comparatively scanty. Incantations make up an important element in the popular poetry of the Finns, and Comparetti has argued effectively to show that the primary sense of the Finnish *runo* was a magic spell.[17] But it is not clear that there was much development in the direction of personal satire. In old Germanic poetry there can be no question as to the prevalence of the *Zauberlied*,[18] and there is also testimony, though not so abundant as one could wish, to the existence of the *Spottlied* from a very early time.[19] That the two types probably stood in close relation, it is one of the purposes of the present discussion to show. But the existence of the destructive satirists on Germanic territory is not altogether a matter of inference. Their practices seem to be contemplated in an ecclesiastical canon of the year 744.[20] A definite case also seems to be furnished by the story of *Hug timidus*, in the ninth century, whose servants sang against him and inspired such terror that the victim did not dare step out of doors.[21] Coming down to later ages, it is well known that in Iceland of the saga period, satirical poems were greatly feared and the poets were strictly dealt with in the laws;[22] and even in the seventeenth century Isaac de la Peyrère, a French traveller in Iceland, testified to the belief that the wound given by a mad dog was "scarce more dangerous than [the] venomous satyrs" of the poets.[23] It is possible, moreover, that the common name for a poet in the West Germanic languages (Anglo-Saxon *scop*, Old High German *scof*) contains the same root as the verb "to scoff." The etymology is not well enough established to be used as proof of the importance of satirical verse among the West Germanic peoples; but on the other hand, such evidence from other literatures as has here been presented removes any serious objection, on semasiological grounds, to the association of the two groups of words.[24]

The poets of the Celts seem to have been famous, even in antiquity, for their use of satire and malediction. One of the oldest classical references to Celtic literature, a well-known passage in Diodorus Siculus, perhaps derived by him from Posidonius, says that the bards, "singing to instruments like lyres, praise some men and abuse others."[25] And down to modern times, in both the main branches of Celtic

literature, the Gaelic and the Brythonic, the twofold function of the
bards, to praise and to blame, has been well recognized and freely
exerted. Their supernatural power, too, has never ceased to be feared;
and it was related of no less a poet than Dafydd ap Gwilym, almost
a contemporary of Chaucer, that he killed a literary antagonist by the
virulence of his verse.[26] On the whole, as might be expected, the magic
aspect of the satirist's work was more emphasized in the early ages of
lower civilization, and it is consequently conspicuous in Irish literature,
which preserves most abundant evidence concerning those periods.
Irish also exhibits very clearly the close connection between the poetry
of magic malediction and the poetry of mockery and abuse, and shows
the importance of satire, of whatever sort, as an element in the life of
simple peoples. Numerous provisions concerning satirists appear in the
ancient law of the land; their maledictions are even recognized among
the sanctions of treaties; rules for the making of satires are laid down
in the native treatises on poetry; and in the ancient popular sagas the
part of satirist is played again and again by important poets, whose
power often determines the fate of national heroes.

Some of the evidence of these peculiar conditions will be taken
up in the pages that follow. But a brief explanation of the Irish terms
for satire ought perhaps to be given first. Satirists are often referred
to in Irish texts by the general words for poet (*file, bard, licerd, aes
dana*, etc.), druid (*drui*), or seer (*fáith*); and it has already been
pointed out that the classes named are freely confused, or at least
exchange their functions, in the older sagas.[27] With specific reference
to satire the terms most frequently employed are *aer* and *cáined* and
their derivatives. Common use is also made of *ainmed*, "blemishing,"
imdergad, "reddening," and *rindad*, "cutting"; all of which seem to
have reference primarily to the physical effects of the satirist's attack.
Somewhat less frequent in occurrence are *ail*, "disgrace," *aithgiud*,
"sharpening" (?), *aithisiugud*, "reviling," *ainfhialad*, "dishonoring,"
cuitbiud, "laughter, ridicule," *ecnad*, "reviling" (sometimes used in the
religious sense of "blaspheming"), *mifhoclad*, "speaking ill," and
sinnad, of which the primary sense is not clear. The word *glám*,
especially in the phrase *glám dichenn*, usually refers to a special
form of incantation which will be described later, but it is sometimes more loosely employed;[28] and *groma*, likewise, appears in the
laws to be associated with a particular process called the *glasgabail*.[29]
Of only occasional, or even rare, occurrence are *dul*, explained in
Cormac's Glossary as *cainte*, "satirist";[30] *runa*, once used in the laws
for satires;[31] and *bired* or *berach*, uncertain both in form and in mean-

ing, but apparently applied to a woman-satirist in a passage of the laws.[32] The word *crosan*, also, of which the usual meaning is "juggler" or "buffoon," sometimes means "satirist" as well.[33] Names for satire and the practitioners of the art are thus seen to be rather numerous in the Irish language, and they describe various aspects of the satirists' work. Some of them are restricted in application, but the majority are used loosely, and appear frequently in combination of two or three even when referring to a single satirical performance. It is noteworthy, moreover, that in their use no distinction is made, or at all events steadily maintained, between the natural and the supernatural, between the satire of magic malediction and the satire of mockery or abuse.

To come to the actual accounts of the Irish satirists, frequent mention of them is made in the various tracts of the Brehon laws, which preserve, as is well known, most valuable evidence of the conditions of ancient Irish life. It is clear that satirical attacks were a common form of injury in all classes of society.[34] In the law of distress (i.e., the law relating to the seizure of property to be held for the enforcement of a claim) it is provided that three days' stay shall regularly be allowed in cases of ordinary satire, slander, betrayal, or false witness;[35] but five days' stay is the prescribed period for other offences, among which are the blemish of a nickname, satirizing a man after his death, and satire of exceptional power (?).[36] In these passages satire is classified with "crimes of the tongue." Elsewhere, as in the law relating to *eric*-fines, satirizing and assault are treated together,[37] and again, these two forms of injury are associated with the stealing of a man's cattle or the violation of his wife.[38] The damages allowed for satire, as for other injuries, depend in part upon the rank of the person injured. It is more serious to satirize a king's son than a lower chief,[39] and a henchman has a smaller indemnity than a chief of *aire-fene* rank.[40] From several places it appears that satire was in some way to be resisted;[41] and a distinction is made between lawful and unlawful satire, comparable, as O'Curry has pointed out, to the distinction in the English law of libel.[42] Just as in the case of fasting against an enemy or a debtor—a familiar old Irish method of enforcing a claim or extorting a benefit[43]—so in this matter of persecution by poets, the law seems to have recognized, and to have sought to regulate, an ancient custom which was liable to dangerous abuse.

In the treatise on Customary Law there is a general analysis of crime (Irish *eitged*, a term which apparently had the general meaning of "excess" or "abnormality"), and several kinds of satire are men-

tioned, though the distinctions among them are not made very clear.[44]
Eitged of words is said to comprise spying, satirizing, and nicknaming.
"White *eitged*" is distinguished from "black *eitged*," the white of
flattery from the black of satire. "Speckled *eitged*" is explained as
referring to the three words of warning, *gromfa gromfa, glamfa
glamfa, aerfa aerfa,* which the English translator of the laws, for lack
of specific equivalents, renders "I will *grom*-satirize, I will *grom*-
satirize; I will *glam*-satirize, I will *glam*-satirize; I will satirize, I will
satirize." *Aeraim* (future *aerfa*) is the most usual word for "satirize,"
as already stated;[45] *glamfa* is said by the Irish commentator on the
passage to refer to the *glam dichenn*, which will be described later;[46]
and *gromfa* is similarly connected with the *glas-gabail*, a procedure of
uncertain character.[47] That "speckled *eitged*" is fundamentally of
magical nature is clear from the whole account of it.

Another legal compilation, the Heptads,[48] designates seven kinds
of satire and discusses the "honor-price" appropriate to each: "There
are with the Feine seven kinds of satire for which *dire* is estimated;
a nickname which clings; recitation of a satire of insults in his absence;
to satirize the face; to laugh on all sides; to sneer at his form; to
magnify a blemish; satire which is written by a bard who is far away,
and which is recited."[49] This classification, which is clearly the product of custom rather than of pure logic, is not altogether clear, even
with the glosses of the native commentators. But the passage shows
the usual association of mockery, invective, and magical injury. It is
followed by regulations, which need not be repeated here, concerning
the payment of honor-price to the aggrieved man and his descendants.

In decidedly the greater number of passages in the laws satire
is treated as a kind of misdemeanor and the satirist condemned. Thus
satirists are classed among the men for whom no one may go surety;[50]
and woman-satirists, along with thieves, liars, and bush-strumpets, are
said to have no claim to an honor-price.[51] Similarly, the son of a
woman-satirist, like the son of a bondmaid, is declared to be ineligible
to chieftaincy.[52] And the same disparagement of the class appears in
the definition of a demon-banquet as "a banquet given to the sons of
death and bad men, i.e., to lewd persons and satirists, and jesters, and
buffoons, and mountebanks, and outlaws, and heathens, and harlots,
and bad people in general; which is not given for earthly obligation or
for heavenly reward—such a feast is forfeited to the demon."[53] In all
these places reference seems to be made primarily to a low sort of
sorcerers and traffickers in personal abuse. But the satirist was not

always so conceived by the makers of the laws. Just as there was a distinction, already referred to, between lawful and unlawful satire, so the poet was sometimes praised and rewarded, rather than blamed, for his exercise of the satirizing function. It may be doubted whether an honor or a reproach to the order is implied by the law that puts the house of a satirist, along with that of a king and that of a thief, among those into which it is forbidden to drive cattle seized in distraint;[54] but other references are less ambiguous. Because of his office as eulogist and satirist alike, the poet is mentioned among the men who have the special privilege of speaking in public.[55] In another place, poets are declared to have peculiar rights and claims because of their services in composing lawful praise on the one hand, and on the other hand, in levying taxes in territories where "points of satire" are regarded and where "points of weapons" are not.[56] And the same power of the poets which is reckoned as a means of enforcing tribute, is also invoked in treaties as a sanction of their observance.[57] The satire employed for such purposes was doubtless for the most part wizardry, but it may have included some ridicule and some appeal to the public opinion of the tribe.[58] At all events, by virtue of its exercise, the satirists obtained a considerable degree of recognition as public servants.

The formal recognition, and even the Christian adoption, of the old satire, with all its magic elements, is further strongly implied in the prescription of the ceremony for the *glám-dichenn*. This is preserved, not in the laws, though the *glám-dichenn* is frequently named there, but in one of the Middle Irish treatises on versification,[59] which describes the procedure against a king who refuses the proper reward for a poem. First there was fasting on the land of the king, and a council of thirty laymen and thirty bishops and thirty poets as to making a satire; and it was a crime to prevent the satire after the reward for the poem was refused. Then the poet himself with six others, on whom the six degrees of poets had been conferred, had to go at sunrise to a hilltop on the boundary of seven lands; and the face of each degree of them toward his own land, and the face of the ollave there toward the land of the king whom he would satirize, and the backs of them all toward a hawthorn which should be on the top of the hill, and the wind from the north, and a slingstone and a thorn of the hawthorn in every man's hand, and each of them to sing a stave in a prescribed metre into the slingstone and the thorn, the ollave singing his stave before the others, and they afterwards singing their staves at once; and each was then to put his stone and his thorn at the butt of the hawthorn. And if it were they that were in the wrong, the earth of the hill would swallow them up. But if it were the king that was in the wrong, the earth would swallow up him and his wife and his son and his horse and his arms and his dress and his hound. The curse (*glám*) of the *Mac fuirmed*[60] fell on the hound; the curse of the *fochloc* on the dress; the curse of the *doss* on the arms; the curse of the *cano* on the wife; the curse of the *cli* on the son; the curse of the *anradh* on the land; the curse of the ollave on the king himself.[61]

Whether this elaborate ceremony was actually in common practice does not matter fundamentally to the present discussion. It may have been largely invented, or at least embellished, by some *file* with a turn for magical liturgy. Certainly the thirty bishops are suspicious participants; and references to the *glám dichenn* in Irish literature do not usually suggest such a complicated affair. The bishops, however, it is to be observed, do not actually have a part in the *glám dichenn*, but only in the preliminary council which sanctions the proceedings. There is plenty of evidence, moreover, as will appear later, that Irish poets did join in companies for making or pronouncing satires; and the characteristic features of the ceremony here described—the fasting, the sympathetic magic, and the assumed retroaction of the unjust curse—are all unassailable elements of popular practice or belief.

The passages cited from the Brehon laws, or used in explanation of them, seem to show pretty clearly the importance of poetic malediction and satire in the life of the ancient Irish, and the impression derived from the laws is borne out by frequent references in the heroic tales and historical documents. In texts of the strict Old Irish period—that is, those preserved in Old Irish manuscripts—no actual accounts of satire have been noted by the writer, though some of the words regularly used for it already occur in documents of the time.[62] In view of the fact that the Old Irish texts are chiefly glosses, the lack of such material is not surprising. But Cormac's Glossary, which is generally conceded, though the manuscripts of it are Middle Irish, to be a work of the ninth or tenth century, and which is therefore one of the earliest documents preserving any considerable quantity of native Irish tradition, contains a score or more of references to the custom. Several words are there explained as having to do with the satirist or his work. *Leos* is defined as "a blush wherewith a person is reddened after a satire or reproach of him"; and one meaning of *ferb* is said to be "a blotch which is put on the face of a man after a satire or false judgment."[63] A similar conception of the physical effect of satire (which will be discussed again later) appears in the definition of *rinntaid,* "*nomen* for a man of satire, who wounds or cuts each face." Both *groma* and *glam* are defined, and the latter explained as coming *ab eo quod est clamor.* The etymology, like that proposed for *cainte,* satirist,—"i.e., *canis,* a dog, for the satirist has a dog's head in barking, and alike is the profession they follow"— has no value in the eyes of modern science, but such comments are of some incidental interest. And this is particularly true of the etymology proposed for *file,* poet, "from poison (*fi*) in satire and splendour (*li*) in praise." The derivation is again impossible, but in associating the word for poet with the "poison of satire" Cormac anticipates, on the semasiological side, the modern theories, already mentioned, with regard to the Germanic words "scop" and "scoff."[64]

More interesting, however, than any of these definitions[65] are four actual pieces of old satirical verse which Cormac has preserved among his citations. Under *riss,* "story," a line is quoted and declared to come from the poem of Coirpre mac Etaine against Bres mac Elathain, the first satire which was made in Ireland. Under *cernine,* "dish," another line from the same poem is cited; but Cormac no- where gives the rest of the satire. In the saga of the Second Battle of Moytura,[66] however, the whole story is told to which allusion is made in the passages cited. According to this account, Coirpre, the poet of the Tuatha, Dé Danann, once came a-guesting to the house of Bres. "He entered a cabin narrow, black, dark, wherein there was neither fire nor furniture nor bed. Three small cakes, and they dry, were brought to him on a little dish. On the morrow he arose, and he was not thankful. As he went across the garth, he said:

> Without food quickly on a dish;
> Without a cow's milk whereon a calf grows;
> Without a man's abode under the gloom (?) of night;[67]
> Without paying a company of story-tellers—let that be Bres's condition."

As a result of the verse it is said that nought save decay was on Bres from that hour.

Under the word *Munnu*, interpreted as *Mo Fhinnu*, a pet name, the following quatrain is quoted and said to come from the satire of Maedoc Ferna against Munnu, the son of Tulchan:

> O little vassal of mighty God!
> O son of Tulchan, O Shepherd!
> She bore a troublesome child to a family,
> The mother that bore thee, Fintan!

Other evidence concerning this satire has apparently not been preserved; in fact some very similar lines are quoted in the commentary on the Martyrology of Oengus and attributed to Columbcille.[68]

A third quatrain, which also appears, as Stokes points out, to be of satirical character, is quoted under the word *rer*, "blackbird."

> Hard to thee[69] the little stripling,
> Son of the little blackbird!
> Have thou every good thing ready before him,
> O little head (that is, O head of a little goose)!

The son of the little blackbird is doubtless the poet Flann Mac Lonain, whom the Four Masters call "the Virgil of the race of the Scots"; and the person addressed is Finnguine, King of Cashel, known as Cenngegain, "head of a little goose." The lines contain little more than word-play on the diminutive formations in the names, and the circumstances referred to are unknown.[70]

A typical story of satire, as it was employed among the Irish, is attached to a fourth stanza, quoted by Cormac under the word *gaire*, "shortness (of life)." The lines are said to have been uttered by Nede, the son of Adnae, against Caier, his uncle, the king of Connaught, and the whole episode is narrated in the version of Cormac's Glossary in the Yellow Book of Lecan.[71] "Caier," as the tale goes, "had adopted Nede as his son, because he had no son at all. The mind of Caier's wife clave unto Nede. She gave an apple of silver unto Nede for his love. Nede consented not, and she promised him half the realm after Caier, if he would go in unto her. 'How shall this happen to us?' said Nede. 'Not difficult,' said the woman, 'make thou a satire on him, so that a blemish come upon him. Then the man with the blemish shall be no longer king.' 'Not easy to me is this thing; the man will not make refusal to me. There is nothing in the world in his possession that he will not give me.' 'I know,' said the woman, 'a thing that he will not give thee, namely, the dagger that was brought him from the lands of Alba he will not give thee; he is forbidden to part with it.' Nede asked Caier for the dagger. 'Woe is me,' said Caier, 'I am forbidden to part with it.' Nede made a *glám dichenn* upon him, and three blisters came forth on his cheeks. This is the satire:

> Evil, death, short life to Caier!
> Let spears of battle wound him, Caier!
> Gaier...! Caier...! Caier under earth,
> Under ramparts, under stones be Caier![72]

Caier arose next morning early (and went) to the well. He put his hand over his countenance. He found on his face three blisters which the satire had caused, namely, Stain, Blemish, and Defect, to wit, red, and green, and white. Caier fled thence that none might see the disgrace, until he was in Dún Cermnai with Cacher, son of Eitirscél. Nede took the realm of Connaught after him. He was there till the end of a year. Grievous unto him was Caier's torment. Nede went after him to Dún Cermnai, seated in Caier's chariot, and Caier's wife and his greyhound were with him. Fair was the chariot that went to the fort! His face told how it was with him. 'Whose is that color?' said every one. Said Caier: 'Twas we that rode on his high seat by the seat of the charioteer.' 'That is a king's word,' said Cacher, son of Eitirscél. (Caier was not known to him up to that time.) 'No, truly, I am not,' said Caier. With that Caier fled (?) from them out of the house, till he was on the flagstone behind the fort. Nede went, in his chariot into the fort. The dogs pursued Caier's track until they found him under the flagstone behind the fort. Caier died for shame on seeing Nede. The rock flamed at Caier's death, and a fragment of the rock flew up under Nede's eye, and pierced into his head." The exact manner of Nede's punishment is differently described in a stanza on the justice of his fate, with which the account ends:

> A stone that happened to be under Caier's foot
> Sprang up the height of a sail-tree,
> Fell—not unjust was the decree—
> On the head of the poet from above.

A number of elements in this story are of interest to the student of early institutions and beliefs: the symbolical use, for example, of the apple of silver,[73] or the peculiar prohibition (Irish *geis*, a kind of taboo) which forbade Caier to part with his dagger,[74] or the provision that a king with a bodily blemish must abdicate his throne.[75] But attention must here be called rather to what concerns the satire itself—to the poet's effort to find an excuse for his attack, to his final punishment for unjust satire, in spite of his ruse, and to the detailed account of the blemishing effect of his maledictory verse. The pimples, blushes, or other kinds of disfigurement produced by satire have been several times referred to in passages previously cited. Here in the story of Caier three blotches, red, green, and white, are definitely mentioned, and called Stain, Blemish, and Defect. The allegorical interpretation may be relatively late, though such treatment of abstract qualities is by no means without parallel in early Irish literature. But the general conception of facial disfigurement as the result of magic persecution or even as a punishment for some form of misbehavior is very widespread. Among the Irish the affliction was visited not only on the victim of an incantation, as in the case of Caier, but sometimes on the poet himself,[76] if his satire was unjust, and also on a judge who rendered an unjust verdict.[77] Somewhat similar is the case of Bricriu, mentioned in the Scéla Conchobair maic Nessa, who had a boil rise from his forehead whenever he tried to withhold a secret.[78] And many readers will recall, what is at bottom the same idea, the Greek belief, mentioned by Bacon in his essay "Of Praise," that "he that was praised to his hurt should have a push rise upon his nose; as we say that a blister will rise upon one's tongue that tells a lie."[79] That there is a physiological basis for all such notions no one, in these days of psychotherapy, will be disposed to deny.[80]

Of the four satirical pieces that have been quoted from the Glossary of Cormac, two, it is to be noted, are really incantations, and two are rather mocking than maledictory in tone. Thus the examples of satire in an early document show the same confusion of different types that was observed in the references to the subject in the laws. And this close association of incantational verse with other forms of poetry will frequently appear in the accounts of satirists to be cited from Irish sagas.

In the further illustration of the subject from these sources no attempt will be made to follow a strict chronological order of events. Some of the saga material to be used is doubtless older, at least in substance, than Cormac's Glossary, and the examples taken from that work have fully established the existence of satire, in the senses under discussion, in the Old Irish period. The practice of it has survived among the Gaels, as will be shown later,[81] down to the present time.

Beyond these general statements of chronology it is not necessary to
go. And there is, in fact, no reason for insisting on the antiquity of the
evidences with regard to this custom, since nobody will contend (as
is often contended with regard to the much-debated elements of Celtic
and Arthurian romance) that the Irish borrowed it from other peoples
of medieval Europe.

It is noteworthy, as has already been remarked, that tales of
destructive satire are associated with some of the most conspicuous
poets in Irish history and saga. The man who was perhaps most
famous for the exercise of this dangerous power was Aithirne the
Importunate, who was so representative a satirist that in the metaphorical language of poetry *sciath Aithirni*, "the shield of Aithirne,"
became a "kenning" for satire.[82] His ruthless exactions, from which
he derived his sobriquet, are described in the saga of the Siege of
Howth,[83] where he is declared to have been "a hard, merciless man,"
"a man who asked the one-eyed for his single eye, and who used to
demand the woman in child-bed." So much was he feared that when,
in the course of his bardic circuit, he approached the borders of
Leinster, the people came forth to meet him and offered him jewels
and treasures not to come into their country, so that he might not
leave invectives. And any man would give his wife to Aithirne, or the
single eye out of his head, or whatever Aithirne might desire of jewels
and treasures. As the result of an enforced contribution of women
and cattle, levied by him on the men of Leinster, came about the siege
of Howth and a war between Leinster and Ulster.[84]

That Aithirne sometimes met his match appears from a short
story in the Book of Leinster, which describes his defeat at the hands
of another poet.[85] Because of his niggardliness, it is declared, Aithirne
never ate his full meal in a place where any one could see him. He
proceeded, therefore, on one occasion to take with him a cooked pig
and a pot of mead, in order that he might eat his fill all alone. And
he set in order before him the pig and the pot of mead when he beheld
a man coming towards him. "Thou wouldst do it all alone," said the
stranger, whilst he took the pig and the pot away from him. "What
is thy name?" said Aithirne. "Nothing very grand," said he:

> "*Sethor, ethor, othor, sele, dele, dreng, gerce,*
> Son of Gerluscc, sharp sharp, right right, that is my name."

Aithirne neither got the pig, nor was able to make rhyme to the

satire. It is evident that it was one come from God to take away the
pig; for Aithirne was not stingy from that hour forth.

The use of the ordinary Irish word for satire (*aer*) here, where
no personal attack or invective is involved, shows the range of its employment. The lines of the strange visitor are of course to be regarded
as a spell, and the contest to which Aithirne is invited is really a contest in magic power. In fact, many of the stories of verse-capping, with
which popular literature abounds,[86] are something more than tests of
poetical skill, and the whole literary type known as the debate, or
Streitgedicht, owes more than is commonly recognized to the ancient
practice of competition between rival magician-poets. But that matter
must be left for investigation and discussion at another time.

To return to Aithirne, the usual result of refusing his requests
is seen in the saga of Aithirne and Luaine, which belongs to the cycle
of King Conchobar of Ulster.[87] After the death of Deirdriu, it is
related, Conchobar was in great sorrow, and no joy or beauty could
appease his spirit. The chief men of Ulster urged him to search the
provinces of Erin, if perchance he might find therein the daughter of
a king or a noble, who would drive away his grief for Deirdriu, and
to this he assented. After a long search his messengers found Luaine,
the daughter of Domanchenn, the one maiden in Ireland who had
upon her the ways of Deirdriu in shape and sense and handicraft; and
when Conchobar beheld her there was no bone in him the size of an
inch that was not filled with long-lasting love for the girl. She was
betrothed to him, and her bride-price was bound upon him. When
Aithirne the Importunate and his two sons heard of the plighting of
the maiden to Conchobar, they went to beg boons of her. At sight of
her they gave love to her, and besought her to play the king false.
On her refusal they made three satires upon her, which left three
blotches on her cheeks, namely Stain and Blemish and Disgrace, which
were black and red and white. And thereupon the maiden died of
shame. When Conchobar learned of her death, great silence fell upon
him, and his grief was second only to his grief for Deirdriu. He took
counsel with the Ulstermen concerning the punishment of Aithirne
and his sons. Luaine's father and mother urged revenge, but Cathbad,
the Druid, gave warning that Aithirne would send beasts of prey
against them, namely Satire and Disgrace and Shame and Curse and
Fire (?) and Bitter Word. In the end they decided upon Aithirne's
destruction; and after the funeral rites had been celebrated for Luaine,
the Ulstermen followed Aithirne to Benn Aithirni, and walled him in

with his sons and all his household, and killed Mor and Midseng, his two daughters, and burnt his fortress upon him. But the doing of that deed, it is said, seemed evil to the poets of Ulster. Although the magician in Aithirne so much outweighs the poet, yet the bards took up his cause, and Amairgen, the chief poet, Aithirne's fosterling and pupil, made a lamentation upon him.

Aithirne and the kings with whom he is associated belong distinctly to the field of saga, but similar tales are told of poets who lived within the historical period or in relation with historical persons. Dallan Forgail, of the sixth century, the traditional author of the Amra Choluimb Chille, is said to have composed both songs of praise and satirical verses upon Aed mac Duach in an effort to obtain from him, by fair means or foul, his famous shield, the *Dubh-Ghilla*.[88] And the death of Niall of the Nine Hostages, one of the chief leaders of the marauding Scots at the beginning of the fifth century, was directly due, according to one account,[89] to strife engendered by a satirist. Echu, the son of Enna Censelach, the tale relates, when on his way from the house of Niall to his own people in Leinster, sought food at the house of Laidchenn, Niall's poet. Laidchenn refused Echu hospitality, and Echu revenged himself later by destroying the poet's house and killing his son. Thereupon for a whole year Laidchenn kept satirizing and lampooning and cursing the men of Leinster, so that neither grass nor corn grew with them, nor a leaf, to the end of a year. Niall also went to Leinster, and forced the people to give him Echu in bonds as a hostage; but Echu broke his chains, and slew nine champions who came up to kill him, and rejoined his people. A second time Niall demanded that the Leinstermen give up Echu, and when this was done, Laidchenn began to revile Echu and the Leinstermen, so that they melted away before him. But Echu let fly a champion's stone, which he had in his belt, and it hit Laidchenn in the crown of his forehead and lodged in his skull. Echu was exiled from Ireland, but this did not put an end to the feud, and afterward, in Alba, Niall himself fell by an arrow from Echu's hand. While the satires of Laidchenn are plainly of the nature of spells, it is clear that he was regarded in Irish tradition as a real poet, and not a mere pronouncer of charms. Poems on the history of the kings of Leinster, ascribed to him, though not to be taken as authentic, will be found in the Rawlinson Manuscript B 502.[90]

With the satires of Laidchenn, which blighted the whole face of Leinster, may be compared the spells attributed to Ferchertne, another great poet of the heroic age, before whom, according to a passage in the Táin Bó Cúalnge (The Cattle-Spoil of Cooley), the lakes and streams sank when he blamed them and rose when he praised them.[91] They bring to mind also the threat of Forgoll, the poet, in the Voyage of Bran, when upon occasion of a disagreement with Mongan, he declared that he would satirize Mongan and his father and his mother and his grandfather; singing spells upon their waters so that no fish should be caught in their river-mouths, and on their woods so that they should bear no fruit, and on their plains so that they should be barren of produce.[92]

Enough has been said to show the association of satire and malediction with Irish poets of high station. The frequency of the practice in the life of the people is further indicated by many passages in the sagas. In the great central tale of the Ulster cycle, the Táin Bó Cúalnge, for example, satirists appear in several important episodes. The account of Ferchertne and his spells has just been referred to. Redg, another satirist, is employed against Cuchulainn when the latter is holding at bay all the army of Connaught. He is sent to ask Cuchulainn for his spear; and upon Cuchulainn's refusal he threatens to take away his honor. Then Cuchulainn lets him have the spear in the back of his head, and kills him.[93] Again, when Ferdiad, the companion of Cuchulainn's youth, refuses to take part against him, Medb sends the druids and the satirists and the hard-attackers to him, that they may make three satires to hold him, and three imprecations (*glamma dicend*), that they may raise the three blotches on his face, Shame and Blemish and Disgrace, so that if he does not die at once he may die before the end of nine days, if he will not go into the fight. And Ferdiad yields, preferring to fall before the spears of bravery and warfare and prowess rather than before the spears of satire and insult and abuse.[94] On another occasion two female satirists from the camp of Connaught stand over Cuchulainn and weep in hypocrisy, predicting the ruin of Ulster.[95] And again, the Morrigan herself the battle-goddess, appears to Cuchulainn in a similar guise.[96] In the text of the Táin Bó Cúalnge she is not called a satirist, but she applies the name to herself in the Táin Bó Regamna, where she plays the same part.[97]

A few more illustrations of destructive satires may be cited from the great collection of early Irish topographical legends which is known as the Dindsenchas.[98] In the account of Mullaghmast,[99] Maistiu, by whose name that of the place is explained, is said to have refused certain demands of Gris, the female rhymester, who so maltreated her with blemishing satires that she died thereof before her. The Dindsenchas of Dublin[100] affords another instance of death from the verse of a poetess, but in this case the poem is described as a sea-spell. Dub, the wife of Enna, discovered that her husband had another wife, Aide, the daughter of Ochenn. In jealousy, then, Dub chanted a sea-spell before Ochenn's house, so that Aide was drowned with all her family.[101] In still another case, in the Dindsenchas of Fafaind,[102] the result of the satirist's verses is not death but disfigurement, as has been noted several times before. Aige, the sister of Fafne, the poet, was transformed into a fawn by her enemies, and then slain by the king's men. Thereupon Fafne went to blemish the king, and raised the customary three blotches upon him. In punishment for this Fafne was arrested and put to death.

It is apparent from a number of passages cited, and particularly from the description of the *glám dichenn*,[103] that satirists often plied their work in companies. A whole body of "druids and satirists and hard-attackers" were sent by Mebd to force Ferdiad into battle.[104] Kings had bands of satirists in their employ,[105] and poets are sometimes grouped with other forces to be counted upon in war.[106] In the tale of the Second Battle of Moytura, for example, when the leaders of all the crafts are asked in turn what help they can give against the Fomorian enemies, the *file* promises, on behalf of his fellow-poets, to make a *glám dichenn* which will satirize them and shame them and take away their resistance.[107] And in the Dindsenchas of Carman, hostile enchanters appear in open opposition.[108] Carman and her sons, according to the story, came from Athens, and she ruined the land with spells and songs and incantations while the sons destroyed by plundering and dishonesty. But the Tuatha Dé Danann sent Ai of their poets and Cridenbél of their satirists and Lugh Laebach of their druids and Bé Cuille of their witches to sing upon them, and the men were driven out, and Carman held as a prisoner behind them. The joint action of enchanters seems also to be referred to in the Dindsenchas of Laigen, which says that the druids of Ireland nearly exterminated by their songs the tribe of the Gaileoin.[109]

In the light of so many accounts of maledictive work of poets it will not appear strange that Cormac thought the "poison of satire" to be one element in the composite of *file*, or that Ferchertne and Nede, in a highly technical "Colloquy" on the poets' profession, several times refer to satire among its characteristic features.[110] Nor is it to be wondered at that the poets as a class came to be greatly feared. In some verses ascribed to St. Columba it is written, "Blessed is he who is praised; woe to him who is satirized!" And again, "Woe to the land that is satirized!"[111] And Ferchertne, in an interesting and typically Irish elaboration of the familiar list of signs before judgment, predicts, among other calamities, that "every man will buy a lampooner to lampoon on his behalf."[112] It was a general belief, sometimes explained by reference to the sacredness of the poet's person, that no request of his should ever be denied, and there was undoubtedly a strong feeling that poets were entitled to be rewarded for their work. But the real motive for yielding to their exactions seems often to have been the fear of their attacks, whether in maledictive verse or in some other form of magic persecution. And that they had other means than the poetic of enforcing their demands is suggested by Cormac's description of the *briamon smetrach*,[113] an operation which they performed on a man who refused them aught. They ground his ear-lobe between their fingers until he died. The supernatural power of the poets was even conceived as lasting beyond their own lives; and it is related of Cuan O'Lothchain, a famous poet who was murdered in 1024, that his murderers became putrid in a single hour. "That," the annalist says, "was the miracle of a poet!"[114]

As a result of the terror they inspired, the poets commonly got what they asked for, even from the boldest of saga heroes. Thus Cridenbél the satirist regularly obtained on demand the best bits of the Dagda's supper, though the Dagda's health was the worse for it; and it was only by a trick that the importunate sorcerer was disposed of.[115] So also Lugaid the king, when solicited by Ban-bretnach, the woman-satirist of the Britons, complied with her demand and lay with her, and became the father of Conall Corc;[116] and it is related of a certain MacSweeney that, when unable to remove a ring which a poet had asked for, he hacked off finger and all rather than not grant the request.[117] Of Leborcham, the nurse of Deirdriu, it is said that she was a woman-satirist and no one dared refuse her aught;[118] and of MacConglinne, who was great at both eulogy and satire, that he was called *Anéra* (the negative of *era*, "denial") because there was no denial of his requests.[119]

Even the Christian saints, it would appear, were not exempted from such demands or by any means superior to the fear of them. For when St. Columba was cutting wood for the church of Doire, certain poets came to him to seek a boon. He told them he had no gift for them there, but that if they would come home with him they should

receive one. They replied that if he did not give the gift then and
there they would satirize him; and Columba was seized with such
shame at this threat that smoke rose from his forehead and he sweated
exceedingly. He put up his hand to wipe away the sweat, and it became
a talent of gold in his palm, and he gave the talent to the poets.
"Thus," the narrator concludes, "did God save the honor of Columbcille."[120] In a story of similar purport the honor of St. Patrick is saved
by the miraculous provision of food for a company of minstrels or
jugglers; but in this instance the petitioners, after receiving their boon,
are swallowed up by the earth in punishment for their insolence.[121]
Vengeance of like character is visited on three poets who threaten to
defame St. Laisren;[122] and, in general, when the satirists confront the
saints, their sorcery is forced to succumb to a higher power.

The community as a whole also sometimes found means, according to the historians, of resisting the demands of the poets, and Geoffrey
Keating reports traditions of at least three banishments of the order.[123]
On the first occasion, in the time of King Conchobar of Ulster, when
the poets were about to set out for Alba, they were taken under protection by Cuchulainn and retained by him for seven years. On their
second banishment they were retained by Fiachna mac Baedan, and
on their third by Maelcobha mac Deamain, both also kings of Ulster.
A fourth attempt to expel them from the country was made by King
Aed mac Ainmiri at the celebrated assembly of Drumceat. But St.
Columba intervened on the poets' behalf and arranged that they
should be allowed to remain, though with their numbers reduced. His
action, Keating observes, is commemorated in the stanza:

> The poets were saved by this means,
> Through Colum of the fair law;
> A poet for each district is no heavy charge,—
> That is what Colum ordained.

The same abuses of the poets which stirred up hostile legislation
called forth much unfavorable comment in Irish literature, and in
one case they produced a counterblast which ranks among the best
pieces of humorous writing in Middle Irish. This is the Imtheacht na
Tromdháimhe (Proceedings of the Great Bardic Institution), which
has been several times referred to.[124] The account of Senchan and the
mice, already quoted from it, shows the spirit of extravagant burlesque
which pervades the whole, and which can hardly be reproduced in a

condensed summary of the story. The chief episodes are as follows: The bards, under Senchan, their newly elected chief, decided to make a professional visit to Guaire, the king of Connaught, who had never been satirized for lack of hospitality; and out of special consideration for him they took with them only thrice fifty poets, thrice fifty students, thrice fifty hounds, thrice fifty kinswomen, and thrice nine of each class of artificers. Guaire greeted them all cordially, only regretting that he could not give a personal welcome to each member of the large company; and they were quartered in a great mansion and told to ask for whatever they might desire. "It was, however, a great difficulty to procure all things for them; for it was requisite to give to each of them his meals apart and a separate bed; and they went to bed not any night without wanting something, and they arose not a day without some of them having longing desires for some things that were extraordinary, wonderful, and rare, and difficult of procurement. It was a task for all the men of Ireland to find that which was longed for, and unless the person who desired it obtained it within twenty-four hours, it was useless ever after to procure it for him." Muireann, the wife of Dallan Forgail, on the very first night moaned aloud and declared that she should die unless she could have "a bowl of the ale of sweet milk, with the marrow of the ankle-bone of a wild hog; a pet cuckoo on an ivy tree between the two Christmases; her full load on her back, with a girdle of yellow lard of an exceeding white boar about her; and to be mounted on a steed with a brown mane, and its four legs exceedingly white; a garment of the spider's web around her, and she humming a tune as she proceeded to Durlus." Another woman of the company desired a skirt full of blackberries in January, and also that Guaire's people might all be stricken down with disease. For the fulfillment of these and other equally preposterous demands Guaire sought the aid of Marban, his brother, the holy hermit; and by miracles of heaven the king's honor was saved, like that of the saints in the stories previously related.

When all the desires of the company had been fulfilled, they sat down to a great feast. Senchan, however, took whimsical offence at the hearty eating of the servants, and refused all food. Guaire in distress sent a favourite steward to prepare a wild goose and serve it to Senchan with special care. But Senchan refused it because the young man's grandfather was chip-nailed. And when a favourite damsel of Guaire's household was sent, Senchan would not take food from her hands because her grandmother had once pointed out the road to lepers. At last, after several days' abstinence, Senchan consented to eat a hen's egg, but the mice got at it, with results that have already been described. When Senchan was saved by St. Kieran from the clutches of Irusan, the great cat, he complained at his release, for he would rather by his death have given occasion for the satirizing of Guaire.

Marban, in the meantime, though a saintly hermit, had lost all patience with the unreasonable demands of the poets, and determined to obtain some redress. Accordingly he made his way to their mansion, declared that he was connected with poetry through the grandmother of his servant's wife, who was descended from poets, and claimed his choice of music from the company. Then he demanded the performance of a *cronán* (a low humming tune) till he should declare that he had enough. He would not be satisfied with the ordinary *cronán*, but insisted on the bass or guttural *cronán*, in the hope that they would break their heads, feet, and necks, and that their breathing would be the sooner exhausted. One company of singers after another was worn out by the performance. Efforts were made to put off Marban with riddle contests, but he always defeated his antagonists in questions, and then reverted to his first demand—"Perform as much *cronán* as we desire." At last, when no one else could respond, Senchan himself had to perform, and he made such exertions at the guttural *cronán* that his eye burst out upon his cheek. Marban was satisfied with this revenge, and restored the eye to its place. Then he laid bonds upon the bards to obtain for him the saga of the Cattle-Spoil of Cooley; and the rest of the story is taken up with their adventures in discharge of the obligation.

In this way the Imtheacht na Tromdhaimhe is brought into connection with the old saga-cycle. But it is really a comparatively late work,[125] and in effect, as has already been said, a satire on the satirists. Satire in the loose or primitive sense furnished material for satire in the stricter definition of the word. It would not be fair to say that the one passed over into the other, and no such suggestion is here intended. The Imtheacht is cited rather as a significant piece of testimony to the extensive development of the old satire of malediction.

It would be easy to multiply references to satire from all branches of early Irish literature, but the passages which have been discussed illustrate the more important aspects of the subject. And it is beyond the compass of the present study to trace the history of satire through Irish literature of the modern period. Suffice it to say, of this later development, that although real satire, as opposed to incantational

verse, increases as time goes on, the old conception of the destructive
satirist, the poet with superior power, whom it is dangerous to displease,
has never disappeared among the Gaels of either Ireland or Scotland.[126] But the village rhymester of to-day, though he may, like
Chaucer's Somonour, have

> In daunger . . . at his owene gyse
> The yonge girles of the diocyse,

is far less important in power or influence than the magician-poet of
saga times. He represents, so far as one can judge, the expiration of a
tradition or custom which in medieval Ireland was still vigorous and
productive of results in literary development.

For the practices of the old Irish satirists have, in addition to
their merely curious interest, a wider bearing on literary history. Attention has already been called[127] to their connection with the development of the "flyting," or verse debate, a matter which cannot further
be treated at this time. And their obvious relation to the beginnings of
ordinary satire also deserves more consideration than it has received
from students at the subjects.[128] One might hesitate just now, when
fashion among critics and scholars is turning against *Liedertheorien*
and doctrines of popular origin, to lay stress upon such a development.
The folklorists and ballad collectors are charged, not unjustly, with
many extravagances: with ill-judged enthusiasm for poor productions,
just because they are popular; with wild speculation about popular
composition; and with a kind of easy-going satisfaction in the collection of popular parallels as if they explained the mature products of
art. Nevertheless, in spite of its peccant humours, the study of folk
literature has yielded solid results, and the "thrice-battered Grimm,"
as Mr. Gummere once called him, is not to be abjured as a Philistine
god. Popular or communal composition, in some such reasonable sense
as Mr. Gummere also has most fully defined and illustrated, must be
recognized as a significant fact in the history of poetry. Popular material, in various forms of mythology and tradition, has entered into the
highest products of art, and the understanding of it is often essential
to the comprehension of Chaucer or Shakespeare or Goethe. In a word,
the historian of poetry will never again be at liberty to disregard the
popular basis of the poetry of art.

Now satire, which belongs conspicuously to the poetry of art,
doubtless owes little, in its developed phases, to such simple products

as the quatrains of Nede and Coirpre. Yet it is unquestionably a very old poetic form, originating in early stages of society and having definite relations with various kinds of popular verse. On one side a source has been found for it in the rude, rustic songs of mockery which exist among many peoples.[129] In another aspect its connection with gnomic writing is well recognized; and one scholar has gone so far, in discussing old Germanic poetry,[130] as to assume that people who possessed a gnomic literature must also have had satire. The close association of these two types could also be admirably illustrated from Irish literature, which furnishes, in such collections of proverbial morality as the ancient Instructions of Cormac, many passages of well-developed satire.[131] But a still more intimate and essential relation seems to exist between satire and the kind of verse that has been described in this paper. And it is interesting to find that an observation by M. Brunetière, whom nobody will accuse of undue partiality for popular literature, points towards its recognition. He concludes an admirable survey of the general history of satire with the following definition:[132] "Opposer, en nous moquant d'eux, ou en les invectivant, —c'est affaire de tempérament,—notre manière de penser, de sentir, ou de voir à ceux qui ne voient, ni ne pensent, ni ne sentent comme nous, tel est, on l'a pu voir, le trait essentiel et commun qui relie les unes aux autres toutes les formes de la satire. Le poète Archiloque, ayant sur la fille de Lycambe des vues que Lycambe n'approuvait point, il les exprima d'une façon si virulente que Lycambe, et même sa fille, dit la légende, s'en pendirent. Voilà le fond de toute satire." The French critic, though chiefly concerned in his essay with the more elaborate and literary forms of satire, yet finds its essential nature to be personal invective. If his observation is sound, and it is certainly not unreasonable, the old Irish satirists were in the main line of development, though very far up the line; and the evidence with regard to them shows that the poetry of enchantment must also be included in the reckoning. For in the days of the magician-poet invective, mockery, and malediction are seen to have been almost inseparably bound together.

NOTES

[1] Sidney's Works, ed. 1724, 3. 52.
[2] Ed. 1665, p. 35.

3 Jonson's Works, ed. Gifford (1875), 5. 518.

4 As You Like It, act iii, Scene 2. Other references to the subject, some of them of considerably later date, will be found in Ben Jonson's Staple of News, act iv, Scene 1 (Gifford's ed., 5. 271); Randolph's Jealous Lovers, act v. Scene 1; Rhymes against Martin Marprelate, cited by Nares from Herbert's Typographical Antiquities, p. 1689 (the whole poem printed in D'Israeli's Quarrels of Authors, 2. 255–63); Sir William Temple's Essay on Poetry, in his works (ed. 1757), 3. 418; Swift's Advice to a Young Poet (ed. Scott, 9. 407); and Pope's version of Donne's Second Satire, line 23. Most of these passages were cited in Nares' Glossary, under *Rats Rimed to Death*; for further discussion see an article by Todd, Proceedings of the Royal Irish Academy, 1855, pp. 355ff.

5 O'Curry's materials were presented in Dr. Todd's paper in the Proceedings for 1855. He mentions one instance of rat-rhyming in 1776, and another about 1820. Cases of the same sort among the Highland Gaels are cited by the Rev. Alexander Stewart in Twixt Ben Nevis and Glencoe (Edinburgh, 1885). A long spell said to have been composed and successfully used by a farmer on the Island of Lismore is given by Stewart on pp. 4ff. Somewhat different from these stories of rat-rhymers is the case related by Giraldus Cambrensis (Gemma Ecclesiastica, Rolls Series, 161) of St. Yvor the bishop, who by his curse expelled the rats (majores mures, qui vulgariter rati vocantur) from an Irish province because they had gnawed his books. This was conceived by Giraldus as a Christian miracle, and is cited, along with the story of St. Patrick and the snakes, to illustrate the fearful effects of excommunication. Still another method of disposing of rats is familiar to everybody in the legend of the Piper of Hamelin.

6 Edited and translated by O. Connellan in the Transactions of the Ossianic Society, vol. 5, Dublin, 1860. The Irish title means simply the Circuit of the Burdensome Company, but the tale is usually referred to in English by Connellan's rendering, as given above.

7 British treatment of Irish history has long been a grievance to Irish writers. Perhaps the best way of getting at the traditional accounts of the "wild Irish" is by consulting the rejoinders of such native writers as Keating in his Forus Feasa air Eirinn, or Lynch in his Cambrensis Eversus. See also the Rev. Dr. T. J. Shahan's survey of the subject in the Am. Cath. Quarterly Review, 28. 310ff.

8 For references to Scot and Temple, see pp. 1, 3, above.

9 For a further account of the Irish terms, see pp. 6ff.

10 The confusion among these different classes is well set forth, with illustrative passages, by C. Plummer, Vitæ Sanctorum Hiberniæ, 1. pp. clx–clxii. Compare also pp. 18ff. for examples of the combination of different magic arts by poets and poetesses.

11 For a convenient survey of the evidence concerning the use of incantations in Greek and Roman civilization, see an article on Græco-Italian Magic, by F. B. Jevons, in Anthropology and the Classics (Oxford, 1908), pp. 93ff.

12 The story seems more likely to have been a late invention. For the authorities, and a possible explanation of its origin, see Croiset, Histoire de la Littérature Grecque (1890), 2. 180. And the death of Bupalus, the victim of Hipponax, of which Sidney's Bubonax (p. 1), seems to show a confused memory, is of similarly doubtful authority.

13 For certain evidences of ancient popular Spottlieder in Greece and Italy, which suggest conditions similar to those among Germans and Celts, see Usener, Rheinisches Museum, 56. 1ff.; Hirt, Die Indogermanen (1905), 2. 478–79, 728. One cannot help suspecting in the light of the Irish material to be here discussed, that there was more of a magic element than Usener recognized in the old Italic poems of abuse.

14 For a full statement of the theory see Goldziher, Abhandlungen zur arabischen Philologie (Leiden, 1896), pp. 1–105. Goldziher's article contains much material of interest to students of European popular poetry. His main conclusion is briefly restated and indorsed by M. J. de Goeje, Die arabische Literatur, in Kultur der Gegenwart, orientalische Literaturen, pp. 134ff. Compare also Brockelmann, Geschichte der arabischen Literatur (1901), pp. 7ff.

15 Professor G. F. Moore called the writer's attention to the fact that Rückert, in his translation of the Hamāsa, employed the term Schmählieder for all such poems, just as writers on Irish have called them "satires." Freytag, similarly, in his edition of the Hamāsa, translated the Arabic subtitle (Bāb el-Hija') as Caput Satyrarum, and the Arabic Hija' has acquired this general sense. But Goldziher (see particularly pp. 26ff. of his article) argues that it meant originally a curse or spell; thus it constitutes an interesting parallel to the development of the Irish aer.

16 This is consistent with the view expressed by De Goeje, op. cit., p. 134.

17 See Comparetti, Il Kalevala, o la Poesia Tradizionale dei Finni (Reale Accademia dei Lincei, Roma, 1891), pp. 23ff.

18 See E. Mogk, Kelten und Nordgermanen, p. 12; also his article in the Arkiv for Nordisk Filologi, 17. 277ff. In the latter place he even argues that the Zauberlied was the chief form of early Germanic poetry, and that the oldest Germanic names for poems (ljoð, galdr, and the Finnish runo, borrowed from Germanic) had reference primarily to spells.

19 For evidence concerning early Spottlieder see Kögel's Literaturgeschichte, vol. 1, part i, pp. 55ff., 208; vol. 1, part ii, pp. 164–65; also Kögel's article in Paul's Grundriss (2d ed.), 2. 48ff., 68ff. The very early instance mentioned in Ausonius (Moselle, 167), of the probra sung against seris cultoribus among the Treviri has been counted by some scholars as Germanic, and by others as Celtic, or even as Roman. See Kögel, vol. 1, part i, p. 55; C. Jullian, Rev. Arch. 40. 321; Martin, Gött. Gel. Anz., 1893, p. 128. Brandl, in his article on Altenglische Literaturgeschichte, in Paul's Grundriss (2d ed.), 2. 974, mentions the Anglo-Saxon dreamas, "gesellschaftliche Lieder," and conjectures that the Spottlied (bismerléoþ) must have figured prominently among them.

20 On the canon see Müllenhoff in Haupt's Zeitschrift, 9. 130. There is some doubt, it should be said, concerning its application to Germanic conditions; and in general, as Professor Wiener has collected material to show, it is necessary to be cautious in deriving from ecclesiastical canons, which were taken over literally from one council to another, evidences as to local beliefs and practices.

21 The story is told in Thegan's Life of Louis the Pious, chapter 28, and is cited by Kögel, Literaturgeschichte, vol. 1, part i, p. 208.

22 Cf. Weinhold, Altnordisches Leben, pp. 341ff., 465; Finnur Jonsson, Den Oldnorske og Oldislandske Litteraturs Historie, 2. 18, 133–39; and for a number of references to sagas, Vigfusson's Dictionary, under danz, flim, and nið.

23 The quotation is from the English version of the Relation de l'Islande of La Peyrère (in Churchill's Collection of Voyages and Travels) (1704), 2. 437. See Farley, Scandinavian Influences in the English Romantic Movement (Harvard Studies and Notes, vol. 10), pp. 19ff.

24 On the etymology of scop there is still considerable difference

of opinion. The word was formerly held to have a long vowel and was brought into connection with *scieppan* (compare the relation of ποιητής and ποιέω). When the vowel was seen to be short, this etymology became harder to support; but Kögel in his Literaturgeschichte, vol. 1, part i, pp. 140ff., still defended it, assuming a theoretic *skupó- with *Tiefstufe* of the *Ablaut*. In Paul's Grundriss (2d ed.), 2. 34, however, he changed his explanation and proposed to connect the word with the root *seq-, sqe-*, in ἔννεπε, Lat. *insece*, and perhaps the Anglo-Saxon *specan*. In favor of the association with "scoff" see Kluge, Engl. Stud. 8. 480, quoted with approval by Gummere, Old English Ballads (1894), p. xxxii. This explanation is adopted in the New English Dictionary, under *scop*, and in Torp's Wortschatz der Germanischen Spracheinheit (Fick's Wörterbuch), 3. 469. The Irish *fáith*, "poet" (cognate with Lat. *vates*), and the Welsh *gwawd*, "mockery," perhaps show a similar relation in meaning. See Zimmer, Die keltischen Literaturen (in Kultur der Gegenwart), p. 77n. The old Norse *skald*, if related to *scold, schelten*, etc., would furnish another parallel. This etymology, defended in Vigfusson's Dictionary, p. 541, is rejected by several later writers, though no other has been clearly established in its place. Compare Lidén in Paul and Brauné's Beiträge, 15. 507ff.; Mogk, in Paul's Grundriss (2d ed.), 2. 657; and F. Jonsson, Litteraturs Historie, 1. 329ff.

25 Diodorus, v. 32. 2. Οὗτοι δὲ μετ᾽ ὀργάνων ταῖς λύραις ὁμοίων ᾄδοντες οὓς μὲν ὑμνοῦσιν, οὓς δὲ βλασφημοῦσι. M. Camille Jullian, in a discussion of this passage (in Revue Archéologique, 40. 321), cites also classical testimony on the use by the ancient Celts of invectives in battle. This custom, which is frequently referred to in both Celtic and Germanic sagas, is closely related to the other forms of satire under consideration. See Goldziher, Abhandlungen zur arabischen Philologie, pp. 26–27, for similar observations with regard to Arabic.

26 For the strife between Dafydd and Rhys Meigen see Barddoniaeth Dafydd ap Gwilym (1789), pp. xi. ff., 452ff.; also L. C. Stern in the Zeitschrift für keltische Philologie, 7. 26ff.

27 See p. 3.

28 For the *glám dichenn* see pp. 108, below; for other uses of the word, and some suggestions as to its fundamental meaning, see Windisch's edition of the *Táin Bó Cúailnge* (Irische Texte, Extraband), p. 241.

29 On the *glas-gabail* see p. 8 and n. 47.

30 For references to satire in Cormac's Glossary see pp. 10ff., above.

31 Ancient Laws, ed. O'Curry, 5. 230.

32 *Ibid.* 5. 456ff.

33 See Todd's edition of the Irish version of Nennius (Irish Archæological Society, 1848), p. 162; also Kuno Meyer's Contributions to Irish Lexicography, under *crosan*. A peculiar use of the word appears in the *Senadh Saighri*, ed. by Meyer in the Gaelic Journal, 4. 108.

34 With the references to satire in the Irish laws should be compared the treatment of the subject in Italic and Germanic laws, already referred to. See particularly Usener on Italische Volksjustiz in Rheinisches Museum, 56. 1ff., and Weinhold, Altnordisches Leben, pp. 341ff.

35 Ancient Laws of Ireland, 1. 152, 162, 231 (published by the Government, Dublin, 1865–1901). The language of the English translation is quoted, except where there is special reason to depart from it.

36 Ancient Laws, 1. 185, 237. The last phrase is translated conjecturally. See d'Arbois de Jubainville, Études sur le Droit Celtique, 2. 181. For discussion of certain inconsistencies in the laws of distress, see the same work, 2. 159ff.

37 *Ibid.* 2. 156; 5. 143, 156.

38 *Ibid.* 5. 512.

39 *Ibid.* 2. 156.

40 *Ibid.* 4. 348, 352.

41 *Ibid.* 5. 168, 172.

42 *Ibid.* 1. 58; 5. 168, 172, 388. For O'Curry's comment see the Proceedings of the Royal Irish Academy, 1855, p. 357.

43 On fasting as a means of distraint, see an article by the present writer in the Putnam Anniversary Volume (Cedar Rapids, Ia., 1909), pp. 567ff.

44 Ancient Laws, 3. 92ff.

45 See p. 6.

46 See p. 9.

47 The *glas-gabail* is mentioned, but not explained, in the Ancient Laws, 5. 216. In the same volume, p. 230, it is glossed *glama gnuisi,* "satirizing the face." If this refers to the disfigurement by

blisters, the *glas-gabail* does not seem to be anything very different from the *glam dichenn*, at least in its effects.

48 Ancient Laws, 5. 228.

49 The last sentence contains one or two obscure words which are not translated. With regard to the distinction between author and reciter, it is to be noted that the Roman Twelve Tables provided for the punishment of both (*si quis occentauisset siue carmen condidisset*). Cf. Usener, Rheinisches Museum, 56. 3.

50 Ancient Laws, 5. 225. Cf. also d'Arbois de Jubainville, Études sur le Droit Celtique, 2. 26.

51 Ancient Laws, 176. For the association with strumpets, cf. also pp. 202–4.

52 Ancient Laws, 5. 456.

53 *Ibid.* 3. 25.

54 *Ibid.* 5. 266–68. Compare also the law (5. 235) which exempts poets, with kings, bishops, insane men, and others, from responsibility for paying their sons' debts.

55 *Ibid.* 1. 19.

56 Ancient Laws, 5. 12.

57 See Revue Celtique, 16. 280; Annals of Clonmacnoise, p. 39; and Aislinge Meic Conglinne, ed. Kuno Meyer, pp. 44ff.; all cited by Plummer, Vitæ Sanctorum Hiberniæ, 1. cii–ciii.

58 An example of satire against a tribe, which was apparently of the nature of invective or insult rather than of incantation, is cited from the Leabhar Breac in the Miscellany of the Irish Archæological Society, 1. 179ff.; see also O'Donovan's edition of O'Daly's Tribes of Ireland (Dublin, 1852), p. 17n. The Cinel Fiacha of Westmeath are asserted to be of plebeian origin. In anger at the insult they murder the satirists.

59 Translated by O'Curry, Manners and Customs, 2. 216ff.; Atkinson, Book of Ballymote (Facsimile), p. 13a; and Stokes, Revue Celtique, 12. 119–20; and summarized and discussed by Thurneysen, Mittelirische Verslehren, pp. 124ff. Thurneysen questions the antiquity of the tradition, at least as part of the *Verslehren*. But the substance of the passage does not look like a late invention.

60 This and the following terms refer to the various degrees of poets.

61 Stokes's translation (in Revue Celtique, 12. 119), somewhat condensed, is followed in the present account.

62 See particularly Ascoli's Glossarium Palaeohibernicum under *air* and its compounds.

63 There is a similar explanation in the Amra Choluimb Chille. See p. 17.

64 See p. 5.

65 For other references to the subject in Cormac, not mentioned above, see the articles on *aithrinne, doeduine, dul,* and *trefhocal.*

66 See Stokes's edition and translation, Revue Celtique, 12. 71. The quatrain is also given in some manuscripts of the Amra Choluimb Chille; cf. O'Beirne Crowe's edition, p. 26 (from the Lebor na h-Uidhre), and Stokes's edition (from Ms. Rawl. B. 502) in Revue Celtique, 20. 158. The story is told separately in Yellow Book of Lecan, p. 137b, and also (apparently) in Trinity College Ms. H. 3, 17. See the Catalogue of Mss. in Trinity College, Dublin, p. 352.

67 The readings of this line differ in the manuscripts, and the translation is uncertain.

68 See the notes to the Martyrology, under Oct. 21 (Stokes's edition for the Henry Bradshaw Society, p. 226).

69 This is Stokes's rendering of *uindsi chucat*; perhaps it should rather be translated "here comes to thee."

70 On Flann mac Lonain see O'Reilly, Irish Writers, pp. lviii. ff.; O'Curry Manners and Customs, 2. 98–104; Todd's edition of the Cogadh Gaedhel re Gallaibh (Rolls Series), p. x; Hennessy's edition of Chronicon Scotorum (Rolls Series), p. 175.

71 See Stokes's Three Irish Glossaries, pp. xxxvi. ff. Stokes's translation, slightly condensed by the omission of doubtful words and of glossarial passages, is here followed. Part of Nede's satirical stanza is quoted at the end of the account of the *glám dichenn* in the metrical treatise already referred to. See p. 9, and Thurneysen, Mittelirische Verslehren, p. 125.

72 Several words in the quatrain are of uncertain meaning.

73 Compare the gifts of Finnabair to Ferdiad, Táin Bó Cúalnge, L. W. Farraday's translation (London, 1904), p. 100. See also Gaidoz, La Réquisition d'Amour et le Symbolisme de la Pomme (Annuaire de l'École des Hautes Études, 1902), with reviewer's remarks in Revue Archéologique, 1902, 1. 134; Lot, in Romania, 27. 560n.; Foster, on the Symbolism of Apples in Classical Antiquity, in Harvard Studies in Classical Philology, 10. 43ff.; and Leite de Vasconcellos, in Revista Lusitana, 7. 126ff.

74 For illustrations of the *geis*, from early Irish sagas, see an article by Miss Eleanor Hull, in Folklore, 12. 40ff.

75 For this requirement that the king shall be free from all deformities or blemishes see Ancient Laws, 1. 73; 2. 279; 3. 85. Compare also the story of Nuada of the Silver Hand, discussed by Rhys, Hibbert Lectures, p. 120.

76 See Revue Celtique, 20. 422, and *Liber Hymnorum*, ed. Atkinson, p. 173.

77 See Ancient Laws, 4. 16; also Revue Celtique, 24. 279.

78 See Ériu, 4. 21, 32.

79 Cf. Theocritus, Idylls, ix. 30; xii. 24. The Greek idea was apparently rather that the flatterer himself had the push rise upon him. For further illustration of the Irish belief, see D. Fitzgerald in the Revue Celtique, 6. 195 (citing a South African parallel).

80 Both Rhys (Hibbert Lectures, pp. 324ff.) and Zimmer (Keltische Literaturen, in Kultur der Gegenwart, pp. 50–51) have discussed the physiological side of the question.

81 See p. 24.

82 See Revue Celtique, 26. 24.

83 Edited and translated by Stokes, Revue Celtique, 8. 47ff. See also O'Curry's Manuscript Materials, pp. 266ff.

84 Rhys (Hibbert Lectures, p. 325) observes in Aithirne's defence that the disparaging account of him comes from the Book of Leinster, and that the Leinstermen were his hereditary foes.

85 Quoted and discussed by Rhys, Hibbert Lectures, p. 332.

86 General references on the subject of verse-capping are hardly necessary here. For some discussion and illustrations, see Gummere, The Beginnings of Poetry, pp. 400ff. Early Irish instances (with parallels from other literatures) are noted by Stokes in the translation of Cormac's Glossary (Ir. Arch. Society), p. 138; see also Irische Texte, 4. 92ff., 303.

87 Edited and translated by Stokes, Revue Celtique, 24. 272ff.

88 See the Imtheacht na Tromdháimhe, ed. Connellan (1860), pp. 12ff.

89 See the story of Niall's death, from Ms. Rawl. B. 502, edited and translated by K. Meyer, Otia Merseiana, 2. 84ff. Cf. O'Curry, Manners and Customs, 2. 70ff.

90 See the collotype facsimile, edited by Kuno Meyer, introduction, p. ix, and text, pp. 116ff.

91 Táin Bó Cúalnge, ed. Windisch (Irische Texte, Extraband), p. 789.

92 The Voyage of Bran, Meyer and Nutt, 1. 49.

93 See the Táin Bó Cúalnge, Windisch's edition, p. 273. And compare a similar episode in the Aided Conchulainn, Revue Celtique, 3. 78ff.

94 Táin Bó Cúalnge, Windisch's edition, p. 441.

95 Ibid. p. 829.

96 See the Táin Bó Cúalnge, Lebor na h-Uidre version, Miss Farraday's translation (Grimm Library), p. 74.

97 See the Irische Texte, ed. Windisch and Stokes, vol. 2, part ii, p. 258.

98 References are made here to Stokes's edition and translation of the prose portion of the Dindsenchas from the Rennes Ms., Revue Celtique, vols. 15 and 16. An edition of the metrical Dindsenchas has been begun by E. Gwynn in the Todd Lecture Series of the Royal Irish Academy (vols. 7 and 8).

99 Revue Celtique, 15. 334ff.

100 Ibid. p. 326.

101 A somewhat similar tale of a jealous wife is told in the Latin Vita Coemgeni (Plummer's Vitæ Sanctorum Hiberniæ, 1. 250ff.). Colman, the son of Carbre, finding his first wife incompatible, put her away and took another. But the rejected woman was powerful in magicis artibus, and sang spells which destroyed all the children of her successor. At last one of them (Faelan) was saved by a miracle of St. Coemgen. The way in which different magic arts were combined in these dangerous women of poetry is shown again by the tale of Dreco (Druidess and female poet), who prepared a poisonous liquor which killed the twenty-four sons of Fergus Redside. See the Dindsenchas of Nemthenn, Revue Celtique, 16. 34.

102 Revue Celtique, 15. 306; and compare Gwynn's Metrical Dindsenchas, 2. 66ff.

103 See pp. 9ff.

104 See p. 18.

105 Compare Revue Celtique, 22. 294.

106 At this point Arabic literature again furnishes interesting parallels. Cf. Goldziher's remarks on the use of the Hija' as an "Element des Krieges" (Abhandlungen zur arabischen Philologie, p. 36).

107 Revue Celtique, 12. 91.

108 *Ibid.* 15. 311.

109 *Ibid.* 15. 299.

110 The Colloquy of the Two Sages (Agallam in da Suaradh), edited and translated by Stokes, Revue Celtique, 26. 23ff.

111 Revue Celtique, 20. 44.

112 See the Colloquy, Revue Celtique, 26. 40.

113 See Cormac's Glossary, under *bri*; also Revue Celtique, 26. 55.

114 See Annals of Ulster, ed. B. MacCarthy (Rolls Series), under the year 1024.

115 See the Second Battle of Moytura, Revue Celtique, 12. 65.

116 See the Coir Anmann, under Conall Corc (Irische Texte, 3. 310).

117 See the Publications of the Ossianic Society, 3. 297.

118 Irische Texte, 1. 71.

119 Aislinge Meic Conglinne, ed. Kuno Meyer, p. 43.

120 See O'Donnell's Life of Columbcille, edited by R. Henebry, Zeitschrift für keltische Philologie, 4. 296–98. The same life says later (*ibid.* 5. 42) that Columbcille was weakly indulgent in rewarding poets and rhymers.

121 Compare Stokes, the Tripartite Life of St. Patrick, pp. lx, 204.

122 See De Smedt and Backer, Acta Sanctorum Hiberniæ (1888), col. 796. Other instances of relations between the satirists and the saints are noted by Plummer, Vitæ Sanctorum Hiberniæ, 1. ciii.

123 See Keating's Forus Feasa air Eirinn, Irish Text Society edition, 3. 78ff.

124 See p. 2.

125 The text is late Middle Irish. In some parts old material is made use of. Compare, for example, the story of the leper, in the latter part of the Imtheacht, with the similar narrative in Cormac's Glossary, under Prull.

126 An extended study of modern Irish satire is greatly to be desired. Interesting illustrations both of real literary satire and of the incantational type are referred in O'Donovan's introduction to O'Daly's Satire on the Tribes of Ireland (Dublin, 1864). The Pairliament Chloinne Thomáis, edited by Stern in the Zeitschrift für keltische Philologie, 5. 541ff., may also be mentioned as a representative satirical document of much interest. For the survival of destructive or incantational satire there is plenty of evi-

dence in the editions of the modern Irish poets. See, for example, in addition to the references already given on rat-rhyming (p. 96, above), Hardiman's Irish Minstrelsy (1831), 2. 358n.; O'Daly's Poets and Poetry of Munster (Second Series, 1860), p. 218n.; Dinneen's edition of Egan O'Rahilly (Publication of the Irish Text Society), pp. xxxi. ff.; Hyde's edition of Raftery, Abhráin Atá Leagtha ar an Reachtuire (1903), pp. 15ff.; Lady Gregory, Poets and Dreamers (1903), pp. 8ff.; and with special reference to Scotland, Zeitschrift für keltische Philologie, 2. 28. Hyde points out that even the praise of the poets is feared, and it is believed that no man who has had a song made about him will live long.

127 See p. 16.

128 This relation, which has been clearly involved in most of the preceding discussion, has doubtlessly been observed by nearly all scholars who are familiar with Celtic literature, but due account has not been taken of it in general discussions of satire. That it has not escaped the keen vision of Professors Kittredge and Gummere, in their investigations of popular poetry, is apparent from a note in Gummere's Old English Ballads (1894), p. xxxiv.

129 Such, for example, as the Etruscan *fescennina*, and the Germanic *Schnaderhüpfl*. Compare Gummere, Beginnings of Poetry, pp. 400ff.; Hirt, Die Indogermanen, 2. 728; and Erich Schmidt, Anfänge der Literatur (Kultur der Gegenwart), pp. 19ff.

130 Kögel, in Paul's Grundriss der Germanischen Philologie (2d ed.), 2. 48.

131 The Instructions of King Cormac Mac Airt (*Tecosca Cormaic*) have been edited by Kuno Meyer in the Todd Lecture Series of the Royal Irish Academy, vol. 15 (Dublin, 1909).

132 See La Grande Encyclopédie, under *Satire*.

G. L. HENDRICKSON

Satura Tota Nostra Est

It may be doubted whether any word in the vocabulary of literary nomenclature is used more frequently or covers a wider territory than "satire." It pertains not only to literature, but also to the casual utterances of daily life. It is not peculiar in passing beyond specific compositions which are called by this name, for the same thing is true of other words such as "tragedy," or "comedy," or "lyric"— names which may also be applied to situations of daily life, to plots and scenes of stories or novels, as well as to the formal compositions of the playwright or poet. But satire, I venture to believe, is a term more widely used than any of these. It is an indispensable label not only for scenes and situations of private and public life, but essential for the characterization of parts of almost every form of literary expression. Satirical comedy goes without saying; only less obvious is satirical epigram, satirical ballad, satirical novel; satirical essay and sermon are familiar and doubtless satirical tragedy may be instanced. In fact with the eclipse of formal satire and the paucity of deliberate satirists, we have almost forgotten that satire is primarily the designation of a form of literature. We have extended the word to designate a certain manner of humorous or ironical criticism of that which appeals to us as false, or pretentious, or insincere; oftentimes to mere banter of novelty or queerness. The wide need which the word satisfies may be seen from the fact that while the Latin used only the nominal form *satura*, subsequent times have extended it by verbal, adverbial, and adjectival forms. "Tragedize" and "lyricize" are curiosities of the dictionary, comedy has yielded no verb, but "satirize" is in everyone's working vocabulary. The word in its various forms has become an inevitable term of characterization for some part of the

From *Classical Philology*, XXII (Jan. 1927), 46–60. Reprinted by permission of the editors of *Classical Philology*.

literature of all times and all peoples; for oriental and Greek writings which existed while the Latin tongue, which furnishes the name, was still unrecorded. Apart from the Roman satirists themselves and the literature which they have immediately influenced, there is an immense literature of satire (specific or incidental) which, with greater or less volume according to the times and the temper of men, has come down through the centuries to our own day. Roman satire is in comparison to the whole a tenuous rivulet—a rivulet however to which, apart from its intrinsic value and subsequent influence, an accidental importance attaches from the fact that in all the Western tongues it has furnished the name to the great stream, of which it is not the source but only a tributary. The great mass of this literature of satire belongs to post-Roman times; and yet if we could survey in its fulness Greek satire from the Homeric period down to Julian we should still have to acknowledge that the Roman contribution, though influential beyond its bulk, is small in comparison.

It must seem therefore somewhat of a paradox to read in the comparative survey of Greek and Roman literature which Quintilian presents in his tenth book the much-quoted dictum: *satura quidem tota nostra est,* "Satire however [that is in contrast to the other literary forms reviewed which were Greek as well as Latin] is wholly ours." We cannot here resort to the easiest resolution of the paradox by simply declaring the statement untrue, and inspired either by patriotic pride or limited vision. Quintilian was above all things conscientious and honest: he sometimes, as in comedy, depreciates Roman literature unduly, and certainly he was well enough read in Greek to recognize its satire, as in fact he does in commenting on Attic comedy. His statement therefore presents a problem to investigate, for on the face of it, as naturally understood and ordinarily translated, it is very obvious that satire is by no means wholly Roman. So far in fact is this from a general truth that it would be easy to defend the thesis that satire is not even characteristically Roman. For just as the Romans as a nation lacked imaginative and poetical instinct, so as a nation they lacked whimsical play in the discernment and expression of the lighter contrasts and absurdities which make for the best satire—the drolleries of Aristophanes, the subtleties of Lucian. The one quality of related kind in which the Romans sometimes claimed a superiority over the Greeks was vigor and raciness of abusive raillery. It was with this that the clever and fluent hybrid Greek was put to rout by the virulence and venom (*pus atque venenum*) of the sturdy Prenestine, Rupilius Rex, in the scene of Horace's early satire (i. 7). But whatever the racial endowment of the two peoples may have been,[1] whatever the Roman *veteres atque urbani sales,* which Cicero preferred to Attic wit, the Greek literature of humor and satire had an antiquity and abundance which Rome could never match.

Such a statement need scarcely constitute a challenge to proof, and in its defense it will scarcely be necessary for me to undertake a review of Greek satirical literature.[2] Some significant aspects of it however may be touched upon briefly to set in proper light the final solution of the problem proposed. Passing over early Greek satire such as may be or has been discerned in Homer, Hesiod, the iambic and gnomic poets, we come to Aristophanes, the supreme satirist of Athens —perhaps of all time. And yet of Aristophanes the satirist, in one sense we have had rather too much. For just as ancient criticism allotted to him an absurd role as a censor and teacher of private morality, so modern criticism has been extravagant in making of him a zealous national reformer in the field of politics, religion, education, and poetry. To be sure for this high seriousness of purpose appeal may be made to various utterances of the poet himself (e.g., *Wasps* 1030): "who came in the mood of a Heracles forth, to grapple at once with the mightiest foes." But to take a comedian's words strictly at their face value and build up from them a conception of character is to miss the humor which often lies behind them. Doubtless he has his likes and dislikes, even some bitter animosities, but to speak as Mr. Lucas has done most recently[3] of his "ceaseless torrent of anger and disgust and scorn" for Euripides is to interpret with credulity much that was merely a rich mine of material for comic effect before a responsive audience. The profession of seriousness, of high moral purpose, where all mankind knows that there is nothing serious, is in itself a source of comedy. The point needs no elaboration, but let me illustrate. In one of Gilbert's pleasant farces the Mountebank Bartolo sings.

> Though I'm a buffoon, recollect
> I command your respect.
> I cannot for money
> Be vulgarly funny,
> My object's to make you reflect.
>
> Other clowns make you laugh till you sink:
> I don't. I compel you to think.

The older German and English criticism of Aristophanes has been very insistent upon his use of ridicule and jest for ultimate ends artistic, moral, political, patriotic—that is for satire. It is time, I venture to think, to urge per contra that his satire is for the most part not the end, but the means, the material—τὸ τέλος, γέλως.

The moral obsession of literary criticism in later antiquity conceived of old comedy sternly as a reforming agent in the battle against vice. It had no conception of the satire of pure fun, like the comic operas of Gilbert let us say, which is less concerned with actual wrong and its reform than with the playful persiflage of the trite, the conventional, or the pretentious. From such a school of serious moralists the brief treatises on comedy (περὶ κωμῳδίας) which have come down as prolegomena to Aristophanes are derived. They are little concerned with old comedy as drama or poetry, but measure it by the canons of ethical value or instruction. They tell with obvious historical distortion that the invention of comedy was found to be a wholesome thing for the community as a deterrent of vice, and that therefore its openness and vehemence of attack received sanction. Of comedy as an element of joyous festival and the license of its carnival spirit in girding at everybody they have no adequate appreciation.

It is out of such Aristophanic criticism that the Latin definition of satire proceeded: *carmen apud Romanos maledicum et ad carpenda hominum vitia archaeae comoediae charactere compositum.* Whether this goes back of Diomedes to Suetonius, or back of him to Varro (as Leo urged), its elements are present in the familiar opening lines of Horace, explaining the *provenance* of Lucilian satire. The Horatian version I have advanced reason for assigning to the prolegomena of the edition of Lucilius, which Valerius Cato was preparing in Horace's time, and if this be correct we may assign this formulation of the function of satire to a period not long subsequent to Lucilius himself. The definition which Diomedes gives contains scarcely a hint of wit or humor as an essential ingredient of satire, except in so far as they are implied in the words *archaeae comoediae charactere,* which however refer rather to boldness of personal attack. The significant element of the definition is contained in the words *ad vitia hominum carpenda.* Satire is conceived of as an instrument of reform in the battle against human vice or sin. It proceeds, like the scholastic criticism of Aristophanes, from a moral, quasi-religious, point of view, which measured all literature by its ethical contribution. Of the pleasant satire of irony, innuendo, or mere incongruity it takes no account. However, definitions fortunately are narrower than the material from which they are drawn, and yet it must be acknowledged that that which in

antiquity came to be recognized as satire *par eminence* was restricted
unduly to the rebuke of vice.

To trace this narrower conception of the function of satire back
to its source, through the general philosophical propaganda of later
antiquity, to the so-called diatribes of early Cynics, has been the study
of many scholars in the past quarter of a century. The ultimate source
itself need not be named too precisely, but just as the later philosophies look to the personality of Socrates as their origin, so Socrates
himself may be thought of as the pioneer in giving the color of satire
to moral instruction and the pursuit of virtue. It is interesting to reflect that in the *Clouds* of Aristophanes we have in dramatic, almost
spectacular, juxtaposition the wit of the greatest spontaneous satirist
of antiquity playing with the character who may be called the source
of that conscious ethical satire which was destined to monopolize in
large measure the subsequent development of this literary category.
Nor is it accidental, for with Socrates we enter upon a long period of
Greek intellectual life which is marked by preoccupation with ethical
problems, with the too self-conscious cult of virtue. The gay, thought-
less satire of old comedy, sometimes too sharp but always merry, had
run its course, apart from archons' edicts or political changes.[4] It
passed over in some degree into new comedy, refined and subtilized,
especially in the direction of character portrayal, but for the most part
what we know of Alexandrine and post-Alexandrine satire is largely
confined to the literature of philosophical propaganda, of exhortation
to repentance and right living (*recte vivere*). Its goal was, in religious
phrase, conviction of sin: ὁ σκώπτων ἐλέγχειν θέλει ἁμαρτήματα τῆς
ψυχῆς. Of Menippus of Gadara and Bion of Borysthenes there is no
need to say more in this context than to call to mind that the satires
of Varro were called by him Menippean, and that Horace refers to his
own as Bionean. These designations in themselves are enough to show
that Quintilian's apparent claim of Roman originality cannot mean
exactly what it seems to say. The popular literature of moral exhortation received apparently from Bion a form and style which came to
dominate the utterances of every school. When Horace, in enumerat-
ing his three types of literary composition—odes, iambics, and satires
—calls the latter *Bionei sermones*, it may be suspected that he uses
the epithet merely *honoris causa* of an "inventor" (εὑρέτης), as the
clearest indication of a type of literature for which no more specific
designation (like *carmina* or *iambi*) was available.[5]

Greek never developed a specific designation for that which we call satire, nor did it create fixed forms for its expression. Satire is to be found in many places; most abundantly in comedy, the new as well as the old, and here it is satire of the more universal type. The moral satire of Bion was conveyed in the form of the lively prose harangue, a kind of sermon. In Menippus, with more conscious literary art, the dialogue seems to have been the prevailing vehicle, the trick and atmosphere of which we catch again in Lucian. There were besides the philosophic parodies of Timon in hexameter verse (σίλλοι), and most recently we have come to know the satirical moralizings of Phoenix of Colophon and Cercidas of Megalopolis in loosely constructed iambics and scazons. Not to attempt completeness of enumeration one may add the gastronomic studies of Archestratus—possible source of the dinner *motif* which plays a considerable role in Roman satire—and allude briefly to the mime and epigram as forms for conveying satirical observation.

In vocabulary κωμῳδεῖν is the word which approaches most nearly and most often to our "satirize." Many other words could be instanced giving a particular color to the given situation or intention. But the one comprehensive term which embraces satire in all its forms and nuances is simply "laughter"— γέλως, γελᾶν —the laughter of amusement and raillery, of irony, of scorn, of anger, penetrating the mask of pretense, demolishing false and restoring true values by the solvent of reality. A good deal of philosophy underlies the scholastic language of the Anonymus περὶ κωνῳδίας (in Kaibel, p. 14, 49) : η δὲ κωμῳδία συνίστησιν τὸν βίον.

That all mankind is caught in the toils of false values, and wastes life in the pursuit of worthless ends, is the more or less common teaching of all the philosophies. In the face of such error some argued, others inveighed, but Democritus merely laughed; and in this late and perhaps fabled story of Democritean laughter we have the most clearly defined theory of the function of satire that antiquity affords: ὗτος ἐγέλα πάντα, ὡς γέλωτος ἀξίων πάντων τῶν ἐν ἀνθρώποις.

Among the pseudepigraphic *Letters* of Hippocrates there is preserved a pedantic, but quaint jest in the form of a series of letters, which play upon the traditional reputation of the people of Abdera for stupidity.[6] It may be thought of I imagine as an aetiological story to explain the proverbial Ἀβδηριτικόν (Cicero *ad Att.* vii. 7). The opening letter contains the request of the senate and people of Abdera to Hippocrates, to come with all speed to avert disaster from their city, threatened with dire peril: because their most famous citizen, Democritus, seems from his behavior threatened with loss of reason. Forgetting everything, and most of all himself, he remains awake night and day, laughing at everything great and small. While others go about all the varied business of life he laughs at them all whether sad or gay. Passing over the details of the correspondence—the questions of Hippocrates, his preparations to leave his practice in Cos, the securing of the necessary simples, and a fast ship—Hippocrates at length arrives and is shown the patient. He finds him in his pleasant garden absorbed in study and writing down observations made upon sundry animals which lay dissected before him. On introducing himself Hippocrates is cordially received and recognized as the great physician. Inquiring the nature of these studies he learns that Democritus is composing a treatise upon madness (περὶ μανίης)—"How apropos!" he murmurs half aloud, with tactless forgetfulness—and to this end is studying the nature and seat of the bile in animals. Hippocrates expresses his interest and congratulates Democritus on enjoying leisure for such study, which is not permitted to himself. "But why not, Hippocrates?" asks Democritus. "Because," I replied, "my lands, my house, my children, my investments, sickness or death in the family, a wedding feast, or some such thing, deprive me of the opportunity of such leisure." Hereupon the man lapsed back into his usual malady and burst into a loud and jeering laugh (ἀνεκάγχασε καὶ ἐπετώθασε). "Why do you laugh?" said I. "At the blessings or the misfortunes of which I spoke?" But at this the man laughed all the more, while the Abderitae, looking on at a distance, smote their foreheads and rent their hair in dismay; for as they told me afterward he had never laughed quite so loud or so long before. But not to follow the scene further, Democritus explains in a long harangue the folly of mankind which provokes his laughter, convinces Hippocrates of the justice of it, and of his own perfect sanity. Thereupon Hippocrates takes his leave and proclaims to the waiting Abderitae—"true Abderitae they!" —that Democritus is the sanest of men, the only one in fact of his city sane, and able to make others wise and sane—a conclusion of familiar paradox: "It was the dog that died!"

This odd and apparently little-used document is a veritable mine of satirical τόποι composed with considerable wit and ingenuity. Its novelistic conception affords merely a piquant setting for a characteristic Cynic "diatribe" upon the general vitia hominum. I have thought it worth reporting because it shows in naïve objectivity a theory of the role of satire as it had become fixed in time antedating the Roman satirists, even if much subsequent to Democritus himself.[7]

Early Roman literary theory, dealing not yet with a literary genus, but merely with the personality of Lucilius (*character Lucilianus*), emphasized in him his freedom and boldness of personal attack. Thus, since it was apparently the natural assumption that all Roman writing must be associated with some Greek prototype, this criticism with absurd exaggeration proclaimed him a close follower of Attic old comedy (*hinc omnis pendet*)—a judgment based less upon old comedy itself than upon the treatises περὶ κωμῳδίας. When at a later time (in the early days of Horace) this *character Lucilianus* became generalized to cover the conception of a Roman *satura*, there came into the definition and idea of satire a notion of vehement personal attack which is in fact quite alien to all Roman satire subsequent to Lucilius. This point of view persisted curiously, so far as the name and theory are concerned, down to the latest times. Its echoes in Horace, Persius, and Juvenal are familiar, and in English literature with better justification (for no Roman satire is so venomous and personal as Dryden, Pope, and their compeers) it lasted down to Gifford and Byron.[8] But in reality from Horace on, except for some sonorous threats, satire is by definition abstract and general, and in its use of names quite harmless. Its subject matter is the rebuke of examples of vice: *quemvis media elige turba: aut ob avaritiam aut misera ambitione laborat*, etc. This of course in its end is not different from the aim of moral philosophy in general. Apart from the metrical form it would perhaps be difficult to assign a specific element of differentiation between the popular Greek literature of moral persuasion and Roman satire, unless it lie precisely in larger insistence on wit or humor as its essential spirit.[9]

To cite in illustration the familiar and somewhat overworked Horatian *ridentem dicere verum* is doubtless superfluous. More subtle and more clever is the allegory in *solventur risu tabulae* to signify that laughter prevails against the most unyielding barriers, and may make palatable the bitterest truth. Persius is accounted a Stoic of the strictest sect, and we do not think of the Stoics as humorists. But if his humor is not always subtle nor his wit trenchant, let no one doubt that humorous intention lies behind his extravagance of phrase, his occasional obscenities, and much that may seem overwrought and hysterical. His purpose is defined for us most compactly in the familiar phrase *ingenuo culpam defigere ludo*. More interesting however and more specific in its implications of theory is the opening of the first satire:

> O curas hominum, o quantum est in rebus inane!
> ....
> tunc, cum ad canitiem et nostrum istud vivere triste
> aspexi, ... tunc, tunc .... cachinno.

This, it will be seen, is nothing characteristically Persian, nor Roman: it is merely the absorption and passing on of the fable or tradition of Democritean laughter. Juvenal is more specific (10, 51) in his reference to the Abderitan:

> ridebat curas nec non et gaudia volgi, interdum et lacrimas,

and it is a reasonable belief that from such familiar source he drew the characterization of his own purpose,

> quidquid agunt homines, votum timor ira voluptas
> gaudia discursus, nostri farrago libelli est,[10]

—not of course as a mere panorama of human life, but as affording material for satire, ὡς γέλωτος ἀξίων πάντων τῶν ἐν ἀνθρώποις— *quidquid agunt homines*.

Wherever then we turn in Roman satire, whether regarding the subject matter or the tone and manner of treatment, everywhere we find Greek theory and Greek literary practice antecedent. With much of this literature Quintilian must have had some acquaintance, even though much of his criticism merely passes on older coin already current. We revert then to the problem from which we started and ask what was meant by his dictum, "Satire is wholly ours."

It has been the general practice of criticism faced with this problem to defend Quintilian by affirming that satire *is* Roman, because in a peculiar degree it is permeated with the Roman spirit, the Roman practical point of view in ethics, and the atmosphere of the larger and more complex social life which, in the ancient world, was only developed at Rome. True as these statements may be in whole or in part, they are yet irrelevant; for while they may explain some traits of Roman satire they do not explain Quintilian. The same thing could be said of several other departments of literature which Quintilian recognizes as common to both Greek and Latin. Yet it does not occur to Quintilian to disassociate Roman history, or elegy, for example, from their Greek counterparts, although both of these forms received a very definite and peculiar Roman development. What then does he mean, and do we translate him correctly when we render "Satire is wholly ours"? Apparently, yes; but we create a dilemma like this: either Quintilian did not know Greek satire, or he did not speak the truth; and neither of these alternatives is acceptable.

The true solution of the difficulty lies in the two words set over against each other, *satura* and *satire*. We seem to be setting two equivalent and identical words side by side; but are we? One is a word, the history of which as recognized literary nomenclature had scarcely more than begun in Quintilian's time; the other is the same word inflated with the associations of twenty centuries of use, and the experience of all the peoples who have derived their literary vocabulary from the ancient world. To understand what the word *satura* meant to Quintilian we must put a check upon too facile identification of *satire* with it, and consider two things: first, the history of the word; and second, the habits of literary classification in antiquity.

The earliest occurrence of the word *satura* in literary association —whether in the form *satura* or *per saturam*—is as a title, probably humorous or playful in the first instance, of the miscellaneous poems of Ennius. Used in the same sense by Lucilius and Varro, it passed over in Horace's time to a designation of the Lucilian satire as a type, and in this sense first occurs at the beginning of Horace's second book (*sunt quibus in satura videor nimis acer*). It is used once again by him in the same book with emphasis on its form—*saturis musaque pedestri*. Yet these tentative efforts of Horace to employ the word did not serve to give it currency. Horace himself was evidently shy of its use. In the first book of the satires, where he talks much of the literary form and its relation to Lucilius, he had not employed the word, nor again fifteen years later, in his *Letters*, with all their discussion of literary and social problems, does he revert to it. The idea of satire he expresses variously with the general resources of the language, but the name itself must have seemed to him too little current for appropriate use, and still carried with it too definitely the suggestion of its origin as the designation of a mere miscellany. Such an explanation is made plausible from the circumstance that in Sallust, the archaizer, at a time contemporary with Horace's early work, we find recurrence of the phrase *per saturam*, which for nearly a century had dropped out of use.

During all the remaining period of the Augustan age (except for a disputed passage of Livy), in all the literary gossip of the Elder Seneca (which might naturally have furnished frequent occasion for its employment), in the abundant satire of the philosopher Seneca, in the satirical romance of Petronius, and in the very satires of Persius, the word still remains unused. We must therefore conclude, not that its absence is due to the defect of our record, but that the word was slow in gaining recognition and in conveying a definite suggestion of manner and tone. This can scarcely have been otherwise when we consider that side by side there were produced works so divergent in manner as Horace's and Varro's, yet bearing a common name. The same thing appears from the information which Porphyrio gives in his comment on the letter to Julius Florus (i. 3) : *cuius sunt electae ex Ennio Lucilio Varrone saturae.* The distinction which Quintilian (and later Diomedes) draws between *satura* as commonly understood in his day, and the older meaning of a miscellany, cannot be earlier than Augustan, and was probably brought about by the classical rank to which Horace's work attained.

Not until the Flavian period does the word emerge again, and show something like currency and a fixed connotation. Statius uses it once in an enumeration of the literary work of the dilettante Vopiscus, and Martial twice. Only in the passage under discussion does Quintilian use the word as the designation of a literary type or genus.[11] However he does thus use the word without apology or explanation, so that it is clear from his (as from Martial and Statius) that the word was now current in this meaning. But it is significant to note that in all of these instances, Horace, Statius, Martial, Quintilian, the word is always the name of the concrete literary genus itself; it has not yet gone beyond this, a situation reflected in the fact that the noun, the name, alone was in use, and that the need for adjectival or other extensions had not yet arisen. The whole vast territory covered by our current usage to indicate the satirical spirit or, as we say simply, satire, with no thought of literary genus or specific compositions, was not yet embraced in the word. This restriction of scope we may illustrate crudely by the word "sonnet," which in an analogous way is restricted and concrete, with no large inclusiveness of connotation beyond the designation of a type of poetry in a certain form.

The importance of a recognized form must not be overlooked in this connection. In Greek for example the whole body of iambic and comic poetry might be called the γένος σκωπτικόν. Under this general rubric there are many forms: iambics, comedy, satyr-drama, mime, silloi, and others. These names connote a general spirit of raillery— σκώπτειν —expressed in a definitely recognized form. But of these two elements it is form which yields the particular classification of any given piece of literature. Thus for example the second epode of Horace is, in accordance with our usage, a perfect "satire" of the man who professes the deepest feeling for country life, and yet cannot be torn from his Wall Street. But neither Horace nor Quintilian could have called it a "satire."

From these illustrations it should be clear what I mean by saying that the word "satire" remained at the stage of a particular connotation, certainly down to Quintilian's time. Thus when he says *satura tota nostra est* he means that the special type of literature created by Lucilius, dominated by a certain spirit, clothed in a certain metrical form, fixed by the usage of a series of canonical writers, and finally designated by a name specifically Latin, is Roman and not Greek. And in this sense the correctness of his statement requires no qualification. His words do not in the least mean that he denies "satire," as we use the word, to Aristophanes for example. He recognizes it of course, but he could not yet think of applying to his manner or spirit the name of "satire." He has in fine no consciousness of saying what we understand by such a translation (though it is apparently verbatim) as "satire is wholly ours." The confusion of our rendering lies in the fact that we do not in consciousness differentiate between the word as a *verbum proprium*, concrete and specific, and the same word inflated by metaphorical shift to embrace a multitude of ideas which are related to the Roman meaning only by likeness.

We are now in position to explain (in some degree at least) what has seemed a paradox, the extraordinary infrequency in Roman literature of a word which is constantly upon our lips in any literary discussion. For in fact, as we have seen, the word had as yet only a fraction of the meaning we attach to it. For ninety per cent or more of the occasions that we find to use "satire," or its apparent derivatives, the Roman would employ *risus, ridere*, or some analogous word suited to the special color of his thought. The extension of the word *satura* to include the satirical spirit in a comprehensive way calls for more careful study. The existence of a large body of satire like Juvenal's may have been influential in creating a consciousness of need, though no one of the four examples in Juvenal can be interpreted as other than concrete and proper. The first indisputable example of the word as a descriptive term, referring to a literature which was neither Roman nor in canonical form, but only in the general vein of Roman satire, is found in Apuleius (*Florida* ii. 20), who refers to Xenocrates as the "author of satires." His meaning is obviously that Xenocrates wrote works similar in spirit to Roman satire: that is, Apuleius uses metaphor. But so soon as a noun enters the domain of metaphor it clamors for extension. Here the Romans found ready at hand a Greek word of similar meaning and of almost identical form, σάτυρος, with a rich family of derivatives, σατυρικός, σατυρίζειν, σατυριστής, and these they appropriated to add to the slender dower of their native *satura*. Few of us I imagine are conscious that in using the series "satire," "satiric," "satirist," "satirize," we are dealing with words unrelated etymologically. Latin usage is confined to the noun *satura*, but it is not from it that our common words "satirical" and "satirize" are derived. From the third or fourth century on *satyricus* (= σατυρικός) begins to function as an equivalent for *scriptor saturarum*. Thus by degrees the true etymology of *satura*, as a Latin word, was lost, and, with modified orthography (*satyra*), derivation from the Greek σάτυρος took its place. Thus in early modern times it seems to have been held quite universally that satire was derived from the Greek satyr-drama, and John Hall in a Latin epigram, prefatory to his *Toothless Satyrs*, plays with the conceit of satire as a new sort of monster, a female satyr,[12] a creature without horns. Support was doubtless given to this conception by the current form of the word, which down to Dryden's time was commonly written "satyr" and probably pronounced as a trochee or pyrrhic with closed *a* and short final syllable, rhyming[13] with "nature" (pronounced "nátur," like "figure, figgur"). Our modern semi-spondaic pronunciation, "sátìre," is probably a vocal accommodation to the apparent length of the last syllable in the French form *satire*, which was introduced into English by Dryden's authority. The false etymology current in early modern times was finally exploded by Casaubon, in his famous of Roman satire and the Greek satyr-drama in the year 1605. But the older view still prevailed: when Milton speaks of satire as "born out of a tragedy" he has in mind obviously the satyr-drama which followed upon the tragic trilogy, and even one of the latest of English writers[14] speaks of satire as "begotten by Pan, the goat-footed."

NOTES

¹ Dionys. Hal. vii. 72. 11: παλαιὰν καὶ ἐπιχώριον οὖσαν τοῖς Ῥωμαίοις τὴν κέρτομον καὶ σατυρικὴν παιδιάν.

² Surveyed by Geffcken in *N. Jahrbb.*, XXVII (1911), 393ff. and 468ff.

³ *Euripides and His Influence*, Boston, 1923.

⁴ Cf. Starkie, Introduction to the *Clouds*.

⁵ The usage of the past few decades has made current somewhat arbitrarily the term "diatribe" as the specific name of this literary manner. As a convenient designation it may and doubtless will continue to be used, but it is an arbitrary and recent restriction of a much more comprehensive word. See the acute and learned observations of O. Halbauer, *De diatribis Epicteti* (diss.), Leipzig, 1911.

⁶ They are Nos. 10–17 in Littré, IX, 320ff. (Kühn, *Medic. Graec.*, XXIII, 775ff.). The longest and most essential letter is No. 17 (Littré, pp. 349ff.). On the character of the text, the date (under Tiberius or Caligula), the names, etc., cf. the able discussion of Diels, *Hippokratische Forsch., Hermes* LIII (1918), 57ff., to whom I owe my acquaintance with the material.

⁷ The two earliest allusions seem to be Cicero *De Orat.* ii. 235, *de risu . . . viderit Democritus*, and Horace *Epp.* ii. 1. 194, *si foret in terris rideret Democritus*. The treatise of Democritus περὶ εὐθυμίας seems the most likely source of the tradition, but with apparent distortion of cheerfulness to satirical laughter.

⁸ Cf. Jerome *Epp.* xxii. 32, *nomen taceo ne saturam putes*, and xl. 2 (Jerome has written against vice in general; his opponent considers it personal), *te clamitas designari . . . et satiricum scriptorem in prosa stulte arguis*. Cited by Weston, *Lat. Sat. Writing Subsequent to Juvenal* (Yale diss., 1915), p. 99.

⁹ Cf. the suggestive paper of C. W. Mendell, "Satire as Popular Philosophy" (in *Classical Philology*, XV (1920), 138ff.), who however underrates the role of humor in Roman satire.

¹⁰ The first part of this declaration of purpose is Democritean, the second part *nostri farrago libelli* looks like a periphrasis of *satura (per saturam)*.

¹¹ In ix. 2. 36, *in satura tradit Ennius*, and in ix. 3. 9, *in satura*, citing a line of Persius, the word is employed to designate the source of an illustration.

¹² Cf. Lucret. iv. 1169, *simula Silena ac satura est*.

[13] Cf. Dryden's characterization of Doeg (*Absalom and Achitophel*, part II):

> "Spiteful he is not though he wrote a satyr,
> For still there goes some thinking to ill-nature."

[14] Mr. Gilbert Cannan in *Satire*, London, 1914.

RONALD A. KNOX

On Humour and Satire

Whoever shall turn up in a modern encyclopaedia the article on humming-birds—whether from a disinterested curiosity about these brightly coloured creatures, or from the more commonplace motive of identifying a clue in a crossword—will find a curious surprise awaiting him at the end of it. He will find that the succeeding paragraph deals with the geological formation known as a *humus*; or if his encyclopaedia be somewhat more exhaustive, with the quaintly named genius of Humperdinck. What will excite his speculation is, of course, the fact that no attempt is made by his author to deal with humour. Humour, for the encyclopaedist, is non-existent; and that means that no book has ever been written on the subject of humour; else the ingenious Caledonian who retails culture to us at the rate of five guineas a column would inevitably have boiled it down for us ere this. The great history of Humour in three volumes, dedicated by permission to the Bishop of Much Wenlock, still remains to be written. And that fact, in its turn, is doubly significant. It means, in the first place, that humour, in our sense of the word, is a relatively modern phenomenon; the idea of submitting it to exhaustive analysis did not, for example, present itself to the patient genius of John Stuart Mill. And at the same time it is an uncommonly awkward and elusive subject to tackle, or why have we no up-to-date guide to it from the hand of Mr. Arnold Bennett?

Assuredly this neglect is not due to any want of intrinsic importance. For humour, frown upon it as you will, is nothing less than a fresh window of the soul. Through that window we see, not indeed a different world, but the familiar world of our experience distorted

From *Essays in Satire*, London, 1928, pp. 15–43. Reprinted by permission of Sheed & Ward, London, and the late Monsignor Knox's Literary Executor.

as if by the magic of some tricksy sprite. It is a plate-glass window, which turns all our earnest, toiling fellow-mortals into figures of fun. If a man awoke to it of a sudden, it would be an enlightenment of his vision no less real than if a man who had hitherto seen life only in black and grey should be suddenly gifted with the experience of colour. More, even, than this; the sense of humour is a man's inseparable playmate, allowing him, for better or worse, no solitude anywhere. In crowded railway-carriages, in the lonely watches of a sleepless night, even in the dentist's chair, the sense of humour is at your side, full of elfin suggestions. Do you go to Church? He will patter up the aisle alongside of you, never more at home, never more alert, than when the spacious silences of worship and the solemn purple of prelates enjoins reverence. I could become lyrical, if I had time, over the sense of humour, what it does for men and how it undoes them, what comfort lies in its companionship, and what menace. Enough to say that if I had the writing of an encyclopaedia the humming-birds should be made to look foolish.

Humour has been treated, perhaps, twice in literature; once in the preface to Meredith's *Egoist*, and once in Mr. Chesterton's book, *The Napoleon of Notting Hill*. What it is still remains a mystery. Easy enough to distinguish it from its neighbours in the scale of values: with wit, for example, it has nothing to do. For wit is first and last a matter of expression. Latin, of all languages, is the best vehicle of wit, the worst of humour. You cannot think a witty thought, even, without thinking in words. But humour can be wordless; there are thoughts that lie too deep for laughter itself. In this essay I mean to treat humour as it compares with and contrasts with satire, a more delicate distinction. But first let us make an attempt, Aristotle-wise, to pin down the thing itself with some random stab of definition. Let us say that the sphere of humour is, predominantly, Man and his activities, considered in circumstances so incongruous, so unexpectedly incongruous, as to detract from their human dignity. Thus, the prime source of humour is a madman or a drunkard; either of these wears the semblance of a man without enjoying the full use of that rational faculty which is man's definition. A foreigner, too, is always funny: he dresses, but does not dress right; makes sounds, but not the right sounds. A man falling down on a frosty day is funny, because he has unexpectedly abandoned that upright walk which is man's glory as a biped. All these things are funny, of course, only from a certain angle; not, for example, from the angle of ninety degrees, which is described by the man who falls down. But amusement is habitually derived from such situations; and in each case it is a human victim that is demanded for the sacrifice. It is possible, in the mythological manner, to substitute an animal victim, but only if the animal be falsely invested with the attributes of humanity. There is nothing at all funny about a horse falling down. A monkey making faces, a cat at play, amuse us only because we feign to ourselves that the brute is rational; to that fiction we are accustomed from childhood. Only Man has dignity; only man, therefore, can be funny. Whether there could have been humour even in human fortunes but for the Fall of Adam is a problem which might profitably have been discussed by St. Thomas in his *Summa Theologiae*, but was omitted for lack of space.

The question is raised (as the same author would say) whether humour is in its origins indecent. And at first it would appear yes. For the philosopher says that the ludicrous is a division of the disgraceful. And the gods in Homer laugh at the predicament of Ares and Aphrodite in the recital of the bard Demodocus. But on second thoughts it is to be reflected that the song of Demodocus is, by common consent of the critics, a late interpolation in Homer; and the first mention of laughter in the classics is rather the occasion on which the gods laughed to see the lame Hephaestus panting as he limped up and down the hall. Once more, a lame man is funny because he enjoys, like the rest of us, powers of locomotion, but employs them wrong. His gait is incongruous—not unexpectedly so, indeed, for the gods had witnessed this farce daily for centuries; but the gods were children, and the simplest farces always have the best run. No doubt the psychoanalysts will want us to believe that all humour has its origin in indecency, and, for aught I know, that whenever we laugh we are unconsciously thinking of something obscene. But, in fact, the obscene, as its name implies, is an illegitimate effect of humour. There is nothing incongruous in the *existence* of sex and the other animal functions; the incongruity lies merely in the fact of mentioning them. It is not human dignity that is infringed in such cases, but a human convention of secrecy. The Stock Exchange joke, like most operations on the Stock Exchange, is essentially artificial; it does not touch the real values of things at all. In all the generalizations which follow it must be understood that the humour of indecency is being left out of account.

Yet there is truth in the philosopher's assertion that the ludicrous is a division of the disgraceful, in this sense, that in the long run every joke makes a fool of somebody; it must have, as I say, a human victim. This fact is obscured by the frequency with which jokes, especially modern jokes, are directed against their own authors. The man who makes faces to amuse a child is, objectively, making a fool of himself; and that whole *genre* of literary humour of which *Happy Thoughts*, the *Diary of a Nobody*, and the Eliza books are the best-known examples, depends entirely on the fact that the author is making a fool of himself. In all humour there is loss of dignity somewhere, virtue has gone out of somebody. For there is no inherent humour in things; wherever there is a joke it is Man, the half-angel, the half-beast, who is somehow at the bottom of it. I am insisting upon this point because, on a careless analysis, one might be disposed to imagine that the essence of satire is to be a joke directed against somebody. That definition, clearly, will be inadequate, if our present analysis of humour in general be accepted.

I have said that humour is, for the most part, a modern pheno-menon. It would involve a very long argument, and some very far-reaching considerations, if we attempted to prove this thesis of humour as a fact in life. Let us be more modest, and be content for the present to say that the humorous in literature is for the most part a modern phenomenon. Let us go back to our starting-point, and imagine one pursuing his researches about humming-birds into the *Encyclopaedia Britannica* of 1797. He skims through a long article on Mr. David Hume, faced by an attractive but wholly unreliable portrait of the hippopotamus. Under "Humming-bird" he will only read the words "See Trochilus." But immediately following, he will find the greater part of a column under the title "Humour." Most of it deals with the jargon of a psychology now obsolete, and perhaps fanciful, though not more fanciful, I think, than the psychological jargon of our own day. But at the end he will find some valuable words on humour as it is contrasted with wit. "Wit expresses something that is more designed, concerted, regular, and artificial; humour, something that is more wild, loose, extravagant, and fantastical; something which comes upon a man by fits, which he can neither command nor restrain, and which is not perfectly consistent with true politeness. Humour, it has been said, is often more diverting than wit; yet a man of wit is as much above a man of humour, as a gentleman is above a buffoon; a buffoon, however, will often divert more than a gentleman. The Duke of Buckingham, however, makes humour to be all in all," and so on. "Not perfectly consistent with true politeness"—oh, admirable faith

of the eighteenth century, even in its decline! "The Duke of Buckingham, however"—a significant exception. It seems possible that the
reign of the Merry Monarch saw a false dawn of the sense of humour.
If so, it was smothered for a full century afterwards by an overpower-
ing incubus of whiggery. The French Revolution had come and gone,
and yet humour was for the age of Burke "not perfectly consistent
with true politeness."

One is tempted, as I say, to maintain that the passing of the
eighteenth century is an era in human history altogether, since with the
nineteenth century humour, as an attitude towards life, begins. The
tone of Disraeli about politics, the tone of Richard Hurrell Froude
about all the external part of religion, seems to me quite inconceivable in any earlier age. But let us confine ourselves to literature,
and say that humour as a force *in literature* is struggling towards its
birth in Jane Austen, and hardly achieves its full stature till Calverley.
I know that there are obvious exceptions. There is humour in Aristophanes and in Petronius; there is humour in Shakespeare, though not
as much of it as one would expect; humour in Sterne, too, and
in Sheridan. But if you set out to mention the great names of antiquity
which are naturally connected with humorous writing, you will find
that they are all the names of satirists. Aristophanes in great part,
Lucian, Juvenal, Martial, Blessed Thomas More, Cervantes, Rabelais,
Butler, Molière, La Fontaine, Swift—humour and satire are, before
the nineteenth century, almost interchangeable terms. Humour in art
had begun in the eighteenth century, but it had begun with Hogarth!
Put a volume by Barrie or Milne into the hands of Edmund Burke—
could he have begun to understand it?

You can corroborate the fact of this growth in humour by a
complementary fact about our modern age, the decline of *naïveté*. If
you come to think of it, the best laughs you will get out of the old
classics are laughs which the author never meant to put there. Of
all the ancients, none can be so amusing as Herodotus, but none,
surely, had less sense of humour. It is a rare grace, like all the *gratiae
gratis datae*, this humour of the *naïf*. Yet it reaches its climax on the
very threshold of the nineteenth century; next to Herodotus, surely,
comes James Boswell. Since the dawn of nineteenth century humour,
you will find unconscious humour only in bad writers, Ella Wheeler
Wilcox, and the rest. Humour kills the *naïf*, nor could any great
writer of to-day recapture, if he would, Boswell's splendid unself-
consciousness.

Under correction, then, I am maintaining that literature before the nineteenth century has no conscious humour apart from satire. I must now pass on to an impression which all of us have, but an impression so presumptuous that we seldom have the courage to put it into words. It is this, that humour, apart from satire, belongs to the English-speaking peoples alone. I say, the English-speaking peoples, a cumbrous and an unreal division of mankind. But, thank God, you cannot bring any preposterous ethnographical fictions in here. Not even Houston Stewart Chamberlain ever ventured to congratulate the Germans on their sense of humour; not even the Dean of St. Paul's will dare to tell us that the sense of humour is Nordic. The facts speak for themselves. Satire still flourishes on the Continent; Anatole France was no unworthy citizen of the country of Voltaire. There is satire, too, among the Northern peoples; I believe that if I expressed my private opinion as to who was the world's greatest satirist I should reply, Hans Andersen. Only in spots, of course; but the man who wrote the *Ugly Duckling* and the *Darning Needle* and the *Story of the Emperor's New Clothes* seems to me to have a finer sense of the intrinsic ludicrousness of mankind than Swift himself. Satire is international, as it is of all ages; but where shall humour be found, apart from satire, on the Continent of Europe? Who, unless he were a laugher at the malicious or the obscene, ever picked up the translation of a foreign book in search of a good laugh? Who ever found a good joke in a Continental illustrated paper? Cleverness of drawing abounds, but the captions beneath the drawings are infantile. I have seen a Swedish illustrated supplement, and I do not believe there was a single item in it which would have been accepted by *Comic Cuts*. I am told that the humorous drama of modern France forms a complete exception to this statement of the facts. I am content to believe it; there must, of course, be exceptions. I put forward the rule as a rule.

Some, no doubt, on a hasty analysis, would limit the field still further by saying that humour is purely English. And it would be easy to defend this contention by pointing to the fact that the English enjoy their joke very largely at the expense of their neighbours. Nothing belongs more decisively to the English-speaking world than the anecdote. We are for ever telling stories, and how many of those stories are about a Scot (we call it a Scotchman), an Irishman, a Jew, or an American? But this, if our definition of humour was a sound one, is in the nature of the case. A foreigner is funny, because he is like

ourselves only different. A Scot or an Irishman is funny to the Englishman because he is almost exactly like himself, only slightly different.
He talks English as his native tongue, only with an incorrect accent;
what could possibly be funnier? A Scot is more funny than a French-
man just as a monkey is more amusing than a dog; he is nearer the
real thing.

But, in fact, all such judgments have been distorted beyond
recognition by national hypocrisy. It is the English tradition that the
Irish are a nation brimming over with humour, quite incapable of
taking anything seriously. Irish people are in the habit of saying things
which English people think funny. Irish people do not think them
funny in the least. It follows, from the English point of view, that
Ireland is a nation of incorrigible humorists, all quite incapable of
governing themselves. The Scot, on the other hand, has an unfortunate
habit of governing the English, and the English, out of revenge, have
invented the theory that the Scot has no sense of humour. The Scot
cannot have any sense of humour, because he is very careful about
money, and drinks whisky where ordinary people drink beer. All the
stories told against the Scottish nation are, I am told, invented in
Aberdeen, and I partly believe it. There is (if a denationalized Ulster-
man like myself may make the criticism) a pawkiness about all the
stories against Scotland which betrays their Caledonian origin. The
fact is that the Scottish sense of humour differs slightly from the
English sense of humour, but I am afraid I have no time to indicate
the difference. There is humour in the country of Stevenson and
Barrie; and if the joke is often against Scotland, what better proof
could there be that it is humour, and not satire?

Whatever may be said of Americans in real life, it is certain that
their literature has humour. Personally I do not think that the Americans are nearly as proud as they ought to be of this fact; Mark Twain
ought to be to the American what Burns is to the Scot, and rather
more. The hall-mark of American humour is its pose of illiteracy. All
the American humorists spend their time making jokes against themselves. Artemus Ward pretended that he was unable even to spell.
Mark Twain pretended that he had received no education beyond
spelling, and most of his best remarks are based on this affectation of
ignorance. "What is your *bête noire?*" asked the revelations-of-char-
acter book, and Mark Twain replied, "What is my which?" "He
spelt it Vinci, but pronounced it Vinchy; foreigners always spell better
than they pronounce"—that is perhaps one of the greatest jokes of

literature, but the whole point of it lies in a man pretending to be worse educated than he really is. Mr. Leacock, as a rule, amuses by laughing at himself. America, on the other hand, has very little to show in the way of satire. Lowell was satirical, in a rather heavy vein, and Mr. Leacock is satirical occasionally, in a way that seems to me purely English. I want to allude to that later on; for the present let it be enough to note that the Americans, like the English and the Scots, do possess a literary tradition of non-satirical humour.

Thus far, we have concluded that the humorous in literature is the preserve of that period which succeeds the French Revolution, and of those peoples which speak the English language under its several denominations; unless by the word humour you understand "satire." It is high time, obviously, that we attempted some definition of what satire is, or at least of the marks by which it can be distinguished from non-satirical humour. It is clear from the outset that the author who laughs at himself, unless the self is a deliberately assumed one, is not writing satire. *Happy Thoughts* and *The Diary of a Nobody* may be what you will; they are not satire. *The Tramp Abroad* is not satire; *My Lady Nicotine* is not satire. For in all these instances the author, with a charity worthy of the Saints—and indeed, St. Philip Neri's life is full of this kind of charity—makes a present of himself to his reader as a laughing-stock. In satire, on the contrary, the writer always leaves it to be assumed that he himself is immune from all the follies and the foibles which he pillories. To take an obvious instance, Dickens is no satirist when he introduces you to Mr. Winkle, because there is not the smallest reason to suppose that Dickens would have handled a gun better than Mr. Winkle. But when Dickens introduces you to Mr. Bumble he is a satirist at once, for it is perfectly obvious that Dickens would have handled a porridge-ladle better than Mr. Bumble did. The humorist runs with the hare; the satirist hunts with the hounds.

There is, indeed, less contempt in satire than in irony. Irony is content to describe men exactly as they are, to accept them professedly, at their own valuation, and then to laugh up its sleeve. It falls outside the limits of humorous literature altogether; there is irony in Plato, there is irony in the Gospels; Mr. Galsworthy is an ironist, but few people have ever laughed over Mr. Galsworthy. Satire, on the contrary, borrows its weapons from the humorist; the satirized figure must be made to leap through the hoops of improbable adventure and farcical situation. It is all the difference between *The Egoist* and *Don*

Quixote. Yet the laughter which satire provokes has malice in it always; we want to dissociate ourselves from the victim; to let the lash that curls round him leave our withers unwrung. It is not so with humour: not so (for instance) with the work of an author who should have been mentioned earlier, Mr. P. G. Wodehouse. To read the adventures of Bertie Wooster as if they were a satire on Bertie Wooster, or even on the class to which Bertie Wooster may be supposed to belong, is to misread them in a degree hardly possible to a German critic. The reader must make himself into Bertie Wooster in order to enjoy his Jeeves, just as he must make himself into Eliza's husband in order to enjoy his Eliza. Nobody can appreciate the crackers of humour unless he is content to put on his fool's cap with the rest of the party.

What, then, is the relation between humour and satire? Which is the parent, and which the child? Which is the normal organ, and which the morbid growth? I said just now that satire borrows its weapons from the humorist, and that is certainly the account most of us would be prepared to give of the matter off-hand. Most things in life, we reflect, have their comic side as well as their serious side; and the good-humoured man is he who is content to see the humorous side of things even when the joke is against himself. The comic author, by persistently abstracting from the serious side of things, contrives to build up a world of his own, whose figures are all grotesques, whose adventures are the happy adventures of farce. Men fight, but only with foils; men suffer, but only suffer indignities; it is all a pleasant nursery tale, a relief to be able to turn to it when your mind is jaded with the sour facts of real life. Such, we fancy, is the true province of the Comic Muse; and satire is an abuse of the function. The satirist is like one who should steal his little boy's water-pistol and load it with vitriol, and so walk abroad flourishing it in men's faces. A treacherous fellow, your satirist. He will beguile the leisure of an Athenian audience, needing some rest, Heaven knows, from the myriad problems of a relentless war with powerful neighbours, by putting on a little play called *The Birds.* Capital; we shall enjoy that. Two citizens of Athens, so the plot runs, take wings to themselves and set out to build a bird city, remote from the daily instance of this subnubilar world. Excellent! That is just what we wanted, a relief for tired brains! And then, the fellow has tricked us, it proves, after all! His city in the clouds is, after all, only a parody of an Athenian colony, and the ceremonies which attend its inauguration are a burlesque, in the worst possible taste, of Athenian colonial policy. We came here for a holiday, and we are being treated to a sermon instead! No wonder the Athenian audiences often refused the first prize to Aristophanes. Skip twenty-one centuries, and find yourself in the times of the early Georges. There has been a great vogue, of late, for descriptions of travel in strange countries; and now (they are saying in the coffee-houses) the Dean of St. Patrick's, Dublin, has written a burlesque of these travel narratives, about countries that never existed at all—the ingenious dog! And then, as we read, it dawns upon us suddenly that Lilliput and Brobdingnag are not, after all, so distant, so imaginary; in fact, we have never really got away from the England of the Georges at all. The spirit of satire has overlooked us, like a wicked fairy, and turned the milk of human kindness sour as we churned it.

My present thesis, not dogmatically asserted but rather thrown out as if for discussion, is that this way of viewing the relations between humour and satire is a perversion of history. To think of satire as a particular direction which humour may happen to take, a particular channel into which humour may be diverted, is to neglect, surely, the broad facts as we have stated them above. Humour is of an age, satire of all ages; humour is of one particular civilization, satire of all countries. Is it not, then, more reasonable to suppose that satire is a normal function of the human genius, and humour that has no satire in it a perversion of the function, a growth away from the normal? That our sense of the ridiculous is not, in its original application, a child's toy at all, but a weapon, deadly in its efficacy, entrusted to us for exposing the shams and hypocrisies of the world? The tyrant may arm himself in triple mail, may surround himself with bodyguards, may sow his kingdom with a hedge of spies, so that free speech is crushed and criticism muzzled. Nay, worse, he may so debauch the consciences of his subjects with false history and with sophistical argument that they come to believe him the thing he gives himself out for, a creature half-divine, a heaven-sent deliverer. One thing there is that he still fears; one anxiety still bids him turn this way and that to scan the faces of his slaves. He is afraid of laughter. The satirist stands there, like the little child in the procession when the Emperor walked through the capital in his famous new clothes; his is the tiny voice that interprets the consciousness of a thousand onlookers: "But, Mother, he has no clothes on at all!"

Satire has a wider scope, too. It is born to scourge the persistent and ever-recurrent follies of the human creature as such. And, for anybody who has the humility to realize that it is aimed at him, and not merely at his neighbours, satire has an intensely remedial effect; it purifies the spiritual system of man as nothing else that is human can possibly do. Thus, every young man who is in love should certainly read *The Egoist* (there would be far less unhappiness in marriage if they all did), and no schoolmaster should ever begin the scholastic year without re-reading Mr. Bradby's *Lanchester Tradition*, to remind him that he is but dust. Satire is thus an excellent discipline for the satirized: whether it is a good thing for the satirist is more open to question. *Facit indignatio versum*; it is seldom that the impetus to write satire comes to a man except as the result of a disappointment. Since disappointment so often springs from love, it is not to be wondered at that satirists have ever dealt unkindly with woman, from the days of Simonides of Amorgos, who compared woman with more than thirty different kinds of animals, in every case to her disadvantage. A pinched, warped fellow, as a rule, your satirist. It is misery that drives men to laughter. It is bad humour that encourages men first to be humorous. And it is, I think, when good-humoured men pick up this weapon of laughter, and, having no vendettas to work off with it, begin tossing it idly at a mark, that humour without satire takes its origin.

In a word, humour without satire is, strictly speaking, a perversion, the misuse of a sense. Laughter is a deadly explosive which was meant to be wrapped up in the cartridge of satire, and so, aimed unerringly at its appointed target, deal its salutary wound; humour without satire is a flash in the pan; it may be pretty to look at, but it is, in truth, a waste of ammunition. Or, if you will, humour is satire that has run to seed; trained no longer by an artificial process, it has lost the virility of its stock. It is port from the wood, without the depth and mystery of its vintage rivals. It is a burning-glass that has lost its focus; a passenger, pulling no weight in the up-stream journey of life; meat that has had the vitamins boiled out of it; a clock without hands. The humorist, in short, is a satirist out of a job; he does not fit into the scheme of things; the world passes him by.

The pure humorist is a man without a message. He can preach no gospel, unless it be the gospel that nothing matters; and that in itself is a foolish theme, for if nothing matters, what does it matter whether it matters or not? Mr. Wodehouse is an instance in point, Mr. Leacock nearly so, though there is a story in *Arcadian Adventures with the Idle Rich* about the amalgamation of two religious bodies on strictly commercial lines, which comes very close to pure satire. Barry

Pain is a humorist who is seldom at his best when he attempts satire; the same fate dogged Mark Twain, though I think he would have liked to be a satirist. Mr. A. A. Milne is in a similar case, and so indeed are all the modern *Punch* writers by the terms (you might say) of their contract. No contrast is more surprising than the contrast in atmosphere between the letterpress of *Punch* before 1890 and its letterpress since. The old *Punches* are full of very bad satire; there is hardly anything else in them; it is all on the same sort of level as *John Bull* in its Bottomley days—anti-aristocratic, anti-foreign, anti-clerical, very much like some rag of the Boulevards. To-day, it is the home of superbly finished humour—humour cultivated as a fine art. But satire is absent.

Some of the greatest humorists have halted between two destinies, and as a rule have been lost to satire. Sir W. S. Gilbert, a rather unsuccessful satirist in his early days, inherited the dilemma from his master, Aristophanes. *Patience* is supreme satire, and there is satire in all the operas; but in their general effect they do not tell: the author has given up to mankind what was meant for a party. Mr. Chesterton is in the same difficulty; he is like Johnson's friend who tried to be a philosopher, but cheerfulness would keep on coming in. The net effect of his works is serious, as it is meant to be, but his fairy-like imagination is for ever defeating its own object in matters of detail. But indeed, Mr. Chesterton is beyond our present scope; for he is rash enough to combine humour not merely with satire but with serious writing; and that, it is well known, is a thing the public will not stand. A few modern authors have succeeded, in spite of our latter-day demand for pure humour, in being satirists first and last: Samuel Butler of *Erewhon*, and W. H. Mallock, and Mr. Belloc, I think, in his political novels. The very poor reception given to these last by the public proves that there is more vinegar in them than oil.

Humour, if we may adopt for a moment the loathsome phraseology of journalism, has "come to stay." It is, if our analysis be true, a by-product and in a sense a waste-product; that does not mean that it has no significance. A pearl is a by-product, and from the fishmonger's point of view a waste-product; but it has value so long as people want it. And there is at present a public demand for humour which implies that humour should take its place among the arts, an art for the art's sake, not depending on any fruits of practical utility for its estimation. There is art in O. Henry, though he does not scourge our vices like Juvenal; there is art in Heath Robinson, though he does not purge our consciences like Hogarth. What rank humour is to take as compared with serious writing is, perhaps, an unanswerable problem; our histories of nineteenth-century literature have not yet been bold enough to tackle it. It is probable, I think, that humour is relatively ephemeral; by force of words humour means caprice, and the caprice of yesterday is apt to leave us cold. There is a generation not yet quite dead which says that nothing was ever so funny as the *Bongaultier Ballads.* The popularity of the *Ingoldsby Legends* is now, to say the least, precarious; and I doubt if the modern youth smacks its lips as we did over the *Bab Ballads* themselves. Read a book of A. A. Milne's, and then turn to an old volume of *Voces Populi*, and you will realize that even in our memory humour has progressed and become rarefied. What reputations will be left unassailable when the tide has receded, it would be rash to prophesy. For myself, I like to believe that one name will be immortal at least, that of Mr. Max Beerbohm. Incomparably equipped for satire, as his cartoons and his parodies show, he has yet preferred in most of his work to give rein to a gloriously fantastic imagination, a humorist in satirist's clothing. One is tempted to say with the prophet: May I die the death of the righteous, and may my last end be like his!

Meanwhile, a pertinent question may be raised, What will be the effect of all this modern vogue for pure humour upon the prospects of satiric writing? We are in danger, it seems to me, of debauching our sense of the ridiculous to such an extent as to leave no room for the disciplinary effect of satire. I remember seeing Mr. Shaw's *Press Cuttings* first produced in Manchester. I remember a remark, in answer to the objection that women ought not to vote because they do not fight, that a woman risks her life every time a man is born, being received (in Manchester!) with shouts of happy laughter. In that laughter I read the tragedy of Mr. Bernard Shaw. He lashes us with virulent abuse, and we find it exquisitely amusing. Other ages have stoned the prophets; ours pelts them instead with the cauliflower bouquets of the heavy comedian. No country, I suppose, has greater need of a satirist to-day than the United States of America; no country has a greater output of humour, good and bad, which is wholly devoid of any satirical quality. If a great American satirist should arise, would his voice be heard among the hearty guffaws which are dismally and eternally provoked by Mutt, Jeff, Felix, and other kindred abominations? And have we, on this side of the Atlantic, any organ in which pure satire could find a natural home? I believe the danger which I am indicating to be a perfectly real one, however fantastic it may sound—the danger, I mean, that we have lost, or are losing, the power to take ridicule seriously. That our habituation to humorous reading has inoculated our systems against the beneficent poison of satire. Unhappy the Juvenal whom Rome greets with amusement; unhappier still the Rome, that can be amused by a Juvenal!

I am not sure, in reading through this essay again, that there is any truth in its suggestions. But I do not see that there can be any harm in having said what I thought, even if I am no longer certain that I think it.

The Greatest Satire
is Nonmoral

"The frantic rage which Dryden's satire provoked was because of
that *coolness* always to be discovered at the centre of his scorn."
Professor Saintsbury

There is no man's "shop" but must appear somewhat cynical to the
outsider. To overhear two physicians conferring is enough to make
the flesh of the bravest creep. That is classical. But it is the same with
every profession. (Most pure business sounds to the outsider and non-
business man like a confabulation of convicts of course, engaged in the
preparation of some novel *coup de main*.) And the craft of the satirist
must perforce retain a few of the more brutal fashions of thinking
that are proper to his occupation. You know our Hogarth's face, in a
nightcap?—it is like a bulldog, in a sense—the most brutal of animals,
the *matador par excellence*.

There is, again, a whole world of difference between the satirist
—so extended as to mean all artists not specifically beauty-doctors,
as I have ordained here—and the "realist." Yet the "materialism" of
the matter of the grotesque is liable to shock. We shall be committed
to an examination of all those controversial values pertaining to that
naked world of the *Satyricon*, of *Volpone*, of the *Médecin malgré
Lui*. We shall have to weigh the dictum of Taine.[1]

"Au plus bas degré sont les types que préfèrent la littérature
réaliste et le théatre comique, je veux dire les personnages bornés,

Chapter I and a passage from Chapter II ("Mr. Wyndham Lewis"),
from *Men Without Art*, London, 1934; reprint, New York: Russell &
Russell, 1964, pp. 103–14, 121–24. Reprinted by permission of Mrs.
Wyndham Lewis and Russell & Russell.

plats, sots, égoïstes, faibles et communes..." against the opposite dictum of Flaubert?[2]

"Il n'y a ni beaux, ni vilains sujets... on pourrait presque établir comme axiome, en se posant au point de vue de l'art pur, qu'il n'y en a aucun, le style étant à lui tout seul une manière de voir les choses."

And then *style* is of course a magician who can convert a ragged crone into an object of great beauty. It is *style* that checkmates subject-matter every time, and turns to naught the beauty-doctor laws of the metaphysician. But merely to decide, upon an aristocratic principle, which, in the view of Nietzsche, gave the *Mahomet* of Voltaire the palm over all subsequent and less "classical" compositions, will scarcely satisfy a public of today. Flaubert stands accused of more than vulgarity: he is arraigned, by one of the masters of the catholic revival, for his turpitude in employing, in deliberate isolation, instincts that issued, certainly, in what he called "style," but which were intended for the service of a more elevated principle. "La faute de Flaubert est grave, aussi. L'art substitué à Dieu, cela l'engage dans une voie... périlleuse."[3]

It will be our duty to take into account the various motives which may decide a man to go and live among such vulgar and imbecile personages as satire, and comedy, require. In the case of Flaubert, to go no farther than he, "style" was not the whole of the story. Like any Christian martyr he went and established himself in the centre of the bourgeois body—he regarded himself as possessing "a message" of sorts—if only that of a plumber. And he dies at his post, struck down by the bourgeois, while at his unsavoury work, there is no dispute at least on that head. Hear Mauriac, his accuser: "puisqu'il ne pouvait plus se soustraire a l'étude du Prudhomme moderne, eh bien, il prendrait le taureau par les cornes; cette énorme bêtise bourgeoise deviendrait le sujet de son livre, il l'incarnerait, ce serait son chef-d'oeuvre.... Le Bourgeois... s'installe à sa table, se couche dans son lit, remplit ses journées et ses nuits, et finit par le prendre à la gorge. Le Bourgeois a eu sa peau enfin; il a, à la lettre, assassiné Flaubert. L'alchemiste de Croisset est mort victime des expériences qu'il tentait sur la créature humaine: il éliminait l'âme du composé humain, pour obtenir de la bêtise à l'état pur: elle l'a asphyxié."[4]

We shall be in these pages, as we are in real life, haunted by this BOURGEOIS of Flaubert. Like a pneumatic carnival personage, incessantly expanding as the result of the fierce puffing of the Marxist into his ideologic bladder, the Bourgeois of Flaubert has assumed portentous proportions.

We are informed by Albalat that Gautier and Flaubert when they met, upon the occasion of the latter's periodic visits to Paris, would sit down and discuss "the bourgeois" for hours together. "Flaubert detested the 'bourgeois' in overalls as much as the 'bourgeois' in plus fours. When Theophile Gautier and he addressed themselves, at one of their séances, to the declamatory abuse of the 'bourgeois,' they worked themselves up to a great pitch of lyrical rage, became as red as turkey-cocks and were obliged afterwards to change their linen (*ils . . . devenaient rouges comme des coqs et se voyaient forcés de changer de chemise*)."

They really took their "bourgeois" seriously! And these two charming and intelligent men, thundering away at each other in the past (an echo of their voices may still be caught, on a quiet afternoon) opposed to the bourgeois—but what do you suppose? It sounds absurd, in our present dispensation, but it was *the artist* that these two Frenchmen were thinking about, and "bourgeois" meant nothing really but the enemy of art. They were as simple as a couple of noisy peasants—in a sense: and *art* filled the whole of their minds and bodies. A passion for a concrete realization of all the mysterious energies with which they were wound up like clocks, possessed them night and day. These two French craftsmen, drenching their shirts with perspiration as they cursed for hours on end the wicked giant who was the great enemy of their craft, were far more mad than Blake, I think. And as to Blake's "prolonged vindication of the cause of all the artists in the world," they did a good deal of that, too, between them.

These will be the sort of subjects among which we shall be picking our way. We shall interrogate these great profane figures composed of "pure art"—these *hommes-plumes* compact of *mots justes*—and see what messages they may have for our even more *be-bourgeoised* period: we shall not be prevented from speculating as to what is our antithesis—with "bourgeois" where it was before, but bigger and weaker, but "artist" somehow changed, and perhaps paired off with some other abstraction. For the politician—whose art is anything but the *mot juste*—has pushed away the artist and now stands where the latter once stood, keeping all to himself the "burgess-gentleman." But if we have to range far afield before we have done with the questions which, one after the other, we shall find this critical enterprise calls up, we will now start with satire pure and simple, and join issue at once with the moralist, who regards satire as belonging pre-eminently to his domain.

There is no prejudice so inveterate, in even the educated mind, as that which sees in satire a work of edification. Indeed, for the satirist to acquire the right to hold up to contempt a fellow-mortal, he is supposed, first, to arm himself with the insignia of a sheriff or special constable. No age, for many centuries, has been so lawless as ours—nothing to compare with Capone it is said, for instance, has ever been known in America. And perhaps for this reason an unnatural sensitiveness to law and order is noticeable in all of us: and in the field of the ethical judgement, as much as in that of the civil law, is this the case. Perhaps that is the reason why, in this defence of the art of satire, I give the place of honour to the moral law, and settle accounts with that source of interference first.—As to the law of libel, the anomalies and injustices of that have often been canvassed: I do not propose here to add to that already considerable body of criticism. It is rather the subtler forms of interference, generally neglected, which I have in mind and am proposing to pass under review.

I am a satirist, I am afraid there is no use denying that. But I am not a moralist: and about that I make no bones either. And it is these two facts, taken together, which constitute my particular difficulty. It is contended, against the satirist, that since man is not autonomous—and who but will agree to that I hope?—he cannot arm himself with laughter and invective, and sally forth to satirical attacks upon his neighbour, without first acquiring the moral sanction of the community—with whose standards and canons of conduct he must be at one—and first advertising himself as a champion of some outraged Mrs. Grundy. So, with Mrs. Grundy on the one side, and Dr. Bowdler on the other, and with a big crocodile tear in his eye (at the thought of the pain he may have to inflict), he sets himself in motion. That is the popular picture. The more sophisticated picture would today only differ from this in the nature of the preparations prescribed: a short prayer for absolution regarding the blood he was about to spill, or if the god had the features of Demos, an invocation to his bloody fist—a brief class-war-dance, with a "more power to my elbow incantation!" And so forward to battle, the Geneva Bible in the breast-pocket. But, whatever else it may be, it must be represented as a

salutary expedition, undertaken on behalf of something with an in-
fallible title to the moral judgement-seat.

There is of course no question that satire of the highest order
has been achieved in the name of the ethical will. Most satire, indeed,
has got through upon the understanding that the satirist first and
foremost was a moralist. And some of the best satirists have been that
as well. But not all. So one of the things it is proposed to do in these
pages is to consider the character, and the function of, non-ethical
satire; and if possible to provide it with a standing, alongside the
other arts and sciences, as a recognized philosophic and artistic human
activity, not contingent upon judgements which are not those specifically of the artistic or philosophic mind.

"The frantic rage which Dryden's satire provoked in his opponents" has been attributed, by Professor Saintsbury, to a *coolness* always to be discovered at the centre of his scorn. Further, Dryden
dispensed with the protective moralistic machinery of the classical
satire. It was, in short, not because his opponents were *naughty* that
Dryden objected to them, but because they were *dull*. They had sinned
against the Reason, rather than against the Mosaic Law. This it was
that aroused the really "frantic rage"! For all those satirized by
Juvenal, or smarting beneath the scourges of most other satirists, of
the classical or modern age, have been able at a pinch to snigger and
remark that "Yes, they *knew* that they were very wicked!" and to
make, even, of such satire an advertisement.

But if you remove from satire its moralism, then it has no
advertisement value whatever for the victim—then it is doubly deadly,
and then also the satirist is doubly hated by those picked out for attack.
And society also, the implicit ally of the moralist, is in a sense offended
(though the way society takes it depends upon the society—ours luckily
does not stand upon its moral dignity very much).

It could perhaps be asserted, even, that the greatest satire *cannot*
be moralistic at all: if for no other reason, because no mind of the
first order, expressing itself in art, has ever itself been taken in, nor
consented to take in others, by the crude injunctions of any purely
moral code. This does not mean that the mind in question was wanting
in that consciousness of itself as a rational subject, which is never
absent in an intellect of such an order: but that its abstract theory,
as well as its concrete practice, of moral judgements, would differ
from the common run, and that their introduction would merely
confuse the issue. The artistic impulse is a more primitive one than

the ethical: so much is this the case—so little is it a mere dialect of the rational language in which our human laws are formulated, but, on the contrary, an entirely independent tongue—that it is necessary for the artist to change his skin, almost, in passing from one department into the other. You cannot with the same instruments compass a work of edification and a work of beauty—and satire may be "beautiful," rather in the way that mathematics claims to be that—with a rational handsomeness peculiar to it; and even such a tubthumper as Bunyan, being an artist, is there as witness to that fact, as has often been pointed out. With the person predestined to an artistic vocation, cheerfulness, or mood of a yet more anomalous order, *will* keep breaking in: so it is better, perhaps, to admit them at the start.

But how can satire stand without the moral sanction? you may ask. For satire can only exist in *contrast* to something else—it is a shadow, and an ugly shadow at that, of some perfection. And it is so disagreeable, and so painful (at least in the austere sense in which we appear to be defining it here) that no one would pursue it *for its own sake,* or take up the occupation of satirist unless compelled to do so, out of indignation at the spectacle of the neglect of beauty and virtue. —That is I think the sort of objection that, at this point, we should expect to have to meet.

Provisionally I will reply as follows: it is my belief that "satire" *for its own sake*—as much as anything else for its own sake—is possible: and that even the most virtuous and well-proportioned of men is only a shadow, after all, of some perfection; a shadow of an imperfect, and hence an "ugly," sort. And as to *laughter*, if you allow it in one place you must, I think, allow it in another. Laughter—humour and wit—has a function in relation to our tender consciousness; a function similar to that of art. It is the preserver much more than the destroyer. And, in a sense, *everyone* should be laughed at or else *no one* should be laughed at. It seems that ultimately that is the alternative.

When Addison introduced the word "genius," to take the place of the word used up to that time, "wit," he did us all a disservice. Wit as a generic term for all those possessed of an excellent judgement, would tend (apart from the advantages resulting from its less pretentious sound) to marshal the gifted upon the *laughing* side of the world. But that little change of a popular monosyllable made all the difference, and today *the laugh* is not wholly respectable: it requires to be explained, if not excused.

But satire is a special sort of laughter: *the laugh* alone possesses great powers of magnification. But *the laugh* that magnified Falstaff till he grew to be a giant like Pantagruel, is not the laugh of the satirist, which threw up the Maids of Honour in Brobdingnag. Now, no one resents the size of Falstaff: he is a routine figure of fun; the jolly toper. But everyone resents the scale of the Maids of Honour, and resents the sounds of the cataracts heard by Gulliver when they made use of their *pots de chambre*. But I will produce the Maids of Honour, so that our sense of what we are discussing should become first hand.

"The Maids of Honour often invited Glumdalclitch to their apartments, and desired she would bring me along with her, on purpose to have the pleasure of seeing and touching me. They would often strip me naked from top to toe and lay me at full length in their bosoms: wherewith I was much disgusted: because, to say the truth, a very offensive smell came from their skins: which I do not mention or intend to the disadvantage of those excellent ladies, for whom I have all manner of respect. . . . That which gave me most uneasiness among these Maids of Honour, when my nurse carried me to visit them, was to see them use me without any manner of ceremony, like a creature who had no sort of consequence. For they would strip themselves to the skin, and put on their smocks in my presence, while I was placed on their toilet directly before their naked bodies, which, I am sure, to me was very far from being a tempting sight, or from giving me any other emotions than those of horror and disgust. Their skins appeared so coarse and uneven, so variously coloured, when I saw them near, with a mole here and there as broad as a trencher, and hairs hanging from it thicker than pack-threads, to say nothing further concerning the rest of their persons. Neither did they at all scruple, while I was by, to discharge what they had drunk, to the quantity of at least two hogsheads, in a vessel that held three tuns."

These are very painful passages. There is no question here of the mere he-man vulgarity of the egregious Scottish surgeon, Smollett. It is much more uncomfortable than that, not alone for the nice-minded but without exception for all the spokesmen of Mr. Everybody.

In this painful effect of true satire we might expect to find the main avenue of attack of the moralist—he might say that it was *ill-natured* instead of *good-natured*, as is mere burlesque. But it is not to that that we must look today, when we are taking our measures of defense, as being the spot likely to draw the fire of the ethical batteries.

The painful nature of satire was recognized by Hazlitt, but promptly misunderstood; for he was looking for something in satire which under no circumstances belongs there, and which in consequence he could not find.

"Bare-faced impudence, an idiot imbecility, are his dramatic commonplaces," he writes of Ben Jonson. So, although one would have thought that Ben Jonson had acquitted himself to admiration of what is after all, in the narrowest sense, the satirist's job, the good Hazlitt finds fault with him for that very reason—because, in fact, Hazlitt did not at all like satire.

The very reasons Hazlitt finds to attack Ben Jonson, do, it seems to me, exactly describe a master of that kind of art: and actually, what Hazlitt says could be applied, with more aptness, to other writers than to Ben Jonson—writers, to my mind, even more important than the author of *Volpone*. This point is one of such significance for an understanding of satire in general, that I will quote the entire passage.

"Shakespeare's characters are men; Ben Jonson's are more like machines, governed by mere routine, or by the convenience of the poet, whose property they are. In reading the one, we are let into the minds of his characters, we see the play of their thoughts, how their humours flow and work.... His humour (so to speak) bubbles, sparkles, and finds its way in all directions, like a natural spring. In Ben Jonson it is, as it were, confined in a leaden cistern, where it stagnates and corrupts; or directed only through certain artificial pipes and conduits to answer a given purpose.... Sheer ignorance, bare-faced impudence, or idiot imbecility, are his dramatic commonplaces—things that provoke pity or disgust, instead of laughter."[5]

But why should not idiot imbecility provoke laughter? Obviously the answer is: Because, being found in a human being, it is "letting down" the species, and so to laugh at it would be unethical and *inhuman*. Physical deformity, again, is often comic. Many dwarfs are highly grotesque (superbly grotesque, one may say without offence in the case of dwarfs), and they even relish the sensation of their funniness. But most people only laugh covertly at such spectacles, or sternly repress a smile. For, they would say, these are "things" which should "provoke pity or disgust, instead of laughter." Such is the Anglo-Saxon point of view.

But the dago is different. Dwarfs, in Spain, are the object of constant mirth, on the part of their "normal" fellow-citizens. Everyone pokes fun at them, there is no hypocrisy, as with us, and the dwarf gets on very well indeed. He is treated as a pet animal, and enjoys himself very much. Also, since he has a great deal of practice, from morning till night, he often ends by being a first-class clown. In short, neither disgust nor pity is experienced by these dagos where their dwarfs are concerned. They feel perhaps that God has made them a present of these hideous oddities to be their sport: and the dwarf feels that too, and is quite puffed-up with his own importance and proud of his god-sent job.

And, after all, pulling long faces at the dwarf, and surrounding him with an atmosphere of inhuman pity, is bad for the dwarf. It is better to explode with laughter at the sight of him—better for all concerned. So far so good: but what of the shell-shocked man, for instance? He is often very funny, and it is very difficult not to laugh. But that is like laughing at the contortions of a dying man, and it would be too brutal a society that made a habit of laughing at its shell-shocked persons—especially as it would be to the society of the laughters to which ultimately the responsibility for these disfigurements would have to be brought home. Therefore there is no society that does not refrain from guffawing at the antics, however "screamingly funny," of its shell-shocked men and war-idiots, and its poison-gas morons, and its mutilated battle-wrecks.

But here is also a principle, of use in the analysis of the comic. *Perfect laughter*, if there could be such a thing, would be inhuman. And it would select as the objects of its mirth as much the antics dependent upon pathologic maladjustments, injury, or disease, as the antics of clumsy and imperfectly functioning healthy people. At this point it is perhaps desirable to note that in general human beings display no delicacy about spiritual or mental shortcomings in their neighbours, but only physical. To be a fool with a robust body can be no more pleasant for the person in question than being an intelligent dwarf: yet no one scruples to laugh at the former, but parades a genteel sensitiveness regarding the latter. Infinitely more pain is inflicted by laughter provoked by some non-physical cause than by that provoked by the physical. So do not let us take too much for granted that we can put our finger blindfold upon the *supreme* "cad."

Our deepest laughter is not, however, inhuman laughter. And yet it is non-personal and non-moral. And it enters fields which are

commonly regarded as the preserve of more "serious" forms of reaction. There is no reason at all why we should not burst out laughing
at a fœtus, for instance. We should after all only be laughing *at ourselves!*—at ourselves early in our mortal career.

Returning to Hazlitt's misunderstanding; in Swift, in Dryden,
in Pope, it is not the "natural," "bubbling" laughter of Shakespearean
comedy that you should expect to find, any more than you would
look for a jovial heartiness in a surgeon at work, or, if you like (to
take a romantic illustration), in an executioner. It would decidedly
be out of place. *Laughter* is the medium employed, certainly, but there
is laughter and laughter. That of true satire is as it were *tragic*
laughter. It is not a genial guffaw nor the titillations provoked by a
harmless entertainer. It is tragic, if a thing *can* be "tragic" without
pity and terror, and it seems to me it can.

But when Hazlitt speaks of the characters "like machines,
governed by mere routine," there, I think, he gives himself entirely
away. For what else is a character in satire but that? Is it not just
because they are such *machines, governed by routine*—or creatures
that stagnate, as it were "in a leaden cistern"—that the satirist, in the
first instance, has considered them suitable for satire? He who wants
a jolly, carefree, bubbling, world chockfull of "charm," must not
address himself to the satirist! The wind that blows through satire is as
bitter as that that predominates in the pages of *Timon* or *King Lear.*
Indeed, the former *is* a satire. And *Hamlet*, for instance, is very much
that too—a central satire—developing now into comedy, now into
tragedy.

Laughter is again an anti-toxin of the first order. As a matter
of fact *no* man (as I have hinted above)—any more than the shell-
shocked man—should be laughed at. It is unfair, therefore it is
"caddish," to laugh at *anybody*: we all, as much as the shell-shocked
man, really could cry *cad*, or have cad cried for us, at an outburst of
mirth at our expense. And this does not only apply to the obviously
defective. It is unnecessary to enumerate the tragic handicaps that
our human conditions involve—the glaring mechanical imperfections,
the nervous tics, the prodigality of objectless movement—the, to other
creatures, offensive smells, disagreeable moistures—the involuntary
grimace, the lurch, roll, trot or stagger which we call our *walk*—it is
only a matter of degree between us and the victim of locomotor-ataxy
or St. Vitus's dance. . . . .

By making a great deal of noise ourselves we at least drown the alarming noise made by our neighbours. And the noise that, above all others, has been bestowed on us for this purpose is the bark which we describe as our *laugh*. I approve of a *barking man* myself—I find that I have less occasion, with his likes, to anticipate a really serious *bite*. So laughter is *per se* a healthy clatter—that is one of the first things to realize about it.

An illustration of this principle, in a parallel order of feeling, is furnished by Henry James, where he is discussing the virtue in a novelist of hard work—and the clatter and bustle which, as it were, accompanies it. Put *laughter* for *hard work*, and you will see what I mean, I think. These are the words of that great puppet-manufacturer:

> "It is, as you say, because I 'grind out' my men and women that I endure them. It is because I create them by the sweat of my brow that I venture to look them in the face. My *work* is my salvation. If this great army of puppets came forth at my simple bidding, then indeed I should die of their senseless clamour."

· · ·

But to return again to Satire: Satire is *cold*, and that is good! It is easier to achieve those polished and resistant surfaces of a great *externalist* art in Satire. At least they are achieved more naturally than can be done beneath the troubled impulse of the lyrical afflatus. All the nineteenth-century poetry of France, for instance, from the *Fleurs du Mal* onwards, was stiffened with Satire, too. There is a stiffening of Satire in everything good, of "the grotesque," which is the same thing—the non-human outlook must be there (beneath the fluff and pulp which is all that is seen by the majority) to correct our soft conceit. This cannot be gainsaid. Satire is *good*!

But so far in these pages we have been accepting the term Satire without stopping to define it. (To define it anew, of course; for the historic definition is far too narrow for what such a definition would have to include today.) Satire in reality often is nothing else but *the truth*—the truth, in fact, of Natural Science. That objective, non-emotional truth of the scientific intelligence sometimes takes on the exuberant sensuous quality of creative art: then it is very apt to be called "Satire," for it has been bent not so much upon pleasing as upon being true.

No work of fiction, however, is likely to be only "satire," in the sense that a short epigrammatic piece, in rhyming couplets (an Epistle of Pope) would be. For again it is necessary to return to the fact that fiction-satire is narrative: a great part of it is apt to be of a most objective nature, cast in a mould very near to the everyday aspect of things. It will only appear "grotesque," or "distorted," of course, to those acustomed to regard the things of everyday, and everyday persons, through spectacles *couleur-de-rose*.

But there is the "truth" of Satire and there is the "truth" of Romance.—The term Satire suggests off-hand some resolve on the part of the "satirist" to pick out disobligingly all that is objectionable and ill-favoured in a given system of persons and things, and to make of that a work of art. Certainly such a "satire" as *The Apes of God* is not that. Indeed often it is nothing but people's vanity that causes them to use that term at all: often they are, in what they call "satire," confronted with a description of their everyday life as close to the truth as that found in any other artistic formula. It is merely a formula based rather upon the "truth" of the intellect than upon the "truth" of the average romantic sensualism.

Must we say, then, that "Satire" is merely a representation, containing (irrespective of what else may be included in it) many of those truths that people do not care to hear?

What is "the truth" regarding any person? What is the objective truth about him?—a public and not a private truth? What is that in a person, or in a thing, that is not "satire," upon the one hand, or "romance," upon the other? Is there such a purely non-satiric, non-romantic truth, at all? Such questions may at all times with advantage be asked; but the very core of the satiric impulse is of course involved in them.

All men are *some* sort of hero to themselves: equally there is no man who is not, to *somebody or other*, a disagreeable person, as unsightly as a toad, or else a first-class figure of fun. How are we to reconcile these opposites—the seeing-of-ourselves-as-others see-us, and the self-picture? It is difficult to see how the objective truth of much that is called "Satire" can be less true than the truth of lyrical declamation, in praise, for instance, of a lovely mistress. There is, in both cases, *another* truth, that is all. But both are upon an equal intellectual footing I think—only the humanly "agreeable" is more often false than the humanly "disagreeable." That is unavoidable, seeing what we are.

Natural Science is a disagreeable study in its way (this was acutely recognized by Leonardo da Vinci, himself a man of science, as well as, in his role of plastic artist, a master of vitalist illusion). What interests and delights *the individual*, again, is, *sub specie aeternitatis* far less interesting, much less delightful. The values proper to the specific organism have to be accounted for, that we all know. So, to conclude, do not let us arbitrarily describe as "Satire" all that is disagreeable to ourselves. That would be a misnomer. For it may not be *satire* at all!

As well as being a satire, *The Apes of God* is a book made of the outside of things. And it is also a book of *action*. By certain critics it was described, even, as an orgy of *the externals* of this life of ours (cf. "Mr. Lewis could be described as a *personal-appearance* satirist," etc.). But that is a compliment. Its author lays great store by that *externality*, in a world that is literally inundated with sexual viscera and the "dark" gushings of the tides of *The Great Within*. Call him a "personal-appearance writer" and he is far from being displeased! You please *him* by that, even if *he* displeases so many people (it would appear) by treating of their *externals* in the way that he does—just by being so *personal-appearance*!

Hazlitt, to return to him again for a moment, must be credited with seeing that "the fault ... of Shakespeare's comic Muse is ... that it is too good-natured and magnanimous." That is the fault also, no doubt, of Hazlitt's *criticism*. And there were, and have been since, many satirists far more apt to bring out this fault in Hazlitt than was "rare Ben Jonson."—Shakespeare's comic muse "does not take the highest pleasure in making human nature look as mean, as ridiculous, and contemptible as possible," writes Hazlitt. "It is in this respect, chiefly, that it differs from the comedy of a later, and (what is called) a more refined, period ... vanity and affectation, in their most exorbitant and studied excesses, are the ruling principles of society, only in a highly advanced state of civilization and manners. Man can hardly be said to be a truly contemptible animal, till, from the facilities of general intercourse ... he becomes the ape of the extravagances of other men."

There must, however, even according to this account, be some first exemplar—some *original* ape! This Rousseauesque picture of man's original perfection does, even in the statement, halt, and seems to point, in spite of itself, to the conclusion that in some form or other that original "ape" was man!

Again, if you insist, as does Hazlitt, that it is "when folly is epidemic, and vice worn as a mask of distinction, that all the malice of wit and humour is called out, and justified, to detect the imposture, and prevent the contagion from spreading," the answer you must expect is as follows: At what period of history has folly *not* been epidemic (allowing for ups and downs and for more and less) : when has "vice" not been an advertisement, and virtue a handicap?— Certainly Hazlitt's attitude to "man" is sentimental. The Tudor dramatists were as much surrounded by epidemics of folly as were the later Stuart writers. There was here a seesaw of opinions and of tastes —neither age was quite civilized enough.

But (in conclusion) the justification of "all the malice of wit" must be more securely grounded than this theory of human corruption succeeding upon a state of original blessedness would allow, so simply stated as that.

NOTES

[1] *L'art et la Morale.* Ferdinand Brunetière.

[2] Quoted by I. J. Bondy, *Classicisme de Ferdinand Brunetière.*

[3] *Trois grands hommes.* F. Mauriac (Editions du Capitole).

[4] *L'art et la Morale.* Ferdinand Brunetière.

[5] *The English Comic Writers.* Hazlitt.

The Elizabethan
Satyr-Satirist
and His Satire

RENAISSANCE THEORIES OF SATIRE

All forms of Renaissance satire were supported by an ample critical theory. To it, with few exceptions, writers of verse satire in England during the sixteenth century turned for guidance, and Jonson evidently took care to fashion his new comical satire in such a way as not to contravene any of its tenets. These principles in their simplest and most popular form were known to every Elizabethan schoolboy, for they appeared in an essay prefaced to practically all the editions of Terence which were printed, either in England or on the Continent, between 1500 and 1600. The essay was written by Aelius Donatus, a grammarian of the fourth century. After giving an account of Terence's life, he presents a brief history of the development of tragedy and comedy in classical times.

Donatus, like Scaliger, believes *satyra* to be the legitimate heir of *vetus comoedia*. He assumes that the writers of old Greek comedy abused their freedom so scandalously that they had to be restrained. *Satyra* was thus devised to avoid a legal prohibition without destroying an author's freedom to criticize and correct his contemporaries as he chose. But, unlike Scaliger, Donatus accepts without reservation the theory that *satyra* was, in both a literal and an imaginative sense,

Editor's title. The selections are Chapter II ("The Prevailing Forms of English Satire, 1588–1599"), sections iii–vi, in *Comical Satyre and Shakespeare's 'Troilus and Cresida'*, San Marino, California, 1938, pp. 24–53. Reprinted by permission of the Huntington Library.

the utterance of satyrs. And he and all the world knew that they were dirty and lascivious woodland deities. Partly because the satirist assumed that he was the heir to the nature and functions of the satyr, he was allowed to attack the faults of the citizens in whatever harsh and savage manner he chose to adopt. But he was forbidden to identify any wrongdoers by name. In the course of time the citizens objected to even this anonymous form of rebuke. It, too, cast a very unfavorable light upon the life of the community and indirectly upon the individuals who composed it. Consequently, they silenced the authors of *satyra*. Though balked for a second time, the impulse toward satire was irrepressible and it promptly invented for itself still another form, called *nova comoedia*.[1]

Donatus clearly regards *vetus comoedia, satyra,* and *nova como-edia* as allied types of corrective writing, one succeeding the other in a direct line of descent. Ignoring the proper literary form of such writing, he prescribes its moral tone and its methods of castigation, and he explains that its very existence depends upon social sanctions. Although he could hardly have had any clear idea of the nature of the early Latin satura, his theory of the origin of satire is less in accord with that of Scaliger and Jonson than with that of modern scholars who hold that satire was not a metamorphosis of *vetus comoedia* but the outgrowth of a native folk drama called *satura*.[2] The present belief that this was a crude play is based on a famous passage in the seventh book of Livy's history. There he says that during a virulent attack of the plague the consuls ordered stage plays to be performed as a means of appeasing the wrath of the gods. From Etruria were summoned actors who, while dancing to the music of the flute, sang and illustrated the meaning of their songs with appropriate gestures. Tuscan imitators of their simple professional art added antiphonal jesting, and lengthened and ordered both the music and the verses until "complete satyres [impletas modis satyras]" came into being.[3]

Latin satire as written by Horace suggests a connection with an earlier histrionic form of literature. It is full of short dramatic scenes, the most famous of which is undoubtedly the author's encounter with the bore—a dialogue, with the action of the participants clearly indicated.[4] Horace also puts his attack on legacy hunters into the form of a colloquy, between Ulysses and Tiresias.[5] He writes introductions to other satires which are pure dramatic dialogues. Such, for example, is Horace's meeting with Catius as he is rushing home to write down some new recipes that he has just had given him.[6] Sometimes a little dramatic scene appears in the midst of a satire, as, for example, the dialogue between an excluded lover and his slave. This is in itself a colloquy within the envelope of a still more ambitious dialogue,[7] between Horace and Damasippus, soon after the latter's conversion to Stoicism. The first satire of Persius is a dialogue between Persius and an ill-natured critic who tries to dissuade the author from writing satire.

These dramatic characteristics of Latin satire were recognized by the critics and scholars of the Renaissance, even though they did not know their provenance. Certainly no contemporary of Jonson would have attributed the vestiges of drama in the Roman satire to its descent from satura by way of some lost "fabulae togatae." Such knowledge as is to be found explicit in Livy seems to have been completely and strangely forgotten during the Renaissance. A few critics accepted the tradition that Latin satire was a late equivalent of *vetus comoedia*, but the common belief was that the form was descended from the satyr play, of which Euripides' *Cyclops* was the only extant example. On the basis of mere verbal similarity between "satire" and "satyr," they reared an elaborate critical structure.

This theory appears in simple outline in the work of Polydore Virgil. He writes:

> The Satires had their name of uplandishe Goddes, that were rude, lassivious and wanton of behavor.
> There bee twoo kyndes of Satyres, the one is both emong the Grekes and Romanes of auncient tyme used, for the diversitie of Meters, muche like a Comody, sayving that it is more wanton. ... The second maner of Satires is very railyng onely ordeined to rebuke vice, and devised of the Romaines, upon this occasion When the Poetes, that wrote the olde Comodies, used to handle for their argumentes, not onely fained matters, but also thynges dooen in deede, whiche although at the firste, it was tollerable, yet afterwarde, it fortuned by reason that thei inveighed so liberally & largely, at their pleasure, against every man that there was a law made, that no man should from thencefurthe reprehend any man by name. Then the Romaines in the place of those Comodies, substituted suche Satires, as thei had newly imagined.[8]

Virgil's pronouncement, in its confusion of various types of early drama, is characteristic of the critical opinion of the time. He seems to regard "satyre" as a mixture of *vetus comoedia,* satyr play, and a postulated primitive Latin comedy to which he is not able to give the name "satura."

The same confusion between satire and satyr play, and concerning the relation of both to *vetus comoedia,* appears in the English critics of the late sixteenth century—in none more picturesquely than in Puttenham. He begins with the conventional idea that literature originated in man's eagerness to honor his gods. It next naturally assumed the function of a preacher bent on correcting human faults. The grave and wise men of that early time, possessing no large halls in which to assemble people, took advantage of the occasions when the folk were gathered in some hallowed place for worship of their deities, to utter salutary rebukes. Because this direct method of correction made the people ashamed rather than afraid, the ancient poets invented

> three kinds of poems reprehensive, to wit, the *Satyre,* the *Comedie,* & the *Tragedie*: and the first and most bitter invective against vice and vicious men, was the *Satyre*: which to th'intent their bitternesse should breede none ill will, either to the Poets, or to the recitours, (which could not have bene chosen if they had bene openly knowen) and besides to make their admonitions and reproofs seeme graver and of more efficacie, they made wise as if the gods of the woods, whom they called *Satyres* or *Silvanes,* should appeare and recite those verses of rebuke, whereas in deede they were but disguised persons under the shape of *Satyres* ... whereupon the Poets inventours of the devise were called *Satyristes.*[9]

Puttenham regarded old comedy as the successor to this sort of satire, devised when the earlier form of rebuke

> seemed not to the finer head sufficiently perswasive, nor so popular as if it were reduced into action of many persons, or by many voyces lively represented to the eare and eye, so as a man might thinke it were even now a doing.[10]

Naturally, some of the characteristic methods of satire were bequeathed to old comedy, which

> followed next after the *Satyre,* & by that occasion was somwhat sharpe and bitter after the nature of the *Satyre,* openly & by

expresse names taxing men more maliciously and impudently then became, so as they were enforced for feare of quarell & blame to disguise their players with strange apparell, and by colouring their faces and carying hatts & capps of diverse fashions to make them selves lesse knowen. But as time & experience do reforme every thing that is amisse, so this bitter poeme called the old *Comedy*, being disused and taken away, the new *Comedy* came in place, more civill and pleasant a great deale and not touching any man by name.[11]

A slightly different view is presented by Thomas Lodge. Though believing that "satyre" succeeded rather than preceded tragedy, he, too, regards the Greek form as the first expression of dramatic satire. His account of the history of the early stage is equally a product of his imagination. He believes that after the first poets had composed hymns of thanksgiving to the gods for plentiful harvests, they invented a kind of didactic play which presented

the miserable fal of haples princes, The reuinous decay of many cou[n]tryes, yet not content with this, they presented the lives of *Satyers*, So that they might wiselye under the abuse of that name, discover the follies of many theyr folish fellow citesens. and those monsters were then, as our parasites are now adayes: suche, as with pleasure reprehended abuse.[12]

In the various ways above enumerated, relations between indefinitely conceived and largely imagined satyr plays, *vetus comoedia*, and satire were asserted by the critics of the Renaissance. Satire, they taught, was in origin a rude form of ridicule designed to purge simple men of their faults and was composed to serve as the characteristic utterance of crude sylvan gods—hence its harshness and license. Jonson was familiar with these doctrines.

This widely held belief in the close relationship between satire and satyr play is responsible for part of the Renaissance theory about the proper emotional tone of satire. The first and most important postulate was that satire, having originated in the mouths of the uncouth shaggy creatures of the Greek forests, ought to maintain the roughness and harshness which characterized their legendary actions. Even occasional obscurity might be more than tolerated; it might be cherished as proof that the coarseness of these pristine goat-songs had not been refined away. The inchoate roughness of Lucilius, the severity of Juvenal's invective, and the bitterness and obscurity of Persius confirmed the Renaissance satirists in their determination to be downright and raw. Adrian Junius in his *Nomenclator* expresses the popular view: "Satyra, Invectium in mores poema, Σατύρα à Satyrorum petulantia dicta. Un esguillon des vices. A nipping kind of poetrie, tawnting and sharpelie shewing men their faults."[13] Puttenham develops the same idea. He writes: "There was yet another kind of Poet, who intended to taxe the common abuses and vice of the people in rough and bitter speaches, and their invectives were called *Satyres*, and them selves *Satyricques*. Such were *Lucilius, Juvenall* and *Persius* among the Latines, & with us he that wrote the booke called Piers plowman."[14]

Bitterness and bluntness were approved by the literary critics, but these virtues were never to descend to the vices of railing, scoffing, or scurrility. Such forms of ridicule were appropriate in the mouth of a buffoon but never in the writing of a self-respecting satirist. Puttenham expresses the accepted opinion in a comment he makes upon Skelton. He calls him "a sharpe Satirist, but with more rayling and scoffery then became a Poet Lawreat, such among the Greekes were called *Pantomimi*, with us Buffons, altogether applying their wits to Scurrilities & other ridiculous matters."[15]

The early writers of English satire repeatedly asserted that their purpose was serious and their methods restrained. None of them conceived the term "satire" as exclusively applicable to any one literary form: it described many different combinations of reformatory social purpose and literary tone. Barclay in his Prologue to *The Ship of Fools* (1509) shows how loose was his conception of the genre, by stating that the Latin poets wrote "satyrs which the greks named Comedyes." In using the word "satyr," apparently for the first time in the English language, he indicates what meaning he attached to the term. It was primarily the reprehension of folly; yet it is correctly used to describe the work of the "olde Poetes Satyriens" who devoted their efforts to reproving of "the synnes and ylnes of the peple."[16] That is to say, Barclay makes no distinction between the correction of sin and the purgation of folly, either or both services being the proper business of the satirist.

Barclay expresses in the same preface another idea, which was to become an important article of faith in the satirist's credo. He insists that the correct method of his art is that of complete realism. His purpose is to force every man to behold in *The Ship of Fools* the course of his own life and his misgoverned manners, "as he sholde beholde the shadowe of the fygure of his visage within a bright Myrrour." The notion rescues satire from its age-long subservience to allegory and marks the beginning of a new conception of the art and of its adoption of an entirely different intellectual procedure. Yet Barclay, while advancing these ideas, retains his faith in the importance of the service which satire renders to society.

The moral dignity of satire continues to be reasserted by all those who write it. Sir David Lindsay, it will be remembered, called his late morality play *Ane Satyre of the Thrie Estaits, in commendation of vertew and vituperation of vyce* (1602), first presented before James V in 1540.[17] In choosing this title for his play, he was perhaps only attempting to enhance its importance in the eyes of the learned. But his deeper purpose was evidently to emphasize its realism and the harsh, direct way in which it attacked the series of courtiers who took the guise of contemporary figures. Or, to paraphrase Professor W. Roy Mackenzie,[18] Lindsay wished to announce that he had transformed the general stimulations to righteous living exercised by the older moralities into a daring exposure of conditions at a court which he knew.

The author of the tragedy of Collingbourne in the 1563 edition of *A Myrrour for Magistrates* puts into the mouth of his protagonist a denunciation of tyrants, under whose reign the free expression of the salutary social corrective of satire is violently suppressed and its practitioners condemned to death. The rhyme for which Collingbourne was convicted and executed,

> The Cat, the Rat, and Lovel our Dog,
> Do rule al England, under a Hog,

used the conventional methods of art approved in all healthy societies and sanctified by the work of Horace and Juvenal, and also by the authors of "tragicke playes." Yet the tyrant whom his lines indirectly struck would not endure the deserved sting. Under the rule of such creatures the life of a satirist is perilous:

> Be rough in ryme, and then they say you rayle,
> Though Juvenal so be, that makes no matter:
> With Jeremye you shal be had to jayle,
> Or forst with Marciall, Ceasars faultes to flatter,
> Clarkes must be taught to clawe and not to clatter:

> Free Hellicon, & franke Pernassus hylles,
> Are Helly hauntes, & ranke pernicious ylles.[19]

George Gascoigne explains, in his dedication of *The Steele Glas* to Lord Grey of Wilton, that the work had been composed to make amends for the love poems in the composition of which he wasted his youth. This idea is developed in the commendatory verses by Nicholas Bowyer which preface the volume:

> From layes of Love, to Satyres sadde and sage,
> Our Poet turnes, and travaile of his time,
> And as he pleasde, the vaine of youthful age,
> With pleasant penne, employde in loving ryme:
> So now he seekes, the gravest to delight,
> With workes of worth, much better than they showe.[20]

The foregoing passages reveal another characteristic of these English satires. In writing them their authors were consciously devising an antidote to the influence of the popular poetic cult of Petrarchism and its manifold developments. They thus took seriously the discharge of their corrective moral functions. They looked their world in the face and distinguished the fair lineaments from the foul. They protected the good, reproved the vicious, and reprehended and exposed the foolish. In brief, they served as vigilant policemen and social teachers to the entire community.

Another characteristic which satire was supposed to have inherited from the satyr play is reflected in Jonson's work. This was its peculiar mixture of comedy and tragedy, of grave and gay. Horace in his *Ars Poetica* explains the origin of the phenomenon, in a passage which was familiar to all the critics of the Renaissance. The lines as they appear in Sir Theodore Martin's spirited translation are the following:

> The bard who strove of yore in tragic strains
> To win the goat, poor guerdon of his pains,
> Anon brought woodland satyrs in, and tried,
> If grave with gay might somehow be allied.
> For only by the lure of things like these,
> That by their novelty were sure to please,
> Could audiences be kept, who were, no doubt,
> By the religious service half tired out,

> And, being flushed with wine could scarce restrain
> The lawless humours of their mad-cap vein.[21]

The Italian critic Cinthio, also assuming that this mixed emotional
character of satire is due to its retention of many features of its
parent satyr-play, analyzes briefly the resultant aesthetic effects. He
believes that they resemble those of tragicomedy, in that satire combines the emotional appeals of both tragedy and comedy. That is to
say, satire moves the reader both to laughter and to pity and terror.[22]

Sir Philip Sidney, in his *Apologie for Poetrie*, also conceives satire
to hold a middle course between mirth and anxiety aroused by the
tragic potentialities of the human passions. He bases his vindication
of "the Satirick," not upon the strength of its moral imperative, but
upon the ability of its playful spirit to "make a man laugh at folly,
and at length ashamed, to laugh at himselfe." Thus, while playing
about our midriff, satire is able to make us "feele, howe many head-
aches a passionate life bringeth us to."[23]

Erasmus' use of the burlesque encomium or farcical panegyric,
uttered by Folly herself in his *Moriae Encomium*, fortified the tradition that moral correction might be seasoned with mirth. He lightens
with a smile the serious countenance expected a satirist. Thus, in
order to deride urbanely and wittily, Erasmus invented the wise fool.
His "confessions" express a similar irony. These artful substitutions
of semidramatic devices for the direct methods of classical formal
satire revealed to later writers effective ways of transferring satire to
the stage in a form harmonious with the traditional gaiety of popular
vernacular comedy.

THE TEMPER OF ENGLISH FORMAL SATIRE, 1593–1599

The English writers of formal satire and epigram who expressed
themselves with increasing fervor and boldness from 1593 to June 1,
1599, illustrate almost all the theories which have just been reviewed.
They gave popular currency to the emancipated critical spirit and
to the literary methods which Jonson and Marston later tried to
preserve in their satiric plays.

Meres, in a famous passage in *Palladis Tamia*, lists the satirists
whom he believes to be the English equivalents of Horace, Lucilius,
Juvenal, Persius, and Lucullus: the author of *Piers Plowman*, Lodge,
Hall, Marston, and Guilpin.[24] These formal satirists assumed the role

of reformer. They conceived their business to be not so much the derision of folly as the exposure of vice. They were dominated by Juvenal's *saeva indignatio* and their methods were deliberately severe. They worked themselves up into a state of vociferous indignation; their voices became strident and their lash played upon the prisoners of evil with cruel abandon. In exhibiting this savage temper these writers were professing faith in their literary descent from the wild, uncouth satyrs. "I am a Satyre," cries William Rankins, "savage is my sport."[25] The satirists also invoke the harsh spirit of Juvenal and of Persius. Their favorite symbols are the instruments of castigation and judicial torture: the scourge, the lash, the rack, the strappado. Hall has an even more horrific desire—to loose upon the wicked world "the snaky tresses of th'*Eumenides*."[26] In two passages he strikes the note which all of the contemporary writers of satire repeat:

> Go daring Muse on with thy thankless taske,
> And do the ugly face of vice unmaske.[27]

> The *Satyre* should be like the *Porcupine*,
> That shoots sharp quilles out in each angry line,
> And wounds the blushing cheeke, and fiery eye,
> Of him that heares, and readeth guiltily.[28]

Guilpin exclaims that writers of satire and epigram

> Are Antidotes to pestilentiall sinnes,
> They heale with lashing, seare luxuriousnes,
> They are Philosophicke true *Cantharides*
> To vanities dead flesh.[29]

Naturally men who cultivated that sort of spirit had no use for stoicism and even less for laughter. They thought that the true satirist should be ruled by melancholy or by that feeling of general and profound discontent, with the human situation, which the Elizabethans called "malcontent."[30] On occasions this spirit became contaminated with disgust or Timon-like cynicism. Such melancholy or bitterness your true satirist could force to yield not tedium but a sober amusement, by converting the aversion caused by all sorts of mad conduct into derision of idiots and fools. Marston explains this salutary transformation in the following lines:

> From out the sadness of my discontent,
> Hating my wonted jocund merriment

(Only to give dull time a swifter wing),
Thus scorning scorn, of idiot fools I sing.[31]

But Marston is firm in his conviction that mirth should be rigorously excluded from a satirist's mind when he contemplates vice, and equally firm in his belief that the writer's excoriation of it should awaken no impulse toward laughter. Yet he does admit that when the satirist seeks merely to display and purge "humours"—a word which he uses in the sense of "social affectations"—then merriment and jesting are appropriate.[32] The distinction which Marston makes between the tone of satire intended to correct vice and that devoted to the control of social folly, and his attempt to establish a different critical method for each, constitute an important pronouncement. Possibly the distinction was suggested by Jonson's treatment of "humour" figures in *Every Man Out of His Humor*. But the Prologue, with the famous declaration that in his play he intends to "sport with humane follies, not with crimes," did not appear in the early quarto version of the comedy. In any case, the distinction is original with neither Jonson nor Marston. It appears in the work of some of the Italian critics of the sixteenth century. Castelvetro, for example, distinguishes between faults which are the result of folly and those due to evil, and between the attitudes to be taken toward them.[33]

Besides these formal satirists, an almost equally large group of writers of satiric epigrams flourished during the same decade. The most important were Sir John Davies, Sir John Harington, Thomas Bastard, and John Weever.[34] The publication of collections of epigrams by Robert Crowley in 1550 and John Heywood in 1562 marked the beginning of serious imitation of Martial in English literature.[35] Though their Latin master composed epigrams of many sorts, both of the English writers regarded the form as best suited to satire. And it is true that a majority of Martial's epigrams were satiric. He devoted much of his ridicule to the immorality prevalent in Rome during the turbulent and socially corrupt days of Nero and Domitian. He never became severe or hortatory, but was content to express amusement, cynical contempt, and, on rare occasions, disgust. Where Juvenal revealed intellectual penetration and moral fervor, mounting easily to exaggerated intensity and even violence of expression, Martial remained cool, urbane, and a little superficial. The difference between the attitudes of these two Romans represents the difference which

Renaissance critics discerned between the satire and the epigram. From Crowley to Guilpin[36] the latter form was considered simply a short satire, retaining some of the conciseness of an inscription and some of the ingenuity of a planned witticism. It certainly expressed a less severe moral tone and employed a less headlong method of attack than did satire. The writers of epigram thus appropriately dealt not with sins but with minor social absurdities. An epigram of Davies and one of Sir John Harington may serve to illustrate this fact. Clearly in imitation of Martial's account of a *bellus homo*[37] is Davies's poem, "Of a Gull":

> Oft in my laughing rimes I name a gull,
> But this new terme will many questions breede;
> Therefore at first I will expresse at full
> who is a true and perfect gull indeede.
>
> A gull is he who feares a velvet gowne,
> And when a wench is brave, dares not speake to her:
> A gull is he which traverseth the towne,
> And is for marriage knowne a common wooer.
>
> A gull is he, which while he prowdly weares
> A silver hilted rapier by his side,
> Indures the lies and knockes about the eares,
> whilst in his sheathe his sleeping sword doth bide.
>
> A gull is he which weares good hansome cloathes,
> And stands in presence stroking up his haire,
> And filles up his unperfect speech with othes,
> But speakes not one wise word throughout the yeare:
> But to define a gull in termes precise,
> A gull is he which seemes, and is not wise.[38]

A more trivial epigram of Martial's[39] is expanded by Harington in his "Of Galla's goodly Periwigge":

> You see the goodly hayre that *Galla* weares,
> 'Tis certain her own hair, who would have thought it?
> She sweares it is her owne: and true she sweares:
> For hard by Temple-barre last day she bought it.
> So faire a haire, upon so foule a forehead,
> Augments disgrace, and showes the grace is borrowed.[40]

The first poem is a portrait; the second, ridicule of a silly affectation.

But each, despite the light, humorous tone, in the last line dismisses the subject with evident scorn.

Whether directed against vice or merely against folly, whether its spirit of correction be furious and headlong or merely indulgent and humorous, the satire and epigram were both asserted to be impersonal in their ridicule. Therefore no man innocent of the faults attacked need take offense at the harshness of the satirists. They reiterate their reassuring message in phrases that echo certain expressions of Horace which appear in the first satire of his second book. In a dialogue between the author and Trebatius, the latter warns his friend that his attacks on the parasite and the spendthrift frighten even those who are untouched by his derision of men guilty of such faults. They fear that their follies, whatever they are, will be the object of his next attack. Horace's answer is, "Why should innocent persons tremble at the punishment meted out to the guilty? When Lucilius began to expose secret foulness, did Laelius or Scipio Africanus or other innocent men take offense?"[41]

Donatus, in the passage already quoted, makes this idea familiar to the minds of all sixteenth-century schoolboys, insisting that not individuals but general faults were the proper objects of satire.[42] Hence satire, as Horace first said,[43] galls only those who deserve censure. But, unfortunately, almost every reader is subject to some vice or folly. For that reason satire never has been, and never will be, a popular form of literature.

These ideas became a commonplace of Renaissance criticism. The English satirists under discussion repeatedly enunciated them. For example, Lodge in *A fig for Momus* writes of his satire, "In them (under the names of certain Romaines) where I reprehend vice, I purposely wrong no man, but observe the lawes of that kind of poeme: If any repine thereat, I am sure he is guiltie, because he bewrayeth himselfe."[44] This assertion is repeated throughout the works of the whole school, with only slight variations."[45] The assertion that everyone who took exception to these writers' excoriation of any vice, presented thereby prima-facie evidence that he practiced it and so justly gave the general admonition a personal application, must have been infuriating to the critics of the movement. They were blithely stigmatized as persons made desperately uneasy by the public revelation of the vices to which they in their hearts knew themselves to be addicted.

THE OBJECTS OF SATIRICAL ATTACK, 1593-1599

The phases of the satiric movement which have already been discussed have revealed the literary traditions which controlled many of the practices of English writers. Some of the objects against which they directed their scorn and ridicule were also drawn from the pages of the Latin satirists. But much of their corrective zeal was stimulated by the contemporary social and economic abuses already briefly analyzed. Joseph Hall and Thomas Bastard attack most directly the evils due to the economic dislocations of their world. Bastard more than once reveals his understanding of the part that profitable raising of sheep had played in precipitating the agrarian crises. The following lines are typical:

> Sheepe have eate up our medows & our downes,
> Our corne, our wood, whole villages & townes.[46]

Elsewhere he attacks with bitter indignation the men responsible for the inclosure of common lands:

> I know where is a thiefe and long hath beene,
> Which spoyleth every place where he resortes.
> He steales away both subjectes from the Queene
> And men from his owne country of all sortes.
> Howses by three, and seaven, and ten he raseth,
> To make the common gleabe, his private land.[47]

Hall, particularly in the fourth and fifth books of *Virgidemiarum*, also attacks inclosure, rack-renting, and other widespread devices of landlords to compel their tenants to contribute more amply to their income. The heirs of Lolio, Hall foresees, will be guilty of various ingenious forms of oppression:

> When perch't aloft to perfect their estate
> They racke their rents unto a treble rate;
> And hedge in all the neighbour common lands,
> And clogge their slavish tenant with commaunds.[48]

In another passage Hall describes the poverty and squalor of the poor tenant, who, nevertheless, in order to keep that little which he has, must haunt his landlord's hall, bearing flattery and gifts:

> The smiling Land-Lord shows a sun-shine face,
> Faining that he will grant him further grace;
> And lear's like *Aesops* Foxe upon the Crane,
> Whose necke he craves for his *Chirurgian;*
> So lingers of the lease until the last,
> What recks he then of paynes or promise past?[49]

Nor does the miserly regrator and hoarder of grain escape Hall's militant scorn:

> Ech Muck-worme will be rich with lawlesse gaine
> Altho he smother up mowes of seeven yeares graine,
> And hang'd himselfe when corn grows cheap againe.[50]

Such passages could be greatly multiplied. They reveal the moral ardor with which the satirists attacked contemporary economic abuses and suggest that they adopted the tone of Juvenal because their own indignation was as hot as his. Orthodox critical tradition met an urgent present need.

The threat which the beneficiaries of the new economic revolution made to the established social classes was also clearly seen by the English satirists. They derided both the upstart courtier and his imitator in the upper ranks of the prosperous merchants. Attacks on the life of a courtier had, as we have suggested, become a convention of English literature by the end of the sixteenth century. They had been directed against the hypocrisy, falsehood, debauchery, and cruelty prevalent at court, and the resultant wretchedness of the situation of a professional suitor for royal favor.[51] Ridicule of such general aspects of court life, when it appears in the work of the new formal satirists, should be regarded as traditional and of purely literary provenance.[52] But many of the attacks upon the courtiers' ways clearly refer to specific conditions prevailing at Queen Elizabeth's court. Donne, for example, describes the sycophant who knows

> When the Queene frown'd or smil'd, and he knowes what
> A subtle States-man may gather of that;
> He knowes who loves; whom; and who by poyson
> Hasts to an Offices reversion;
> He knowes who'hath sold his land, and now doth beg
> A licence, old iron, bootes, shooes, and egge-
> shels to transport; Shortly boyes shall not play

> At span-counter, or blow-point, but they pay
> Toll to some Courtier.[53]

Marston in *The Scourge of Villainy* shows that the courtier's eagerness to obtain monopolies is part of his desperate search for the money which he must have if he is to "jet it jollily" before the Queen.[54]

All of the writers derided the follies and pretensions of the upstart, with a moral fervor which today seems inappropriately intense. Their zeal is proof that they regarded these insignificant dandies as symptoms of social disintegration which it was their duty to check. Hence their exposure of the fantastic pretensions of the pushing new capitalist was an indirect assertion of the innate fineness of the ideals of the old landed aristocrats. These gentlemen they sought to recall from their avaricious bickering at court, which was not only blinding them to their hereditary social values but also weakening the bonds which until then had united them into a strong social class. Therefore, what now seems exaggerated concern with a negligible folly was to the satirists a menace of social revolution.

Other objects attacked by the formal satirists are either less clearly of immediate social consequence or mere constituent elements of a literary tradition. All of the seven deadly sins are assailed, and particularly those which had been singled out by Juvenal and Persius —hypocrisy, greed, gluttony, dishonesty of all sorts, and especially avarice and lust.[55] The new forms which avarice assumed during the sixteenth century were those most often excoriated; hence the satire of greed should be regarded as realistic and contemporary. How much of the persistent attack upon lust reflects an existing situation and how much represents conscientious imitation of earlier writers of epigram and satire, is difficult to say. Martial devoted many of his poems to describing sexual sins and abnormalities, although in a tone that is seldom severe. Sometimes his verses merely give range to wanton desires, but more often they express a kind of taunting ridicule. His favorite procedure is to use comment upon a sexual matter as careful preparation for a jest or a *jeu de mots*. For example, he refers to the Lesbian practices of a certain Bassa in order to say, "You have invented a monstrosity which may serve as an answer to the Theban riddle, 'How can a woman commit adultery without a man?' "[56] Such poems are probably no proof of Martial's own immorality or of his delight in brooding over obscenity. He tells us as much: "Lasciva est nobis pagina, vita proba."[57] In writing such stuff he was realistically satisfying the taste of the decadent Romans for whom his works were composed. He was merely giving them the "jocosa carmina" that they expected. *The Rime* of Francesco Berni, written between 1518 and 1536, and *The Dialogues* of Pietro Aretino, may have furnished the English satirists with another excuse, as good as the example of Martial, to concentrate their attention upon all forms of licentiousness. Yet they never adopted the careless delight of those men in the presence of sexual nastiness. Juvenal's fierce aversion to the phenomena seemed to them the proper attitude to take. In particular, his violent rebuke of women's debauchery and lust fascinated them and fixed the tone of their treatment of this subject, which was harmonious with that expressed in the traditional medieval satire of women.

In spite of all these literary precedents, the preoccupation of all the members of this English school with the sins and perversions of sex is so marked that a critic must assume either that the satirists, in particular Marston, were pathologically attracted to the unsavory subject or that lustful practices constituted in their time the most dangerous enemy to social decency. Today these attacks seem not so much warnings from evil as revelations of "what every old roué should know."

Joseph Hall sounded the summons to this massed attack by devoting his second satire to expressions of indignation against the treatment of lewd and obscene subjects in poetry.

> Now is *Pernassus* turned to a stewes:
> And on Bay-stocks the wanton Myrtle grewes.
> *Cythêron* hill's become a Brothel-bed,
> And *Pyrene* sweet, turned to a poysoned head
> Of cole-black puddle.[58]

In his ninth satire, which is a hostile criticism of the current interest of poets in such themes, he singles out for attack some nameless writer of bawdry, a graceless fellow who

> Rymed in rules of Stewish ribaldry,
> Teaching experimentall Baudery.[59]

In one of his academical satires, Hall warns a certain Labeo to "write better" "or write none." Later in the poem it appears that he means "write cleanly, Labeo, or write nothing." Still farther along, he laments the recent publication of English translations of foreign erotica. He asks:

> But who conjur'd this bawdie *Poggies* ghost,
> From out the *stewes* of his lewde home-bred coast:
> Or wicked *Rablais* dronken revellings.[60]

Guilpin attacks the same sort of poets, who

> Are Panders unto lusts, and food to sinnes,
> Their whimpring Sonnets, puling Elegies
> Slaunder the Muses; make the world despise,
> Admired poesie, marre *Resolutions* ruffe,
> And melt true valour with lewd ballad stuffe.[61]

The various works constituting the body of the literature to which Hall refers are, for the most part, too well known to need enumeration here. The movement culminated in such famous erotic poems of the early 1590's as Marlowe's translation of Ovid's *Elegies*, his *Hero and Leander*, the *Epigrammes* of Sir John Davies, Chapman's *Ovids Banquet of Sence*, and Shakespeare's *Venus and Adonis*. The principal source of the movement was Ovid's more licentious works, notably the *Ars Amatoria* and the *Amores*. This literature was written largely to pander to the taste of young profligates like the Earl of Southampton. Its popularity seems thus not to have been so much the *cause* as the *result* of an unhealthy interest in every sort of sex practice, normal and abnormal.

Whatever the reasons for emphasis upon the exposure of licentiousness, the fact is incontrovertible. The first satire in the fourth book of Hall's *Virgidemiarum* is ostensibly devoted to all the sins that fear exposure, or, as he puts it, to all who detest his open rhymes. His method in dragging them into the light will be very much like that of the Roman Fescennine satires described by Livy, which did not hesitate to be licentious themselves when occasion offered. This statement should prepare his readers for the attack upon libertines, both male and female, in Juvenal's furious temper, which occupies the entire latter half of the poem. The third satire of Marston's *The Scourge of Villainy*, with even more scandalous detail, lashes all sorts of strange forms of lust and licentiousness.

Moreover, satires ostensibly on other subjects betray almost an obsession of the writers' minds by an interest in matters of sex. Marston devotes his fourth satire, for example, to showing that slight faults are severely punished but "damned deeds" are praised. The evidence he presents is chiefly drawn from the licentiousness of the gods. Even many of the figures of speech with which these poets choose to decorate and illumine their themes are taken, as it were, from the stews. Donne's third satire is a striking instance of the curious preoccupation of the entire group. His subject is the futile search for true religion. Yet the metaphors which he employs to expose various reprehensible attitudes toward religion are largely drawn from the life of prostitutes. The following passage is typical:

> . . . . . . Careless Phrygius doth abhorre
> All,[62] because all cannot be good, as one
> Knowing some women whores, dares marry none.[63]

This somewhat repulsive characteristic of the formal satires needs no further illustration. It is patent to everyone who reads them.

Other reflections of the work of Juvenal and Persius appear in the details of the English poems which seem, at first sight, to be personal experiences of the authors. Even Hall's severe criticism of his fellow poets was almost surely suggested by similar attacks in the writings of his Latin masters. Persius, in his first satire, asserts the superiority of his work to that of Labeo, who presents a collection of "Bravos!" and "Beautifuls!" as evidence of literary excellence. Juvenal, in his first satire, similarly exalts his realistic achievements. They are, he maintains, vastly better than the compositions of poets who continue to tell tales of Hercules or to celebrate romantic wonders like the bellowing of the Minotaur. Such vaporings of an outmoded mythology, or even recapitulations of the adventures of Aeneas, have little to recommend them except that they are safe forms of poetic activity. They offend no one. But how can an author justify his absorption in such literature of escape in an age which is distorted into ugliness by all sorts of social enormities?

Hall frequently writes in just this Juvenalian vein. In his introduction to *Virgidemiarum*, called "His Defiance to Envy," he similarly strikes at the verbal extravagance and the chimerical imagination which characterized the poetry of Spenser and that of Ariosto, whose *Orlando Furioso* had just appeared in Sir John Harington's English translation (1591). Works like these "musty moral types," along with related forms of ambitious literary achievement, he renounces:

> Rather had I, albee in carelesse rymes,
> Check the mis-ordred world, and lawless Tymes.

In the third satire of the first book he derides the "huf-cap terms, and thundring threats," of popular tragedy. A direct reference to "Turkish *Tamberlaine*" suggests that Hall regarded Marlowe as one of the worst purveyors of bombast. In the seventh satire of the same book, Hall ridicules the sonneteers; in the eighth, the poets who meddle with holy things; and in lines like

> "Now good S. *Peter* weeps pure *Helicon*"

and

> "Great *Salomon*, sings in the English Quire"

he refers specifically to Robert Southwell's *Saint Peter's Complaint* and to Markham's *Sion's Muse*. But Hall's most extended attack is upon Labeo, whose name, at least, he derived from Persius' first satire. His voluminous muse seems to have busied herself with English translations of Homer, Poggio, and Rabelais. The literary activity of no known contemporary of Hall's assumes just this catholic form. The English Labeo is best regarded as a type figure representing each and every one of the assiduous and tasteless Elizabethan translators. In fact, all of Hall's satires of literature are most sensibly viewed, not as expressions of personal animus against fellow authors or as documents in the history of literary quarrels, but as an extension and application of an artistic method of two admired Latin models. This statement is equally true of the other satirists who participated in the movement. Personal allusions, when present, are fugitive, never carefully sustained or logically developed. To search for personal lampoons in the satires is to adopt the wrong approach toward them and can only result in distorting them and missing their larger significance.

A complete enumeration of the sins, excoriated in Roman satire, which reappear in the writings of the English satirists of the period would not serve the purposes of the present study. Alden,[64] in speaking of Hall's contributions, says, "Without exception (save in the case of alchemy and one or two others, excluded for obvious reasons) the vices and follies in these satires are those of classical satire." That is an exaggerated statement. As we have shown, many of the individuals ridiculed had no prototype in Latin satire. They represent social abuses and social follies created by economic phenomena of sixteenth-century England—a fact which enhances the value of the work of the English satirists. It establishes a nice balance, in their poems, between respect for literary tradition and concern with pressing social problems. It justifies their reiterated assertions that they have introduced into English literature, and domesticated there, a highly regarded type of classical literature.

THE METHODS OF ENGLISH FORMAL SATIRE, 1593–1599

The artistic methods developed by these authors of formal satire are of importance for this study because of the strong influence which they exerted upon the construction of the comical satires. Imitators of Latin literature that they were, they found indirect and weak the early English way of classifying individuals for censure according to type or social function. They preferred to follow their classical models in presenting sin and folly as traits of clearly conceived individuals. Accordingly, they created semidramatic figures who at first bore a naïvely simple relation to the particular human frailty under pitiless observation, as indicated, in the work of Lodge for instance, by such a phrase as "Example be thou *Hepar*."[65] Figures serving such a purpose demanded three distinct services from their creators: they had to be introduced with much identifying detail, exhibited in characteristic action, and finally deflated and discomfited. If not forced to endure some sort of humiliation, they would not have served as salutary warnings, and their authors' intentions could not be pronounced unmistakably satiric.

These three stages in the exemplary career of folly or sin can be clearly discerned within the narrow compass of some of the epigrams of this school. Guilpin's poem, "Of Cornelius," may serve as a specimen. The first lines swiftly identify him:

> See you him yonder, who sits o're the stage,
> With the Tobacco-pipe now at his mouth?
> It is *Cornelius* that brave gallant youth,
> Who is new printed to this fangled age.

The next lines describe his clothes and the manner in which he circulates among his acquaintances. These are his crowning absurdities. The last lines expose him as a counterfeit:

> Yet this Sir *Bevis*, or the fayery Knight,
> Put up the lie because he durst not fight.[66]

Guilpin employed the same method in his satires, which are a mere sequence of expanded epigrams, each dealing with the addicts of a certain vice. For example, his fourth satire is a warning against jealousy. Among those afflicted with its ravages is Severus. His suspicions of his wife's virtue drive him to wild savagery. He beats her, swaggers among her maids, and ends by

> . . . . . . wreeking his teene
> Upon her ruffes and jewels, burning, tearing,
> Flinging and hurling, scolding, staring, swearing.[67]

This conduct is outrageous enough to pronounce verdict upon itself. But the author fulfills his obligations to his artistic form by devoting four lines to a heated assertion of the desperate character of Severus' guilt, in a succession of mordant similitudes:

> Hee's as discreet, civill a gentleman,
> As *Harry Peasecod*, or a Bedlam man,
> A drunken captaine, or a ramping whore,
> Or swaggering blew-coate at an ale-house doore.[68]

A series of such portraits commonly unites to form these satires. The derided figures thus constitute a kind of procession of the various slaves to passion who march through the poem. Guilpin's fifth satire, in which he reviews the creatures whom he meets as he walks in Paul's is a poem of this sort. Many of Marston's best satires are designed on a like model. In all of them the emotional climax is formed by the few lines of direct rebuke with which the author dismisses his characters. For example, after exhibiting a pseudo gallant who is all face and clothes, he drives him out of his poem in a burst of surprising severity:

> Is this a man? Nay, an incarnate devil,
> That struts in vice and glorieth in evil.[69]

Such treatments of the fools and knaves are character sketches of a sort, but they should be clearly differentiated from the technical "character" as invented by Theophrastus and widely developed by English writers of the seventeenth century. The method adopted by

Theophrastus in all of his short character sketches is the same. It is, to quote Professor Edward C. Baldwin, "simplicity itself. It consists in defining a quality, and then proceeding to enumerate the things the type of man embodying that quality may be expected to do under given conditions."[70] The character is never strongly individualized. There is no description of his clothes, his appearance, or his peculiar attitudes. His actions, being various—different under different circumstances—are never set in a definitely visualized milieu. In all these ways the "character" was much more remote from the needs and methods of comic drama than the "satiric sketches," the prototype of which is to be found not in Theophrastus but in Martial.[71]

The English satires often display other dramatic characteristics than those to be found in this portrait. Most of them are adaptations of familiar aspects of Latin satire. Horace, in particular, was fond of dialogues and presented many human encounters in which he indicated clearly the action and even the gestures of the participants. His painful experience with the bore is the best-known of these semi-dramatic works. His English disciples availed themselves of similar devices. John Donne's first satire is but another version of Horace's encounter. A motley humourist meets the poet and insists on walking along the street in his company. The fantastic actions of the foolish fellow, as he passes different persons, are presented in a quasi-dramatic way, as the following lines will show:

> Now leaps he upright, Joggs me, & cryes, Do you see
> Yonder well favoured youth? Which? Oh, 'tis hee
> That dances so divinely; Oh, said I,
> Stand still, must you dance here for company?
> Hee droopt, wee went.[72]

Such a passage contains dialogue and clearly indicated action, as does all the rest of the poem. The bore leaves the poet only when he spies his Love in a window and flings away

> "Violently ravish'd to his lechery."[73]

In the latter part of Donne's fourth satire an even more effective dramatic scene is presented. The poet sees in a dream a crowd of suitors at court. The setting is the Presence Chamber, the time is "ten a clock and past." At this hour to the court come

> . . . . All whom the Mues,
> Baloune, Tennis, Dyet, or the stewes,
> Had all the morning held.[74]

These intellectual derelicts are followed by the ladies, whom the men accost. The two groups at once fall to praising each other—the men the women's beauty, the women the men's wit. Upon the stage thus set enters a typical courtier. He has stopped at the threshold to put his clothes in order and to indulge in elaborate furbishing and prinking. Then

> . . . . . . a Lady which owes
> Him not so much as good will, he arrests,
> And unto her protests protests protests.[75]

While these two ceremoniously plague each other in this way, Glorius enters. He is a fellow who affects in all his manners a rough carelessness. Hence he rushes in as if to shout an alarum, caring not whose cloak his spurs tear or whom he spits upon.

> . . . . . . He keepes all in awe;
> Jests like a licenc'd foole, commands like law.[76]

As the boor begins to dominate the assembly, the poet leaves the Presence by passing through the great chamber, which is hung with tapestry depicting the seven deadly sins. He wonders why.

Here is an ensemble scene composed with the adroitness of a skilled dramatist and an experienced stage manager. The characters who emerge as the spawn of the trifling atmosphere generated by the throng are depicted with just those details indispensable for an actor who might play the part. For example, instead of describing at length the appearance or the costume of Macrine, Donne indicates definitely what the fellow should do with his clothes, what posture he should assume at his entrance, what lady he should first accost, and what kind of remark he should make to her.

While beholding the dramas played out by these satirically conceived and vividly drawn figures—in fact, while responding to each of the literary devices employed by these poets—the reader is continually aware that the admonitory author is at hand. We see every character through his eyes; the illustrative anecdotes are all his; he intrudes, at frequent intervals, with angry rebuke. He is at once detective, prosecutor, and judge. The evils exposed are those which arouse his moral aversion and his derision, and the correction is the product of his invention. Practically all of the characteristics of English formal satire which have been enumerated in this chapter reappear in the comical satires which took over their office. The authors of these plays derided the same social enormities and follies; they assailed them in the same temper; and, in striving for exposure, discomfiture, and reform, they translated many of the details of method of the older form into the vernacular of the stage and its accessories. In fact, one may fairly say that the distinguishing features of formal satire, transferred to comical satire, largely determined its peculiar dramatic character.

NOTES

1 This passage is a summary of the following important sentences in Donatus' essay: "Sed cum Poëtae abuti licentius stylo, & passim laedere ex libidine coepissent plures bonos: ne quisquam in alterum carmen infame proponeret, lege lata, silvêre. Et hinc de inde aliud genus fabulae, id est satyra sumpsit exordium. quae à satyris, quos illotos semper ac petulantes deos scimus esse, vocitata est. etsi aliunde nomen traxisse prave agresti modo, de vitijs civium tamen sine ullo proprij nominis titulo carmen esset. Quod item genus comoediae nultis obfuit Poëtis, cum in suspicionem potentibus civibus venissent illorum facta descripsisse in peius, ac deformasse genus stylo carminis.... Hoc igitur, quo suprà diximus modo, coacti omittere satyram, aliud genus carminis... novam comoediam reperêre Poetae." ("Terentii vita, et de tragoedia ac comoedia non pauca, ex Aelio Donato," in *P. Terentii comoediae opera des Erasmi Roter. Castigatae* [Basle, 1534], sig. B3r & v.)

2 Cf. H. M. Hopkins, "Dramatic Satura in Relation to Book Satura and *Fabula Togata*," *Transactions and Proceedings of the American Philological Association*, XXXI, l–li.

3 Here is presented, first the Latin text of the pertinent passage, and then Philemon Holland's Elizabethan translation of it:

"Caeterum parva quoque (ut ferme principia omnia) & ea ipsa peregrina res fuit. Sine carmine ullo, sine imitandorum carminum actu, ludiones ex Hetruria acciti, ad tibicinis modos saltantes, haud indecoros motus more Thusco debant. Imitari deinde eos inventus, simul inconditis inter se jocularia fundentes versibus cepere: nec absoni à voce motus erant. Accepta itaque res, saepiusque usurpando excitata. Vernaculis artificibus, quia hister Thusco verbo ludio vocabatur, nomen histrionibus inditum: qui non sicut ante Fescennino versu similem incompositum temere ac rudem alternis jacebant, sed impletas modis satyras descripto iam ad tibicinem cantu, motuque congruenti peragebant." (*Titi Patavini Romanae historiae principis, libri omnes* [London, 1589], p. 186.)

"But (as all beginnings lightly are) a small thing (God wot) it was at first: without song and meetre, without gesture and action suitable unto song and verse, and the same also meere outlandish. For the plaiers, who were sent for out of Hetruria, as they daunced the measures to the minstrell and sound of flute, gestured not undecently withall, after the Tuscane fashion. But in processe of time the youth began to imitate and counterfeit them, jesting pleasantly besides one with another, and singing in rude rimes and disordered meetre: and their gesture was sorting with their jestes and ditties. Thus was this thing first taken up, and thus with much use and often excercise, practised. And heereupon our owne countrie Actors and artificiall professours of this feate, were called *Histriones*, of *Hister* a Tuscane word, which signifieth a plaier or dauncer. But these uttered not (as they used afore time) in their turnes one after another, disordred, confused, and rude verses, like to the loose and baudie Fescenine rimes: but went through and rehearsed out, whole Satyres, full of musicall measures, with a set consert of song also, to the instrument of the minstrell, and with gesture agreeable therunto. Certaine yeares after, *Livius*, who was the first that after the use of Satyres, ventured to set forth an Enterlude, ..." (*The Romane Historie Written by T. Livius of Padua. ... Translated out of Latine into English, by Philemon Holland* [London, 1600], p. 250.)

4 *Satires* I. ix.

5 *Ibid.*, II. v.

6 *Ibid.*, iv.

7 *Ibid.*, iii. 259–71.

8 *An abridgement of the notable worke of Polidore Vergile ... Compendiously gathered by Thomas Langley* (London, 1551), fols. xix, xviii[r & v]. The first edition of this translation was published in 1546.

9 *Puttenham, Arte of English Poesie*, sigs. E4[v]-F.

10 *Ibid.*, sig. F.

11 *Ibid.*, sig. F r & v.

12 Lodge [*Reply*], sig. C2ᵛ. This supposed connection between satire and the satyrs of Greek mythology was almost universally held until the appearance in 1605 of Isaac Casaubon's *De satyrica Graecorum poesi et Romanorum satira, libri duo.*

13 Adrianus Junius, *The Nomenclator, or Remembrancer... Written...in Latine, Greeke, French and other forrein tongues: and now in English,* by John Higins (London, 1585), p. 11.

14 *Op. cit.*, sig. E2ᵛ.

15 *Ibid.*, sig. Iᵛ.

16 "Satyra inter- | This present Boke myght have ben callyd nat
pretatur re- | inconvently the Satyr (that is to say) the
prehentio. | reprehencion of foulysshnes. but the neweltye
of the name was more pleasant unto the fyrst
actour to call it the Shyp of foles: For in lyke
wyse as olde Poetes Satyriens in dyvers Poesyes
conjoyned repreved the synnes and ylnes of the
Speculum | peple at that tyme lyvynge: so and in lyke
stultorum. | wyse this our Boke representeth unto the iyen
of the redars the states and condicions of
men: so that every man may behold within
the same the cours of his lyke and his mysgov-
erned maners as he sholde beholde the shadowe of the fygure of the visage within a
bright Myrrour."

(Sebastian Brant, *Shyp of Folys,* tr. Alexander Barclay [London, 1509], fol. xɪɪᵛ.)

The first sentence of this passage, in the Latin of Locher as quoted by Barclay, is, "Potuisset praesens his noster libellus/ non inconcinne satyra nuncupari: sed auctorem novitas tituli dilec- tavit, sicuti enim prisci satyrici: variis poematibus contextis: scelera ac pravitates mortalium reprehendebant." (*Ibid.*, fol. xɪɪ.)

17 For the text, see *The Works of Sir David Lindsay of the Mount, 1490–1555,* ed. Douglas Hamer (Scottish Text Society, 3d Ser.; Edinburgh), II (1931).

18 *The English Moralities from the Point of View of Allegory* (Boston, 1914), p. 94.

19 *A Myrrour for Magistrates* (London: Thomas Marshe, 1563), "Howe Collingbourne was cruelly executed for making a foolishe rime," ll. 69–70, 8–14.

20 *The Steele Glas. A Satyre compilled by George Gascoigne Esquire. Togither with the Complainte of Phylomene. An Elegie devised by the same Author* (London: Richard Smith, 1576), sig. A4ʳ ᵃⁿᵈ ᵛ.

21 Ll. 220–24:

"Carmine qui tragico vilem certavit ob hircum,
mox etiam agrestis Satyros nudavit et asper
incolumi gravitate jocum temptavit, eo quod
illecebris erat at grata novitate morandus
spectator, functusque sacris et potus et exlex."

22 "La satira e imitazione di azione perfetta di dicevoli grandezza, composta al giocoso ed al grave con parlar soave, le membra della quale sono insieme al suo luogo per parte, e per parti devise, representata a commovere gli animi a riso, el a convenevole terrore e compassione.... "Insieme giacosa e grave—la fa diversa dalla comedia e dalla tragedia, delle quali la prima e composta al piacevole, l'altra al grave. Ed essendo ella insieme partecipe della piacevolezza dell' una, e della gravita dell' altra, non e nè questa nè quella.... A commovere terrore e compassione—la separa della comedia e la fa dissimule alla tragedia il dire ad essa—conveneole. Perchè ciò mostra che non si movono nella satira gli affette con quella forza colla quale si movono nella tragedia. E cosi è un alcuna parte la satira simile alla comedia, in alcune alla tragedia, ed in alcune altre è dissimile dall' una e dall' altra." ("Lettera overo discorso di Giovambattista Geraldi Cintio sopra il comporre le satire atte alle scene," in *Scritti estetici biblioteca rara publicata da G. Daelli*, Vol. LIII [Milano, 1864], 134 *et passim.*)

23 "The Satirick, who

Omne vafer vitinum, ridenti tangit amico.

Who sportingly never leaveth, until hee make a man laugh at folly, and at length ashamed, to laugh at himselfe: which he cannot avoyd, without avoyding the follie. Who while

Circum praecordia ludit,

giveth us to feele, howe many head-aches a passionate life bringeth us to. How when all is done,

Est ulubris animus si nos non deficit aeguus."
(*Apologie for Poetrie*, sig. F3.)

24 "As *Horace, Lucilius, Juvenall, Persius* & *Lucullus* are the best for Satyre among the Latines: so with us in the same faculty these are chiefe, *Piers Plowman, Lodge, Hall* of Imanuel Col-

ledge in Cambridge; the Authour of *Pigmalions Image, and certaine Satyrs; the Author of Skialetheia.*" (Francis Meres, *Palladis Tamia* [London, 1598], p. 283ᵛ.)

²⁵ *Seaven Satyres, Applyed to the weeke* (London: W. Fernbrand, 1598), No. 1 ("Contra Lunatistam"), sig. A5.

²⁶ *Joseph Hall, Virgidemiarum, Sixe Bookes. First three Bookes, Of Tooth-lesse Satyrs* (London: T. Creede, 1597); *The three last Bookes. Of byting Satyres* (London: R. Bradocke, 1598), Lib. 5, Satire 3, sig. F4.

²⁷ *Ibid.*, Lib. 1, Prologue, sig. Bᵛ.

²⁸ *Ibid.*, Lib. 5, Satire 3, sig. F3ᵛ.

²⁹ Edward Guilpin, *Skialetheia. Or, A Shadowe of Truth, in certaine Epigrams and Satyres* (London: J. Roberts, 1598), "Satyre Preludium," sig. Cᵛ.

³⁰ For the meaning of this term, cf. O. J. Campbell, "Jacques," *The Huntington Library Bulletin*, No. 8 (Oct., 1935), pp. 71–79.

³¹ *The Scourge of Villainy*, Satire 10, ll. 1–4 (*The Works of John Marston*, ed. A. H. Bullen [London, 1887], III, 367).

³²   ".............Come, sporting Merriment,
          Cheek-dimpling Laughter, crown my very soul
          With jouisance, whilst mirthful jests control
          The gouty humours of these pride-swoll'n days,
          Which I do long until my pen displays."
                              (*The Scourage of Villainy*, Satire 11,
                              ll. 6–10 [*Works*, III, 371].)

³³ Cf. Ludovico Castelvetro, *Poetica d'Aristotle, vulgarizzata* (Basilia, 1576), p. 92, where he draws a sharp line between "turpitudine procedente de schiocchezza" and "turpetudine procedente de malvagità," and the ways in which each is to be corrected.

³⁴ The important works of these men are: Sir John Davies, *Epigrammes* (1590?); Sir John Harington, *Epigrams* (1615, 1618; but almost surely written between 1591 and 1599); Thomas Bastard, *Chrestoleros. Seven bookes of Epigrames* (1598); John Weever, *Epigrammes in the oldest cut, and newest fashion* (1599).

³⁵ The best study of Martial's direct influence on the English epigram of the sixteenth and seventeenth centuries is T. K. Whipple, *Martial and the English Epigram, from Sir Thomas Wyatt to Ben Jonson* ("University of California Publications in Modern Philology," X [1920–25], 279–414).

36   The Satyre onely and Epigramatist,
        (Concisde Epigrame, and sharpe Satyrist)."
                                    (Guilpin, *op. cit.*, sig. C.)
37 *Epigrams* III. lxiii. This similarity has been pointed out by
Whipple (*op. cit.*, p. 339).
38 *Epigrammes and Elegies. By J. D. and C. M.* (Middleborough
[1590?]), Epigram 2, sig. A3ᵛ.
39 Cf. Whipple, *op. cit.*, pp. 346–47.
40 *The Most Elegant and Witty Epigrams of Sir John Harrington*
(London, 1618), Bk. 2, No. 66, sig. F8ᵛ.
41   "..................quid? cum est Lucilius ausus
        Primus in hunc operis componere carmina morem,
        detrahere et pellem, nitidus qua quisque per ora
        cederet, introrsum turpis, num Laelius et qui
        duxit ab oppressa meritum Karthagine nomen
        ingenio offensi aut laeso doluere Metello
        famiosis que Lupo cooperto versibus?"
                                    (*Satires* II. i. 62–68.)
42 Haec quae Satyra dicitur, eiusmodi fuit, ut ... de vitijs civium
tamen sine ullo proprij nominis titulo carmen esset." (See n. 16,
above.)
43 *Satires* I. iv. 25–33.
44 T[homas] L[odge], *A fig for Momus: Containing Pleasant
varietie, included in Satyres, Ecologues, and Epistles* (London:
printed for Clement Knight, 1595), sig. A3ᵛ.
45 E.g., Lodge, in the first satire in *A fig for Momus*, says that
men hate to be even reminded of great and unusual deformities:

        "Thus, though mens great deformities be knowne,
        They greeve to heare, and take them for their owne."
                                    (Sig. B2.)

Sir John Davies asserts that the epigram is subject to the same
law of anonymity. He is scornful of those ignorant enough to
believe that the epigram can properly become an instrument of
personal lampoon:

        "But if thou find any so grosse and dull,
        That thinks I do to private taxing leane,
        Bid him go hang, for he is but a gull,
        And knowes not what an Epigramme doth meane:
        Which taxeth under a particular name,
        A generall vice that merites publike blame."
                            (*Epigrammes and Elegies. By J. D. and
                            C. M.*, Epigram 1, "Ad Musam," sig. A3.)

46 *Chrestoleros,* Lib. 4, Epigram 20, sig. G5^v.

47 *Ibid.,* Lib. 3, Epigram 22, sig. F$^{r\ \&\ v}$.

48 *Virgidemiarum,* Lib. 4, Satire 2, sig. C2^v.

49 *Ibid.,* Lib. 5, Satire 1, sig. E5^v.

50 *Ibid.,* Lib. 4, Satire 6, sig. D7.

51 Cf.: (1) John Skelton, *The Bowge of Court* (*ca.* 1520); (2) Sir David Lindsay, *The Testament, and Complaynt, of our Soverane Lordis Papyngo* (1530); (3) Alexander Barclay, *Eclogues,* I, ll. 825ff.; (40) Sir Thomas Wyatt, "Satires," 11, ll. 19ff., 52ff.

52 Such, for example, is the fifth satire of John Donne. (*The Poems of John Donne,* ed. Herbert J. C. Grierson [Oxford, 1912], I, 168–71; cf. also Marston, Satire 2, ll. 87–106 [*Works,* III, 272–73].) Sycophancy was traditionally associated with an atmosphere of vice, as Donne asserts in these bitter lines:

> ".......Aretines pictures have made few chast;
> No more can Princes courts, though there be few
> Better pictures of vice, teach me vertue."
>
> (*Poems,* I, 161.)

53 *Poems,* I, 162.

54
> "Aulus will leave begging monopolies
> When that, 'mong troops of gaudy butterflies,
> He is but able jet it jollily
> In piebald suits of proud court bravery."
>
> (Satire 4, ll. 84–86 [*Works,* III, 328].)

55 These same sins had been exposed in many of the early prose tracts which have been hastily reviewed above—for example, in Stubbes, *Anatomy of Abuses,* Lodge, *An Alarum against Usurers,* and Nashe, *Pierce Penilesse.* The influence of the characters depicted in this literature of exposure, upon those appearing in the formal English satires, is a large subject, deserving special investigation. The ultimate literary sources of the figures attacked in the satires is not a matter of first importance to the present study.

56 This is a translation of the sense, not the literal meaning, of the following lines:

> "Commenta es dignum Thebano aenigmate monstrum,
> hic, ubi vir non est, ut sit adulterium."
>
> (*Epigrams* I. xc. 8–9.)

57 *Ibid.,* iv. 8.

58 *Virgidemiarum,* Lib. 1, Satire 2, sig. B3^v.

59 *Ibid.*, Satire 9, sig. C3. It is probably impossible to discover just whom Hall meant. The description best fits the work of Pietro Aretino, which was widely known in England during the last two decades of the sixteenth century.

60 *Ibid.*, Lib. 2, Satire 1, sig. C7^v.

61 *Skialetheia,* sig. B8.

62 I.e., "All religions."

63 Satire 3, ll. 62–64 (*Poems,* I, 156).

64 *Rise of Formal Satire,* p. 123.

65 *A fig for Momus,* Satire 5, l. 35 (sig. G^v).

66 *Skialetheia,* Epigram 53, "Of Cornelius," sig. B4$^{r \& v}$.

67 *Ibid.*, Satire 4, sig. D3^v.

68 *Ibid.*

69 *The Scourge of Villainy,* Satire 7, ll. 26–27 (*Works,* III, 345).

70 Edward Chauncey Baldwin, "The Relation of the English 'Character' to Its Greek Prototype," *PMLA,* XVIII (N.S., XI), 415.

71 Martial seldom writes an epigram containing the three essential characteristics of the best satiric portrait: (1) a description of the appearance and actions of the individual satirized; (2) the presentation of the character in dramatic terms; and (3) his scornful dismissal in the last line or two of the epigram. However, a few meet all these requirements. An examination of poems LXII and LXIII in Book III of the *Epigrams* will illustrate the points at issue. Epigram LXII satirizes a foolish spendthrift, Quintus, by describing his purchases. For example, Martial cries, "You buy slave boys for a hundred thousand, and often two hundred thousand, sesterces apiece," etc. (l. 1: "Centenis quod emis pueros et saepe ducenis"). At the end of the poem, Martial deflates the fellow in two lines: "Do you think, Quintus, that the purchase of these things is an indication of a large intelligence? You are mistaken. These are the things that a petty mind wishes to buy" ("Haec animo credis magno te, Quinte, parare?/falleris: haec animus, Quinte, pusillus emit"). Epigram LXIII is a more complete prototype for the satiric portrait, in that the description of the fool is more clearly dramatic in method. The poem presents the actions of Cotilus, a typical "bellus homo" or fop. He spends his time dallying with his curls, humming tunes which have been imported into Rome from the Nile or the Gades, and waving his arms in

time with various musical measures. Or he lolls among the
ladies, forever whispering into the ear of one of them. He runs
from one party to another, purveying such gossip as who is in
love with whom, or such information as the long pedigree of a
famous race horse of the day. Martial ends Cotilus' little hour
of stage strut with these scornful lines: "Is this, this thing a
fop, Cotilus? Then is a fop, Cotilus, a very thrashy thing"
("Quid narras? hoc est, hoc est homo, Cotile, bellus?/res
pertricosa est, Cotile, bellus homo"). In such an epigram the
English satirists could have found a model for all the essential
elements of their portraits.

72 Satire 1, ll. 83–87 (*Poems*, I, 148).

73 *Ibid.*, l. 108.

74 Satire 4, ll. 175–77 (*Poems*, I, 165).

75 *Ibid.*, ll. 210–12.

76 *Ibid.*, ll. 227–28.

H. W. FOWLER

Humour, Wit, Satire, Etc.

humour, wit, satire, sarcasm, invective, irony, cynicism, the sardonic.
So much has been written upon the nature of some of these words, &
upon the distinctions between pairs or trios among them (wit &
humour, sarcasm & irony & satire), that it would be both presumptuous & unnecessary to attempt a further disquisition. But a sort of
tabular statement may be of service against some popular misconcep-
tions. No definition of the words is offered, but for each its motive or
aim, its province, its method or means, & its proper audience, are
specified. The constant confusion between sarcasm, satire, & irony, as
well as that now less common between wit & humour, seems to justify
this mechanical device of parallel classification; but it will be of use
only to those who wish for help in determining which is the word that
they really want.

From *A Dictionary of Modern English Usage*, Oxford, 2nd ed., revised
by Sir Ernest Gowers, 1965, p. 252. Reprinted by permission of the
Clarendon Press, Oxford.

	MOTIVE OR AIM	PROVINCE	METHOD OR MEANS	AUDIENCE
humour	Discovery	Human nature	Observation	The sympathetic
wit	Throwing light	Words & ideas	Surprise	The intelligent
satire	Amendment	Morals & manners	Accentuation	The self-satisfied
sarcasm	Inflicting pain	Faults & foibles	Inversion	Victim & bystander
invective	Discredit	Misconduct	Direct statement	The public
irony	Exclusiveness	Statement of facts	Mystification	An inner circle
cynicism	Self-justification	Morals	Exposure of nakedness	The respectable
The sardonic	Self-relief	Adversity	Pessimism	Self

DAVID WORCESTER

From The Art of Satire

INVECTIVE

The Engine of Anger

In the formation of any kind of satire there are two steps. The author
first evolves a criticism of conduct—ordinarily human conduct, but
occasionally divine. Then he contrives ways of making his readers comprehend and remember that criticism and adopt it as their own. Without style and literary form, his message would be incomprehensible;
without wit and compression it would not be memorable; without
high-mindedness it would not "come home to men's business and
bosoms." Juvenal's ringing words, "difficile est saturam non scribere,"
have given many thousands of readers the concept of a man forced by
frightful wrongs to pour his indignation, careless of whether he has
any hearers or no. In reality, Juvenal's phrase is a brilliant stroke of
rhetoric. Intense suffering does not often leave a man in a literary
frame of mind. Even if the sly Roman rhetorician had himself experienced the bygone ills that he denounces, he need have felt no
difficulty in refraining from satire. People threatened with suffering or
forced to watch others suffer are far more apt to "take pen in hand"
than the man who has spent ten years in a mercury mine or who has
been run down by a drunken driver. Feminine readers may find in
this observation a possible explanation for the fact that no woman has
ever made a mark in satire.

From *The Art of Satire*, Cambridge, Mass.: Harvard University Press,
1940, pp. 13–19, 37–38, 40–51, 77–83, 111–12. Copyright 1940 by the
President and the Fellows of Harvard College; 1968 by Eloise Worcester Spencer Wade. Reprinted by permission of the publishers.

Juvenal's words pertain to our second step—that of appeal to the reader. Without expressing any opinion, he transfixes our attention by the awful suggestion of his remark, and we anxiously await his criticism. It is this necessity of winning the reader's sympathy that makes satire a paradoxical subject. The satirist must simultaneously appear amiable to his audience, hostile to his enemies. Where the audience is small and prejudiced, the problem hardly exists. If you undertook to denigrate the character of Hitler before a company of Jewish refugees, you would find no great difficulty in appearing amiable; but if you sought fame in the wider field of literature, among casual, impartial, and even hostile readers, you would find the trick of riding two horses at once less easy than it looks. It takes genius to be able to boast with Erasmus and Dryden of the applause of your victim. Erasmus wrote,

> The Pope himself read the Moria and laughed. His only comment was this: "I am glad our Erasmus is the Moria himself"; and yet I deal with no one more scathingly than with the Popes.[1]

Dryden observes of the character of Zimri, or Buckingham, in *Absalom and Achitophel,*

> It is not bloody, but it is ridiculous enough; and he, for whom it was intended, was too witty to resent is as an injury.[2]

Rhetorical devices, then, serve to win the reader and to soften the impact of the writer's destructive or vengeful sentiments. Such devices are all-important for the study of satire. The skill with which they are employed serves as a criterion between good satire and bad. The reader who has trained himself to recognize and appreciate them, like the amateur of music who has trained himself in harmony and counterpoint, receives much because he gives much. What is more to the present point, the presence or absence of such devices determines what is satire and what is not.

Many persons instinctively shrink from satire as they might from a scorpion. Is not satire the expression of controversial heat, of venomous rancor, of the raw, negative emotion out of which humanity struggles to rise, age by age? Granted one dispensation, I hope to show that no such generalization is valid. A writer on lyric poetry feels no obligation to take account of newspaper jingles, yet a writer on satire finds it difficult to assume the same standard of excellence. Oceans of ink have been poured out in acrimonious and shocking libels and invectives; but so have oceans been spent on nauseous obituary verse and summer-verandah romances. In thinking of satire, we should consider the hundreds of works that have risen to the top. The millions below, graduated from acidulous gruel to a thick sludge of hell-broth, are interesting only insofar as they help to explain the principles of great satire.

How easily satirists acquire a bad name! Lucian, the Antichrist, deservedly torn to pieces by dogs; Rabelais, the filthy mocker; Swift, the inhuman misanthrope, not content with crucifying the women who loved him but bent on destroying the virtue and happiness of all mankind; one smiles on encountering these fancies, until damnable iteration brings on ironic melancholy. How little humanity, how little study, are needed to show that these and many other ill-treated satirists are the cleanest and brightest and merriest minded of men! Mark Twain remarked that the presence of only the Best People was enough to damn even heaven.

The content of satire is criticism, and criticism may be uttered as direct rebuke or as impersonal logic. Innumerable intermediate stages, by combining emotion and intellect in different proportions, lead from one pole of blind, human feeling to the opposite pole of divine, or inhuman, detachment. The spectrum-analysis of satire runs from the red of invective at one end to the violet of the most delicate irony at the other. Beyond either end of the scale, literature runs off into forms that are not perceptible as satire. The ultra-violet is pure criticism; the infra-red is direct reproof or abuse, untransformed by art.

In view of the pain, already mentioned, with which persons of delicate sensibilities are apt to regard satire, a large proportion of satiric literature might be expected to consist of direct attack, that is, open name-calling and nose-thumbing. Unquestionably many people hold this belief. To test it, Hugh Kingsmill's twin anthologies, *Invective and Abuse* and *More Invective*, may be consulted.[3] Shuddering anticipation dies as the pages are turned and such old friends appear as Skelton's extravagant burlesque of Wolsey; Prince Hal's mock-denunciation of Falstaff; Donne's lyric "The Apparition"; Jeremy Taylor's meditation on life's ills; the famous verse-portraits of Sir Hudibras, Achitophel, Og, Doeg, Atticus, and Sporus; the King of Brobdingnag's Olympian summing-up of the English nation; Goldsmith's almost jocular mock-epitaph, "Retaliation"; Burke's legal forensic against Warren Hastings; Keats's anguished appeal to Fanny Brawne; and Dickens' humorous description of Mr. Pickwick, routed from Bob Sawyer's rooms by Mrs. Raddle.

The editor writes:

> Invective has been understood in this Anthology to mean direct verbal attack. Irony and satire are therefore, as far as possible, excluded, though the line of demarcation is sometimes indistinct.[4]

Here are grounds for wonder. Are the great verse-portraits to be excluded from "satire" and Swift's masterstrokes from "irony"? Surely, invective must be stretched far beyond its usual acceptation to include such mild and circuitous attacks. An occasional stinger does appear, like Swinburne's letter to Emerson or Browning's lines to Edward FitzGerald. On the whole, however, wrath and hatred find little expression. The crux of the matter lies in the words "*direct* verbal attack." It is the direct attack that people expect to find in satire, particularly in invective-satire, yet in almost every instance the emotion is controlled, the blow is softened, and the approach is indirect. Parody is not direct, nor are irony and mock-heroic. Their whole force may be traced to the fact that they are indirect.

The reason for the scarcity of direct invective in literature is not far to seek. Anger is the most repellent of emotions. It is acute discomfort to be present where a man has fallen into a furious passion. If you are in such a situation, and the object of your acquaintance's rage has no connection with you, you will experience an instinctive craving to escape into humor, to turn the painful situation into a ludicrous one. This is done by withdrawing all sympathy from the blusterer and by taking a more relativistic view of him as a lobster-faced baboon in a fit. A little boy receiving a wigging will concentrate on a purple wart, if such there be, on his tormenter's nose. Anger does not beget anger. Remember the artful self-control of Mark Antony as he whipped the Roman populace to a frenzy of rage by means of the cumulative irony of his "So are they all, all honorable men."

Satire is the engine of anger, rather than the direct expression of anger. Before our sympathy is won, we must be freed from the distress of witnessing naked rage and bluster. Like Mark Antony, the artist must simulate coolness and detachment. Like the vaudeville marksman with his mirror, he must look in one direction while he shoots in the opposite direction. To avoid the possibility of misunderstanding, it may be emphasized that the actual text of an invective piece is the only subject under discussion. A satire may be inspired by rage; it may produce rage in its readers; but ninety-nine times out of a hundred, rhetorical analysis of its language will reveal the widest differences between its style of attack and the style of a rattling good set-to between man and wife, or between a Communist lecturer and a member of the American Legion. To write in cold anger is to show detachment in language; to write in lofty anger is to affect disregard of an opponent; to write in cutting anger is to hold a victim in the icy grasp of irony. Mark Twain's *To the Person Sitting in Darkness* (1901) provoked a wilder furor than any other American satire before or since. His exposure of the looting and extortion practised by our missionaries in China was described by friends and foes as savage, blistering, and vitriolic. So it was—in its intent and in its effect, but not in its manner or its language.

Mark Twain prefaces his article with a newspaper dispatch, telling how a missionary had first collected 300 taels for each of 300 murdered native Christians and then had imposed a fine of thirteen times the total amount.[5] The Catholics, having lost 680 in the uprising, demanded 750,000 strings of cash and 680 *Chinese heads!* Mark Twain's opening words are:

> By happy luck, we get all these glad tidings on Christmas Eve —just in time to enable us to celebrate the day with proper gayety and enthusiasm. Our spirits soar, and we find can even make jokes: Taels, I win, Heads you lose.[6]

With the same amused detachment, he proceeds in a leisurely way to roast the missionaries; but they are roasted by chilling irony, just as Bird's-Eye peas come to the pot already half cooked by the action of extreme cold. Nor does he depart at any time from the tone of irony. Clearly, some attention is due to the devices whereby detachment becomes the propelling force of strong emotion.

•   •   •

One pressing question remains. If satire uses the technique of wit and the comic, how is it to be distinguished from "pure" comedy? Clearly, no academic formula can be used to plot a sharp dividing line. Like the problem of what constitutes good taste, the question is one on which unanimity is impossible. Two general principles are useful in deciding whether to call a given piece of writing a satire or a form of pure comedy, such as farce, skit, extravaganza, and so on. First we should consider the closeness with which the camera pursues the object of satire. If the comic devices are applied to a single object or group of related objects, if a sense of unity is produced by the common bearing of diverse illustrations, we are on the side of satire. If the operations of wit are promiscuous and casual, the presumption is in favor of comedy.

Secondly, we may consider the degree of virulence in the comic devices. Here we find use for the foregoing remarks on detachment, time-lag, and participation of the reader with the author. At one end of the scale, harsh derision denotes satire; at the other end, gentle banter and mild amusement denote comedy. The final conclusion is reached by a comparison of two readings, one closeness of pursuit, the other the intensity of condemnation. Young's *Satires*, for example, are mild in feeling but earn their name by strict attention to business. Artemus Ward and Finley Peter Dunne are comic rather than satiric artists; many satirical touches are to be found in them, but these strokes do not combine into a single, sustained object. Swift writes with passion under iron control, and pursues his object relentlessly; hence he belongs to satire.

The laughter of comedy is relatively purposeless. The laughter of satire is directed toward a preconceived end. Comedy demands little of the audience. Reading Stephen Leacock's delightful *Nonsense Novels* may be compared to lying in a hammock and being pleasurably tickled. A half-hour with *Jonathan Wild*, on the other hand, makes the brain reel with the constant effort of unraveling the irony and capturing Fielding's true meaning.

BURLESQUE

Satire by Comparison

In making the rounds of an amusement park, you can always find people "laughing like a swarm of flies" in front of the eccentric mirrors. You draw near to one of them and see a squat, obese goblin goggling at you. With a pang of surprise, you observe that the monster wears your clothes, mimics your gestures, and is, in horrid fact, you. Before the next mirror, behold yourself shot up into the wasted wreck of a giant, with pipestem arms and elongated horse-face. These two experiences have introduced you to burlesque in its simplest form.

It has been shown how invective-satire, compelled to gain the sanction of society, uses wit mechanisms to circumvent mankind's prejudice against naked rage. Derision is the purpose of invective-satire. The reader has no choice in accepting the subject of condemnation, for it is held steadily before his eyes; yet he derives some sense of self-determination, for example from the simile, which permits him to make a comparison and draw his own deductions from it. The reader would sympathize with the condemnation still more, if the simile could be expanded from a brief trope into a literary vehicle capable of carrying a multiple-series of comparisons between the ideal and the real. He could then see how a man's deeds compare with his words, how the operation of a law fulfils the purpose for which it was enacted, how far a would-be hero falls short of true greatness.

Burlesque is just such a vehicle. It is a kind of extended simile. "Look here, upon this picture, and on this," says the author. The reader looks first on one, then on the other, and decides for himself whether the mirrored image faithfully reproduces the object. Of course, in satire it does not do so, for the satirist secretly aims at exposing a discrepancy in the strongest possible light. Once he has exposed it, the fewer words the better, for his insistence on pointing the moral will rob the reader of his share in the game. So long as he abstains from sermonizing, he has the reader with him. Far from using the goad of invective, he lures his audience by posing as a passive agent, letting the condemnation come home to roost by analogy. The reader then appears to himself to draw his own independent conclusions.

The reader's sense of participation is given an extra fillip by suppression of one term of the simile. We do not find a parody printed side by side with its original. It is the reader's part to supply knowledge of the model. He must hold up the model, and the author will furnish him with a distorted reflection of it. Herein lies the strength of burlesque, and its weakness. So long as the author can depend on his audience for the necessary information, he need not utter a word of reproach or obloquy; his audience will provide the curses, and he will yet "have a thank" for his good offices. And yet, knowledge that seems to one age to be graven in adamant seems to the next to have been written in the sand. The *Batrachomyomachia,* or Battle of Frogs and Mice, finds a small audience today although it parodies Homer, the Bible of the ancient world. Likewise all the machinery of the mock-heroic—the invocations, epithets, and set speeches so delicious to the eighteenth century—raises only an occasional smile today. Dryden, in writing *Absalom and Achitophel,* must have been confident that his allegory would be comprehended at sight by readers born hundreds of years to come. How many today can read it for the first time without recourse to Bible or to "Notes"? Just as invective dies when the social occasion that countenanced it passes, so burlesque withers away when the knowledge that supports it is forgotten.

Two courses are open if we wish to use the method of comparison to show up a man's shortcomings. We may draw a picture of a low fellow engaged in vicious or trivial pursuits and endow him with the features of our victim. These features, perhaps degraded and brutalized, are not altered past recognition. The first reaction of the audience on recognizing the likeness is one of pure comedy. And comic enough it is to see a hawk's bill doing duty for a human nose, or a human face translated into a fox's mask. The satiric reaction is overlaid on the comic. Comparing what we know of the real man with the caricaturist's distorted image, we single out a hawk-like rapacity in his character, or a foxy duplicity. Once this quality has been impressed on our minds, we shall find it hard to think of the man without remembering it. Thus by altering the true image, by degrading it and presenting it without dignity, the artist acts like the first of the two mirrors, the glass that reduces the spectator to a fat goblin. This process of diminishing and degrading the object is the method of low burlesque.

Low burlesque creates a standard below its victim and makes the reader measure him against the standard. Fox ethics, for example, are lower than human ethics. When the reader is led to regard a man as a fox, whatever foxy qualities the man possesses are thrown into sharp relief. In the same way, a piano with the loud pedal held down will give back whatever note is sung into it. Low burlesque calls forth these sympathetic notes or hidden affinities.

It is clear that we can obtain a second scale of comparison by placing our standard, not below the victim, but above him. Holding him up against a standard obviously too elevated for him will make his shortcomings stand out sharply. If he conceives of himself as an exalted personage, let him be invested with the trappings and dignities of a real hero, retaining only his proper features. His pretentiousness will then stand out, to the exclusion of all other qualities. The artist in this instance does the work of our second mirror. He draws us out to an unconscionable length. We seem to knock at the stars with our exalted head, until our legs, too frail to support such eminence, give way. Great then is our fall, and hugely pleasing to bystanders. It is this principle of magnification that gives us high burlesque.

Both forms of burlesque differ importantly from invective-satire. Invective-satire is the direct and didactic expression of opinion, relieved from tedium and bad taste by comic mechanisms. Burlesque is mimetic. The author acts a part; he pretends to be Tennyson writing a poem, but he is careful to give himself away by the triviality of his subject. Lucian poses as a venerable philosopher, and when he has won the reader's respect gives him a flirt over the head with his bladder. Rabelais, in pedant's skull-cap and slops, overwhelms one with erudition that proves on closer examination to serve no other end than nonsense. The burlesque artist puts on an act for his audience. He must keep the show going and at the same time step out of his part and assure the audience that it is only a show. Consequently burlesque requires of an author more detachment and higher aesthetic gifts than does invective.

The indirect, mimetic, and aesthetic qualities of burlesque give us one set of criteria for dividing it from invective. The use of the comic is a second means of discrimination. Invective employs the comic in various ways, as small, palliative tropes or units of rhetoric, secondary to the main design. The comic element in burlesque is enlarged until it takes the proportions of the central design or "fable." The core of *MacFlecknoe* and of the *Dunciad* is the crowning of a monarch of dullness. *The Battle of the Books* shows animated volumes engaged in Homeric warfare. *The Praise of Folly* is a mock-oration by a mock-goddess. The frame of these and of countless other burlesques is in itself purely comic. Satire enters only when specific persons or man-made conditions are recognized as the source of the distorted reflection in the burlesque. To a reader entirely ignorant of history, *Hudibras* would be pure comedy, with only a trace of satire. Children find in *Gulliver's Travels* a story of funny little men and funny big men. They lack all knowledge of the true objects so curiously reflected in the satiric mirror of Swift's mind. Burlesque, then, first moves us to the purposeless laughter of pure comedy by its ludicrous plot or frame. This explains the mechanics whereby most of the greatest satires con-

vey an air of geniality and warm humanity. The critical or corrective
laughter of satire enters when the story is recognized as a mirror in
which the actions or conditions of men are purposely distorted.

High and Low Burlesque

Such are the differences between invective-satire and general
burlesque. A further extension of the same principles serves to divide
low from high burlesque. Low burlesque invites the reader to compare
its subject with what is base and sordid. A satirist might, for example,
represent Aeneas as a vagabond and Dido as a fishwife. He would then
be creating a sort of expanded simile. The laughter to which his
degrading comparison gives rise is derisive, scornful, and self-congratulatory. Since it is of the same sort that arises from calling names,
low burlesque is evidently half-brother to invective-satire. High burlesque, on the other hand, depends not on noticing similarities but on
noticing differences. Contrast rather than comparison is its method.
In reading *MacFlecknoe* we care nothing for any actual resemblance
Shadwell may bear to a monarch of letters. We are all eagerness to
learn how *unfit* he is for his heroic setting. We love to see him
magnified in one line, but only for the pleasure of seeing him knocked
down in the next. What we are faced with in high burlesque is a simile
in reverse, a simile without similitude. We must invert the comparison
before we arrive at the sense. High burlesque, then, partakes of irony,
which must preserve its fiction with scrupulous care. There will of
course be clues to tell us to reverse the literal meaning of an ironical
argument, but they are cunningly concealed. So long as the fiction is
transparent, and the author lets us see behind the mask, and the
knock-down blow is given in public, we are still in the realm of burlesque. The conclusion of *MacFlecknoe* gives us a brilliant illustration
of the art of building up with one hand and knocking down with the
other:

> The hoary prince in majesty appear'd,
> High on a throne of his own labours rear'd.
> At his right hand our young Ascanius sate,
> Rome's other hope, and pillar of the state.
> His Brows thick fogs, instead of glories, grace,
> And Lambent dulness play'd around his face.
> As Hannibal did to the altars come,

> Swore by his sire, a mortal foe to Rome;
> So Shadwell swore, nor should his vow be vain,
> That he till death true dulness would maintain:
> And, in his father's right, and realm's defence,
> Ne'er to have peace with art, nor truce with sense.

Conventionally, high burlesque treats a trivial subject in an elevated manner, and low burlesque treats an elevated subject in a trivial manner. Professor R. P. Bond, after a study of English burlesque poetry from 1700 to 1750, finds grounds in contemporary criticism for further discrimination. Parody and mock-heroic belong to the family of high burlesque. Both use the grand manner for trifling themes, but parody adopts the manner of a specific work, while mock-heroic copies a whole class of writing. Conversely, travesty and the Hudibrastic poem are branches of low burlesque. Travesty imitates a particular model, the Hudibrastic a general type.[7] These distinctions may be expressed graphically thus:

	SPECIFIC	GENERAL
High	Parody	Mock-heroic
Low	Travesty	Hudibrastic

No better schematization is possible, yet difficulties arise when one attempts to sort out poems and assign them quickly and easily to their proper pigeon-holes. Seldom is a burlesque poem true to type throughout. Cogitation is usually necessary to determine whether the prevailing manner is diminishing or degrading; and when the object of imitation is specific at one moment, general at the next, classification may become so laborious that it breaks down of its own weight. Prose evades exact labels more readily than verse. With all its virtues, neither this nor any other scheme may be applied thoughtlessly and automatically. The incongruity inherent in satiric and humorous writing and the elasticity of critical terms in common usage will convert any rigid system of definitions into a bed of Procrustes.

In the preceding chapter, mention was made of the time-lag, or interval between the perception of the spoken or printed word and the full comprehension of the author's meaning. The greater the time-lag, it appeared, the sharper the sense of the comic and of the author's detachment. It is as though the time spent by the author in aiming his shaft gave him a chance to let his emotions cool and to approach his subject through reason. There is a progressive increase in the time-

lag as we ascend each of the steps between abuse, invective-satire, low
burlesque, and high burlesque. In the last, it is incumbent on the
reader to provide his own knowledge of the object of satire and to
reverse the burlesque magnification in terms of that knowledge. Satire
is thus at two or three removes from its object. It is well mixed with
the comic and free from blustering wrath. So far as "over-awing vice"
is concerned, high burlesque is worse than useless. Often it treats its
victim with reverent admiration. Dryden's satirical portraits in the first
part of *Absalom and Achitophel* are the greatest in the language because of the civil, well-bred manner in which he speaks. He seldom
needs to raise his voice, thanks to his marvelous talent for rhetoric.

Of all the types of satire—here classified as invective, burlesque,
and irony—burlesque offers the greatest freedom to the artist and
exacts the most from him in terms of creative invention. Burlesque is
imitative, it is true, yet the imitation goes no deeper than surface and
form. Once an affinity with the model has been established, the more
extravagant and ludicrous the action the better the public is pleased.
Unless the author has skill in creating original incidents, the work is
likely to drag. *MacFlecknoe* has enough action for its length. The
Dunciad has not; the heroic games of poets, critics, and booksellers
give the second book a backbone that is wanting in the third book
with its tedious visions and in the fourth with its lengthy prophecies.

Burlesque, as it is close to the art of the clown, calls for nimble
friskings. It can no more afford to stand still than a play can. The
great masters amaze and delight by the perpetual motion of their drol-
ling antics. Erasmus burdened himself in the *Praise of Folly* with an
abstract, philosophical subject. Yet his inventive genius keeps us constantly diverted, until it tires and invective-satire supplants burlesque
in the second half of the book. Following the technique of his master,
Lucian, he personifies his subject as a goddess and employs a hundred
specific touches to make us actually see her as she delivers her
harangue, and see likewise the expressions on the faces of her auditors.
Once launched on her mock-encomium, the goddess gives an un-
equaled display of intellectual juggling, sporting with it, and treating
it in true burlesque fashion, as Diogenes in Rabelais treated his tub:

> There, I say, in a great vehemency of his Spirit, did he turn
> it, veer it, wheel it, whirl it, frisk it, jumble it, shuffle it, huddle
> it, tumble it, hurry it, joult it, justle it, overthrow it, evert it,
> invert it, subvert it, overturn it, beat it, thwack it, bump it, batter

it, knock it, thrust it, push it, jerk it, shock it, shake it, toss it, throw it, overthrow it upside down, topsiturvy, arsiturvey, tread it, trample it, stamp it, tap it, ting it, ring it, tingle it, toul it, sound it, resound it, stop it, shut it, unbung it, close it, unstopple it.[8]

Erasmus's language is concrete and picturesque, never abstruse. His style, like Rabelais's, shows that delightful mingling of scholarly niceness with the salty idiom of the common man which is the hallmark of most great satire. To be sure, there is no central narrative, but neither is there a moment's tedium. The ideas go by us so fast and in such odd disguises that we seem to be trying to take in all three rings of the circus at once.

Invention, motion, forward movement—these are indispensable for good burlesque. The admirers of *The Hind and the Panther* are scholars every one. For the general reader, the triviality of the fable breaks down the illusion of burlesque-satire. Dryden has used the animal-allegory simply to lend objectivity to his remarks on a painful subject. The action is practically static; the distorted reflection is promised but never delivered; hence he has not so much used as abused the burlesque convention.

•   •   •

Verbal Irony

Irony might be defined in two words as an impractical joke. To see a top-hatted dandy slip on a banana-peel is always pleasant. But the pleasure becomes truly exquisite to the watcher who has seen the banana-peel in advance or perchance placed it where it would do the most good. While the jest of irony is played with ideas, instead of slippery or blunt objects, the distinction between the initiated and the about-to-be-initiated still remains. The little audience (Horace's *pauci lectores*) is quick-witted enough to see the trap in advance; the "many-headed vulgar" rush blindly to meet their fate. In a practical joke a single victim is enough, and comedy is the result. In literature the percipients of irony always feel themselves to be members of a small, select, secret society headed by the author. The victims, by implication, are legion. Satire enters when the few convict the many of stupidity. The implication of a large audience is not always justified by the fact.

The New Yorker owes its success to the skill with which its editors charm five million readers into the illusion of belonging to an aloof, sophisticated, esoteric, and fastidious minority. Critics of its sometimes mastodonic irony in turn plume themselves on being the true *cognoscenti.*

> So, naturalists observe, a flea
> Has smaller fleas that on him prey;
> And these have smaller still to bite 'em,
> And so proceed *ad infinitum.*[9]

The ironist appeals to an aristocracy of brains. It requires mental exertion to comprehend even the simplest and crudest form of irony—sarcasm. Sarcasm is derived from a Greek word that means "flesh-tearing." When someone smiles pityingly at your criticism of a novel and remarks, "Of course, we all know you could write a much better book if you only would," your flesh is torn, so to speak, but it is not the going in of the barb that wounds, but rather the pulling out. For the words build you up only to knock you down; you must perceive the intentional inversion of meaning and translate back into the original, to your own hurt, if you would not appear a blockhead and natural butt.

When we dislike a writer's irony, we call it sarcasm. The word has unpleasant connotations, and we reserve it for obvious double-dealing in words, such as appears in conversation or in written jibes and taunts. Sarcasm is irony, none the less. *The Arte of English Poesie* (1589) mentions "ironeia, or the dry-mocke," and the *New English Dictionary* cites as the earliest use of the word "irony" a passage from Wynken de Worde (1502) in which "yronye of grammar" occurs when "a man sayth one & gyveth to understande the contrarye." Sarcasm is then a form of verbal irony, produced by an inversion of meaning. It may be distinguished from the more literary kinds of irony by the fact that it never deceives its victim. It carries its sting exposed; and lest it should be misunderstood, it has established a set of non-verbal conventions to accompany it—a curl of the lip, a special intonation and falling inflection, and often shaking or nodding of the head. Such obvious self-advertisement means that the time-lag between hearing and comprehending is much shorter than it would be in a purely ironical speech, delivered without change in voice or expression. When portracted, sarcasm quickly degenerates into "heavy sarcasm." No settled habit of speech is more wearisome and vexatious, for a long string of sarcasms is a series of jokes on the hearer which the speaker noisily explodes and relishes in advance.

As a substitute for fist-fights, corporal punishment, and invective, sarcasm has become indispensable in social intercourse. Any reader who finds this observation cynical is invited to try the experiment of living for a week, or even a day, without allowing a sarcastic utterance or intonation to cross his lips. Even the Lord found it expedient to meet Job's reasonable complains with a crushing sarcasm:

> Canst thou draw out leviathan with an hook? . . . Wilt thou play
> with him as with a bird? or wilt thou bind him for thy maidens?

The existence of a double audience—an esoteric and an exoteric —is rather implied than real when sarcasm is used. There are few too dull to scent the reversed meaning. Writers, dealing with the subtleties of frozen language instead of the ephemeral spoken word, naturally produce a purer irony than do speakers, formal orators excepted. When they set down words and sentences that express the opposite of their real meaning, they have no warning flags to fly, no special intonations of the voice, no raising of the eyebrows. The reader discovers the deception for himself, unravels the contradiction, and feels happily at one with the author. Irony of inversion involves a longer time-lag than invective, burlesque, or sarcasm, and it demands that the reader join more energetically with the author in the act of artistic creation.

It is scarcely necessary to give examples of irony of inversion, since every grand, artistic lie, told with a poker face, belongs to this category. My own favorites are from Chaucer. In *The Nun's Priest's Tale*, Chauntecleer, the know-it-all cock, tells his dame that, sure as Gospel,

> *Mullier est hominis confusio,—*
> Madame, the sentence of this Latyn is,
> "Womman is mannes joye and al his blis."[10]

In *The Merchant's Tale*, the "faire, fresshe" May, after one brief interview with her husband's squire, resolves to love him though she is but a four days' bride. By way of comment, the Merchant adds a single line—Chaucer's favorite line, it has been called, from its use elsewhere:

> Lo, pitee renneth soone in gentil herte![11]

Earlier in the same tale is the startling observation, already noted:

> Whan tendre youthe hath wedded stoupying age,
> Ther is switch myrthe that it may nat be writen.[12]

Irony of inversion ordinarily compels the reader to convert apparent praise into blame. Its shocking power is greatest when it is thus used to shatter complacent truisms and unthinking optimism. Occasionally contempt and insult are to be understood as praise. Swift's disconcerting way with with his friends was to address them in terms of reproach and abuse, and then, by a fine stroke of wit, to convert the whole into a compliment. In *Jonathan Wild*, Fielding represents Heartfree's simplicity and benevolence as low sentimentality and want of spirit. Stevenson in his celebrated defense of Father Damien ironically acknowledges the blemishes in Damien's character and makes them appear faint shadows that only set off the brilliance of his hero's virtues. But Swift, after all, was a virtuoso in irony, and Heartfree is only a counterpoise to Jonathan Wild, the prince of rogues, and Stevenson was answering a bill of indictment, point by point. The negative function of irony in making approval explode into dislike is more frequent and more effective than the reverse method. Irony is a form of criticism, and all irony is satirical, though not all satire is ironical. Skepticism and pessimism and melancholy are the ironist's and he is content to have it so. Lucian boldly declares:

> I profess hatred of pretension and imposture, lying, and pride. ...However, I do not neglect the complementary branch, in which love takes the place of hate; it includes love of truth and beauty and simplicity and all that is akin to love. But the subjects for this branch of the profession are sadly few.[13]

Swift echoes this conclusion, saying, "The materials of panegyric, being very few in number, have been long since exhausted.[14]

It is in the mock encomium that irony of inversion reaches its greatest concentration and brilliance. Mention has been made in the preceding chapter of the *jeux d'esprit* in this kind by Lucian, Erasmus, and Rabelais. The encomiums of sponging, of folly, and of debt are orations, which classical sources in Roman *satura* and in the Greek *spoudaiogeloion* and mime-literature in general. Fielding breathed the spirit of the mock encomium into a modern form, that of the full-length novel (most burlesque novels of the eighteenth century were as long as their models). *Jonathan Wild* furnished a model for *Barry Lyndon*, although Thackeray's genius falls below Fielding's in the dexterous handling of irony and in intellectual power. In recent years Aldous Huxley has transferred the mock encomium to the field of the Utopia. Burlesque Utopias containing occasional satire existed before *Brave New World*, but Huxley's Utopia-in-reverse is in a class by itself. To the reader who satisfies the inordinate demands made upon him, it offers a carefully worked out criticism of life. In its mirror writing, every comment or surface meaning requires only to be reversed before falling into its place in Huxley's social philosophy.

Of all the themes that lend themselves to ironical panegyric, none has proved so fruitful as the theme of *Jonathan Wild*—the Great Man. Peacock may be allowed to speak for his predecessors in his succinct way:

> Marry, your hero guts an exchequer, while your thief dis-embowels a portmanteau; your hero sacks a city, while your thief sacks a cellar: your hero marauds on a larger scale, and that is all the difference, for the principle and the virtue are one: but two of a trade cannot agree: therefore your hero makes laws to get rid of your thief, and gives him an ill name that he may hang him: for might is right, and the strong make laws for the weak, and they that make laws to serve their own turn do also make morals to give colour to their laws.15

Treatment of this theme had gradually become more and more ironical since the Renaissance, as a few illustrations will show. Following upon the satiric invectives of Erasmus and More against war and those who made it, Rabelais uttered a burlesque snarl against a certain King Anarchus:

> These devillish Kings which we have here are but as so many calves, they know nothing, and are good for nothing, but to do a thousand mischiefs to their poor subjects, and to trouble all the world with warre for their unjust and detestable pleasure: I will put him to a trade, and make him a crier of green sauce.16

Burton speaks his mind on the Great Man, but uses his words, angrily ironical in themselves, to construct a detached and whimsical indict-

ment of human folly. In the following extract, we meet Alexander,
who was to become the proverbial example of the Great Man:

> Every nation had their Hectors, Scipios, Caesars, and Alex-
> anders!... These are the brave spirits, the gallants of the world,
> these admired alone, triumph alone, have statues, crowns, pyra-
> mids, obelisks to their eternal fame, that immortal genius attends
> on them.... Alexander was sorry, because there were no more
> worlds for him to conquer, he is admired by some for it, *animosa
> vox videtur, et regia,* 'twas spoken like a Prince; but as wise
> Seneca censures him, 'twas *vox iniquissima et stultissima,* 'twas
> spoken like a Bedlam fool....
>
> One is crowned for that for which another is tormented....
> A poor sheep-stealer is hanged for stealing of victuals, compelled
> peradventure by necessity of that intolerable cold, hunger, and
> thirst, to save himself from starving: but a great man in office
> may securely rob whole provinces, undo thousands, pill and poll,
> oppress *ad libitum,* flea, grind, tyrannize, enrich himself by spoils
> of the commons, be uncontrollable in his actions, and after all,
> be recompensed with turgent titles, honoured for his good service,
> and no man dare find fault, or mutter at it.[17]

Dramatic Irony

The distinction between the world of uninitiate, common souls
and the select few who share some special knowledge underlies every
form of irony. This distinction must have been bitterly ruminated by
Swift when he found that his defense of the Established Church in
A Tale of a Tub had made him an object of horror in the eyes of pious
Queen Anne, who thereafter refused to hear of his preferment. Defoe
in the pillory must likewise have pondered the truth of the proverb,
"nothing succeeds like success." And who can read the thoughts of the
unfortunate man, trembling on the verge of religious conversion, to
whom his mentor, Canon Ainger, innocently sent Samuel Butler's
diabolical pamphlet, "In Defense of the Miraculous Element in Our
Lord's Ministry upon Earth"?

The sense of belonging to a privileged minority arises from verbal
irony in solving the puzzle of inversion or understatement, and from
irony of manner in penetrating the disguise of the *ingénu.* When the
field of observation is enlarged from words or personalities to life as a
whole and the ways of Providence, the sense of esoteric knowledge is

conveyed through dramatic irony. The conflict of good and evil is the central fact of intellectual experience. From age to age, man wrestles with chaos, seeks to discover universal laws, and devises orderly, uniform arrangements of the universe. Social institutions, in the Occident at least, support that search for certainty by proclaiming the benevolence and justice of God, the fairness of the moral law, or the conquest of nature by the laboratory. Religion, philosophy, and science together provide the faith that is the motive power of civilization. From this body of belief is derived the "knowledge of life" of the masses. The dangers of such a system are those that confront the *alazon* in comedy: overstatement, overconfidence, failure to preserve the inconspicuous moderation wherein safety lies. Opposed to this general, vulgar knowledge is the private knowledge of the *eiron*: the horror of becoming a Pollyanna, the realization that blind chance can destroy all that the heart holds dear, the conviction that pride goeth before destruction, the observation that knowledge brings sadness, the suspicion that the universe is indifferent, or even hostile, to man. It was not for nothing that God forbad Adam and Eve to eat the fruit of the Tree of the Knowledge of Good and Evil. In every attempt to regularize the cosmos, some allowance must be made for the Imp of the Perverse, for the jealousy of the gods, for the panurgic principle.

•   •   •

NOTES

[1] P. S. Allen, ed., *The Praise of Folly* (Oxford, 1925), p. xvii.

[2] "Essay on Satire," Walter Scott, ed., *The Works of John Dryden* (London, 1808), XIII, 95. Dryden overestimates the magnanimity of his butt. See IX, 272.

[3] London, 1930.

[4] *Invective and Abuse*, p. 1.

[5] It later appeared that the fine was actually one-third of the damages. "Thirteen" was a cable-error.

[6] Mark Twain, "To the Person Sitting in Darkness," *Europe and Elsewhere* (New York, 1923), p. 252.

[7] R. P. Bond, *English Burlesque Poetry, 1700–1750* (Cambridge, Mass., 1932), pp. 3–17. The term "mock-heroic," it may be

noted, does duty for other forms of general high burlesque, including mock-ode, mock-eclogue, and mock-didactic.

8 Rabelais, Author's Prologue to the Third Book.

9 Swift, "On Poetry."

10 *Canterbury Tales*, VII, 3164–3166.

11 *Canterbury Tales*, IV [E] 1986.

12 *Canterbury Tales*, IV [E] 1738–1739.

13 *Works* (trans. H. W. and F. G. Fowler, Oxford, 1905), I, 215.

14 Preface to *A Tale of a Tub*.

15 T. L. Peacock, *Maid Marian* (London, 1891), pp. 166–67. See also p. 103....

16 Book II, Chapter xxxi.

17 *The Anatomy of Melancholy* (London, 1887), pp. 28–31....

MARY CLAIRE RANDOLPH

The Medical Concept in English Renaissance Satiric Theory

No reader of English satire in the Renaissance can have failed to note the popular vogue for medical imagery in the critical statements defining and characterizing satire. To the Renaissance critic and satirist, satire is a scourge, a whip, a surgeon's scalpel, a cauterizing iron, a strong cathartic—all in one; its mission is to flay, to cut, to burn, to blister, and to purge; its object is now a culprit, a victim, a criminal, and now an ailing, submissive patient, a sick person bursting with contagion; and the satirist himself is a whipper, a scourger, a barber-surgeon, an executioner, a "doctour of physik."

Neither can the reader of English satire have failed to note that this Renaissance fashion for medical vocabulary dealing with Man's physical body[1] figures much less prominently once the seventeenth century rationalistic philosophies have made close contact with the main current of English satire. In the later seventeenth century, Man's critical attention is fastened for the most part on his Reason, his Will, the workings of his mind, and his place in and relation to society; and satire acquires a new and quieter vocabulary of comparatively exact philosophical and psychological terms,[2] while the greater part of the old popular medical metaphor drops away, trailing some interesting but highly conventional remnants. The satirist becomes in neo-classic theory a philosopher and moralist instead of the short-gowned barber-surgeon of Renaissance metaphor; and the vices and follies earlier characterized as ulcers, tetters, and pustules become "ruling passions"

From Studies in Philology, XXXVIII (April 1941), 125–57. Reprinted by permission of the editors.

which temporarily divert Man's Reason from the norm of right Judgment and which must be subdued and conquered by his Will acting
under the spur and direction of Ridicule. It is the eighteenth century
satirist's business to use Ridicule judicially so that Man will be persuaded to use his Will to pursue a strictly rational course of behavior
and to preserve with dignity his allotted place in the center of the
Great Chain of Being. To a large extent, an intellectual nomenclature
—Will, Judgment, Reason, Ridicule—thus becomes current and fashionable as the earlier medical vocabulary had been current and fashionable.

It is this predominant fashion for medical vocabulary and imagery in English Renaissance satiric theory[3] with which this paper is
concerned. Because the neighboring Celtic satire seems in various ways
to place a similar emphasis on the functions of satire in relation to the
physical body, a brief survey of that aspect of Celtic satire is offered
at the outset as a preface to the more detailed survey and analysis of
the medical concept in English Renaissance satiric theory. This is not
done with the intention of proving unequivocally that the first has influence on the second, but rather with the intention of drawing attention to certain similarities.

I

Nearly thirty years ago Professor Fred Norris Robinson pointed
out in some detail what an "intimate and essential relation seems to
exist" between satire, even of the highly intellectualized sort, and early
Irish incantation and spell.[4] Professor Robinson's parallel investigations
in other literatures prompted him to posit tentatively the theory that
sophisticated or literary satire has certain of its roots deep in primitive
magic and spell-winding and that after a long period of development
there emerges something like personal invective devoid of supporting
magic, and that that personal invective is a factor contributing to
moral, philosophic satire as an art-form. To aid his readers, Professor
Robinson cautiously called the magical lines, "incantational satire" and
the non-magical lines, "real satire."

"Incantational satire," which appears to have been chiefly personal curses and direct imprecations reenforced by sympathetic magic
and uttered with the prime intent of blasting the human body, must
have been well-nigh universal among primitive peoples. Researches and

relics (such cursing-stones) show it to have been wide-spread among the Mediterranean peoples, Greeks, Latins, Arabs, and Hebrews.[5] Students of satire, attempting to piece out the background of the genre, are particularly interested in curses and imprecations when the magic trappings begin to fall away, and the malefic words stand alone, relying on their own power. Obviously we cannot accurately tell at this distance where magical imprecation ends and the thing that Professor Robinson calls "real satire" begins, any more than we can date the preserved pieces with any certainty.

The great body of this incantational satire and of the early non-magical forms is unfortunately lost to us. In Greek literature almost the sole instances of such unaided word-power are the uncertain legends of Archilochus' iambics, which presumably caused Lycambes and his daughter to hang themselves, and the similarly doubtful stories of the powerful iambics of Hipponax and Simonides of Amorgos. Whole continuities of early satiric forms from the classic literatures, both Greek and Latin, are lost to us.[6] The same thing is evidently true of Anglo-Saxon literature, which preserves only charms and a few fleeting references to *bismerleoð* (insult-songs) and *niðing* verses (*nið*, envy, malice, hatred).[7] Early Celtic[8] literature, however, is singularly valuable in that it is comparatively rich in various types of early satiric verses.

One of the striking features of this early Celtic verse is that it was apparently called satire from the very earliest times just as the men and women who pronounced it were called satirists.[9] So important were these satirists and their verses that very few of the ancient heroic tales preserved failed to have a roving, scheming satirist threatening maiden, warrior, or tribal chieftain with his dread satire.

The Celtic satirist, a sorcerer and magician up to a relatively late date, was one of the classes of poets; and as such, his training was long and arduous and his position important. Tribal arrangements gave him by hereditary right certain comprehensive powers and authorities; he was feared, flattered, obeyed, and extravagantly bribed and rewarded above all men, even the druids, whose powers at times seem almost identical with his. We can say that this "satirist" is no more than a befeathered medicine-man and that his verses are but chanted mumbo-jumbo; but even preliminary studies indicate that here may be one source, at least, of a native tradition in English satire.

The Celtic satirist was frankly out for actual blood or "word-death." In many instances he meant to destroy his victim, flesh, bone, nerve, and sinew; his victim's hounds, cattle, horses, pigs, wife, and children (and even their children's children); his trees and grain and pasture-lands, the very fish in his streams.[10] In other cases, he meant to mutilate the victim's face so shamefully that, if it were a man, he could hold no high tribal office; and if it were a woman, she should be repulsive to those who might love her. Few satires or fragments of satires preserved to us fail to include the idea of physical mutilation or destruction, an idea which the early Irish terms for satire and satirists persistently stress. These words may be cited from general texts: *ainmed*, blemishing; *imdergad*, reddening; *rindad*, cutting; and these words from *Cormac's Glossary: leos*, "a blush wherewith a person is reddened after a satire or reproach of him; "*ferb*," a blotch [or ulcer?] which is put upon the face of a man after a satire or false judgment"; and *rinntaid*, "*nomen* for a man of satire, who wounds or cuts each face."[11] *Glas-gabail*, or facial satire, is one of the seven kinds of satire and is apparently the kind most frequently recited against women (cf. *Heptad* XXVI and accompanying commentary). *Heptad* XV mentions "the son of a rindile who yields not right nor justice to any person," and the glossator says, "i.e., the son of a man who engraves (scarifies) a person with his tongue, the satirist."[12] The *Brehon Laws*, the *Senchus Mor*, and other legal tracts yield many more references of the same character.[13] Thus, when a Celtic satirist uttered his three words of warning, he might just as well have said three times, "I shall without fail contrive to cause your certain death, either immediately or within the year, either by direct or by indirect means."

Cairbre mac Etaine, for instance, one of the most overbearing and dreaded of ancient Celtic satirists, deprived Bres mac Elathain, his host, of food, cattle, shelter, and possessions in a brief pronouncement of slightly more than a score of words, "and nought save decay was on Bres from that hour"; it was he also who drained opposing Fomorian warriors (famous wizards themselves) of their physical power to bear weapons and fight.[14] Scheming Nede of Connaught, well knowing the ancient Celtic law that no man with a blemish on his body could be king, cunningly usurped his uncle Caier's throne by blistering him with a *glám dichenn*: thre blisters arose overnight on his face, a red one named Stain, a green one called Blemish, and a white one called Defect. Caier then had to flee his country to escape public disgrace.[15] It is said that Laidchenn of the Scots so vigorously satirized and cursed the Leinstermen that no grass, no corn, no single leaf grew in Leinster for an entire year.[16] These examples could be multiplied many times with but slight variation in the essential pattern.

When we look closely at Nede's famous lines on Caier, however, we can find no evidence of any magical rite or ceremony having accompanied them. They appear to be only a vindictive personal imprecation against Caier's body, and their chief malefic character- istic seems to be simply the repetition of Caier's name:[17]

> Evil, death, short life to Caier!
> Let spears of battle wound him, Caier!
> Caier . . . ! Caier . . . ! Caier under earth,
> Under ramparts, under stones be Caier![18]

But Caier received the usual physical punishment in the form of three multicolored blemishes and finally died of shame after a year of exile and hiding; and so Nede's lines must belong to the group of magical incantations.

It seems very likely that when the magical rites fell away from the words and when the satirists abandoned their pierced round curs- ing-stones, their sharp white thorns, and their black north winds blowing through hawthorn bushes on high hilltops, there still remained in the folk-mind the fear that for long ages had associated itself with the satirists' movements and their articles of ritual. Possibly the satirist came to know that he need no longer depend on these external trap- pings to inspire fear of himself and his words, and that the folk-fear had finally become focused and concentrated, either consciously or subconsciously, on the words themselves.[19]

Even taking into account the frequently reiterated warning that Irish verse suffers peculiar losses from translation, we cannot now dis- cover in the surviving remnants of this early satiric verse any intrinsic destructive quality in the words themselves. We must conclude that their power over the organic body rests, not in the actual words, but in the carefully induced fears of the folk-mind. The *Brehon Laws* and minor legal tracts clearly show that the folk attached a dread signifi- cance to words, any words apparently, in a recognizable order, repeated a specific number of times; to special words; to the chiming repetition of a victim's name (or his nickname, if that precious piece of informa- tion could be obtained) ; and to the recurrence of verbal echoes and interlocking rhymes (some rhymes were so deadly as to have been absolutely forbidden by law).

R. A. S. Macalister, professor of Celtic archaeology at University College, Dublin, noted ancient Irish story references to persons dropping dead or dying quickly from shame, grief, or the breaking of a taboo:

> What does all this mean? Such things do not happen, as a rule. The emotions of shame and grief are very real, and in excess, may possibly have grave psychological consequences; but they are rarely lethal.
>
> It seems to me that we must here see evidence of the existence of the remarkable phenomenon known as *thanatomania*, well known to medical and other observers among the aboriginal peoples of Australia or of New Zealand. A man suddenly becomes conscious that he has broken a tabu. For such a one no consolation has any effect; and he has committed an unpardonable sin; his life is forfeit; and, just as certainly as the morrow's sunrise, that man will die—sometimes in strong convulsions.[20]

The hitherto inexplicable deaths resulting so suddenly from the recitation of an apparently harmless quatrain may also have been instances of *thanatomania*; in fact, there seems, so far, no other explanation for it. It is possible that the satirists, like the Indian fakirs, were able to induce in their victims a sort of hypnotic state, a suggestion borne out to some degree by the medical facts that cutaneous sensibility increases markedly when a subject is in that state, and that blisters, wounds and eschars like those of burns, red swellings, and itching inflammations may then be induced simply by verbal suggestion.

The apparently non-magical verses are occasionally on precisely the same subjects beloved by the Latin satirists of the Augustan and Silver Ages, i.e., inhospitality, niggardly portions of food, failure to pay just debts, gluttony, selfishness, ineptitudes of one kind and another, official favoritism, etc. Usually the earlier lines threaten the victim with some physical punishment. Sometimes, however, they seem to be only jeering lampoons, as, for instance, these lines satirizing Crundmail's niggardliness:

> I should not wonder
> if Crundmail's tumble-down house
> used salt for butter,
> their skins are as shrivelled
> as the bark of a dried-up tree.[21]

English soldiers coming into Ireland, particularly the County Meath, during the reigns of Henry VIII and Elizabeth, could still find in abundance both magical and non-magical satiric verses which preserved the old incantational characteristics. At the time of the English Renaissance, Irish satire of all kinds seems inclined to list at incredible length the specific diseases and misfortunes which the satirist means to call down on his victim. Incantational satire has never disappeared in Ireland,[22] not to this day; and he who would distinguish incantational from non-incantational satire is likely to find himself baffled time and again.

This stanza, for instance, from "The Satire of Domhnall na Tuile" of Egan O'Rahilly (d. *ca.* 1570), is not far removed from the most ancient magical cursing, although it is not far removed, either, in method, intent, or time from the English formal satire of the 1590's:

> In revenge for his reproaching a poet descended
> Of the true blood of bright Core of fair Munster,
> I shall file down his entrails, his complexion, his cheek,
> And his heart for the idiotic morose boor.[23]

The following lines (which may well have come out of the curses in *Timon of Athens* or *Troilus and Cressida*) are part of an imprecation which Blind Raftery once directed at a certain offending Shaun a Burca and are quoted here because their concentration on diseases and physical disintegration is typical of a vast block of Irish satire of all periods:

> The feet may you lose from the knees down,
> The sight of the eyes and the movement of the hands,
> The leprosy of Job, may it come down upon you,
> Farcy, erysipelas, and king's evil in the neck.
>
> A shaking argue, hiccough, and gravel on you,
> May that come quick, and the disease of death,
> May your hair fall off from your sullen forehead,
> And may there be no ear on you, but only the place of them.
>
> Disgust and hardship, lameness and corruption on you,
> Running and rout and hatred for you amongst your kin,
> Whitlow under the nails, and disease of the eyes upon you
> And neither marrow nor sap may there be in your bones.[24]

There can be small doubt, even after a necessarily brief survey of this sort, that although Celtic satire may resist definition and classification, its primary intention is relatively clear—to harm, mutilate, or destroy the human body.

II

When we come to deal directly with the omnipresent medical metaphor in English satire of the sixteenth and early seventeenth centuries, we realize that what was apparently real bodily mutilation and destruction in ancient times is here diminished and metamorphosed into harmless but highly significant figures of speech. The satirist, it must be remembered, always makes analogy one of his chief tools in hand; he has with varying degrees of emphasis equated the physical and the moral in all languages at all times; and he always shrewdly utilizes to the full whatever popular lore, prejudice, or concept lies ready to his pen. There were various good reasons why medical imagery[25] should have been in the foreground in Renaissance satire, reasons quite aside from the theory here tentatively suggested that literary satire normally inherits the physical metaphor from its primitive forbears, or to put it another way, that certain initial functional elements of primitive satire normally survive in popular metaphor.

Every one of the Renaissance years was a plague year for England; for the Black Death, fiercest of all scourges, was never really absent, though it might rage more violently in certain years. These were the years, too, when fighting in Ireland, France, and the Low Countries was almost continuous, and when soldiers returning from the wars could almost always be found on England's highways or in the ale-houses, exhibiting to the curious many a gangrenous wound or sore festering from arquebus shot.

Diseases by the score flourished, virtually unchecked. The formal verse satires, epigrams, "comical satyres," and satiric comedies all paint dark pictures of the prevalence of venereal diseases ("the Neapolitan bone-ache," "Scottish fleas," "Galliae Morbus," "Spanish Pip," or "English poxe"). Leprosy in its various stages was still not uncommon; neither was diphtheria, anthrax, the "sweating-sickness," nor "dancing-mania," while typhoid fever, cholera, tuberculosis, puerperal fever, and ergotism ("St. Anthony's fire," "holy fire," or "hell's fire") reached the proportions of pestilences.

For almost all ailments of the flesh, the barber-surgeons, apothe-
caries, vagrant practitioners, and charlatans, as well as the long-robed
doctors of the time, had two sovereign remedies, letting blood or
"lanching," and purging by tartar emetics and sharp cathartics (both
vegetable and mineral). Poisons and their antidotes, nostrums, aphro-
disiacs, soporifics, and medicaments of every kind, from powdered
mummy and unicorn's horn to hollywood and sassafras, were part of
the bourgeois lore of the time.

A knowledge of anatomy began to be developed in the sixteenth
century despite sharp ecclesiastical opposition. The English barber-
surgeon had heretofore studied his "wound-man," a chart showing
where body-wounds might ordinarily be expected in warfare. Any
ailment within the body could be located and operated on only by
guesswork since religion had long been hostile to dissection of the dead.
Despite the so-called Galenic tradition and ecclesiastical opposition,
however, the study of anatomy made very considerable progress in
these years. With the great *Fabrica* (1543) of Andreas Vesalius and
the *Surgery* (1564) of Ambroise Paré, some part of the way to scientific
dissection and anatomical studies was at last opened. Even so, "body-
snatching" and "graveyard-robbing" had to be undertaken with extreme caution by even the greatest of medical men; and it was long
before a fascinated public imagination could see anything more in
anatomizing than the devil's amusement so luridly pictured in countless "medical" pamphlets.

In such an age of constant plagues and wars, when medicine was
still so largely a matter of knowledge and fact, it is to be expected that
literature of every type should reflect Man's concern for his physical
body. And so it does—sermon, sonnet, tragedy, comedy, epigram and
satire.[26]

In the case of satire, however, all critical definitions of the genre
and all critical and exegetical statements concerning its functions,
methods, and essential nature are couched almost exclusively in terms
of the medical concept, a phenomenon which occurs in the case of no
other literary genre.[27] It is the province of this paper to examine that
concept only as it is used to define, describe, and interpret the genre.

These medical metaphors, however, are not all of a kind. Sometimes they seemingly look backward to the ancient idea of the magical
curse as a lethal instrument and of satire as but a means for a man to
achieve personal revenge; more often they represent the more cultured

and sophisticated notion of satire as a sanative agent, a means of curing a man of his moral ills[28] and of providing a normal outlet for the satirist's own irritation at certain social conditions. It is possible, then, in studying Renaissance theoretical statements (from prefaces, title-pages, epigrams, and mottoes, but chiefly from the satires themselves) to observe in closest juxtaposition both the primitive and the cultural aspects of satire, sometimes even within the same verse, paragraph, quatrain, or couplet.

The old magical tradition that satire could actually kill a man outright crops up here and there in English satire far into the eighteenth century. In this connection the vague and hazy legends of Archilochus and Hipponax were always mentioned, as was the Welsh bard, Dafydd ap Gwilyn, living at about Chaucer's time, who was reputed to have killed a literary antagonist by the force of his verse. But if actual stories were few, there was no lack of metaphor reflecting the idea, any more than there seems to have been a lack of tales to the effect that fiercely venomous satire could so shame and trouble a man as to induce chagrin and morbidity leading finally to his suicide.[29]

The Renaissance Englishman had only to look to Scotland on the north of him and to Ireland on the westward to learn at first hand the ferocity of Celtic satire. The virulence and force of the Scottish flytings and pasquils and the incantatory powers of the Highland Madge Wildfires (at some distance the Scotch counterparts of the Irish female satirists) were proverbial with him,[30] as was the dangerous quality of Irish magical verse. Soldiers, officers, civil officials, and Lords-Lieutenant of Ireland had gone over from England steadily both before and during Elizabeth's reign; and not a few of them had learned to their sorrow to be wary of a rhymer.

The Irish themselves have it that a certain English Lord-Lieutenant of Ireland was rhymed to death by Irish bards:

> John Stanley, Deputy of the King of England, arrived in Ireland, a man who gave neither mercy nor protection to clergy, laity, or men of science, but subjected as many of them as he came upon to cold, hardship, famine ... The O'Higgins, with Niall, then satirized John Stanley, who lived after this satire but five weeks, for he died from the virulence of their lampoons.[31]

The English, however, evened the rhyming score when Lord Mountjoy and Sir George Carew employed a renegade Irish satirist,

Angus O'Daly, the Red Bard, or Angus of the Satires, to travel up
and down the four provinces of the island, satirizing the ancient Irish
families and clans (chiefly on the grounds of poverty and inhospitality), a single rann or quatrain to each. The English knew full well
that an Irishman feared nothing in this world so much as a satire
made on his house and that Angus would not be harmed since the
person of the bard was sacred. A maddened servant in Tipperary,
however, forgot himself and stabbed the Red Bard in the throat.[32]

Most of the Renaissance references to Irish magical verse had to
do with rat-rhyming because most of the English soldiery had been
quartered in the County Meath, the "Pale," where Irish rat-rhyming
is said to have originated with the bard, Seanchan Torpeist. Like
Spenser, many a soldier and official must have returned home full of
tale and story from the boggy Emerald Isle. Such references always
note that the Irish can rhyme a man to death as easily as they can
rhyme a rat. Philip Sidney had spoken of it in *An Apologie for Poetrie*
(*ca.* 1581, published 1595):

> I will not wish unto you the Asses eares of *Midas*, nor to bee
> driven by a Poets verses (as Bubonax was) to hang himselfe, nor
> to be rimed to death, as is sayd to be doone in Ireland.[33]

At the funeral of Henry V, the Duke of Exeter ponders on destructive
verses in this wise (*I Henry VI*, I, i, 25–27):

> Or shall we think the subtile-witted French
> Conjurers and sorcerers, that, afraid of him,
> By magic verses have contriv'd his end?[34]

and the *Rhymes against Martin Marre-Prelate* mentions, as a final
threat, the fatal effects of Irish rhyming:

> And this I warn thee, Martin Monckies-face,
>   Take heed of me; my rime doth charm thee bad.
> I am a rimer of the Irish race,
>   And have alreadie rimde thee staring mad.
> But if thou cease not thy bald jests to spread,
> I'le never leave till I have rimde thee dead.[35]

Rosalind, Shylock, and Hamlet all mention rat-rhyming,[36] as
does Reginald Scot in *The Discouerie of Witchcrafte* (1584):

The Irishmen affirm that not only their children but their cattel
are, as they call it, eye-bitten when they fall suddenly sic, &
tearm one sort of their witches eye-biters, only in that respect:
yea, and they will not stick to affirm that they can rime either
man or beast to death.[37]

Ben Jonson in the lines, "To the Reader," appended to *Poetaster*
(1601), connects Archilochean iambics and Irish rat-charming, apparently with the thought that they are very similar indeed:

> ... I could doe worse,
> Arm'd with Archilochus' fury, write Iambicks,
> Should make the desperate lashers hang themselves,
> Rime 'hem to death, as they doe Irish rats
> In drumming tunes;

and Ben's short-lived, variously gifted "son," Thomas Randolph, makes
a similar threat in *The Jealous Lovers* (1632), V, ii:

> ... my poets
> Shall with a satire, steep'd in gall and vinegar
> Rithme 'em to death, as they do rats in Ireland.

Not even the many Renaissance allusions to rat-rhyming, however, offer so much clear evidence of the original destructive intent
of satiric verse in its magical stages as do our English words and
phrases descriptive of satire. If *Cormac's Glossary* proves useful in
illuminating certain phases of ancient satire, so does the modern English vocabulary prove useful in its way. Almost all of our words descriptive of satire preserve the primitive notion of destroying or harming
the human body. Satiric words can be:

blasting	stinging	blemishing	virulent
blighting	bewildering	nettling	bitter
withering	killing	freezing	sharp
excoriating	wounding	biting	deadly
searing	blistering	annihilating	vitriolic
scorching	stabbing	shocking	noxious
scathing	galling	burning	corrosive
devastating	irritating	venomous	malignant
cutting	smarting	barbed	chilling
shrivelling	crushing	caustic	poisonous

With them a satirist can:

brand	back-bite	castigate
stigmatize	flail	brow-beat
"roast"	tongue-lash	cut to the quick
bait	"knock"	stain
bare his fangs	twit	whip

And the victim may:

blench	tremble	droop	chafe
quail	chill	freeze	waste (away)
wince	shiver	languish	
cringe	shudder	pine	
blush	shrink	dwindle	
bridle	wilt	suffer	
quake	burn	recoil	

This is a relatively brief list. In most cases the etymologies of the words lead even more directly back to the original function of incantational satire than do their present surface meanings.

Direct Renaissance references to satire's ancient killing power and even metaphors based on it,[38] however, are relatively few when compared with the countless number of medical figures stressing satire's reaction on the human body for sanative purposes. Sometimes the curative or sanative purpose is implied so casually that one doubts if it is there at all and if the Renaissance satirist is not, after all, in wishful metaphor reverting to the ancient principle of drawing blood for the sake of personal revenge. When attacked, the Latin satirists had always argued their sanative purpose, their solemn intent to accomplish social reforms, as one means of personal defense; but they had employed medical metaphor in that connection with relative infrequency. Horace had praised Lucilius for "rubbing the city down with much salt" (I, x, 3–4) and for "peeling the skins off hypocrites" (II, i, 64); and Persius had followed his lead by similarly commending Lucilius for having flayed the city (I, 114–18); but there is in Horace, Persius, and Juvenal no such wide-spread and persistent use of the metaphor as in English Renaissance satire.

In 1509 Alexander Barclay, freely translating and augmenting James Locher's Latin preface to Brant's *Das Narrenschiff*, spoke in ancient Stoic manner of vices as illnesses and avowed his translator's purpose "to clense the vanyte and madnes of folysshe people of whom over great nombre in the Royalme of Englande." Another churchman, the zealously puritanical Thomas Drant, Archdeacon of Lewes (d. 1578?), first to translate or rather to mutilate hideously the entire group of Horatian satires, incorporated the medical notion into his title, *A MEDICINABLE/ Morall, that is, the two Bookes of Horace Satyres, En-/glyshed accordyng to the/ prescription of saint Hierome/* ... (London, 1566), and also into his title-page motto, "*Antidoti salutaris amaror.*"[39] Hereafter, as satire becomes a rising and increasingly popular genre, it is constantly referred to as a cleansing, bitter medicament.

The satirist's most common metaphorical pose was that of the barber-surgeon. Vice and Folly are referred to as some sort of malignant swelling or pustule. It is interesting to note that whereas the magician-satirist had actually sought to raise sting-blisters and facial blemishes, the Renaissance satirist, under culture influences, seeks metaphorically to cure them. Later, when the theory of satire becomes practically regarbed in the vocabulary of rationalism, the physical blemish becomes the ruling passion or satiric flaw in a man's character. In the sixteenth and early seventeenth centuries, however, satirists were still metaphorically applying "wholesome remedy" to "ugly, foul disease," a remedy first cleansing, that is, stinging, cutting, or burning, and then healing. Vice is often a "canck'red" sore, tetter, ulcer, ringworm, cancer, leprosy,[40] scrofula, or a headed pustule with a heavy core. For example, Feliche says in Marston's *Antonio and Mellida, Part One* (1602), III:

> O, if that candle-light were made a Poet,
> He would prove a rare firking Satyrist,
> And draw the core forth of impostum'd sin.

Whatever the disease, the idea of noxious infection and contagion had to be there, the uglier the better.[41] The satirist's ink was always the metaphorical remedy: it was corrosive copperas, black aconite (drawn from Cerberus' jaws), verjuice (a sour, tart acid from crabapples or other green fruits), gall, vinegar, wormwood and sulphur,[42] salt (cf. "Attic salt"), *aqua fortis* (nitric acid), the deadly spew of the cuttlefish, or perhaps speckled viper's venom. Such ink was to irritate vicious sores, cause them to fester, and finally to heal them of infection. In each case, the ink bit like acid, eating "farther than the marrrow." In the eighteenth century such figures were to be very largely supplanted

by rationalistic terminology: the satirist's weapon or scalpel was Ridicule; the ailment to be pointed out by Ridicule was the ruling passion;
and the curatives were Reason and Judgment; but in the Renaissance
Marston, Hall, Jonson, and their fellows were still speaking chiefly in
terms of the body, not the mind.

The figure of the satirist-physician applying his acid to skin diseases is so common as to appear by the score. Burbidge [*sic*] says in the
"Induction" to Marston's *The Malcontent* (1604) that ". . . such
vices as stand not accountable to law should be cured as men heal
tetters, by casting ink upon them"; and that curious amalgam of ancient concept and classical theory, the melancholy Jacques, declares
that he would "most invectively" pierce through "the body of the
country, city, court."[43] Medical figure, in fact, pervades his theorizing:

> Give me leave
> To speak my mind, and I will through and through
> Cleanse the foul body of th'infected world,
> If they will patiently receive my medicine.[44]

So speak all the various types of satirically minded malcontents, quasi-
malcontents, professional railers, and their kind. Here, Duke Senior
replies in like figure that in reality Jacques is more concerned with a
personal catharsis:

> For thou thyself hast been a libertine,
> As sensual as the brutish sting itself;
> And all th'embossed scores and headed evils
> That thou with license of free boot hast caught,
> Wouldst thou disgorge into the general world.[45]

The satirist's pen is often a searing, cauterizing scalpel which
probes deep and cuts away dead or gangrenous flesh, leaving a clean
wound to heal. Cloven like a satyr's hoof, it oftentimes spouts or drips
oil and fire from its nibs on the evil place and scalds and blisters but
at the same time cauterizes.[46] Sometimes the satirist dips his hot pen
in aconite or the blood of Lycambes and brands his victim's forehead
with ineradicable, everlasting marks of shame, so that, as Jonson says
in his "Dedication" to *Volpone* (1607), ". . . not Cinnamus the barber,
with his art, shall be able to take out the brands; but they shall live,
and be read, till the wretches die." "R. C." in "Epigrammisatiron,"
prefacing *The Times' Whistle* (1614-16), exhibits the conventional
boldness when he commands, "Let ulcer'd limbes and gowtie humours

quake,/Whilst with my pen I doe incision make,"[47] and Cynthia herself orders outright amputation as punishment of the gulls in *Cynthia's Revels* (1601), V, v, "Th'incurable cut off, the rest reforme."

A particularly popular figure, further stressing the pain inflicted on the supposedly acquiescent victim, was that of the satirist's whipping or scourging away infected flesh with a steel flail, a mastix, or the knotted rope or leather thongs of a cat-o'-nine-tails. For fully half a century the idea of a satirist's "untrussing" an offender, stripping him naked, and inflicting deep stripes, cuts, and gashes on his sides was a popular one, as testify numbers of titles, e.g., *The Children of the Chapel Stript and Whipt* (1569); Marston's *The Scourge of Villainy* (1598); "W. J.'s" *The Whipping of the Satyre* (1601); Nicholas Breton's *No Whippinge, nor trippinge: but a kinde friendly Snippinge* (1601); Dekker's *Satiromastix* (1601); and *The Scourge of Folly* (1610) by John Davies of Hereford. Davies' work contained, opposite the title-page, "a neat cut representing Wit scourging Folly, who is mounted upon the back of Time with the hoofs of a Satyr, whose scythe and hour-glass lie on the ground; with a label from the mouth of Wit, 'Nay vp with him if he were my brother.' "[48]

Young bishop-to-be Joseph Hall concocted a similarly fashionable title in 1598 for his collection of satires, *Virgidemiarum*, "a bundle of rods," and sternly exhorted his readers to hold out their "guilty" and their "galléd hides." But it is Marston, rather than any other satirist, who seizes on and fully exploits the fashionable satiric figures of the day. Scourges and rods and lashings are liberally scattered through his lines as are such set formulae as this:

> I am too mild. Reach me my scourge again:
> . . . .
> I strip you nak'd, and whip you with my rhymes,
> Causing your shame to live to after-times.[49]

Lampatho in *What You Will* (III, ii) might easily be describing a Renaissance Jack Ketch instead of a satirist:

> Let me unbrace my breasts, strip up my sleeves,
> Stand like an executioner to vice,
> To strike his head off with the keener edge
> Of my sharp spirit.
> . . . .

Now is my fury mounted. Fix your eyes;
Intend your senses; bend your list'ning up:
For I'll make greatness quake; I'll taw the hide
Of thick-skinn'd Hugeness.

Certain of the methods of medieval torture still in use provided
the satirist with figures useful in giving the illusion of extreme physical
pain inflicted on the victim. Such figures implied no sanative action;
only physical punishment was suggested. Racks are frequently mentioned, as are strappadoes, e.g., Richard Brathwaite's *A Strappado for
the Diuell* (1615).[50]

Anatomical dissection, it has been noted, was an extremely
popular topic; and the general interest in it is reflected in many titles
of collections of satires and epigrams purporting to bring their victims
"to the most perfect light" and "lay them open," e.g., Stubbs' *Anatomie of Abuses* (1583); Henry Hutton's *Follie's Anatomie* (1619);
*Times Curtaine drawne or the Anatomie of Vanitie with other choice
Poems entituled Health from Helicon; by Richard Brathwayte
Oxonian* (1621); *A Brief Anatomie of Women* (1653); and Richard
Head's(?) *The Catterpillars of the State Anatomized* (1659). Single
lines by the hundreds use the anatomizing figure, which is particularly
useful to satire in that it purports to bring out in the open those vices
which ordinarily lurk in shadows and dark corners, unperceived and
unapprehended by the law.

Most significant of all the medical figures, however, is that of
satire's operating as a purge, by way of either phlebotomy, laxative,
or emetic. The satirist's pen pricks his victim's vein and draws off
blood "both corrupt and cleare," e.g., *The Letting of Humours Blood
in the Head-Vaine. With a new Morissco, daunced by seaven Satyres,
upon the bottome of Diogines Tubbe* (1600), by Samuel Rowlands.
The satirist's pills, purges, and laxatives are of various kinds, since
vices and follies are variously represented as a surfeit of food, an excess
of some humour, or even as downright poison demanding instant antidote. Black and white hellebore are often mentioned, rhubarb less frequently. The "Rhamnusian whip," which editors and students have
carelessly supposed to be some sort of actual whip, was in reality a
violent cathartic, sap-green, yielded by the berries of the buckthorn,
Rhamnus catharticus. "R. C." says in the brief poem, "In adulantes
Aulicos," appended to *The Times' Whistle,*

> O how my Muse, armde with Rhamnusiaes whip,
> Desires to scourge your hell-bred villanie.[51]

Asper is quite ready to administer cathartics to the gulls in the "Induction" to *Every Man out of his Humour* (1599):

> They are more infectious than the pestilence:
> And therefore I would give them pills to purge,
> And make them fit for fair societies;

and Edward Guilpin in the "Praeludium" to *Skialethia* (1598) defines satire almost wholly in terms of physical catharsis:

> The Satyre onely and Epigramatist,
> (Concisde Epigrame, and sharpe Satyrist)
> Keepe diet from this surfet of excesse,
> Tempring themselves with such licenciousnes,
> The bitter censures of their Critticke spleenes,
> Are Antidotes to pestilentiall sinnes
> They heale with lashing, seare luxuriousness,
> They are Philosophicke true *Cantharides*[52]
> To vanities dead flesh. An Epigrame
> Is popish displing, rebell flesh to tame:
> . . . . . . sharpe sauce it is,
> To lickerous vanitie, youths sweet amisse.
> But oh the Satyre hath a nobler vaine,
> He's the Strappado, rack, and some such paine
> To base lewd vice; the Epigram's Bridewell,
> Some whipping cheere: but this is follies hell.
> The Epigram's like dwarfe Kings scurrill grace,
> A Satyres Chester to a painted face;
> It is the bone-ach unto lechery,
> To Acolastus it is beggery:
> It is the scourge, the Tamberlaine of vice,
> . . . .
> It is (oh scurvey) to a Lenten rime;
> . . . .
> It's like a Syring to a Hampshire Goose.[53]

The satirist's victim is always enjoined to submit patiently to all these violent flailings, bleedings, probings, brandings, and purgings; for, as he is constantly reminded, they are all for his own ultimate

good. Those who resist are, according to Asper in the "Induction" to
Every Man Out:

> None but a sort of fools, so sick in taste,
> That they contemn all physic of the mind,
> And, like galled camels, kick at every touch.

The details of the victim's physical reactions, that is, the outer
manifestations of an inner catharsis, are usually noted with some care,
however. He blushes, his ears glow, his eyes flash anger, he trembles,
becomes feverish, tears flow down his cheeks, he shakes with chills and
agues, or he simply breaks out in a cold sweat. The scene (I, iv) between Comedy, Tragedy, Mime, and Satire, in Thomas Randolph's
The Muses' Looking Glass (1638) brings together much of the physical
imagery connected with satire and stresses the victim's supposed reactions. Satire is described as one

> . . . whose whip of steel can with a lash
> Imprint the characters of sin so deep,
> Even in the brazen forehead of proud sin,
> That not eternity shall wear it out.
> When I but frown'd in my Lucilius' brow,
> Each conscious cheek grew red, and a cold trembling
> Freez'd the chill soul; while every guilty breast
> Stood fearful of dissection, as afraid
> To be anatomis'd by that skilful hand,
> And have each artery, nerve, and vein of sin,
> By it laid open to the public scorn.
> I have untruss'd the proudest: greatest tyrants
> Have quak'd below my powerful whip, half-dead
> With expectation of the smarting jerk,
> Whose wound no salve can cure. Each blow doth leave
> A lasting scar, that with a poison eats
> Into the marrow of their fames and lives;
> Th'eternal ulcer to their memories.[54]

The satirists themselves were usually referred to as Saturnian
men, i.e., under the astrological domination of "pale Saturnus, the
colde," of all planets the most malignant and most baleful with the
greatest power for evil and the spread of incurable diseases. In one of
the earliest English definitions of satire, Thomas Drant in 1566 had

made an erroneous etymological connection between "satyre" and "Saturn," and had stressed the saturnine character of the satirist:

> Satyre of writhled waspyshe Saturne may be namde
>   The Satyrist must be a wasper in moode,
> Testie and wrothe with vice and hers, to see both blamde
>   But courteous and frendly to the good.
>
> As Saturne cuttes of tymes with equal sythe:
> So this man cuttes downe synne, to coy and blythe.[55]

Besides endowing the satirist with a February face and gloomy disposition, Saturn figured further as the patron power of satirists because he had overwhelming destructive forces at his command. For an excellent summary of the baleful powers assigned to Saturn throughout the Middle Ages and the Renaissance, one may well turn back to Chaucer's *Knight's Tale* (ll.2454–69) wherein Saturn admirably surveys his own strengths:

> My cours, that hath so wyde for to turne,
> Hath more power than woot any man,
> Myn is the drenchyng in the see so wan;
> Myn is the prison in the derke cote;
> Myn is the stranglyng and hangyng by the throte,
> The murmur and the cherles rebellyng,
> The groyning, and the pryvee empoysonyng,
> I do vengeance and pleyn correccioun
> Whil I dwelle in the signe of the leoun.
> Myn is the ruyne of hye halles,
> The fallynge of the toures and of the walles
> Upon the mynour or the carpenter.
> I slow Sampsoun, shakynge the piler;
> And myne be the maladyes colde,
> The derke tresons, and the castes olde;
> My lookyng is the fader of pestilence.

It is when Saturn is in the fixed sign of Leo that he is particularly powerful with his "maladyes colde" and in his role as "fader of pestilence." Professor W. C. Curry quotes William Lilly (*Christian Astrology*, London, 1647) on Saturn's responsibility for

> all impediments of the right ear, teeth, all quartan agues proceeding of cold, dry, and melancholy distempers, leprosies,

rheums, consumptions, black jaundice, palsies, tremblings, vain
fears, fantasies, dropsie, the hand and foot-gout, apoplexies, dog-
hunger, too much flux of the hemeroids, and ruptures.[56]

Saturn's endowment of the satirist with the traditionally melancholy spirit is of particular interest here.[57] Satirists conventionally speak
of themselves as sour and grimly melancholy; and the Renaissance
reader quickly comes to consider in a broad category as Saturnian men
all murmuring malcontents, professional satirists, railers, and dis-
gruntled spectators of the current scene, just as the student of Celtic
quickly groups together druids, poets, satirists, lampooners, smiths, and
leeches. As the latter all have to do with sorcery and destructive magic,
so are the former all characterized by complaint and surly grumbling,
cursing, invective or satire. Many of these sons of Saturn, besides
having naturally saturnine dispositions, are further like the Celtic
satirists and smiths in having some bodily ailment or deformity contributing further to the development of the malcontent mood.[58]

Thersites, in the "comicall satyre," *Troilus and Cressida,* has
a twisted, hunch-backed body, like his Homeric prototype; and he
grumbles almost entirely in terms of boils, scabs, and bowels, lechery,
lice, and red murrains whenever he "opes his mastic jaws." His first
words in the play are:

> Agamemnon—how if he had biles—full, all over, generally? . . .
> And those biles did run—say so? Did not the general run then?
> Were not that a botchy core? . . . Then would come some matter
> from him. I see none now.[59]

More than any other malcontent, railer, or satirist of the time,
Thersites reverts to the primitive satiric principle, marring and harming the human body. Bricriu of the Poison Tongue might very well
have spoken these lines for him:

> If thou use to beat me, I will begin at thy heel and tell what
> thou are by inches, thou thing of no bowels, thou.[60]

Thersites' more formal curses, those having the dignity of an invocation and an "Amen," call down in primitive fashion the most repulsive of diseases while he threatens to "learn to conjure and raise devils"
unless he sees "some issue" of his "spiteful execrations."[61] He amuses
himself by angering Patroclus with an indirect curse:

Now the rotten diseases of the South, the guts-griping, ruptures, catarrhs, loads o' gravel i' the back, lethargies, cold palsies, raw eyes, dirt-rotten livers, whissing lungs, bladders full of imposthume, sciaticas, limekilns i' the palm, incureable boneache, and the rivelled fee simple of the tetter, take and take again such preposterous discoveries.[62]

Satirists deliberately go far out of their way to stress their native surliness, perhaps, one conjectures, to foster a fear and awe similar to that felt by the early Irish folk before their Dubthach Chafertongues and Aithirnes. Renaissance satirists frequently picture themselves as barking dogs, showing their fangs, snapping, and sinking their pointed teeth deep in some sinner's vitals. It will be remembered that Cynic (Greek, Κύων, Κυνός, dog) philosophy had been one important source of the subject-matter of early Roman satire. The Cynic moralists, more or less pessimistic, had tried to present the less academic side of their philosophy to the populace, while Stoicism was recognized as a somewhat more aristocratic mode of thought cultivated by the upper classes. The Renaissance satirist frequently speaks of his "Cynicke satyre." *Cainte* was one of the numerous early Irish terms for satirist listed in *Cormac's Glossary*: "i.e., *canis*, dog, for the satirist has a dog's head in barking and alike is the profession they follow."[63] Canine,[64] cynic, and *cainte* are thus significantly linked together.

The dog motif occurs frequently, both in titles and as extended metaphors in the text.[65] William Goddard's surreptitious piece was called, *A Mastif Whelp, with other ruff-Island-like Currs, fetcht from among the Antipides, which bite and barke at the fantastical humorists and abusers of the time* (n.d.). There were also "T. M.'s" *Microcynicon, Sixe Snarling Satyres* (1599) and Henry Parrot's (?) *The Mastive, or Young Whelp of the Olde Dogge* (1615) with the picture of a mastiff on its title-page.

One of the most common figures concerns the teeth of the satire and its biting quality. Such figures are usually incomplete, and it is difficult to tell just whether satirists conceived of the mythological satyr as having teeth or not. The satyr's cloven hoof, his shaggy sides, and even his howling at sin are mentioned; but the hungry fangs, twitching chaps, and gnashing teeth may belong to some vague satiric Cerberus.[66] Whatever the complete figure intended, the Renaissance satirist had to give metaphorical teeth to his satires. When Joseph Hall divided his *Virgidemiarum* into three books of "tooth-lesse satyres"

and three of "byting satyres," he left open the way for John Milton's
sharp contention nearly fifty years later in the *Apology against
Smectymnuus* (1642) that there could be no such thing as a "toothless" satire:

> ... sure he loved toothless satires, which I took were as improper
> as a toothed sleekstone. ... I will not conceal ye what I thought,
> readers, that sure this must be some sucking satyr, who might
> have done better to have used his coral, and made an end of
> teething, ere he took upon him to wield a satire's whip. ... For
> a satire as it was born out of tragedy, so ought to resemble his
> parentage, to strike high, and adventure dangerously at the most
> eminent vices among the greatest persons, and not to creep unto
> every blind tap-house, that fears a constable more than a satire.
> But that such a poem should be toothless, I still affirm it to be
> a bull, taking away the essence of that which it calls itself. For
> if it bite either, how is it toothless? So that toothless satires are
> as much as if he had said toothless teeth.

Most of the critic-satirists, however, in full accord with Renaissance fashion declared themselves to be "all dog and scorpion," at the
same time insisting, after the classical *lex operis*, that satire is a personally necessary and socially profitable vent for "modest anger" or
"melancholick humour."[67] Puttenham (?) wrote in 1589 that epigrams
(most of which were either extremely satiric or were actually short
satires) were devised because "men would and must needs utter their
splenes in all ordinarie matters also or else it seemed their bowels
would burst."[68] It was "Mother Hubberd's heat of choller" that caused
the excessive severity of the *Tale*, according to Gabriel Harvey,[69] and
"sweet, satyric" Thomas Nashe wrote in *Strange News, or Foure
Letters Confuted* (1592):

> *The tickling and stirring invective vaine, the puffing and swelling
> Satiricall spirit* came upon him. ... Needes hee must cast up
> certayne crude humours of English Hexameter Verses that lay
> uppon his stomache; a Nobleman stoode in his way as he was
> vomiting, and from top to toe he all to berayed him with
> *Tuscanisme.*[70]

Ben Jonson's "gentle Horace," of course, is the Aesculapius to the bad
satirist, Crispinus (Marston), in the famous vomiting scene (V, i) in

Poetaster, and offers him bitter, wholesome pills "mixt with the whitest kind of hellebore," to

> give him a light vomit that should purge
> His brain and stomach of those tumultuous heats.

Marlowe in the First Sestiad (ll.126–7) of *Hero and Leander* (1598) had declared that the suitors, ". . . their violent passions to assuage/ Compile sharp satires";[71] and the gentleman-satirist Quadratus exclaims in *What You Will* (II, i), "My spleen's afire in the heat of hate." It is Jonson's Asper (for in Jonson and Shakespeare native and classical theory stand side by side) who, in the "Induction" to *Every Man Out*, speaks the old classical argument, *"Difficile est saturam non scribere"*:

> Who is so patient of this impious world,
> That he can check his spirit, or rein his tongue?
> Or who hath such a dead unfeeling sense,
> That heaven's horrid thunders cannot wake?
> . . . .
> Who can behold such prodigies as these,
> And have his lips sealed up? Not I: my soul
> Was never ground into such oily colours,
> To flatter vice and daub iniquity:
> But with an armed and resolved hand,
> I'll strip the ragged follies of the time
> Naked as at their birth.

The satirist's justification of his genre as a virtuous and admirable means to a catharsis of his own feelings was thus an integral part of the defense of his work which every satirist, alert to his own interests, was bound to make sooner or later.[72]

III

This paper has sought to direct critical attention to the ubiquitous and varied medical metaphor in English Renaissance satiric theory, its possible relationships and its implications.

First, it has suggested that those metaphors, relatively few in number, which represent satire as having either an actual lethal power or which represent the satirists as taking a sadistic or vengeful pleasure in using satire to harm the human body seem to point backward to similar characteristics of primitive incantational and magical verse, in this instance, that of the Celts. Such metaphors, I have noted, may possibly be the survival of certain initial functional elements of early satiric verse.

Corollary to this suggestion, the paper argues also for the belated recognition of traces of a Celtic strain in English satire (a strain which may logically and suitably be designated a part of our native tradition), as well as for a careful reconsideration of Professor Robinson's statement of nearly thirty years' standing that "a still more intimate and essential relation seems to exist between satire and the kind of verse [early Irish magico-satiric verse] that has been described in this paper."[73] No attempt has been made here to prove that there exists any positive generic affiliations between English and Celtic satire; but the two have been placed in juxtaposition and certain specific similarities have been noted.

Second, it has been suggested that the larger number of medical metaphors representing satire as having a cathartic, that is, a sanative and finally a healing or curative effect on the person satirized, as well as on the satirist himself, seems to point forward to the eighteenth-century development of satire as a philosophical art-form, dealing with the moral bases of human behavior. Corollary implications here are (a) that ample occasion exists for an investigation into the multiple aspects of a theory of satiric catharsis, analogous in some respects to the Aristotelian theory of tragic catharsis;[74] (b) that the whole subject of the various medical aspects of satire is a large and relatively untouched field, competent exploration of which would be a distinct aid to the study of satiric theory; and (c) that, contrary to supposition, satiric imagery in the Renaissance is neither scant nor insignificant.

It should be noted finally that the medical metaphor in English Renaissance satiric theory is only a metaphor serving to cloak philosophical abstractions, which, in the eighteenth century, rely for the most part on their own intellectual terminology without benefit of the interposed medical figures.

NOTES

[1] Medical imagery, or at least imagery relating to the human body, has apparently never been wholly absent from satire at

any period in any literature. It was present in Latin verse satire, and it continues to be present in eighteenth-century English verse satire; but at no time in English satire has it been so omnipresent a fashion as in the verse satire, both dramatic and non-dramatic, of the Renaissance.

2 It is not suggested that these rationalistic terms and concepts were at all new to verse satire, but that their marked and extensive use constituted a prevalent fashion in English verse satire between approximately 1670 and 1750. Various students in the eighteenth century, Ricardo Quintana, for instance, in *The Mind and Art of Jonathan Swift* (Oxford, 1936), use the term neostoicism in this connection because it suggests the antiquity and continuity of the basic concepts of the rationalistic philosophies. As has been pointed out many times, satire in any given period always tends, chameleon-like, to take on the coloring of the dominant rationalistic philosophy of that period.

3 Scattered, informal critical and quasi-critical statements concerning English Renaissance satire, not the satires themselves primarily, comprise the material for consideration here. Satire (or "satyre," as the spelling continued well into the eighteenth century) is in the Renaissance a sprawling inconclusive term, reaching out to include libel, invective, and epigram on the one hand, and Jonsonian comedy on the other. Renaissance and early seventeenth-century critical and lexicographical usages show satiric terminology to have been in a state of confusion. In the main, the Renaissance word "satyre" seems to have meant (1) a poem (2) approaching and practically synonymous with invective, (3) whose mission is didactic—the reprehension of vice and folly.

4 "Satirists and Enchanters in Early Irish Literature," *Studies in the History of Religions* (New York, 1912), pp. 95–130. "Enchant" and "incant" are the same word, of course.

5 See examples noted by W. Sherwood Fox, "Cursing as a Fine Art," *Sewanee Review*, XXVII (1919), 460–77. God's curse for disobedience (*Deuteronomy* 28: 21–29) is a majestic, all-inclusive effort at physical annihilation; but there, of course, divine power replaces the magical power ordinarily invoked by mortal men. Three unidentified Christian psalms are said to be lethal, as is Rune No. 11 of the Finnish *Kalevala*.

6 Many classical scholars have carefully pointed out that intricately heterogeneous, almost lapidarian popular backgrounds of Latin satire, e.g., Fescennine verses, plebeian proverbs, jocular folk slang, Oriental beast fables, satyr-dramas, ancient mnemonic

devices, illustrative *chriea*-like anecdotes, Atellan farces, homilies, rationalized myths, Bionean diatribes, and so on. There is nothing, however, that seems to correspond to the Celtic satiric quatrains.

7 See Felix Grendon, "Anglo-Saxon Charms," *Journal of American Folklore*, XXII (1909), 105–237; Francis P. Magoun, Jr., "Zu den altenglischen Zaubersprüchen," *Archiv. f. d. Studium der neueren Sprachen*, CLXXII (1937), 18, n. 2; and "Strophische Überreste in den altenglischen Zaubersprüchen," *Englische Studien*, LXXII (1937), 1–6.

8 The inclusive term Celtic is used here to indicate that the satiric forms and methods noted in early Irish literature by Professor Robinson seem common to all Goidelic and to most Brythonic branches of the Celts. Scotland, the Hebridean archipelago, Wales, and the Isle of Man have all preserved similar magico-satirical forms.

9 The Celts used the word *aer* indiscriminately to indicate a wide variety of magical spells as well as verse with which no magic seems to have been connected. The line of demarcation is thus very dim and the student must move with caution. Robinson notes (*op. cit.*, pp. 98–101) that Germanic *Zauberlied* or *Spottlied*, Arabic *Hijâ'*, and Finnish *runo* may very possibly be equated with early Irish *aer*.

10 Like witches' potions, satirists' words were frequently devised to blast fertility. Famines were frequent in this land of rocks and bogholes, as testify references to corn with but one grain to the ear; storms and bad weather often destroyed the beechmast and the nuts and washed fish and their spawn from the creek-mouths, but these natural phenomena were probably attributed to satirists' powers.

11 Robinson, *op. cit.*, pp. 103–4; 106; 109.

12 *The Ancient Laws of Ireland*, ed. Eugene O'Curry (Dublin, 1865–1901, 5 vols.), V, 215; 217; 177; 203; 205.

13 *Ibid.*, I, 59; III, 140n.; 352n.; IV, 345; 347; 349; V, 229; 231; 233; 389.

14 "The Second Battle of Moytura," ed. and trans. Whitley Stokes, *Revue Celtique*, XII (1891), 71.

15 *Three Irish Glossaries: Cormac's Glossary, Codex A, O'Davoren's Glossary and A Glossary to the Calendar of Oingus the Culdee*, ed. Whitley Stokes (London, 1862), p. 24. Robinson suggests (*op. cit.*, p. 114) that these allegorical interpretations may have been added later. It is extremely difficult to separate

the chaff from the grain in these ancient dreamland tales; but, regardless of possible manipulation of detail, the general character of the satirist and his satire are outlined with sufficient clarity in a sufficient number of instances to be of the greatest significance and value.

[16] Cf. Eugene O'Curry, *On the Manners and Customs of the Ancient Irish*, ed. W. K. Sullivan (London, 1873, 3 vols.), II, 69–70.

[17] This compares interestingly with the Bolevian and Popean practice of so cleverly ordering their lines "sans rompre le mesure" that victims' names should be impaled on the most heavily stressed syllables in each hemistich, the most lethal point being at the extreme end of the line, e.g., Boileau's *Satire*, IX, 130: "Qu'on est assis à l'aise aux sermons de Cotin."

[18] Robinson (*op. cit.*, p. 113) translates after Stokes from the text in *Cormac's Glossary* (*Three Irish Glossaries*, ed. Stokes, p. 24) and notes that "several words in the quatrain are of uncertain meaning."

[19] Most sorcerers are profoundly convinced of their own powers. Whether or not the ancient Celtic satirist himself believed in the power of his words we cannot now tell.

[20] *Ancient Ireland: A Study in the Lessons of Archaeology and History* (London, 1935), p. 222. Macalister cites Sir James G. Frazer's *Taboo and the Perils of the Soul* (London, 1911), pp. 131–37, for other instances of such deaths. William Seabrook in *Witchcraft: Its Power in the World Today* (New York, 1940), pp. 3–12, agrees that the "elemental key" to this sort of thing is "induced autosuggestion" and describes at some length the psychological processes by which a suggestion "implanted from the outside" begins to take root and "eat in" on a person. Seabrook thinks that the power of ancient witchcraft was lodged solely in the mind and emotions of the victim and that it operated on the principles of mental therapy reversed. The power of the ancient Celtic satiric verses must be similarly explicable.

[21] *The Silver Branch*, ed. Sean O'Faolain (New York, 1938), p. 129. Both text and translation appear in *Abhandlungen der Akademie der k. Wissenschaften zu Berlin*, VII (n.d.), 33.

[22] Various refractions of it appear in the work of Jonathan Swift, who knew much about Irish malediction, e.g., the poem, "On Censure," (1726/27), *The Poems of Jonathan Swift*, ed. Harold Williams (Oxford, 1937, 3 vols.), II, 414:

For let Mankind discharge their Tongues
In Venom, till they burst their Lungs,
Their utmost Malice cannot make
Your head, or tooth, or finger ache;
Nor spoil your shape, distort your face,
Or put one feature out of place.

[23] *The Poems of Egan O'Rahilly*, ed. Rev. Patrick S. Dinneen (Irish Text Society, III [London, 1911, 2nd. ed.]), 239.

[24] *The Religious Songs of Connaught: A Collection of Poems, Stories, Prayers, Satires, Ranns, Charms, etc.*, ed. Douglas Hyde (London, 1906, 2 vols.), II, 273. The curses in Shakespeare's *Henry VI* plays, and in *Richard II*, as well as those in *Timon of Athens* and *Troilus and Cressida*, come to mind with their comparable lists of diseases. The extent to which English Renaissance literature preserves ancient charm, coterie curse, and hilltop incantation has never been assessed. Ancient Celtic remnants crop up everywhere, e.g., Quadratus' charm in Marston's *What You Will* (1607), V, I, and constitute fair argument for those who would maintain that English Renaissance satire, both dramatic and non-dramatic, presents certain aspects very similar to neighboring Celtic satire.

[25] Imagery in both the theory and practice of English satire of this period offers a fertile field for study, Miss U. M. Ellis-Fermor to the contrary (*The Jacobean Drama* [London, 1936], p. 83). Animals with qualities unattractive to man—the ass, ape, bear, fox, lynx, marmoset, mole, wolf, etc.; birds similarly unattractive—the gull, ibis, popinjay, daw, dotterel, widgeon, rook, goose, vulture, eagle; plants and fruits with unpleasant characteristics—fungi, weeds, parasites, Chian figs; reptiles; and stinging insects—wasps, hornets, gnats, gad-flies, and horse-leeches—these are all drawn upon. This was "Armada weather," and so there are sallies and charges against Vice, cannon volleys and musket discharges of words, explosions of powder-mines of jests, campaigns, battering-rams, and bullets of "three-piled hyperboles" in curious juxtaposition with desperate crusader-knights of the early Middle Ages, armed with targes, lances, and the dashing cloak of Virtue. There is, besides, the imagery of astrology, chiefly concerning "icy Saturn" and his influence; of masquerades and masques—mad-caps, whirligigs, and dominoes; and of card-playing—the knave of hearts, clubs, spades, etc. In eighteenth-century satire, all of the bird, beast, and plant imagery was to fit neatly without change into the Great Chain of Being theory.

[26] The Middle Ages had also stressed the fragility of the human

body, its susceptibility to ailment, and its inevitable capitulation to Death. No matter how sophisticated satire becomes, it still has much in common with medieval literature, in particular with the debates between body and soul, *estrifs* between vice and virtue, allegorical presentations of the Seven Deadly Sins, and the popular Backbiter and Detraction characters from the morality plays, as well as with the broad purpose and intent of the morality play. Many eminent churchmen have served youthful apprenticeships to satire, e.g., Barclay, Skelton, Donne, Hall, Swift, Sterne, etc.

27 Comedy, the large species to which the genre satire belongs, is defined only partially in terms of physical imagery; but "comicall satyre," like non-dramatic satire, is also defined by way of medical imagery (cf. the "Induction" to Jonson's *Every Man out of his Humour*). The medical profession, it may be noted, besides contributing imagery and the catharsis analogy to satire, has always been the special butt of satirists. See Eugene Holländer, *Die Karikatur und Satire in der Medizin* (Stuttgart, 1905), pp. 175–77; A. W. Brown, *Molière and his Medical Associations* (London, 1897), *passim*; E. Parkes Weber, *Aspects of Death in Art and Epigram* (London, 1914, 2nd ed.), pp. 161–66; "Dr. Serenus," *Aesculap als Harlekin: Humor, Satire, und Phantasie aus der Praxis* (Wiesbaden, 1911); and Isador H. Coriat, "The Psychology of Medical Satire," *Annals of Medical History*, III (1921), 403–7.

28 Minturno had made this general connection between medicine and satire in 1563 in his *De Arte Poetica* (*L'Arte Poetica del Signor Antonio Minturno*, Napoli, 1725), III, 272: "Come adunque le infermità, e le ferite del corpo direste esser materia della Medicina, come di quelle che in loro si rivolta, cosi le passioni, e le piaghe dell'animo soggetto di questa Satirica Poesia chiamereste. E. pericocchè l'una e l'altra ha per suo fine la sanità, quella del corpo, questa dell'anima; similmente ha cura di sanare, quella con le cose, questa con le parole; quella con amara bevanda, questa con acerba riprensione. Ma, periocchè la Filosofia è medicina di quella malattie, onde l'anima s'inferma, e'l Filosofo riprende per sanarla; intenda il Satirico scrittore, chenon s'appartiene a lui quel, ch'è propio della Filosofia, il trattare delle vertù, e delle coso, che loro si controppongono: ma il riprendere altrui festevolmente, nè senza sdegno con versi, per li costumi ammendare." Cf. Minturno's entire treatment of satire, pp. 271–87; also *De Poeta* (1559), Book V.

29 Pierre Bayle, who had slight sympathy with or belief in the mission and integrity of literary satire, scattered throughout the

Dictionnaire historique et critique (Rotterdam, 1697, 2 vols.) numerous lengthy accounts of how *le genre dangereux* had led to the deaths of such Renaissance figures as Erasmus, Joseph Scaliger, and Isaac Casaubon. See the English translation by Charles Des Maizeaux (London, 1734–38, 5 vols., 2nd ed.), III, 426 a; 464 a, b; 465 a, b; V, 98 b, 765. Isaac D'Israeli also collected numbers of such instances in his *Calamities and Quarrels of Authors* (London, n. d.), pp. 114–30.

30 Scotch satire, a story in itself, is a markedly interesting chapter in the history of Celtic satire. King James VI feared satire inordinately (a fear directly connected with his interest in demonology) and took the most extreme legal measures to curb it. See *A Book of Scottish Pasquils, 1568–1715*, ed. James Maidment (Edinburgh, 1868), p. ix. Thomas Warton later suggested that the proverbial violence of the Scotch satirists might be partially due to their climate (*History of English Poetry* [London, 1774, 3 vols.], II, 321); and James Boswell wrote, "The difference between satire in London and in Scotland is this: In London you are not intimately known so the satire is thrown at you from a distance, and however keen, does not tear and mangle you. In London the attack on the character is clean boxing. In Scotland it is grappling. They tear your hair, get you down in the mire, and not only hurt but disfigure and debase you" (*Boswelliana*, ed. Rev. Charles Rogers [London, 1874], p. 287). The Scotch thistle is often taken as the symbol of the Scottish tendency toward stinging satire, "the satirical itch ... from the regions beyond the Tweed," as Swift wrote in "The Preface" to *A Tale of a Tub* (1704).

31 Rev. J. H. Todd, "On Rhyming Rats to Death," *Proceedings of the Royal Irish Academy*, V (1850–53), 360 (quoted from the entry under the year 1414 in *The Annals of the Four Masters*). Concerning the relations at this period between the Irish satirists and the English, see John O'Donovan's "Introduction to the History of Satire in Ireland," prefacing his edition of Aenghus O'Daly, *The Tribes of Ireland: A Satire* (Dublin, 1852), pp. 13–15; and *Irish Minstrelsy, or Bardic Remains of Ireland; with English Poetical Translations*, ed. J. H. Hardiman (London, 1831, 2 vols.), I, "Introduction," xviii, n. The bards were not above acting as spies, making their way into British camps in minstrel disguise and carrying away enemy news and plans. Spenser wrote a decidedly uncomplimentary account of the Irish bards in his *A Veue of the Present State of Ireland* (*ca.* 1596) and recommended that English laws be framed to deal severely

with them and halt the rebellions they fomented. Neither were such current accounts of Irish affairs as those of Stanyhurst, Camden, Samuel Daniel, Campion, Moryson, and John Davies lacking in sharp comment on the dangerous character of the bards and in plentiful indication that the English had come to close quarters with them. See also Geoffrey Keating, *The History of Ireland* (Irish Texts Society, London, 1902–14, 4 vols.), I, 4–95, *passim*.

[32] O'Donovan; *op. cit.*, pp. 22–24; and Douglas Hyde, A *Literary History of Ireland* (London, 1899), pp. 476–78.

[33] Jonathan Swift's gloss on this particular passage is interesting. After having quoted Sidney is his *Advice to a Young Poet: together with a Proposal for the Encouragement of Poetry in this Kingdom* (1721), he says, "Our very good friend (the Knight aforesaid), speaking of the force of poetry, mentions rhyming to death, which (adds he) is said to be done in Ireland; and truly, to our honour be it spoken, that power in a great measure continues with us to this day."

[34] The *Henry VI* plays, like *King Richard III*, are filled with remnants of Celtic satiric theory, just as *As You Like It* and *Much Ado about Nothing* contain much classical theory of the genre. Richard himself evinces considerable faith in Irish bardic lore (IV, ii, 108–9): "... a bard of Ireland told me once/I should not live long after I saw Richmond." His arm, he says, has been withered by curses and charms (III, iv, 66–71):

> Look how I am bewitch'd. Behold, mine arm
> Is like a blasted sapling, wither'd up.

[35] Quoted in full by I. D'Israeli, *op. cit.*, p. 528.

[36] *AYLI*, III, ii, 185–87; *Merchant of Venice*, IV, i; *Hamlet*, III, iv.

[37] Todd, *op. cit.*, p. 356, quoted from the 1665 edition, p. 35. Even so late as 1660 a political satire was entitled, "Rats Rhimed to Death, or The Rump-Parliament Hang'd up in the Shambles."

[38] The score or more of basilisk figures, for instance, wherein the satirist is the fabulous dragon whose breath or glance is fatal, e.g., Lampatho in Marston's *What You Will* (II, i).

[39] Reference here is to a microfilm of the 1566 edition (British Museum copy, No. T. 773 2).

[40] Cf. Thomas Timme's A *plaine discouerie of ten English Lepers, verie noisome and hurtfull to the Church and common wealth* (1592) and a later political pamphlet, Thomas Edwards' *Gangraena* (1646).

41 Moralists ever protest that satire paints vice and folly in such vivid detail and unforgettable colorings that they attract rather than repel, e.g., R. M. Johnston, "The Extremity of Satire," *Studies Literary and Social* (Indianapolis, 1892), pp. 119–37, which castigates *Vanity Fair* as a remedy far worse than the disease it presumes to cure.

42 John Taylor's *Nipping or Snipping of Abuses* (1614) included "A Cataplasmicall Satyre, composed and compacted of sundry simples, as salt, wormwood, and a little gall, very profitable to cure the impostumes of vice," while *A Cure for the State* (1640) took the form of a medical prescription, and John Cleiveland protested in *The Character of a London Diurnall* (1644), "But I have not Inke enough to cure all the Tetters and Ring-worms of the State."

43 *AYLI*, II, i, 58–59.

44 *Ibid.*, II, vii, 58–61.

45 *Loc. cit.*, 65–69. Cf. Isador H. Coriat, *op. cit.*, pp. 403–7. Dr. Coriat finds in much medical satire and caricature evidence that the satirist has repressed interests and secret pleasures in investigating sexuality, obstetrics, the excrementory organs, etc. Duke Senior here accuses Jacques of having been a voluptuary and of now seeking to vent his spleen and accumulated repressions through satire.

46 Satirists of the time liked to describe Aretino's pen as hot and black, dripping poison, oil, fire, etc.

47 Ed. J. M. Cowper (Early English Texts Society, XLVIII [London, 1871]), p. 2.

48 Thomas Corser, *Collectanea Anglo-Poetica* (Manchester, 1860–65, 5 vols.), V, 93. The cut was reprinted on the title-page of Davies' *A Scourge for Paper Persecutors* (1625) with these lines added under the cut: "O couldst thou whip these Bedlams till they bleed,/Thou whippst in vaine: we'ele whip anon in deed."

49 *The Scourge of Villainy*, Satyre IX ("Here's a Toy to Mocke an Ape indeed").

50 Punishment by strappado consisted of tying the victim's hands across his back, fastening them to a pulley, and letting him fall abruptly from a height, only to be caught up with a violent jerk when about half-way to the ground. Bastinado, that is, cudgeling a victim on the soles of his feet, is more rarely mentioned.

51 *Op. cit.*, p. 135.

[52] A preparation of dried Spanish flies or blister beetles, usually used internally as an aphrodisiac. Here, however, it is apparently used externally in its less commonly noted function as a rubefacient, i.e., to redden and blister flesh. There are numbers of references to satire's having such a function, e.g., Marston's *The Metamorphosis of Pigmalion's Image* (1598), Satire II, "Now, Satire, cease to rub our galléd skins."

[53] A prostitute. Also called Winchester goose.

[54] *Poetical and Dramatic Works of Thomas Randolph*, ed. W. Carew Hazlitt (London, 1875, 2 vols.), I, 189–90.

[55] *A Medicinable Morall* (London, 1566), sig. a. iiii^v (reference here is to a microfilm of a British Museum copy).

[56] *Chaucer and the Mediaeval Sciences* (New York, 1926), p. 130. These things were part of every man's lore in the Middle Ages and the Renaissance, but Robert Greene's *Planetomachia* (1585) and John Lyly's *The Woman in the Moone* (1597) might have served Renaissance satirists as immediate source books of Saturn's malevolent powers and influences, had they needed any.

[57] Other interesting connections may be made, e.g., Saturn was thought to be the planet farthest from the sun and consequently to bequeath a chill and aridity to those under his black sign (in contrast to his ancient function as an agricultural god). Blackness and frigidity, of course, have been satire's very own color and quality from the Celtic hilltop satire (*glám dichenn*), which demanded a cold black wind blowing, to Hegelian analyses of satiric aridity and objective "distance."

[58] The Celtic smith, who is sometimes indistinguishable from the satirist, was traditionally dwarfish and lame, like Vulcan. (See my article, "Celtic Smiths and Satirists: Partners in Sorcery," in a forthcoming issue of *ELH*.) The satirist might be blind, like Dallán Forgaill, or seriously deformed like the "idle, blind man named Cridenbél" who had his mouth "out at his breast."

[59] II, i, 2–3; 5–7; 9–10.

[60] II, i, 52–54.

[61] II, iii, 1–24.

[62] V, i, 20–28.

[63] Robinson, *op. cit.*, p. 114.

[64] John Aubrey wrote of Milton (*Brief Lives*, ed. A. Clark [Oxford, 1898, 2 vols.], II, 67–68): "He pronounced the letter R (*littera canina*) very hard—a certaine sign of a satyrical witt—from John Dryden."

65 Marston, for instance, has scores of references to barking "band-dogs" and snarling satirists.

66 Satyrs and dogs surveying civilized man and snapping and snarling at what they see are not unlike Swift's horses looking at the Yahoos.

67 The Latin satirists had provided ample precedent for such a theory of personal catharsis on the part of the satirist. Lucilius had said that the satiric spirit demanded some outlet: "*evadat saltem aliquid aliqua*" (Frag. 632); and when the cautious Trebatius advised Horace to seek a safer catharsis by swimming the Tiber thrice and drinking much good wine at night, Horace follows Lucilius in declaring that he cannot sleep and querying, "*Quid faciam?...Sequor hunc*" (II, i, 7; 34). Persius also must have his laugh out, "*Quid faciam? sed sum petulanti splene ca chinno*" (I, 12); and Juvenal, the "prynce of all" to Renaissance satirists, explains carefully why he must get his word in: "*...indignatio facit versum*" (I, 79).

68 *The Arte of English Poesie*, reprinted in *Elizabethan Critical Essays*, ed. G. G. Smith (Oxford, 1904, 2 vols.), II, 56.

69 *Ibid.*, II, 229.

70 *Ibid.*, II, 239.

71 Isador H. Coriat (*op. cit.*, pp. 403–7) suggests that satirists, particularly in satires on physicians, medicine, and medical subjects forbidden in polite conversation, take that opportunity for discharge or release of repressed interests, impulses, and curiosities. It has already been noted that obstetrical and sexual subjects are prominent in medical satire as are references to excremental organs, functions, and material, e.g., Rabelais' *Gargantua*, xii, and portions of Swift's *Gulliver's Travels*. Sexual exhibitionism and certain types of satire may be two very different manifestations of the same pathological phenomenon. Dr. Coriat thinks that though such satire may be highly symbolized, it is nevertheless a literary cover for or vicarious fulfillment of obscene or sexual tendencies, general sadism, or hostile impulses toward fellow beings. Extreme license of expression in connection with such subjects is further evidence of repression on the part of satirists. See also C. H. Herford, *Studies in the Literary Relations of England and Germany in the Sixteenth Century* (Cambridge, England, 1886), on "Grobius and Grobianism," pp. 323–88. The lecherous quality of most of the satires against lechery has been noted by many a Renaissance scholar, who has doubted that the satirist was applying a homeopathic cure. Morse S. Allen, for in-

stance, in his *The Satire of John Marston* (Columbus, Ohio, 1920), pp. 116–17, draws attention to the fact that Marston boldly published the extremely lascivious *Pigmalions Image* in the same binding as *The Scourge of Villainy*, which contained a satire (Satyre VIII, "Inamorato Curio,") against libidinous and amorous poets.

[72] There are no formal *apologiae* in English Renaissance satire. The best examples from both classical and modern literatures are: Horace, II, i; Persius, I; Juvenal, I; Régnier, XII; Boileau, XII; and Pope's *Epistle to Dr. Arbuthnot*.

[73] *Op. cit.*, p. 129.

[74] That investigation, tentatively entitled, "A Theory of Satiric Catharsis," for which this paper is intended to serve as partial background, is now complete in MS. form.

MARY CLAIRE RANDOLPH

The Structural Design of
the Formal Verse Satire

The word "formal" in the phrase "formal verse satire" implies that the genre has some specific vertebrate form or architectural design despite its apparently loose-meshed, casually discursive surface. So far as I now know, there exists in English no study which considers what the general aspects of that structural pattern may be. Should an alertly critical reader or student set out to discover how a formal verse satire should be made, he could find nothing or next to nothing within the range of English scholarship to help him to recognize and appreciate the satirical patterns of Horace, Persius, or Juvenal; DuBellay, Régnier, or Boileau; or Donne or Pope or Edward Young. The following condensed treatment, by no means exhaustive, attempts to synthesize available information concerning the form of the formal verse satire.[1]

It is generally agreed that the formal verse satire is the only species or genre within the wide area of the genus Satire to have any sort of identifiable crystallized form or framework. Fluid and elusive as mercury, the Satiric Spirit almost refuses to be bound by any rigid tenets but easily flows into and fuses itself (especially in periods when it encounters episcopal and legal opposition) with other essentially or even temporarily congenial genres—comedy, beast fable, prose narrative, etc.[2] Formal verse satire itself, brittle, fragile, and unstable for all its core of pattern, easily drifts and fades before stern, organized opposition or spins itself out into brief, ephemeral by-products: daredevil lampoons, pasquils, political libels, invective, goliardic ballads and street-songs, fly-by-night pamphlets and corantos. This fugitive

From *Philological Quarterly*, XXI (1942), 368–84. Reprinted by permission of the editors of *Philological Quarterly*.

character of the genre and our long uncertainty as to its ancient origins
and terminology have combined to discourage investigations into form,
a point always neglected in any theorizing about the genre.

The precise pattern and plan of Latin *satura* has long been a
puzzle to classical scholars. Once its deceptively simple exterior is
penetrated, an intricate honeycomb of allusion and inheritance appears. Reduced to simplest terms, the extensive scholarship on the
subject[3] resolves into these conclusions: the formal verse satire, as
composed by Lucilius, Horace, Persius, and Juvenal, was evidently
bi-partite in structure,[4] that is, some specific vice or folly, selected
for attack, was turned about on all its sides in Part A (if one may
arbitrarily call it so) in something of the way premises are turned
about in the octave of a sonnet; and its opposing virtue was recommended in Part B.[5] The arraignment in Part A of the specific vice or
folly was clearly a process of intellection whereby a mode of dialectic
was employed to view the various facets of the subject through the
opaque media of plebeian folk proverb, Oriental beast fable, dramatic
vignette, *chriea*-like anecdote, rationalized myth, Socratic dialogue,
and so on. Thus, a vice was laid open to the light by a sophisticated
exegetical process, almost labyrinthine, in which practically every
known Hellenic literary form was employed. Formal verse satire consequently has an astonishing array of affiliations and relationships with a
myriad phases of world culture since there is almost nothing that
cannot appropriately be poured into its quasi-dramatic mould, as the
name *satura* indicates. On the score of literary organism alone, it owes
specific debts to ancient repetitive incantation,[6] the Old Comedy (in
fact, to all of the Greek comic genres), the Theophrastian character,[7]
the Bionean diatribe, the Socratic or Platonic dialogue, all "frame"
literature, and all gnomic or wisdom literature.

Various scholars have attempted to show that the formal verse
satire of the Augustan period owes all or nearly all of the multiple
aspects of its deceptively intricate structure to various inchoate Greek
forms.[8] Certain theorists have argued that it is most nearly like the
Bionean diatribe, which came closer to achieving crystallized fixity
of pattern than any other satiric type before Lucilius.[9] This Cynic
diatribe was a short conversational disquisition, addressed to an imaginary listener or even to an entire company, autobiographical and
highly informal in character, arranged sometimes in letter form, on a
single ethical thesis or theme, arraigning a single vice and commending the opposing virtue, packed with extremely personal illustrative

anecdotes, animal similes, allegorical personifications, realistic little mime-like scenes or vignettes, reflective soliloquy, citations from and parodies of older writers, witty and caustic comparisons, maxims and *sententiae*, strong contrasts, clever metaphors, and excessively coarse jests and colloquialisms. Attractively gay and spirited and extremely various in content, rhymed and designedly quotable, these diatribes of Bion were very popular and served as influential, easily remembered pieces of philosophic propaganda. They were written in a variety of verse-forms: scazons or choliambics (reserved usually for the severest abuse), dactylic hexameters, elegiacs, iambic trimeters, and tetrameters, trochaic tetrameters, and sotadean measures. The Bionean diatribe thus seems in its jocular exegetical character and in its heterogeneous materials as well as in its dichotomous pattern very like formal verse satire.

Other scholars, the French Paul Lejay, for instance, see in the extremely variable architectural design of the Aristophanic comedy (i.e., *Prologos; Parados; Proagon; Agon; Parabasis*, and *Exodos*) a plan broadly comparable to the similarly variable structure of the Horatian satire.[10] Lejay experimentally sets the comic *Prologos* against satiric prologue; the comic *Agon* against the satirical exegesis or dialectical exposition of a vice; and the comic *Exodos* against the satiric conclusion or exhortation to the opposing virtue. In each of Horace's first four *Satires*, Lejay finds three of the five major elements of the Aristophanic comedy; and, after similar though less successful analyses of the remaining *Satires*, he concludes: "Nous pouvons dire que ses satires ont des vestiges certains d'une influence technique de la comédie ancienne, plus exactement de la comédie aristophanienne, en ce genre la seule dont nous connaissions la structure."[11]

Whatever the genesis of the classical *satura* and whatever its salient contributing factors, the usual structure of formal verse satire seems to be this: An outer shell-like framework encloses the entire piece; more likely than not a combative hollow man or interlocutor, an Adversarius, who may be identified by name and occupation or who may remain shadowy and anonymous, serves as whip and spur to the Satirist, now baiting him with a question, now thrusting in a barbed rejoinder calculated to draw out from him fresh comment and anecdote concerning the vice in question. Sometimes this second figure is only a straw decoy who utters no word but simply listens throughout the Satirist's monologue; sometimes he is a pessimistic, hardheaded Mentor; again he is an annoyingly irrational person who early detaches himself from a crowd and draws near the Satirist; very rarely is he such a one as can cleverly turn the tables on the Satirist himself. The background against which these two talk is ever so lightly sketched in; perhaps it is only half suggested or possibly only barely intimated, but it is nearly always there. Not infrequently it is a moving panoramic background—a street, a royal court, another journey to Brundisium— some setting wherein people pass by and thus provide a steady stream of type-figures on whom the Satirist can comment to the Adversarius. Altogether, then, we have the minimum essentials for the quasi-dramatic genre that formal verse satire is: two actors or participants, a Satirist and his Adversarius; a setting of sorts; and a thesis to be argued.

Within this outer frame lies the satire itself wherein, in what has been called Part A, some irrational behavior of Man, either foolish or vicious, is turned about on a pivot and its various sides and facets mercilessly exposed and illumined by a wide variety of lively exegetical devices. When the conversation begins abruptly and jerkily, as it usually does, and continues elliptically, broken and interrupted here and there, throughout the whole elaborate, studied rhetorical apparatus, frequently without either Satirist or Adversarius being clearly identified as the speaker, the uninitiated reader is apt to feel thoroughly lost. One of the most common editorial and critical accusations against formal verse satire is that its lack of clarifying guide-words and transitions results in extreme confusion of dialogue. What we have now perhaps lost sight of is the fact that classical satire, as it was descended from oral genres, was still in Augustan Rome designed to be recited in public arcade or forum and was probably energetically dramatized as the speaker gave his lines.

To illustrate his thesis, win his case, and move his audience to thought and perhaps to psychological action, the Satirist utilizes miniature dramas, sententious proverbs and quotable maxims, compressed beast fables (often reduced to animal metaphors), brief sermons, sharp debates, series of vignettes, swiftly sketched but painstakingly built up satiric "characters" or portraits, figure-processions, little fictions and apologues, visions, apostrophes and invocations to abstractions—anything and everything to push his argument forward to its philosophical and psychological conclusions in much the same manner as events might push action forward to a dénouement in drama or fiction. In addition to these structural devices, an innumerable variety of purely rhetorical devices is employed to give point, compactness, speed, climax, contrast, surprise, and a score more of the special effects so necessary to good satire. Holding these varied materials together internally is the unifying thesis-thread or core of argument, while the outer frame serves as external enclosure for the entire piece. Thus, whatever simplicity and nonchalance formal satire seems to have is only an assumed simplicity of verbal surface beneath which there exists a skillfully evolved and delicately convoluted development of dialectical argument. The method employed in satire thus connects it with formal dialectic, psychology, and medicine; the end in view, the correction of folly and vice by persuasion to rational behavior, connects it with all didactic literature and with the organized forces of religion and law; while the miscellaneous illustrative materials utilized connect it with all the daily activities of man.

In practice, the negative portion of the formal satire has always outweighed the positive portion, as it must in any satire, formal or informal, verse or prose, since, paradoxically, in the very act of presenting the negative or destructive side of human behavior the satirist is establishing a positive foundation on which he can base his specific recommendation to virtue.[12] Sometimes there is a transition followed by a direct admonition to virtue or rational behavior couched in plain words. Often the admonition to virtue, never psychologically pleasing at best, is only implied throughout Part A or perhaps cleverly introduced by way of quotable proverb and maxim throughout that portion. But it is there, it must be there, spoken or unspoken, if the piece is to be more than mere virulence and fleeting invective. Now, this positive side of satire toward which the whole exegetical and rhetorical procedure is pointed is usually a dogma of a rationalistic philosophy since the essential function of Satire is ever by Ridicule to recall Man from the by-ways of Unreason to the base line of Reason, that is, to present Rational Man as the norm or standard.[13] In any age, Satire never fails to assume the colorations of the dominant rationalistic philosophy of that period: in antiquity, Cynicism and Stoicism; in the Middle Ages, Scholasticism; in the Renaissance, Humanism; and in the neoclassic period, Cartesianism. In antiquity the standard or Rational Man was the *vir bonus*, the tranquil, ideal citizen of the Roman commonwealth whose ideal was the Golden Mean and who preferred the quiet life "at Ulubrae"; in the Renaissance, Rational Man is the Sidneian humanist described in the courtesy books of the period; and in the Age of Enlightenment, he is the *honnête homme*.

It would thus be possible, if a satirist so chose, to build each satire around an essential dogma of a chosen philosophy, and, in a whole cluster of ten or a dozen satires, to present a pragmatic exegesis of that single philosophy. Persius did essentially that for Stoicism, although it is but rarely that a satirist is so closely identified with any single system of thought as is Persius. It would also be possible to select a single broad thesis and to write a group of satires on various aspects of that single thesis as Edward Young did in his seven satires, *Love of Fame, the Universal Passion* (1725–28). In any case, whatever the plan, the positive rational mode of procedure advocated or unmistakably implied in a satire will be the precise opposite of the vice or folly ridiculed; as in the mediaeval morality plays with which formal satire has obvious generic sympathy, the Virtue will oppose the Vice, or more accurately, specific Reason will oppose specific Unreason.

Two further points concerning form should be noted in connection with classical satire. The first concerns the still unsettled question of the satiric epistle. Horace wrote two books of *Epistles*, 19 in the first, 2 in the second, the first book of which appears in every way to be satires, save for title and an added freedom of conversation justified by the fact that the satirist writes informally to friends. The now familiar and unresolved question is posed: may formal verse satires properly be written in letter form?[14] Various satirists have solved the question for themselves by writing a cluster of satiric "epistles" supplementing their satires exactly as Horace had done. In France, Boileau wrote 12 *Epîtres* (1669–98), distinct supplements to his 12 *Satires* (1660–1711); and his very competent predecessor in the genre, Mathurin Régnier, wrote 16 *Satires* (1608), all in the form of familiar letters, besides three additional *épîtres*. In England, Alexander Pope, besides brilliantly adapting nearly one third of the *Satires, Epistles,* and *Odes* of Horace, wrote four original formal verse satires in the epistolary form, the *Moral Essays* (1731–35), like Horace's *Epistles*, so similar to formal satires as to be so considered, though not so titled.

The second point concerns the one set form to be encountered in formal verse satire, the satirist's *apologia pro satura sua* which he seems bound to write sooner or later, and for which there is now a considerable tradition. Lucius R. Shero[15] has analyzed the framework and content of the Latin *apologia*, i.e., the remaining fragments of Lucilius XXX; Horace II, i; Persius I; and Juvenal I, and finds this common pattern: a dissuading Interlocutor or friendly Monitor warns the satirist to be prudent, to transfer his talents and efforts before it is too late to a safer, more popular genre, epic, for instance, or the exceedingly profitable panegyric. The satirist vehemently replies that his passion for satire cannot be restrained, that he must discharge his spleen when provocation evokes it, and that he but follows inexpertly in the Lucilian tradition and writes for sympathetic, understanding folk, cognizant of the demands of that tradition. The Interlocutor's pleas are highly stylized and so are the satirist's rebuttals. At the close, the satirist usually makes some polite concession to the Interocutor; he may, for instance, agree to write only of the dead or of persons without political power. In a way, these stock-in-trade debates are not unlike the mediaeval debates between the body and soul wherein the soul or Muse dissuades and the body persists. Modern *apologiae* of this pattern, simultaneously defining and defending satire, are frequent, e.g., Régnier's XII ("Régnier apologiste de soi-même") ; Boileau's famous IX ("A son Esprit") ; and Pope's *An Epistle to Dr. Arbuthnot*.[16] Swift's *Verses on the Death of Dr. Swift (1731)* is an adaptation of the traditional *apologia* to the Dean's own ironic method.

In England very little serious attention, critical or otherwise, has ever been paid the baffling subject of the form proper to a formal verse satire. It has never been the way of the English critical mind, as it is the way of the French, to busy itself primarily with questions of literary form any more than it is the way of the English creative mind to hinder itself seriously with the strict limitations imposed by certain literary forms; in fact, the native English temperament, inherently opposed to strict schematization and antipathetic to formal moulds of any sort, has always tended to regard the formal verse satire as an artificial genre transplanted from the Mediterranean. The Englishman's taste for moral perfection, however, has always been as lively as his feeling for highly stylized form has been inert; and so he has been constantly drawn to satire because of its moral purpose. That fact accounts for the Englishman's early and continued admiration of Juvenalian *saeva indignatio*, his swift elevation of Juvenal as the "prynce of all" among the Latin satirists, his own constant and wearisome emphasis on the moral mission of satire, and his reiterated intent in the Renaissance to scourge and flay, the more fiercely the better. Among the scores of casual, informal critical statements having to do with verse satire from 1509 to 1692/93, there is not one, so far as I have been able to discover, that has to do with form.

In France, on the other hand, a very great deal, relatively speaking, had always been made of the question of satiric form. At a time when English satirists were marshalling their victims pell-mell into *Cock Lorell's Bote* and many another such capacious craft, the French had carefully divided contemporary society into three strata for the satirists' convenience: *noblesse, église, labeur,* each with specific degrees, hierarchies, and *vices propres.* The satirist began with the *noblesse,* cited the conventional faults, and leisurely pursued his way downward, utilizing prescribed transitions, until he arrived at the lowest division of *labeur.*[17] Highly stylized, geometrically air-tight patterns were devised for half a dozen small, preliminary satiric forms which served as forerunners to the first formal verse satires of DuBellay and Régnier. Nothing like them was ever devised in England, although one occasionally finds some fleeting mention of the French patterns, particularly among the Scotch. Among the pages of the fifteenth- and sixteenth-century *rhétoriqueurs* appear neatly worked out instructions for the making of the *blason*;[18] the Provençal *sirventois*; the completely mechanized *fatras* which admitted of being a *fatras simple* or *double* (with a reversed pattern in the second group of lines), *possible* (coherent) or *impossible* (incoherent):[19] and the satanically clever *coq-à-l'âne.*[20] Although in England there were "comicall satyres," satirical characters in verse, satirical epigrams, and "gulling" sonnets with stings in their specially appended tail verses, there are not, early or late, any such rigorously set and prescribed forms as these of the French *rhétoriqueurs.*

If the Renaissance English satirist thought at all critically of form in connection with verse satire, he left no printed expression of his thoughts. But certain elementary points and connection with the satires of Horace, Persius, and Juvenal were immediately visible to him; indeed, he could hardly escape them. The English satirist noted, for instance, that the ancients had seemingly written their satires in clusters of varying numbers, groupings which were further subdivided into "books." What he perhaps did not know was that the classical satires were primarily intended to be recited aloud and that no "book" (*libellus*) of the ancient form could have contained many more than a thousand lines; consequently, satires had to be preserved in groups or "books" containing approximately that many lines. He noted that Lucilius had reputedly written 30 books of satires; that Horace had written 18 satires, grouped into two books, 10 in Book I, 8 in Book II; as well as two books of epistles; that Persius wrote a cluster of 6 satires, prefaced by what appears to be a prologue of 14 choliambics;

and that Juvenal wrote 16 satires preserved in 5 "sets" or books with *Satire I* often regarded as preface to the entire number. English Renaissance satirists obediently took their cue from this classical precedent and wrote similar clusters of satires, sometimes grouping them arbitrarily into "books" with short prologues, sometimes not, apparently according to whim. Donne, for instance, wrote a cluster of 5 satires, perhaps more; Lodge, 4, although he declared himself to have written a whole *centon*; Hall, 35, the largest collection of satires in the Renaissance, which he chose to break up into three books of "toothless" and three of "bytyng" satires; Rankins, 7; Marston, 11, numbered consecutively through three books, called *The Scourge of Villanie*, besides another group of 5, simply called "Satyres." Seven became an extremely popular number in the early seventeenth century because of the Seven Deadly Sins and the seven planets which presumably regulated human fortunes and human behavior. For new editions Renaissance satirists casually added new satires to their original groupings or eked out slender volumes with satirical epigrams, practices which indicate that the original arrangement had been arbitrarily determined, perhaps by the printer, at the outset.

When the English satirist looked at the lengths of the Latin satires, he found them widely variant. Juvenal's *Sixth Satire,* for instance, contains 661 lines, and is twice the length of any of his other satires (the *Fourth* has only 173 lines); and Persius' longest satire, the *Fifth* (191 lines), immediately follows his shortest, the *Fourth* (52 lines). Finding no special rule in evidence, the Renaissance measured his own pieces by rule of thumb, sometimes extending his "epigrammes" into satires or shortening his "satyres" until they approached a brevity consonant with the theory of epigram.

Classical tradition had taught Renaissance English satirists that formal satire was in direct descent from the Old Comedy and from the Greek satyr-play and should therefore be quasi-dramatic in character. The long persisting lexicographical error connecting English "satyre" with Greek satyros ($\delta\acute{\alpha}\tau\upsilon\rho\sigma\varsigma$) instead of Latin *satura* (a myth dissipated by Casaubon in his *De Satyrica,* Book I) was responsible for the current popular notion that satire should be loose-jointed, crudely devised, and obscurely and harshly worded, a supposition hardly calculated to foster critical investigation into classical Latin form. Still, whatever else they may not have known about the form, Renaissance and early seventeenth-century satirists were certain of the principle that the genre was a semi-dramatic one held together by the figure of the Narrator-Satirist and became extremely clever at devising and reviving dramatic devices to give life and color to what might have been forthright, unadorned imprecation against vice. So far as verse form was concerned, the English satirist early noted that the classical satires were monometric and gradually and naturally, without much critical ado, fixed on his own iambic pentameter with its "grappling-hooks" of rhyme.

From observation and study of the classical satires, then, the English Renaissance satirist learned these elementary things about form: that satires were usually written in clusters of indeterminate number, sometimes introduced by separate prologue or preface; that their lengths were extremely variable; and that they were semi-dramatic and monometric. Those Latin satires dealing directly with satiric theory, Horace's *Fourth* and *Tenth*, Book I, and the *First*, Book II; Persius' *Prologue* and his *First Satire* (the *Fifth* perhaps incidentally) ; and Juvenal's *First Satire*, concerned themselves chiefly with spirit, tone, and ethics, and not at all with form. So far as one can now tell, the English verse satirist of the Renaissance must have decided that the architectural pattern was his own to make and that only the tone, direction, and general external outline of the genre had been marked out for him by the ancients.

John Dryden was the first and he remains almost the only English man of letters to have considered critically the matter of the architectural pattern of formal verse satire and then only in 1692/93 when England's first period of verse satire was long gone by and a second and greater one even then under way. It is the latter portion of Dryden's *A Discourse on the Original and Progress of Satire* (1692/93), perhaps the most generally neglected and inadequately edited major critical essay in our literature, plus the extremely interesting headnotes or "Arguments" to the translations of Persius and Juvenal, which show that Dryden's chief interest at this time was the form proper to formal verse satire. Possibly roused by the bold Bolevian experimentations in the larger aspects of satiric form going on across the Channel,[21] Dryden's interest was fostered by his extensive use of Isaac Casaubon's learned introductory essay of nearly 300 pages, *De Satyrica Graecorum Poesi et Romanorum Satira* as well as Casaubon's copious notes to his great Paris edition of Persius (1605). Dryden says in the *Discourse*:

I will tell you . . . how a modern satire should be made. . . . please

> ... observe, that Persius, the least in dignity of all the three, has notwithstanding been the first, who has discovered to us this important secret, in the designing of a perfect satire, that it ought only to treat of one subject; to be confined to one particular theme; or, at least, to one principally. If other vices occur in the management of the chief, they should only be transiently lashed, and not be insisted on, so as to make the design double. . . . In general all virtues are everywhere to be praised and recommended to practice; and all vices to be reprehended, and made either odious or ridiculous; or else there is a fundamental error in the whole design.[22]

Thus, according to Dryden, one vice and one alone must be the subject of a formal verse satire. If any other vices enter into the design, they must be logical subdivisions of the one chief vice. Dryden immediately compares this precept of unity of design in a satire to unity of action in a drama, a comparison not infrequently echoed here and there in the eighteenth century and even extended to include the unities of place and time. Casaubon had carefully brought the principles of Aristotle's *Poetics* to bear on satire throughout his essay, e.g., in Book II, Chap. III; and Dryden follows Casaubon in remarking that since Horace knew the rules of unity as they applied to drama, he should have applied them to his satires;

> As in a . . . tragi-comedy, there is to be but one main design: and, though, there be an underplot, or second walk of comical characters and adventures, yet they are subservient to the chief fable, carried along under it, and helping to it: so that the drama may not seem a monster with two heads. . . . It is certain, that the divine wit of Horace was not ignorant of this rule,—that a play, though it consists of many parts, must yet be one in the action, and must drive on the accomplishment of one design; . . . yet he seems not so much to mind it in his satires, many of them consisting of more arguments than one; and the second without dependence on the first.[23]

Dryden rejects the very plausible argument that *satura*, as it signifies etymologically a variety of fruits and grains, may properly imply a miscellaneous assortment of literary materials, unless, he specifies, the miscellaneous materials all fall logically under one single, broad heading, so that the variety may be ordered and organized variety. Juvenal, Persius, and Boileau, he notes, have all confined themselves to unity of design in the single satire and have allowed their finished groups of satires to provide the variety traditionally implied in the generic term *satura*. Moreover, Dryden argues, if the satirist insists on variety, he can illustrate these subordinate branches of the major vice with sufficient examples to provide color and change and avoid monotony.[24]

A further point, included in this neo-Aristotelian rule for unity of design within a satire, is that a satirist must offer one single positive precept of moral virtue to balance his attack on the one particular vice. "He is," says Dryden, "chiefly to inculcate one virtue and insist on that."[25] If he has subdivided the chief vice into component parts, then he must offer corresponding minor precepts of moral virtue which will be logical subdivisions of the major precept. Thus, for every vice, major and minor, there must be a precisely corresponding precept of virtue.

But this is not all of Dryden's formula. He sees clearly, as did Persius, that a satirist's entire collection of satires could, if carefully planned, present a unified, practical exegesis of the essential dogmas of some particular rationalistic philosophy:

> Herein then it is, that Persius has excelled both Juvenal and Horace. He sticks to his own philosophy; he shifts not sides, like Horace, who is sometimes an Epicurean, sometimes a Stoic, sometimes an Eclectic, as his present humour leads him ... Persius is every where the same; true to the dogmas of his master ... His kind of philosophy is one, which is the Stoic; and every satire is a comment on one particular dogma of that sect, unless we will except the first, which is against bad writers; and yet even there he forgets not the precepts of the Porch.[26]

The eleven headnotes to the satires translated by Dryden are visible evidence that he had striven to put his theory of bi-partite form to immediate, pragmatic use. In every instance he tries to discover and state exactly what vice has been the satirist's special target of attack. If there are subordinate vices or tangential subtopics, Dryden notes carefully how they logically fall into proper place under the main heading. He takes pains to point out "artful" transitions from Part A to Part B and to note and to phrase carefully the constructive precept to virtue or philosophic dogma offered and stressed by the satirist. Some of the satires very obviously present difficult problems; and occasionally Dryden has to admit outright that Part B, the precept to virtue, is only implied or that the needful transition is blurred or missing altogether.[27]

This concept of symmetrical, interlocking pattern for a formal verse satire which Dryden has outlined in the latter portion of the *Discourse* and attempted to apply in his headnotes is as stiffly geometric in its contrasting parts as the most severely formal eighteenth-century garden. The basic suggestions for it came both directly and indirectly from the pages of Casaubon's 1605 edition of Persius, specifically from the essay, *De Satyrica* . . . , Book II, Chapters III, IV, and V, as well as from certain of the notes.[28] It will be noted that in large outline Dryden's theory of formal satire coincides very well with the theory of form earlier described in this paper.

But the Drydenian formula for the making of a "modern satire" was too mechanically cut-and-dried for any satirist to put to actual use, and so it seems to have been as generally overlooked in the poet's own time as later. Ranking English men of letters, however, even in England's greatest age of satire, wrote very few original formal verse satires. Dryden himself wrote none; Swift, Gay, Addison, Steele, and Arbuthnot wrote none; only Edward Young and Alexander Pope, in company with a certain few of the lesser poets, wrote any formal verse satires that could properly be termed original. Add to these the five formal *Satyres* of John Donne, and one has England's chief original contributions to the genre. Not one of the half dozen or so great English satires, it must be noted, is a formal verse satire. But if English satirists did not themselves create great numbers of original formal verse satires, they so admired the clusters of classical satires that they paid constant, careful lip-tribute to them as the great ancient patterns; they studied and imitated them; they paraphrased and adapted them, altering locale and names in Bolevian fashion; and they translated and edited them—but in actual creative practice they chose to go their own English ways. The formal verse satires of the neo-classical period would be almost negligible in number were it not for the large body of translations and adaptations of Horace, Persius, and Juvenal.

Various reasons suggest themselves in explanation of the English critical neglect of the form of this particular literary genre. Obviously the architectural design or structure of formal verse satire has never been clearly defined or generally understood at any time. Dryden is apparently the only critic in English literature who has come reasonably close to an apprehension of the basic structure of the genre and then only by the aid of Casaubon's suggestions. Even now when twentieth-century classical scholars (mentioned in the footnotes to this paper) have investigated various aspects of the architectural pattern of classical Latin satire, no one of them, so far as I know, has synthesized their scattered materials into anything like a connected, detailed analysis of the form. Thus, it may be that English satirists generally have not clearly recognized and perceived the structure of the genre and have warily preferred to confine themselves to translations and adaptations of the classical patterns. It seems rather more likely, however, that the paucity of original formal verse satire in England may be explicable as one result of the staunch resistance of British temperament to the rigorous schematization and regimented formalism of certain phases of neo-classicism. Formal verse satire is designed with greater syllogistic precision than the sonnet, and its intellectual demands on both writer and reader are specialized, multiple, and stringent. Englishmen have varied the sonnet and the ode forms to suit themselves; in the case of the formal verse satire, however, they have been content, for the most part, with score on score of "adaptations." As a form, formal verse satire was never to be a leading genre in English literature; but its peculiar spirit and temper were to pervade and animate nearly every literary genre in England for a hundred years and more.[29]

NOTES

[1] It has not been possible within the range of this article to describe or list the scores of devices, both rhetorical and structural, and traditional generic conventions contributory to the form.

[2] Censorship has always affected the theory and practice of satire: made it cautiously recommend veiling allegory, fable, subterfuges, keys, and obscurity of diction; seek other channels of expression; or take refuge in minor forms. Satire has had a long battle with the law from the time of the Roman Twelve Tables to the present day when increasing numbers of political cartoonists, the modern approximation of the verse satirists, have been fined and imprisoned.

[3] Important studies bearing on form are: H. Nettleship, "The Original Form of the Roman Satura" (originally written, 1878), *Lectures and Essays* (2nd. ser., Oxford, 1895), pp. 24–43; G. L.

Hendrickson, "The Dramatic Satura and the Old Comedy at Rome," *Amer. Jour. of Philology*, XV (1894), 1–30; H. M. Hopkins, "Dramatic Satura in Relation to Book Satura and the Fabula Togata," *Proceedings of the American Philological Society*, XXXI (1900), 1–51; G. L. Hendrickson, "Satura, the Genesis of a Literary Form," *Classical Philology*, VII (1912), 177–89; C. Knapp, "The Sceptical Assault on the Roman Tradition Concerning the Dramatic Satura," *Amer. Jour. of Philology*, XXXIII (1912), 125ff. (Knapp makes a grievous error when he asserts that to Horace comedy and satire were convertible terms); R. J. E. Tiddy, "Satura and Satire," *English Literature and the Classics*, ed. G. S. Gordon (Oxford, 1912), pp. 196–227; A. L. Wheeler, "Satura as a Generic Term," *Classical Philology*, VII (1912), 457–77; J. W. D. Ingersoll, "Roman Satire. Its Early Name?" *Classical Philology*, VII (1912), 59–65; B. L. Ullman, "Satura and Satire," *Classical Philology*, VIII (1913), 173–94; and "The Present Status of the Satura Question," *Studies in Philology*, XVII (1920), 379–401; and G. L. Hendrickson, "*Satira tota nostra est*," *Classical Philology*, XXII (1927), 46–60.

4 The fact has long been recognized that formal verse satire as a poetic form breaks sharply into two markedly disproportionate divisions—thesis and antithesis, destruction and construction, black and white—with the latter portion being ever the weaker and less striking of the two. Augustin G. C. Cartault in his *Etude sur les Satires d'Horace* (Paris, 1899), p. 347, proposed a grouping of the materials of the *Satires* into ideas of destruction and construction for study purposes (see Oscar E. Nybakken, *An Analytical Study of Horace's Ideas* [Iowa City, Iowa, 1937], p. 12).

5 In simple outline, this is not unlike the form of the ancient beast fable with its attached moral or unlike the bestiary tale with its appended *significatio*.

6 If the beginnings of Greek satire were not so completely lost to us, we should probably discover that the satirist in a less sophisticated age was akin to the magician, prophet, soothsayer, juggler, and buffoon with the sorcerer's power to wreak enormous destruction, as in early Germanic, early Irish, and early Arabic literatures. See F. N. Robinson, "Satirists and Enchanters in Early Irish Literature," *Studies in the History of Religions* (New York, 1912), pp. 95–130; and Mary Claire Randolph, "Celtic Smiths and Satirists: Partners in Sorcery," *ELH*, VIII (1941), 184–97; "The Medical Concept in English Renaissance Satiric

Theory: Its Possible Relationships and Implications," *Studies in Philology*, XXXVIII (1941), 127–59; and "Female Satirists of Ancient Ireland," SFQ, VI (1942), 75–87.

[7] Character-portraiture, the delineation of types by means of focus on the individual, is ever a forerunner or concomitant of satire. Theophrastian characters preceded classical satire; mediaeval type-portraiture preceded the gallery of satirical characters in Chaucer's *Prologue* (*ca.* 1387); vast quantities of such pictorial writing, e.g., *The Ship of Fools* (1509) and its numerous progeny, preceded Elizabethan formal satire; and the seventeenth-century characters were preliminary to the "timeless engravings" of Achitophel, Atticus, Sporus, and Atossa. Satiric efforts in the plastic arts and in portrait-painting, especially caricature, not infrequently flourish in an era of literary satire, e.g., Hogarth's serial "Progresses," *Marriage à la Mode, Gin Alley*, etc. See Thomas Wright, *History of Caricature and Grotesque in Literature and Art* (London, 1839), and F. G. Stephens, *Catalogue of Prints and Drawings in the British Museum* (London, 1870–79, 4 vols.), I.

[8] See Paul Lejay's Introduction (pp. vii-xxxii) to Horace's *Satires* (Paris, 1911); George Converse Fiske, *Lucilius and Horace: A Study in the Classical Theory of Imitation* (Madison, 1920), Chaps. II and III; Mary A. Grant, *The Ancient Rhetorical Theories of the Laughable: The Greek Rhetoricians and Cicero* (Madison, 1924), pp. 7–100; the numerous articles by J. Geffcken, George L. Hendrickson, and B. L. Ullman; and Nicola Terzaghi's recent work, *Per la storia della satira* (Turin, 1932), for extended research in the Hellenic backgrounds of Roman satire.

[9] Terzaghi, *op. cit.*, Part I, "Della Diatriba alla Satira," pp. 7–51. See also M. R. Heinze, *De Horatio Bionis imitatore* (Bonn, 1899); Lejay, *op. cit.*, pp. xv–xvi; and Archibald Y. Campbell, *Horace: A New Interpretation* (London, 1924), pp. 154–56.

[10] *Op. cit.*, pp. xlvii-lxxv.

[11] *Ibid.*, p. lx.

[12] The satiric picture, being negative, is usually heightened to increase the impact of the positive precept. Exaggeration downward, always preserving verisimilitude, however, is regarded as a legitimate artifice of the satirist. Precisely how much satiric exaggeration this side falsehood is justifiable is almost indeterminable. Swift, of course, uses exaggeration downward until it

has passed the line of verisimilitude into the realm of the False and thence beyond into the regions of Fantasia.

13 See C. W. Mendell, "Satire as Popular Philosophy," *Classical Philology*, XV (1920), 138–57. Mendell regards the satiric form as a sort of dilute, shortened, versified Platonic dialogue, a metrical descendant of the popular philosophic essay, a genre from the field of ethics, concerned with the science of behavior. See also B. L. Ullman, "Q. Horatius Flaccus, Ph.D., Professor of *Ethics*," *Classical Journal*, XIII (1917), 258–66; and J. Tate, "Horace and the Moral Function of Poetry," *Classical Quarterly*, XXII (1928), 65–72.

14 See G. L. Hendrickson, "Are the Letters of Horace Satires?" *American Jour. of Philology*, XVIII (1897), 313–24. The satires in Juvenal's last two books (IV and V) are really epistolary moral essays, each addressed to a friend, lacking dialogue, and almost lacking dramatization.

15 "The Satirist's Apologia," *Classical Studies*, Series II, University of Wisconsin Studies (Madison, 1922), 148–67. From its inception as a genre, satire has been apologetic and on the defensive, even occasionally regarded as outside the pale of respectability in some period, but ever justifying its sometimes questionable means by its impeccable, never-to-be-questioned ends. An outcast from Parnassus and under the protection of no Muse, Satire has ever eaten humble-pie and bowed to its betters.

16 In the 419-line dialogue, Arbuthnot the Adversarius speaks approximately a dozen lines, the usual proportion for the second figure. Pope's *Epistle* closely follows its Horatian model (II, i), but the whole piece has been pitched to a higher, sharper tone than in Horace, Boileau, or Swift.

17 Henry Guy, *Histoire de la Poésie française au moyen-âge* (Paris, 1910), pp. 69–70.

18 The *blason* was an exquisitely figured small satiric pattern, lavish in its detail, utilizing flowers, precious stones, parts of the feminine body, medicine, geography, politics, practically everything for subject matter, and concluding in some startling fashion. The *blason* had a tremendous vogue for a time. See Thomas Sebillet, *Art Poétique Françoys*, 1548, Chapitre X, "Du Blason, et de la définition, et déscription" (Gariffe edition, Paris, 1910), pp. 169–73.

19 Bauldet Herenc, *Le Doctrinal de la Seconde Rhétorique* (Langlois, III), and Jean Molinet, *L'art de Rhétorique vulgaire*

(Paris, 1493), quoted by Warner F. Patterson, *Three Centuries of French Poetic Theory* (Ann Arbor, 1935, 2 vols.), I, 123–24; 148–49.

[20] The four *coqs-à-l'âne* of Clément Marot (written 1535–36) are regarded as the most important predecessors of the formal verse satire in France. An agile cock (the satirist) holds a touch-and-go conversation with a stolid donkey (the Adversarius and in this instance the partial butt of the satire). The absurdity of the situation is its very essence: the Aesopic cock, deliberately speaking illogically and disjointedly, outwits the donkey with sprightly enigmas. The term in French satire means a hodge-podge composition in octosyllabic verse without proper transitions or connections, without any evident logic, jumping from one subject to another, the general confusion serving to conceal partially much sharp criticism not infrequently uncouth and vulgar. See my note, "The French *Coq-à-l'âne* as a Satiric Form," N. & Q, CLXXI (1941), 100–102.

[21] Boileau, technician first and moralist afterward, had broken Juvenal's *Third Satire* (on city noises, filth, traffic, thieves, etc.) into two parts, expanding them into his own full-fledged *First* ("Adieux d'un poète à la ville de Paris") and *Sixth* ("Embarras de Paris") *Satires*, and had similarly broken the conventionally stylized classical *apologia* into two parts, his own *Seventh* ("Le Genre satirique") and *Ninth* ("A son Esprit") *Satires*. Besides changing settings and names from Rome to Paris and adapting the Latin satires in other significant ways, he had chosen to unify his own pieces by writing the greater part of them around various aspects of a single thesis, a propaganda thesis—the inept writer and his output of mediocre or bad literature. (It has been noted that Joseph Hall may have had some such idea a century and a half earlier.)

[22] *The Works of John Dryden*, ed. Sir Walter Scott and George Saintsbury (Edinburgh, 1882–93, 18 vols.), XIII, 109; 112.

[23] *Ibid.*, pp. 109–10.

[24] *Ibid.*, pp. 110–11.

[25] *Loc. cit.*

[26] *Works*, ed. Scott-Saintsbury, XIII, 204; 111-12. See the "Argument" to the *First Satire* of Persius, *op. cit.*, XIII, 213.

[27] *Ibid.*, pp. 124, 135, 154, 214, 249.

[28] I hope to show in detail in a later paper the extent of Dryden's dependence on Casaubon, both directly by his own use of

Casaubon's great edition of Persius and indirectly by his reliance on Dacier's neat summary of Book I of the Huguenot editor's work. English scholars have erred in their failure to investigate the relationships existing between the Continental scholars, particularly those at Leyden, and the seventeenth-century satirists. [29] Since writing this paper, I have read and wish to note Professor Elizabeth H. Haight's urbane and competent volume, *The Roman Use of Anecdotes in Cicero, Livy, and the Satirists* (New York, 1940), an investigation into one aspect of the structure of the formal verse satire which is closely linked with much that I have said here.

MAYNARD MACK

The Muse of Satire

It grows plainer every year that literary study in our part of the twentieth century has been considerably stimulated by one important event. This event is the gradual reëmergence of rhetoric—by which I mean the reëmergence of a number of interpretive skills and assumptions about literature that under the name of rhetoric once formed part of the medieval trivium and together with grammar made up a study somewhat resembling what we now call literary explication. As we begin the second half of the century, the signs of this rhetorical quickening seem to me to be multiplying very fast.

To begin with a whimsical example, I notice that my reprint of Puttenham's "Arte of English Poesie" (1589), frequently on loan to students, is well thumbed chiefly at the twelve chapters where the rhetorical figures are named and illustrated. Forty-five years ago, when Gregory Smith reprinted Puttenham in his collection of "Elizabethan Critical Essays," these were precisely the chapters, and the only chapters, he chose to leave out. This is a straw in the wind from readers.

There is ampler evidence from writers. One might cite, at the level of research, the speedy proliferation of studies dealing with aspects of rhetorical history: investigations like J. W. H. Atkins' of classical, medieval, and Renaissance criticism, or T. W. Baldwin's of Shakespeare's grammar school training, or Miss Tuve's of sixteenth-century rhetorical manuals. At the level of practical criticism, one could point to the reappearance of rhetorical concepts in literary discourse. One hears the word *decorum* used nowadays without a sneer; one comes across mentions, though as yet no illuminating discussions, of the "three styles"—high, middle, and low; one even hears the admission that there may be something in genre: "Paradise Lost," Mr. C. S.

From *The Yale Review*, XLI (1951), 80–92. Copyright the Yale University Press. Reprinted by permission of the Yale University Press.

Lewis has been trying to persuade us, is what it is at least as much because it is a *heroic* poem as because it was written by John Milton.

But doubtless the climactic evidence at the critical level is the so-called—the so ineptly called—"new" criticism. The enormous influence of this body of writing can only be properly understood, I think, if we realize that it has been the pioneering phase—that is to say, the most applied and "practical" phase—in a general revival of rhetorical interests and disciplines. Evoked by the absence of a continuing tradition of rhetorical analysis (for the classical tradition was unfortunately discredited by the time the new critics began to write), this criticism has been an effort, often fumbling, often brilliant, to recapture some of the older exegetical skills, or at any rate to formulate their equivalents, for modern use.

Now rhetoric being a body of learning that insists on the recognition of artifice, one of the effects of its renascence is bound to be the reinvigoration of our sense of distinctions between art and life. If we compare ourselves with the nineteenth century in this respect, we realize that we no longer write, or care to read, books like Mrs. Cowden Clarke's on "The Girlhood of Shakespeare's Heroines" (1850–52); nor do we care to inquire, even with so great a critic as A. C. Bradley, where Hamlet was when his father was being murdered, or with Ellen Terry, how the Boy in Henry V learned French: "Did he learn to speak the lingo from Prince Hal, or from Falstaff in London, or did he pick it up during his few weeks in France with the army?" We realize, too, that unlike the nineteenth century we can no longer speak of Shakespeare's "Dark Period" or his "Joyous Comedies," except by enclosing the words in quotation marks. We acknowledge, to be sure, that a playwright and his plays are involved with each other in important ways, but we are much too conscious of artifice to be willing to risk a direct reading from comedy or tragedy to the author's states of mind.

In our dealings with the drama, in fact, most of us are now willing to add to the study of how a work grows or what it does the study of what it is. Inquiries into biographical and historical origins, or into effects on audiences and readers, can and should be supplemented, we are beginning to insist, by a third kind of inquiry treating the work with some strictness as a rhetorical construction: as a "thing made," which, though it reaches backward to an author and forward to an audience, has its artistic identity in between—in the realm of artifice and artifact. With respect to drama, there has lately been building a valuable even if by no means uniformly sound criticism of this kind. But outside the drama, and a few other areas recently invaded, we cannot point to very much. On the subject of poetry in general, Mr. Ricardo Quintana has complained, most of our commentary still "turns out to be either description of our impressions" (i.e., effects), "or reconstruction—largely imaginary—of a precise moment in the poet's emotional history with which we have chosen to equate the poem" (i.e., origins).

One need not share Mr. Quintana's doubt as to the effectiveness of other approaches to feel that in the case of satire, at any rate, what is desperately needed today is inquiry that deals neither with origins nor effects, but with artifice. Criticism of satiric literature has barely begun to budge from the position of Macaulay, Elwin, Leslie Stephen—all of whom seem, at one time or another, to have regarded it as a kind of dark night of the soul (dank with poisonous dews) across which squibs of envy, malice, hate, and spite luridly explode. Here is a sample from 1880, referring to Pope's "Sporus": "that infusion of personal venom"; "the poet is writing under some bitter mortification"; he is "trying with concentrated malice to sting his adversary"; he is "a tortured victim screaming out the shrillest taunts at his tormentor" (Sir Leslie Stephen). Here is a sample from 1925, referring to Pope's epistles and satires in general: at the time of their creation, "they resembled nothing so much as spoonsful of boiling oil, ladled out by a fiendish monkey at an upstairs window upon such of the passers-by whom the wretch had a grudge against" (Lytton Strachey). And here is a sample from 1941, referring to the "Dunciad" —if anything the tone is shriller: "impossible to admire it without an unenviable pleasure in sheer spite"; "the tone of furious indiscriminate hatred"; "the half-crazed misanthropy of the whole poem"; "a general indictment of the human race"; "this universal shriek of loathing and despair" (Gilbert Highet).

In this essay, I should like to ventilate this fetid atmosphere a little by opening a window on one or two rhetorical observations. These observations will be commonplaces, but the record suggests that they can bear repetition. My illustrations will be drawn from Pope, especially from his formal satires, such as the "Epistle to Dr. Arbuthnot"; and my thesis will be that even in these apparently very personal poems, we overlook what is most essential if we overlook the distinction between the historical Alexander Pope and the dramatic Alexander Pope who speaks them.

It is to underscore this distinction that I have ventured in my title to name the Muse. For the Muse ought always to be our reminder that it is not the author as man who casts these shadows on our printed page, but the author as poet: an instrument possessed by and possessing—Plato would have said a god, we must at any rate say an art. And, moreover, the Muse ought to remind us that in any given instance the shadow may not delineate even the whole poet, but perhaps only that angle of his sensibility which best refracts the light from epic, elegy, pastoral, lyric, satire. The fact is not without significance, it seems to me, that though Pope, following the great victories of naturalism in the seventeenth century, had to make do with a minimum of mythology and myth, he never discarded the Muse, either the conception or the term. She appears with remarkable regularity even in his satires, and there, for my present purposes, I am choosing to regard her as a not entirely playful symbol of the impersonality of the satiric genre—of its rhetorical and dramatic character.

Rhetorically considered, satire belongs to the category of *laus et vituperatio*, praise and blame. It aims, like all poetry, in Sidney's phrase, through the "fayning notable images of vertues [and] vices," to achieve "that delightful teaching which must be the right describing note to know a Poet by." And it has, of course, its own distinctive means to this. Prominent among them to a casual eye is the *exemplum* in the form of portrait, like Dryden's Zimri or Pope's Atticus; and the middle style, which stresses conversational speech (more than passion or grandiloquence) along with aphoristic phrasings, witty turns, and ironical indirections. Less prominent but more important than either of these is the satiric fiction into which such materials must be built.

All good satire, I believe it is fair to say, exhibits an appreciable degree of fictionality. Where the fiction inheres in familiar elements like plot, as in "Absalom and Achitophel" or "The Rape of the Lock" or "The Dunciad" or "The Beggar's Opera," its presence is, of course, unmistakable; and it is unmistakable, too, in such satires as Swift's "Argument against Abolishing Christianity" or his "Modest Proposal," where the relation of the speaker to the author is extremely oblique, not to say antithetical. But when the relation is only slightly oblique, as in Pope's formal satires, the fictionality takes subtler forms and resides in places where, under the influence of romantic theories of poetry as the spontaneous overflow of powerful emotions, we have become unaccustomed to attend to it. (How far unaccustomed is seen if we reflect that the extraordinary views of Gulliver in Houyhnhnm-land have been repeatedly cited as identical with Swift's. And this despite the fact that the incidents of the book show the author to be studiedly undercutting his hero-gull and to be using the metaphor of the rational *animal*, the Houyhnhnm, to make it plain that pure rationality is neither available nor appropriate to the human species— just as in the "Essay on Man" Pope's fully rational angels show "a Newton as we show an Ape.")

One aspect of the fictionality in Pope's case resides in the general plan of the formal satiric poem. This, as Miss Randolph has observed in the work of Horace, Persius, and Juvenal, contains always two layers. There is a thesis layer attacking vice and folly, elaborated with every kind of rhetorical device, and, much briefer, an antithesis layer illustrating or implying a philosophy of rational control, usually embodied in some more or less ideal norm like the Stoic *vir bonus*, the good plain man. The contours of a formal verse satire, in other words, are not established entirely or even principally by a poet's rancorous sensibility; they are part of a fiction.

We encounter a further aspect of this fiction when we pause to consider that the bipartite structure just mentioned apparently exists to reflect a more general fictive situation. This situation is the warfare of good and evil—differentiated in satire from the forms it might take in, say, lyric, by being viewed from the angle of social solidarity rather than private introspection; and from the forms it might take in, say, tragedy, by being carried on in a context that asserts the primacy of moral decision, as tragedy asserts the primacy of moral understanding.

Tragedy and satire, I suspect, are two ends of a literary spectrum. Tragedy tends to exhibit the inadequacy of norms, to dissolve systematized values, to precipitate a meaning containing—but not necessarily contained by—recognizable ethical codes. Satire, on the contrary, asserts the validity and necessity of norms, systematic values, and meanings that *are* contained by recognizable codes. Where tragedy fortifies the sense of irrationality and complexity in experience because it presents us a world in which man is more victim than agent, in which our commodities prove to be our defects (and vice versa), and in which blindness and madness are likely to be symbols of insight, satire tends to fortify our feeling that life makes more immediate moral sense. In the world it offers us, madness and blindness are usually the emblems of vice and folly, evil and good are clearly distinguishable, criminals and fools are invariably responsible (therefore censurable), and standards of judgment are indubitable. All this, too, results from a slant of the glass, a fictional perspective on the real world—which, as we know, does not wholly correspond either with the tragic outlook or the satiric one.

Finally, we must note, among these general and pervasive aspects of fictionality in satire, the *ethos* of the satirist. Classical rhetoric, it is well to recall, divides the persuasive elements in any communication from one man to another into three sorts: the force of the arguments employed, the appeal to the interest and emotions of the hearer, and the weight of authority that comes from the hearer's estimate of the speaker's character, his *ethos*. For the satirist especially, the establishment of an authoritative *ethos* is imperative. If he is to be effective in "that delightful teaching," he must be accepted by his audience as a fundamentally virtuous and tolerant man, who challenges the doings of other men not whenever he happens to feel vindictive, but whenever they deserve it. On this account, the satirist's *apologia* for his satire is one of the stock subjects of both the classical writers and Pope: the audience must be assured that its censor is a man of good will, who has been, as it were, *forced* into action. *Difficile est saturam non scribere:* "It is difficult *not* to write satire."

Moreover, the satirist's *ethos* is the *rhetorical* occasion (even though vanity may be among the *motives*) of his frequent citations of himself. As a candid fellow, for instance, and no pretender to be holier than thou:

> I love to pour out all myself, as plain
> As downright Shippen, or as old Montaigne....
> In me what Spots, (for Spots I have) appear,
> Will prove at least the Medium must be clear.

A man, too, of simple tastes, persistent loyalties:

> Content with little, I can piddle here
> On Broccoli and mutton, round the Year;
> But ancient friends, (tho' poor, or out of play)
> That touch my Bell, I cannot turn away.

A man whose character was formed in the good old-fashioned way by home instruction and edifying books:

> Bred up at home, full early I begun
> To read in Greek, the Wrath of Peleus' Son.

> Besides, My Father taught me from a Lad,
> The better Art, to know the good from bad.

Consequently, a man who honors the natural pieties:

> Me, let the tender Office long engage
> To rock the Cradle of reposing Age:

who is sensible of life's true ends:

> Farewell then Verse, and Love, and ev'ry Toy,
> The rhymes and rattles of the Man or Boy,
> What right, what true, what fit, we justly call,
> Let this be all my Care—for this is All:

and who is valued by distinguished friends. If the friends happen to be out of power, or drawn in part from a vanished Golden Age, so much the better for *ethos*: our satirist is guaranteed to be no time-server.

> But does the Court a worthy Man remove?
> That instant, I declare, he has my love.
> I shun his Zenith, court his mild Decline;
> Thus Sommers once, and Halifax were mine.
> Oft in the clear, still Mirrour of Retreat
> I study'd Shrewsbury, the wise and great....
> How pleasing Atterbury's softer hour!
> How shin'd the Soul, unconquer'd in the Tow'r!
> How can I Pult'ney, Chesterfield forget
> While Roman Spirit charms, and Attic Wit?...
> Names which I long have lov'd, nor lov'd in vain,
> Rank'd with their Friends, not number'd with their Train.

By passages of this kind in Pope's satires, the rhetorically innocent are habitually distressed. They remark with surprise that Pope insists on portraying himself in these poems as "lofty, good-humored, calm, disinterested." Or they grow indignant that an epistle like "Arbuthnot" reveals "not what Pope really was, but what he wished others to think him." They fail to notice that he speaks this way only in a certain kind of poem, and so enlarge irrelevantly—though to be sure with biographical truth enough—upon the subject of his vanity. Meantime, on a rhetorical view, the real point remains, which is simply that in passages of this sort, as also in his notes to the "Dunciad," and probably, to some extent, in the publication of his letters (both these enterprises, significantly, accompanied his turning satirist), Pope felt the necessity of supporting the *ethos* a satirical poet must have.

Obviously, the two agents to be considered in the fictive situation are the person speaking and the person addressed. We may, however, dismiss the second, for though he is often a true *adversarius*—a friend calculated like Job's friends to be egregiously mistaken in his views and values—no one, I think, has ever seriously misinterpreted a satire because he failed to see that the *adversarius* was a fiction. It is with the satiric speaker that the difficulty has come. We may call this speaker Pope, if we wish, but only if we remember that he always reveals himself as a character in a drama, not as a man confiding in us. The distinction is apparent if we think of Wordsworth's use of the word *young* in a famous passage from "The Prelude" about the early days of the French Revolution: "Bliss was it in that dawn to be alive, And to be young was very heaven"—and then compare it with Pope's remark to the friend with whom he professes to be conversing in the first dialogue of the "Epilogue to the Satires": "Dear Sir, forgive the Prejudice of Youth." Wordsworth's *young* is determined by something outside the poem, something true (in the years to which the poet refers) of himself in real life. But in real life, when Pope wrote his dialogue, he was already fifty; his *youth* is true only of the satiric speaker of the poem, who is an assumed identity, a *persona*.

This *persona* or speaker has almost always in Pope's formal satires three distinguishable voices. One is the voice of the man I have partly described in connection with *ethos*: the man of plain living, high thinking, lasting friendships; who hates lies, slanders, lampoons; who laughs at flatteries of himself; who is "soft by Nature, more a Dupe than Wit"; who loves of all things best "the Language of the Heart"; and who views his own poetry with amused affection qualified with Virgilian tenderness for the tears of things in general:

> Years foll'wing Years, steal something ev'ry day,
> At last they steal us from ourselves away;
> In one our Frolicks, one Amusements end,
> In one a Mistress drops, in one a Friend:
> This subtle Thief of Life, this paltry Time,
> What will it leave me, if it snatch my Rhime?

Then, secondly, there is the voice of the *naïf*, the *ingénu*, the simple heart: "the Prejudice of Youth." The owner of this voice is usually the vehicle of ironies about matters he professes not to understand, and is amazed by his own involvement in the literary arts. "I lisp'd in Numbers, for the Numbers came"—says this voice, speaking of one of the most carefully meditated poetries in literature. Or else: "Why did I write? What sin to me unknown Dipt me in Ink...?" To the owner of this voice, his proficiency in satire is particularly puzzling. Should it be explained as the by-product of insomnia?

> I nod in Company, I wake at Night,
> Fools rush into my Head, and so I write;

a scheme of personal defense like jiujitsu?

> Satire's my weapon...
> Its proper pow'r to hurt each Creature feels,
> Bulls aim their Horns, and Asses lift their Heels;

or is it a species of harmless madness, a kind of psychosomatic twitch that nothing short of death will stop?

> Whether the darken'd Room to Muse invite,
> Or whiten'd Wall provoke the Skew'r to write,
> In Durance, Exile, Bedlam, or the Mint,
> Like Lee and Budgell, I will Rhyme and Print.

Pope's third voice is that of the public defender. If the first voice gives us the satirist as *vir bonus*, the plain good private citizen, and the second, the satirist as *ingénu*, this one brings us the satirist as hero. A peculiar tightening in the verse takes place whenever this *persona* begins to speak, whether he speaks of the mysterious purposes of

> That God of Nature, who, within us still,
> Inclines our Action, not constrains our Will;

or of the time when

> Inexorable Death shall level all,
> And Trees, and Stones, and Farms, and Farmer fall;

or of his own calling:

> Yes, I am proud; I must be proud to see
> Men not afraid of God, afraid of me.

The satirist as *vir bonus* was content to laugh at flatteries, but the satirist as hero feels differently:

> Fr. This filthy Simile, this beastly Line,
> Quite turns my Stomach—P. So does Flatt'ry mine;
> And all your Courtly Civet Cats can vent,
> Perfume to you, to me is Excrement.

Similarly, the satirist as *ingénu* chose to find the motives of satire in a nervous reflex; the satirist as hero has other views:

> O sacred Weapon! left for Truth's defence,
> Sole dread of Folly, Vice, and Insolence!
> To all but Heav'n-directed hands deny'd,
> The Muse may give thee, but the Gods must guide.

Without pretending that these are the only voices Pope uses, or that they are always perfectly distinguishable, we may observe that the total dramatic development of any one of his formal satires is to a large extent determined by the way they succeed one another, modulate and qualify one another, and occasionally fuse with one another. In a poem like Pope's imitation of the first satire of Horace's second book, the structure is in a very real sense no more than a function of the modulations in tone that it takes to get from the opening verses, where the *naïf* shows up with his little slingshot and his five smooth pebbles from the brook:

> Tim'rous by Nature, of the Rich in awe,
> I come to Council learned in the Law;

through the point, about a hundred lines later, at which we realize that this fellow has somehow got Goliath's head in his hand (and also, the hero's accents in his voice):

> Hear this, and tremble! you, who 'scape the Laws.
> Yes, while I live, no rich or noble knave
> Shall walk the World, in credit, to his grave;

then back down past a window opening on the unimpeachable integrity of the *vir bonus,* instanced in his ties with men whom it is no longer fashionable to know: "Chiefs, out of War, and Statesmen, out of Place"; and so, finally, to a reassumption of the voice of the *ingénu,* surprised and pained that he should be thought to have any but the noblest aims. "Libels and Satires!" he exclaims, on learning the category into which his poems are thrust—"lawless things indeed!"

> But grave Epistles, bringing Vice to light,
> Such as a King might read, a Bishop write,
> Such as Sir Robert would approve————?

Indeed? says the friend; well, to be sure, *that's* different: "you may then proceed."

Though the construction in Pope's satires is by no means always so schematic as in this example, it seems almost invariably to invoke the three voices of the *naïf,* the *vir bonus,* and the hero. And their presence need not perhaps surprise us, if we pause to consider that they sum up, between them, most of what is essential in the satirist's position. As *naïf,* the satirist educates us. He makes us see the ulcer where we were accustomed to see the rouge. He is the child in the fairy story forever crying, "But mamma, the king *is* naked." As *vir bonus,* on the other hand, he wins our confidence in his personal moral insight. He shows us that he is stable, independent, urbane, wise—a man who knows there is a time to laugh, a time to weep: "Who would not weep, if Atticus were he?" And finally, as hero, he opens to us a world where the discernment of evil is always accompanied, as it is not always in the real world, by the courage to strike at it. He invites us, in an excellent phrase of Mr. Bredvold's, to join "the invisible church of good men" everywhere, "few though they may be—for whom things matter." And he never lets us forget that we *are* at war; there *is* an enemy.

We should never have made, I think, so many mistakes about a portrait like "Sporus" if we had grasped the fact that it is primarily a portrait of the enemy (one of the finest Pope ever drew), evoked in a particular context at a particular point. We know, of course, that the lines were based on Pope's contemporary, Lord Hervey, whom he passionately disliked; and therefore we may justly infer that personal animus entered powerfully into their motivation.

But to read with this animus as our center of interest is to overlook the fact that, though the lines may be historically about Hervey, they are rhetorically about the enemy. It is to fail to see that they sum up in an *exemplum* (of which the implications become very pointed in the references to Satan) the fundamental attributes of the invader in every garden: his specious attractiveness—as a butterfly, a painted child, a dimpling stream; his nastiness—as a bug, a creature generated in dirt, a thing that stinks and stings, a toad spitting froth and venom; his essential impotence—as a mumbling spaniel, a shallow stream, a puppet, a hermaphrodite; and yet his perpetual menace as the tempter, powerless himself but always lurking "at the ear of Eve," as Pope puts it, to usurp the powers of good and pervert them. Because the lines associate Sporus with Evil in this larger sense, his portrait can be the ladder by which Pope mounts, in the evolution of the epistle as a whole, from the studiedly personal impatience of the pestered private citizen in the opening lines: " 'Shut, shut the door, good John!' fatigu'd I said," to the impersonal trumpet tones of the public defender on the walls of *Civitas Dei*—"Welcome for thee, fair Virtue, all the past." Without Sporus prostrate on the field behind him, the satiric speaker could never have supported this heroic tone. Something pretty close to the intensity exhibited by this portrait was called for, at just this point, not by the poet's actual feelings about a contemporary, but by the drama of feelings that has been building inside the poem— the fictive war—"the strong Antipathy of Good to Bad," here projected in its climactic symbol.

W. H. AUDEN

Satire

THE OBJECT OF SATIRE

The comic butt of satire is a person who, though in possession of moral faculties, transgresses the moral law beyond the normal call of temptation.

Thus the lunatic cannot be an object for satire because he is not responsible for his actions, nor can the devilish be an object because, while responsible, he lacks the normal faculty of conscience.

Any person who causes serious suffering to the innocent partakes of the devilish and is the object, not of satire, but of prophetic denunication. For example, a black marketeer in sugar is satirizable because the existence of such a black market depends upon the greed of others and to do without sugar is not a serious suffering; a black marketeer in penicillin is not satirizable because those who need it are innocent and, if they cannot pay his prices, die.

The mere fact of transgressing the moral law is not enough to make a person the object of satire, for all men do so, but the average man's transgression is tempered by various considerations, conscience, prudence, reason, competing desires. Most men, for example, desire wealth and are sometimes unscrupulous in their means of obtaining it, but their desire is tempered by laziness. A miser is satirizable because his desire for money overrides all other desires, such as a desire for physical comfort or love for his family. The commonest object of satire is a monomaniac.

From "Notes on the Comic," in *Thought*, XXVII (Spring 1952), 66–69. Copyright 1952 by W. H. Auden. Reprinted in *The Dyer's Hand and Other Essays*, New York, 1962, London, 1963, pp. 383–85. Reprinted by permission of Random House, Inc., New York, and Faber & Faber, Ltd., London.

THE SATIRICAL STRATEGY

There is not only a moral norm but also a normal way of transgressing it. At the moment of yielding to temptation, the normal human being has to exercise self-deception and rationalization, he requires the illusion of acting with a good conscience; after the immoral act, when desire is satisfied or absent, he realizes the nature of his act and feels guilty. He who feels no guilt after transgressing the moral law is mad, and he who, at the moment he is transgressing it, is completely conscious of what he is doing is demonic.

The two commonest satirical devices, therefore, are as follows:

1) to present the object of satire *as if* he or she were mad, i.e., as unaware of the nature of his act.

> Now Night descending, the proud scene was o'er,
> But liv'd in Settle's numbers, one day more.
> > —Pope

The writing of poetry which, even in the case of the worst poets, is a personal and voluntary act is presented as if it were as impersonal and necessary as the revolution of the earth, and the value of the poems produced which, even in a bad poet, varies, is presented as invariable and therefore subject to a quantitative measurement like dead matter.

The satiric effect presupposes that we know that Settle in real life is not a certifiable lunatic for real lunacy overcomes a man against his will; Settle is, as it were, a self-made lunatic.

2) To present the object of satire *as if* he or she were demonic, i.e., completely conscious.

> Although, dear Lord, I am a sinner,
> I have done no major crime;
> Now I'll come to Evening Service
> > Whensoever I have time.
> So, Lord, reserve for me a crown,
> And do not let my shares go down.
> > —John Betjeman

Again, the satiric effect depends upon our knowing that in real life the lady is not wicked, for if she really were as truthful with herself as she is presented, she could not go into a Christian church but would have to attend the Temple of Mammon, and become a formidable criminal.

Satire flourishes in a homogeneous society with a common conception of the moral law, for satirist and audience must agree as to how normal people can be expected to behave, and in times of relative stability and contentment, for satire cannot deal with serious evil and suffering. In an age like our own it cannot flourish except in private circles as an expression of private feuds; in public life, the serious evils are so importunate that satire seems trivial and the only suitable kind of attack prophetic denunciation.

ROBERT C. ELLIOTT

The Satirist
and Society

Two cripples, characters in Yeats' play *The King's Threshold* (1904),
speak:

> SECOND CRIPPLE. If I were the King I wouldn't meddle with
> him [Seanchan, Chief Poet of Ireland in the seventh century];
> there is something queer about a man that makes rhymes. I knew
> a man that would be making rhymes year in and year out under
> a thorn at the crossing of three roads, and he was no sooner dead
> than every thorn-tree from Inchy to Kiltartan withered, and he
> a ragged man like ourselves.
>
> FIRST CRIPPLE. Those that make rhymes have a power from
> beyond the world.

The central notion here is clearly that of the artist as magician—as
one set apart by reason of his gift, one to be regarded with awe, with
reverence and with fear. The notion is not uncommon and in some
respects survives today: "People speak with justice," says Freud, "of
the 'magic of art' and compare artists with magicians. . . ." But Yeats'
lines have a special application; in the play Seanchan is presented as a
symbolic figure: he is The Artist, heroically prepared to die in defense
of the ancient right of the poets. The Middle Irish tale from which
Yeats took the episode, however, presents Seanchan as a particular
kind of artist: he is a satirist, well known for his magical powers, best
known, in fact, as a forerunner of The Pied Piper of Hamlin.[1] In a

From *ELH: A Journal of English Literary History*, XXI (Sept. 1954),
237–48. Reprinted by permission of the Johns Hopkins University
Press. In a greatly revised form, this essay appeared in Elliott's *Power
of Satire* (1960, see below).

fit of pique Seanchan satirized certain mice who had stolen his food;
his riddling verses end:

> You mice, which are in the roof of the house,
> Arise all of you, and fall down.

Ten mice plopped down dead at his feet. There is no mistaking the
magic; and in view of the tradition behind Seanchan (comic as it is)
the remarks of the Cripples in Yeats' play open up richly ambiguous
areas of meaning.

The poet-satirists of Old Ireland were all magicians; they all
had, at least potentially, "a power from beyond the world"; and so
did other, non-Irish satirists. The historical fact has implications for
the forms satire takes, for the language it uses, and, I believe, for
the relation of satirist (ancient and modern) to society.

I

In the *Poetics* Aristotle declares that the earliest division of
poetry occurred when the "graver spirits imitated noble actions, and
the actions of good men" while the "more trivial sort imitated the
actions of meaner persons, at first composing satires, as the former did
hymns to the gods and the praises of famous men." The lampooners
became writers of Comedy, and the Epic poets writers of Tragedy.
"Tragedy—as also Comedy—[he says] was at first mere improvisation.
The one originated with the leaders of the dithyramb, the other with
those of the phallic songs, which are still in use in many of our cities."
Old Comedy then developed, according to Aristotle, out of "satire,"
specifically out of satiric improvisations uttered by the Leaders of the
Phallic Songs. Modern scholars, particularly the classical anthropologists Jane Harrison and F. M. Cornford, have shown in detail how
that development must have taken place. The Phallic Songs were, of
course, ritual performances devoted to increasing the fertility of the
land, the herds, and the people. The ritual seems to have had two
general parts: the invocation of good through the magic influence of
the phallus, and the expulsion of evil by means of the magic power
of satire, invective, lampoon—this last improvised by the Leaders of
the Songs. In the apotropaic part of the ritual the satire might be
hurled at wicked individuals by name or at evil influences generally;

but for our purposes the important consideration is that the satire was thought to be magically efficacious. It was a coercion of certain natural forces through the magical potency of the word.

Here, in this much simplified account of a primitive ritual, is the first indication that in the beginning "satire" is inextricably involved with magic. There is much supporting evidence.

For example, Archilochus, the almost legendary "inventor" of the iambic measure—he flourished in the seventh century B.C.—was thought to have wielded more than natural power in his invectives against his enemies. Archilochus was betrothed to the daughter of Lycambes. For some reason Lycambes broke "the great oath made by salt and table" (as Archilochus says in one of the surviving fragments) and refused to allow the marriage. Archilochus composed iambics of such terrible virulence, or of such uncanny power, that Lycambes and his daughter hanged themselves. A similar story is told of the sixth-century Hipponax, whose iambics, it is said, drove the sculptors Bupalis and Athenis to suicide. We can account for these stories only by recognizing the wide-spread belief from which they spring—the belief, as the classical scholar G. L. Hendrickson puts it, in "the destructive, supernatural power of words of ill-omened invective or imprecation. . . ."

Similar beliefs existed in other cultures. The ancient Arabic satirist, for example, was the seer, the oracle of his tribe. His enormous prestige derived from his role as magician, for his primary function was to compose magical satires, thought always to be fatal, against the tribal enemy. The Arabs thought of their satires concretely as weapons, and as the satirist led his people into battle—his hair anointed on one side only, his mantle hanging loose, shod with only one sandal —he would hurl his magical verses at the foe just as he would hurl a spear; and indeed the satires might be dodged, just as a spear could be dodged, by ducking and bobbing and skipping off.

The most impressive mass of evidence for the early connection of satire and magic, however, exists in the sagas and tales of pre-Christian and early Christian Ireland. Over forty years ago F. N. Robinson brilliantly demonstrated that, in Old Irish society, poetic invective, mockery, and magical malediction were inseparably bound together. The ancient Celtic poet, like his Arabic counterpart, was a seer, his almost unlimited privilege and power deriving unmistakably from his command over preternatural forces. Irish poet-satirists were called upon to levy taxes in areas where, presumably, the sword had proved ineffective as a means of collection—where, as the old laws put it, "points of satire" were regarded, but "points of weapons" were not. The most solemn treaties invoked the satirist's power as a threat to those who might think of violation. And in warfare the satirist had a proudly, even crucially, significant role; witness this brief dialogue from the saga of *The Second Battle of Moytura*:

> "And thou, O Carpre, son of Etain," saith [King] Lugh to his poet, "what power can *you* wield in battle?"
> "Not hard to say," quoth Carpre. "I will make a *glam dicinn*[2] on them. And I will satirize them and shame them, so that through the spell of my art they will not resist warriors."

For these and other public services the Celtic poets were extravagantly rewarded.

Important as the satirist may have been, however, in defending and supporting and holding together the social order, his public role was overshadowed, in ancient legend, at any rate, by his individualistic, almost anarchic practices. Possessed of dreadful power, he exercised it ruthlessly. For example, the poet Nede, prompted by the basest motives, pronounced a satire against his uncle the King; the satire raised three blisters (marks of dreadful shame) on the King's cheek. He fled into hiding, and when a year later Nede found him, the King fell dead of shame at his feet. Certainly the worst of many predatory satirists was Aithirne the Importunate who roamed Ireland from kingdom to kingdom, exacting fantastic levies wherever he went. The one-eyed King Eochaid offered Aithirne whatever his people had of jewels and treasures to buy off the threatened satires. " 'There is, forsooth,' said Aithirne, 'the single eye there in thy head, to be given to me into my fist. . . .' So then the King put his finger under his eye, and tore it out of his head and gave it into Aithirne's fist." Of the King of Munster Aithirne demanded permission to sleep with his wife on the night that she was to give birth to a child. The Queen acceded "for the sake of her husband's honour, that his honour might not be taken away." The people of Leinster came out to meet Aithirne, offering him enormous gifts of jewels and treasures so that he would not leave invectives in their land. Aithirne departed from Leinster with a magic jewel and thrice fifty wives of the princes and nobles. It is something of a satisfaction to record that Aithirne finally came to a bad end. A satire that he had directed at Luaine, beloved of Conchobar, raised the familiar three blisters on her face and caused the girl to die of shame. Conchobar and the Ulstermen walled Aithirne the Importunate up in a fortress and burned the place about his ears.

Some of the great Celtic satirists of legend were able through the magic of their malefic verse to blight the fertility of the land itself —a curious reversal here of the function of satire in the fertility rituals of ancient Greece. For a whole year, it is said, Laidcenn, chief poet of Niall of the Nine Hostages, "kept satirizing and lampooning the men of Leinster . . . so that neither grass nor corn grew with them, nor a leaf, to the end of a year." That satirists could rhyme rats to death, following on Seanchan's lead, was a commonplace belief, well known later to Elizabethan writers; Shakespeare and Sydney refer to it, and Ben Jonson, with specific reference to the legendary powers of satire, writes:

> I could doe worse,
> Arm'd with Archilochus' fury, write Iambicks,
> Should make the desperate lashers hang themselves,
> Rime 'hem to death, as they doe Irish rats
> In drumming tunes. . . .

Still later Sir William Temple, Swift, and Pope are familiar with the tradition, which seems, indeed, to have flourished among the Irish folk well into the nineteenth century. Yeats exploits the mythic associations of the belief in these magnificently bitter lines from "Parnell's Funeral" (1934):

> Come, fix upon me that accusing eye.
> I thirst for accusation. All that was sung,
> All that was said in Ireland is a lie
> Bred out of the contagion of the throng,
> Saving the rhyme rats hear before they die.

One is tempted to tell more tales; but at this point a crucial problem must be faced: is there justification for adopting the translators' usage and calling the kind of magical imprecation discussed above "satire?" I am convinced that a genetic relation exists between magical invective and literary satire, but it would be impossible to explore that relation fully here. There are these facts, however, which Professor Robinson has noted (except for the matter of linguistic continuity, which is a special problem, they apply to the Greek material as well as to the Irish) : the Irish language employs the same words for the incantatory lines of say, Aithirne, as for the literary satire of a later age. The makers of these lines were not mere enchanters, they were poets, *filid*, either historical or legendary, and part of their function as poets was to produce this kind of verse. They frequently attack the same vices as do the later satirists: inhospitality, stinginess, etc. Finally, and very important, their announced method, like that of later satirists, is to ridicule their victims and to shame them.[3] These lines from a fragment of Archilochus are of interest in this connection:

> "Father Lycambes, what, pray, is this thou hast imagined? Who hath perverted the wits thou wast endowed with? Thou seem'st matter for much laughter to thy fellows now."

This evidence seems adequate, at least provisionally, to establish the central point: in its early manifestations in Greece, Arabia, and Ireland satire is intimately connected with magic and the satirist hardly distinguishable from the magician.

II

The magician has always and everywhere been the focus of strong and conflicting feelings on the part of his society. In so far as he uses his great powers to enhance the well-being of society—defending it from its enemies, coercing the powers of Nature into favorable performance, enriching the inner life of society through ritualistic ceremony, etc.—he is honored and revered. Magic, according to Malinowski, "is one of the means of carrying on the established order [and] is in its turn strengthened by [that order]." But the very fact that the socially approved practices of the magician are made possible by the exercise of supernatural power implies a complementary danger. For the powers of the magician are only in a very limited sense amenable to social control; in them is potentiality for benefit, but also for danger, both social and personal. The magician is at once prop and threat to society and to each individual. Consequently, the relation of the magician to society is always colored by the ambivalent emotional attitudes generated by this knowledge. Clearly the situation of the satirist-magician is very similar. His satire may be incorporated into ritual, as in the Phallic Songs, and thus contribute materially to the social cohesiveness which it is one of the functions of ritual to bring about. Or it may be employed in straightforward and warlike defense of his tribe against threat from without. The satirist may even partake of a partial divinity, as did Archilochus, who was destined from birth to be immortal. The man who killed Archilochus in battle was banished from the temple of Apollo for having slain "a servitor of the Muses," and there is some evidence that at his death Archilochus became the center of a cult on his native island of Paros. In these situations the satirist unquestionably inspires emotions of honor and respect and awe. But in other, and possibly more characteristic roles, the satirist becomes the object of fear and hate; as testimony we have many legends where the fear is expressed either directly or symbolically, and we have the evidence of ancient law. Plato proposes legal measures against magical incantations (which would include magical satire); the Roman Twelve Tables invoke the death penalty for defamatory and libelous verse (which was thought to be magically efficacious); and the Irish laws are full of specific injunctions against satire. These latter, however, distinguish between lawful and unlawful satire and provide rewards for "good" satire and punishments for "bad." Here are codified, in legal formulas, the ambivalent attitudes of a society toward its satirists.

When we move from the realm of magic and blisters and incantatory death onto the more familiar ground of literary satire, we must expect some change in the relations of satirist to society. The satirist is no longer a medicine man—half in society and half out, as he mediates between his people and higher powers; his mantic function has been pre-empted by the priest, and the focus of interest in his poetic utterance shifts from concern for its magic potency to concern for aesthetic value. Only in this way can the magic invective of an heroic folk society develop into literary art. Cassirer's statement, in the brilliant final chapter of *Language and Myth*, is precisely to this point, although he happens here to be speaking of pictorial art: "The image ...achieves its purely representative, specifically 'aesthetic' function only as the magic circle with which mythical consciousness surrounds it is broken, and it is recognized not as a mythico-magical form, but as a particular sort of *formulation*."[4] In short, the satirist becomes, instead of a seer, a "mere" poet, writing, as he frequently confesses, in an inferior genre. The distinction is well pointed up by contrasting the magnificent confidence of power of Carpre, whose satire would render the enemy incapable of resisting warriors, with Horace's account to Augustus of the poet's function. "Though he is no hero in the field [says Horace], the poet is of use to the State, if you grant that even by small things great ends are helped." No matter how much the characteristic wry understatement discounts the literal meaning, it is a mighty falling off. But even granting the changed modes of belief and the relatively inferior status of the poet, it is still possible to see in the relationship of the satirist to a more sophisticated society some reflection of the ambiguities we have been considering.

At any rate the law continued to pay close heed to the satirist, and from Horace's day to our own the satirist has skated on the thin edge of censorship and legal retribution. It was forbidden for a time to print satires at all in Elizabethan England; and in totalitarian states today the satirists are among the first to be silenced. This relation with the law has itself been of considerable importance in determining the forms that satire will take and the methods it will use. Freud perhaps throws some light here; he notes that society has progressively stifled our hostile impulses, first by prohibiting the expression of our antagonisms in direct physical action, then by prohibiting violent personal assault in language. But the hostile feelings remain, says Freud, and in order to surmount the restrictions imposed by society, we have developed a new technique of verbal assault—a technique which employs wit. "Wit," writes Freud, "permits us to make our enemy ridiculous through that which we could not utter loudly or consciously on account of existing hindrances; in other words, wit affords us the means of surmounting restrictions and of opening up otherwise inaccessible pleasure sources."

Once wit has been brought into the service of the satiric impulse, then all the stock devices by which the literary satirist achieves his end become available: irony, burlesque, innuendo, the beast fable, the imaginary voyage, allegory—all the devices of indirection which make the study of satire so fascinating and so confusing. The Earl of Shaftesbury, writing in the eighteenth century, had some such idea in mind when he explained the prevalence of irony, raillery, and writing in disguise as resulting from the weight of censorship. " 'Tis the persecuting Spirit has raised the *bantering* one," he says. "The greater the Weight [of constraint] is, the bitterer will be the Satire. The higher the Slavery, the more exquisite the Buffoonery." We might compare this with Kenneth Burke's paradoxical notion that satire thrives best when society attempts to censor it. According to Burke, ". . . the most inventive satire arises when the artist is seeking simultaneously to take risks and escape punishment for his boldness, and is never quite certain himself whether he will be acclaimed or punished."[5] The ancient ambiguity, or something very close to it, is still there.

We have an excellent opportunity to examine the satirist's claims for social approval largely by reason of the literary convention which decrees that he must justify his ungrateful art. From the times of Horace, Persius, and Juvenal down to Boileau, Swift, and Pope and into our own day with men like Wyndham Lewis, the satirist has felt compelled to write an *Apologia*, whether formal or informal, in verse or prose. The Apologies are remarkably similar in their protestations (Mr. Lewis dissenting) ; from them we get a kind of ideal image which the satirist projects of himself and his art. According to the image the satirist is a public servant fighting the good fight against vice and folly wherever he meets it; he is honest, brave, protected by the rectitude of his motives; he attacks only the wicked and then seldom or never by name; he is, in short, a moral man appalled by the evil he sees around him, and he is forced by his conscience to write satire. Juvenal's *"facit indignatio versum"* is the prototype.

The satirist claims, with much justification, to be a true conservative. Usually (but not always—there are significant exceptions) he operates within the established framework of society, accepting its norms, appealing to reason (or to what his society accepts as rational) as the standard against which to judge the folly he sees. He is the preserver of tradition—the true tradition from which there has been grievous falling away.

Society, quite naturally, is dubious. On the most obvious level it points with outrage to the inevitable discrepancy between the ideal image, projected by rhetorical convention, and what it takes to be the actual fact. Swift, or Pope—so goes the reasoning—was a wicked man; therefore we may dismiss his satire. The *non sequitur* is comforting. But the problem on other levels is more complex. Despite society's doubts about the character of the satirist, there may develop a feeling that in its general application the satire has some truth in it—or the feeling that other people may *think* that it has some truth in it. Individuals who recognize characteristics of themselves in the objects of attack cannot afford to acknowledge the identity even to themselves. So they may reward the satirist as proof of piety, while inwardly they fear him. *"Satyr,"* says Swift, *"is a sort of Glass, wherein Beholders do generally discover every body's Face but their Own; which is the chief*

Reason for that kind Reception it meets in the World, and that so very few are offended with it." "Publicly offended," one might add. Publicly the satirist may be honored, but privately he will be feared.

I think of a modern instance, perhaps trivial. Consider the high reputation in academic circles of Mary McCarthy's *Groves of Academe.* We may applaud, but many of us must feel the bite. Perhaps it would be a matter for congratulation to have Miss McCarthy on our faculties; it would hardly be a matter for comfort.

Society has even better reasons for its suspicions. No matter how conservative the rationale of the satirist may be, it is inevitable that the pressure of his art will in some ways run athwart society's efforts to maintain its equilibrium. The satirist usually claims that he does not attack institutions, he attacks perversions of institutions; when, for example, he ridicules a corrupt judge he intends no reflection on the law as such, he is attacking a corruption which has crept into the law. But it seems to be that in the hands of a powerful satirist an attack on a local phenomenon is capable of indefinite extension into an attack on the whole structure of which that phenomenon is part. It is significant, I think, that this imaginative process is essentially a magical one; it works by synecdoche which is one of the foundations of magic. In "mythico-linguistic thought"—to use Cassirer's phrase—the part does not merely represent the whole, it *is* the whole; by the magical process of identification the nail paring or the lock of hair from an enemy *is* the enemy, and it is acted on accordingly. So with our judge —for the process just described is by no means confined to a "mythically bound" society; as a different order of experience, to be sure, it is the way of the imagination when it is bound, in its own way, by the spell of the creative artist. The judge who has been ridiculed by a powerful satirist comes to stand for lawyers in general, and lawyers for the law. What starts as local attack ends up by calling the whole institution into question. Thus the satirical portraits of Chaucer, who seems to have been a thoroughly orthodox Catholic, have often been interpreted as evidence of his revolt against the Church; during the Reformation he and Langland were used for purposes doubtless far removed from their intent. Swift, attacking in *A Tale of a Tub* what he considered corruptions in the Church, unwittingly provided criticism capable of extension into an undermining action against the Church itself. I believe that Swift was deeply committed to the welfare of the Established Church as he saw it; but under the impact of his satire one of the great pillars of society rocked a bit. Swift's strength, as Empson puts it, made his instrument too strong for him. His magic, one might say, was his undoing.

The final point now, which is implicit in what has gone before. The satirist usually claims to be conservative, to be using his art to shore up the foundations of the established order. Between the claim and the reality, however, may lie a tremendous gulf. I take my last example again from Swift. The complexly simple projector of *An Argument Against Abolishing Christianity*, the 'I" of the piece, argues cogently for the retention of nominal Christianity. To restore "real" Christianity, he says, "would indeed be a wild project, it would be to dig up Foundations; ... to break the entire Frame and Constitution of Things; to ruin Trade, extinguish Arts and Sciences, with the Professors of them; in short, to turn our Courts, Exchanges, and Shops into Desarts...." One reads this and one can only say, He is right. Between Swift and the projector, of course, there is a considerable ironic remove, just as there is distance between Swift and some of the meanings set in motion by his creature. One may doubt that Swift the Tory politician, Swift the social man would have had much sympathy with breaking the "Frame and Constitution of Things." But Swift the artist is another matter. The pressure of his art works directly against the ostensibly conservative function which it is said to serve. Instead of shoring up foundations, it tears them down. It is revolutionary.

Society has doubtless been wise, in its old pragmatic way, to suspect the satirist. Whether he is an enchanter wielding the ambiguous power of magic, or whether he is a "mere" poet, his relation to society will necessarily be problematic. He is of society in the sense that his art must be grounded in his experience as social man; but he must also be apart, as he struggles to achieve proper distance. His practice is often sanative, as he proclaims; but it may be revolutionary in ways that society can not possibly approve, and in ways that may not be clear even to the satirist.

NOTES

[1] The original tale is the *Immtheacht na Tromddihme* [*Proceedings of the Great Bardic Institute*]; Owen Connellan's translation appears in Vol. V of *Transactions of the Ossianic Society* (1860). It is a remarkable tale—a satire on the Irish satirists, full of wild burlesque and very amusing. Of the episode from the tale

which he utilized, Yeats says that he "twisted it about and revised its moral that the poet might have the best of it."

2 Translated variously as a "metrical malediction," "extempore satire," "Satire from the Hill-tops," and, most recently, "an endless, biting attack."

3 Ridicule, according to anthropologists, plays an enormously important role in primitive societies. Paul Radin writes: "To avoid [ridicule] a man will go to any length. He may even commit suicide in consequence of it." One thinks of Archilochus's victim, Lycambes, and of others. Radin adds: "The fear of ridicule is thus a great positive factor in the lives of primitive peoples. It is the preserver of the established order of things and more potent and tyrannous than the most restrictive and coercive of positive injunctions possibly could be." *Primitive Man as Philosopher* (New York, 1927), pp. 50–51.

4 Caricature as an art apparently did not develop until late in the sixteenth century; Ernst Kris and E. H. Gombrich account for the fact thus: "Caricature is a play with the magic power of the image, and for such a play to be licit or institutionalized the belief in the real efficacy of the spell must be firmly under control. Wherever it is not considered a joke but rather a dangerous practice to distort a man's features even on paper, caricature as an art can not develop." "The Principles of Caricature" in Kris, *Psychoanalytic Explorations in Art* (New York, 1952), pp. 189–203.

5 Burke, *The Philosophy of Literary Form* (Baton Rouge, Louisiana, 1941), pp. 231–32. In a totalitarian society where control is nearly absolute, satire against the ruling regime is, of course, impossible.

ELLEN DOUGLASS LEYBURN

Animal Stories

> *"prettie Allegories stealing under the formall Tales of beastes,*
> *makes many more beastly then beastes: begin to heare the sound*
> *of vertue from these dumb speakers."*
>
> *Sir Philip Sidney*

Brute creation seems sometimes to exist as a satire on mankind. All
that the allegorist needs to do is to point the parallel. Moralists have
used man's likeness to the animals for instruction in a variety of ways
ranging from the strange edification of the medieval bestiary to the
reproof of the newspaper political cartoon. There has never been a
time when men were not trying to teach each other the lessons to
be learned from the creatures. The Bible is full of such teaching; and
the stories spread under the name of Aesop are probably more widely
known than any other classical literature. The Orient is as rich as the
Occident in this lore; and the African folk tales, many of which reappear with a new set of animal characters in the Uncle Remus stories,
attest the vitality of the genre without dependence on a written language.

Sometimes the teaching is so explicit that the resulting work
cannot be called allegory. This is true of many of the fables of Aesop
and his successors; but it is a significant proof of the value of indirection in art, even the art of pedagogy, that the best and best known of
the Aesopic fables label the moral and leave it as something distinct
and outside the story instead of making it explicit within the narrative.
The ones that do point the lesson within the tale are the least effective
of the group. When the mother of the wayward thrush explains to her

From *Satiric Allegory: Mirror of Man*, New Haven, 1956, pp. 57–70.
Reprinted by permission of the Yale University Press. Copyright ©1956
by the Yale University Press.

son, who wants to make a companion of the swallow, that friendship between those who cannot bear the same climate is folly, we have the feeling that the bird would have learned more by making the experiment and we by watching its outcome. In this fable, the moral is at least dramatized to the extent of being explained to a character within the action. The reader is even more dismayed when the point is simply explained directly to him, as in the fable of Jupiter's not granting horns to the camel because the prayer was for something nature had not intended. The more artistic fables tell the story and stop like true allegories, allowing the reader the pleasure of drawing his own conclusion before he reaches the labeled moral, which remains outside the story.

When the cock tells the fox who has been preaching a general peace among the animals in order to make the cock come down out of the tree, that the dogs are coming, the story is complete with the dramatic ending of the fox's running off. When the fox who has refused to visit the sick lion says that he notices tracks of other animals going to the lion's palace, but none coming away, we know what to think without having the moral further pointed. The moral is left suspended within the tale in all the most familiar of Aesop's fables: The Fox and the Grapes, The Dog in the Manger, The Hare and the Tortoise, The Fox and the Stork, The Dog and His Shadow, and the Country Mouse and the City Mouse. And when any of these reappear in the writings of sophisticated artists, as when Horace retells the last named story, the same rule holds. The artist respects the integrity of the story and the intelligence of the reader and lets the tale make its own point. Perhaps L'Estrange is right in the preface to his edition of the Fables when he says that we are all like children and prefer the pill of moral teaching sweetened with the pleasure of the tale.[1] Nor do we want the pleasure of the allegory spoiled by being told that it is really moral medicine after all. The moral labeled and separated from the tale as is customary in Aesop's stories, we accept without protest because no disguise is presented, and there is therefore no violation of conception; but having the moral stated within the story, where we expect to get it only through the images, destroys the imaginative effect which it has been the whole object of the story to product. The case is somewhat altered in a work like Swift's "Beasts' Confession," where the application is longer than the tale, and the animal allegory serves just as introduction to the classes of mankind who mistake their talents. But even here Swift announces the pointing of the moral as distinct from the tale.

A different sort of problem is created by the animal story which is instruction about man observed from the point of view of the animals. A highly effective example of this use of the beasts is Johnson's *Idler, 22*,[2] in which the old vulture gives instruction to her young about the order of the universe in which man is created as the "natural food of a vulture." The mother bird, in response to the puzzled inquiry as to how man is to be killed if he is so much bigger and stronger than the vulture, replies:

> "We have not the strength of man ... and I am sometimes in doubt whether we have the subtilty; and the vultures would seldom feast upon his flesh, had not nature, that devoted him to our uses, infused into him a strange ferocity, which I have never observed in any other being that feeds upon the earth. Two herds of men will often meet and shake the earth with noise, and fill the air with fire. When you hear noise, and see fire, with flashes along the ground, hasten to the place with your swiftest wing, for men are surely destroying one another; you will then find the ground smoking with blood, and covered with carcasses, of which many are dismembered, and mangled for the convenience of the vulture."—"But when men have killed their prey," said the pupil, "Why do they not eat it? When the wolf has killed a sheep, he suffers not the vulture to touch it till he has satisfied himself. Is not man another kind of wolf?"—"Man," said the mother, "is the only beast who kills that which he does not devour, and this quality makes him so much a benefactor to our species."

In the effort to explain the mystery of human behavior, the mother quotes a wise old vulture of the Carpathian rocks:

> "His opinion was, that man had only the appearance of animal life, being really vegetables with a power of motion; and that as the boughs of an oak are dashed together by the storm, that swine may fatten upon the falling acorns, so men are, by some unaccountable power, driven one against another, till they lose their motion, that vultures may be fed. Others think they have observed something of contrivance and policy among these mischievous beings; and those that hover more closely round them, pretend, that there is, in every herd, one that gives directions to

the rest, and seems to be more eminently delighted with a wide
carnage. What it is that entitles him to such preëminence we
know not; he is seldom the biggest or the swiftest, but he shows
by his eagerness and diligence that he is, more than any of the
others, a friend to vultures."

The impact of the satire here comes from the ironic point of view.
At first the essay seems not allegorical at all since the animals are
not acting in a way that parallels man's actions. But it turns out that
the point of view itself is an allegory of man's assumption that he is
the center of the universe, with all other beings created for his benefit.
This attitude of the vultures, which is perfectly sustained once Johnson
leaves the awkward introduction of the shepherd for the story itself,
contributes an extra level to the irony of the analysis of the reasons why
men kill each other for the "convenience of the vulture."

In addition to the large body of assorted kinds of fables, there
are a great many more strictly allegorical satires with animal characters. The very universality and obviousness of the relation of animals
to man makes at once the appeal of this sort of satiric story and its
special difficulty. Both sides of the parallel are so familiar that it is
hard to keep them in proper balance, and every reader feels himself
competent from his own observation to judge what the writer is doing
with the material. But beyond this recognition of the familiar, there
are certain criteria by which to judge success in the form.

One gift essential to the teller of satiric animal tales is the power
to keep his reader conscious simultaneously of the human traits satirized
and of the animals as animals. The moment he loses hold on resemblance and lets his protagonists become merely animals or merely
people, his instrument has slipped in his hands and deflected his
material away from satiric allegory into something like *Black Beauty*
or *The Three Bears*. But if the writer of animal allegory can successfully sustain and play upon two levels of perception, making us feel
that his animals are really animals and yet as human as ourselves,
he can control the imaginative response. This doubleness of effect is
the central power of great animal stories as different as the *Nun's
Priest's Tale* and *The Tar Baby*. We delight in Chaunticleer and
Pertelote and Brer Rabbit because they are at once real as people and
real as animals. The climax of the Tar Baby story, "Bred en bawn
in a brier-patch, Brer Fox—bred en bawn in a brier-patch!" reminds
us inescapably that this creature is a rabbit exactly while it reminds
us of his resemblance to the human being who by his wit can extricate

himself from any difficulty. Uncle Remus concludes, "en wid dat he skip out des ez lively ez a cricket in de embers," and we find his liveliness irresistible because we see a real rabbit skipping off in a mood that we know as human. So with Chaucer's masterpiece: Pertelote's "Pekke hem up right as they growe and ete hem yn" is often cited as one of Chaucer's wittiest reductions to the animal level in all his mock-heroic scheme. Yet this remark, which reminds the reader with humorous felicity that a hen is speaking, conveys also the quintessence of Pertelote's wifely solicitude. It seems that when she is most a chicken, she is most full of the particular sort of femininity that Chaucer is placing beside masculine roosterishness for amused scrutiny.

Indeed, it is belief in these creatures as animals that accentuates and isolates the human trait singled out for laughing observation. The animal make-up from which the human characteristic emerges throws it into high light and sharpens perception, acting as a proper vehicle for the tenor. Thus the true animal allegory fulfills I. A. Richards' requirement: "the vehicle is not . . . a mere embellishment of a tenor which is otherwise unchanged but the vehicle and tenor in co-operation give a meaning of more varied powers than can be ascribed to either."[3]

Since the whole point of animal satire is to show up humanity by revealing human traits in nonhuman characters, it follows that the few human beings who appear must not be characterized at all lest they break into the allegorical scheme. At the end of the Uncle Remus stories we know no more about "Miss Meadows en de gals" than does the little boy when he first asks, "Who was Miss Meadows, Uncle Remus?" and gets the unenlightening response: "Don't ax me, honey. She wuz in de tale, Miss Meadows en de gals wuz, en de tale I give you like hi't wer' gun ter me." The characterization of Mr. Man is if possible even vaguer: "Des a man, honey. Dat's all."[4] In George Orwell's *Animal Farm*, where the notion of man as tyrannical master is necessary to the imaginative plan, the only human character who really figures after the ousting of Mr. Jones is Whymper, who as his name suggests has no personality at all, and he is never seen by the nonporcine animals from whose point of view the story is told. The *Nun's Priest's Tale* may seem an exception to this rule, for there is a good deal of circumstantial detail in the depicting of the widow who owns the fowls. But when we come to examine the treatment of her "sooty bower" and her "attempree diete," we find that all the attention is given to externals. As a person, the widow has no more identity than do the peasants who own Chaunticleer in Chaucer's sources. The realistic detail of her few possessions and her meager life is all used to sharpen the humor of the elaborate mock-heroic treatment of the cock and his lady. It seems safe to say that there does not exist anywhere a successful animal allegory which includes a vivid human character.

Another outgrowth of the choice of animal characters to throw human traits into bold relief is the concentration upon isolated human characteristics. The successful writer of animal allegory rarely gives his characters more than one human trait at a time. This concentrated singleness of attack might almost be laid down as a second law of the genre, as binding as the first that the animals shall stay both animal and human. It removes the possibility of very complex characterization. The complexity comes from the double consciousness of animal and human attributes; and the force of the tale is almost in proportion to the singleness and simplicity on the human level. This is true even of a fairly sustained piece such as Munro Leaf's *Ferdinand*. The increasingly funny repetition of the comment that Ferdinand just sat down quietly and smelled the flowers whenever he was expected to fight not only endears the bull to us in our belligerent world, but leaves the essence of his character indelibly fixed in our minds. This is all we know of him and all we need to know except that "He is very happy."

The same practice holds in aggregations of stories centered around one character such as the medieval beast epic of *Reynard the Fox*, where Reynard is always cruelly taking advantage of his neighbors, and the Uncle Remus stories, where Brer Rabbit always mischievously turns the tables on his stronger enemies. As Uncle Remus puts it, "Eve'y time I run over in my min' 'bout the pranks er Brer Rabbit ... hit make me laugh mo' en mo'. He mos' allers come out on top, yit dey wuz times w'en he hatter be mighty spry."[5] His invention is boundless, but he is always himself.

> I 'speck dat 'uz de reas'n w'at make ole Brer Rabbit git 'long so well, kaze he aint copy atter none er de yuther creeturs.... W'en he make his disappearance 'fo' um, hit 'uz allers in some bran new place. Dey aint know wharbouts fer ter watch out fer 'im. He wuz de funniest creetur er de whole gang. Some folks moughter call him lucky, en yit, w'en he git in bad luck, hit look lak he mos' allers come out on top. Hit look mighty kuse

now, but 't wa'n't kuse in dem days, kaze hit 'uz done gun up
dat, strike 'im w'en you might en whar you would, Brer Rabbit
wuz de soopless creetur gwine. (pp. 21–22)

The essence of his character revealed in story after story Uncle Remus
summarizes: "dey w'a'n't no man 'mungs de creeturs w'at kin stan'
right flat-footed en wuk he min' quick lak Brer Rabbit" (p. 129).
What most stimulates his intelligence is being in a tight place: "Brer
Rabbit 'gun ter git skeer'd, en w'en dat creetur git skeer'd, he min'
wuk lak one er deze yer flutter-mills" (p. 220).

A corollary of the focus upon single human traits in animal tales
is brevity. The swiftness with which the narrative reaches its climax
sharpens the concentrated effect of the flashing out of the human
motive. Uncle Remus's comment on his hero's character gives the clue
to the simple plot of most of his stories, which without ever seeming
monotonous repeatedly show Brer Rabbit "monst'us busy . . . sailin'
'roun' fixin' up his tricks" (p. 63) to outdo the other animals who
have it in for him: "dem t'er creeturs. Dey wuz allers a-layin' traps
fer Brer Rabbit en gittin' cotch in um deyse'f" (p. 119). Though he
is usually extricating himself from a difficulty, he sometimes initiates
pranks from sheer love of mischief. He is always alert for fun. "Brer
Rabbit, he one er deze yer kinder mens w'at sleep wid her eye wide
open" (p. 93). The illustrations of his ingenuity as it makes the plots
for the tales are endless: he gets Mr. Fox, who has come to fetch him
for revenge to serve as his "ridin' hoss" by pretending to be too ill to
accompany Brer Fox on foot; he gets Miss Cow stuck fast by the
horns in the persimmon tree so that he and all his family can milk
her by promising her a feast of persimmons that she is to shake down
by butting the tree; he scalds Mr. Wolf, who runs into his chest for
protection from the dogs; he gets the bag after Mr. Fox's hunt by
playing dead and tempting Brer Fox to add the rabbit to his game;
on two occasions he nibbles up the butter and manages to let the
'possum and the weasel have the blame; he saves the meat of his own
cow, takes Mr. Man's cow from Brer Fox, and steals Mr. Man's
meat and money by a series of ruses; he often persuades other animals
to take his place in traps by appealing to their greed; he escapes from
the hawk by begging to be allowed to grow big enough to make a
full meal and from the embrace of the wildcat by offering to tell him
how to get turkey meat; he turns the tables on other enemies by
appealing to their perversity in many variations on the Tar Baby

story. Always Brer Rabbit is equal to the emergency. His own ruses succeed and those to outwit him fail. Only the Terrapin and the Crow ever best him, never any of the stronger animals like the Fox, the Bear, and the Lion. After the account of his exploits, Uncle Remus's judgment seems a model of understatement: "Bless yo' soul, honey, Brer Rabbit mought er bin kinder fibble in de legs, but he w'a'n't no ways cripple und' de hat" (p. 208).

Just as the hero of these stories represents always mischievous fooling, so he confronts only one trait in his antagonist in each story. The singleness of impression, which enforces the sharpness, is never violated. But one source of variety from story to story is the range of human traits singled out in the other creatures for Brer Rabbit's laughter. To be sure, laughter is the quality of his prankish intelligence. "Well . . . you know w'at kinder man Brer Rabbit is. He des went off some 'ers by he own-alone se'f en tuck a big laugh" (p. 214). Uncle Remus's adjective for him is "sassy." But the very story of his Laughing Place is another illustration that the weaknesses of the other creatures give him ample scope to exercise his ingenuity in besting them for his own amusement. Here it is Brer Fox's curiosity that makes him the victim. The stories already mentioned show Brer Rabbit playing upon greed, vanity, eagerness for revenge, or sheer cruelty in his more imposing neighbors. The stories of his frightening the other and bigger animals, even the Lion, by playing upon their natural timorousness are especially striking in view of his own physical helplessness. The Lion lets Brer Rabbit tie him to a tree to save him from being blown away by a nonexistent wind; the animals all run from Brer Rabbit when he appears bedecked in leaves; he scares them from the house they have bulit by saying that the cannon is his sneeze and the pail of water his spit; he sets a stampede in motion by simply running past and saying he has heard a big noise; and he outdoes himself in frightening the others by the clatter he makes dressed up in the tin plates they are waiting to steal from him:

> Brer Rabbit got right on um 'fo dey kin git away. He holler out, he did:
> "Gimme room! Tu'n me loose! I'm ole man Spewter-Splutter wid long claws, en scales on my back! I'm snaggle-toofed en double-jinted! Gimme room!"
> Eve'y time he'd fetch a whoop, he'd rattle de cups en slap de platters tergedder—*rickety, rackety, slambang!* En I let you know w'en dem creeturs got dey lim's tergedder dey split de win',

> dey did dat. Ole Brer B'ar, he struck a stump w'at stan' in de
> way, en I ain't gwine tell you how he to' it up 'kaze you won't
> b'leeve me, but de nex' mawnin' Brer Rabbit en his chilluns
> went back dar, dey did, en dey got nuff splinters fer ter make um
> kin'lin' wood all de winter (p. 123).

The human bully is probably the character most roundly mocked by
Brer Rabbit.

In Caxton's version of the medieval stories of Reynard, on the
other hand, the hero is the bully. Surely from the folklorist's viewpoint
one of the most interesting aspects of animal stories is the relationships
among the various groups. The story of Brer Rabbit's rising from the
well by getting the fox to leap into the other well bucket, for instance,
is identical with the story that Erswynd, wife of Isegrim the Wulf,
tells of her being tricked into the well bucket by Reynard. A plot that
is repeated with different characters in both sets of stories is that of
the creature delivered and turning on his deliverer, only to be re-
imprisoned by the judgment of a third party. Rukenaw tells in Caxton
the story of the man's freeing the serpent, who then turns on the man,
with Reynard as the judge who refuses advice until he sees the
contestants in their original positions. In the Uncle Remus version,
the creature under the rock is the wolf, who is freed by Brer Rabbit,
and the judge is Brer Tarrypin (always Brer Rabbit's ally except
when he outruns his speedier friend in the Uncle Remus variant of
the story of the Tortoise and the Hare) who says: "I hates might'ly
fer ter put you all gents ter so much trouble; yit, dey aint no two
ways, I'll hatter see des how Brer Wolf was kotch, en des how de
rock wuz layin' 'pun top un 'im" (p. 278). Then of course the wolf
is left pinned under the rock just as is the snake in the other story.

The intricate ramifications of interrelations of sources for both
sets of stories lie beyond the scope of this study, which is concerned
with the artistry of the telling. But the subject of the representation
of the heroes is an aesthetic problem which is curiously linked with
the larger anthropological relation. It is hard to resist the impression
that somewhere in the course of the development of the two groups
of tales, one hero was set up in deliberate response to the other. Both
are extremely clever; and both triumph over the other animals by
deceits. But the feeling created by the two is totally different. When
Uncle Remus says, "dat seetful Brer Rabbit done fool ole Brer Fox"
(p. 89), we laugh with the rabbit. When Erswynd says, "Ache felle

reynart / noman can kepe hym self fro the[e] / thou canst so wel vttre thy wordes and thy falsenes and reson sette forth,"[6] our sympathy is all with the duped she-wolf. Instead of rejoicing at Reynard's triumphs, the reader shudders at the cruelty of his tricks, which grow in evil from his making Bruin lose "his scalp, ears, and forepaws," in his bloody escape "nearly dead" from the cloven tree, through his preparing for his false pilgrimage by securing a square foot of Bruin's hide for his scrip and two shoes from each by ripping off the pawskins of Isegrim and Erswynd, through his cold-blooded devouring of Cuwart, the Hare, to the horrors of the final fight in which he slips his shaved and oiled body always out of Isegrim's grasp while he blinds the wolf by slapping his face with the tail befouled according to Rukenaw's suggestion, kicking sand into Isegrim's eyes, and treating him with every sort of indignity until he wins with his ugly stratagem leaving Isegrim mutilated and half dead. Parallel to the mounting cruelty of his deeds is the increasing baseness of his false speeches. His deceits instead of tickling the fancy like those of Brer Rabbit make their treachery abhorrent. There is serious hatred of Reynard and serious reason for it:

> Alle the beestis both poure and riche were alle stylle when the foxe spak so stoutly/the cony laprel and the roek were so sore aferde that they durste not speke but pyked and stryked them out of the court bothe two. and whan they were a room fer in the playne they saide. god graunte that this felle murderare may fare euyl. he can bywrappe and couere his falshede. that his wordes seme as trewe as the gospel herof knoweth noman than we. how shold we brynge wytnesse. it is better that we wyke and departe. than we sholde holde a felde and fyghte with hym. he is so shrewde. ye[a] thaugh ther of vs were fyue we coude not defende vs. but he shold sle vs alle.

While the narrative management in *Reynard the Fox*, as in other groups of animal stories is episodic, Caxton's version of the epic has decided organization toward a climax. The increasing tension is craftily arranged. Reynard's first false defense is filled with consummate treachery; but his villainy is greater in his second hoodwinking of the king. When honors are finally heaped upon him after his foul play to Isegrim, perfidy is left triumphant. If we turn from such a spectacle of evil to the merry pranks of Brer Rabbit, we are bound to feel some slight restoring of poetic justice in the fact that Brer

Fox is always defeated in his efforts to outwit Brer Rabbit. Nothing can bring to life the hens and pigeons and other helpless creatures, even Cuwart the Hare himself, whom Reynard has foully murdered; but it is hard to resist the feeling that the sly Brer Fox is suffering some retribution for the sins of Reynard.

This strong difference in response to the two protagonists suggests a third criterion by which to judge the satirist using animal tales for his allegory. The kinds of smartness displayed by Reynard and Brer Rabbit are, of course, different; but much of the difference in the feeling about them is determined by the attitude toward them displayed in the stories. The establishing of a clear point of view toward the animal characters seems as important a requisite for the successful animal tale as does the focusing on a single dominant trait in the animal. The rejoicing of Uncle Remus and his various hearers in the exploits of Brer Rabbit is an incalculable aid to Harris in communicating the same attitude to the reader; but as he repeatedly says in the introductions to his various volumes, he did not create Uncle Remus's point of view. Brer Rabbit is the hero, in the full admiring sense of the word, of the stories as Harris heard them told by Negro after Negro. To be sure, he is a hero that can be laughed at; but the gay satire is directed at the human foibles of the other animals which lead them into Brer Rabbit's traps. In the stories of Reynard, on the other hand, while there is some mockery of the animals who are Reynard's dupes, the appalling comment on human character comes in Reynard himself. Modern experience of the rise of tyrants through cruelty and lies must intensify response to the revelation of iniquity in Reynard; but there can be no doubt that Caxton intends Reynard to be regarded as a villain. We see that Isegrim is as simple-minded as Brer Wolf; but instead of feeling that his stupidity is mocked, we resent the violence done him. We are conscious of the greed of Bruin and Tybert which helps make them prey to Reynard's wiles; Bellin's desire for importance is directly responsible for his being killed as Cuwart's murderer; and Nobel seems a very unsuspecting monarch indeed to be taken in by Reynard's flattery. But many of the fox's victims have no other weakness than physical helplessness. The revealing light of the allegorical satire is turned most searchingly upon the villainous hero himself; and when he is allowed to go off triumphant in the end, the feeling is that the wicked ways of the world have been convincingly displayed.

There is obviously a good deal of social satire, especially of

abuses in the church, in *Reynard the Fox*. This would be in a measure
true of any group of stories presenting a number of animals together.
The mere assembling of individuals suggests some comment on social
structure. Even the fables of La Fontaine display the classes of society,
as does the assembly of birds alone in *The Parlement of Foules*. But
in some animal stories, the central purpose is clearly comment on
society rather than on individual human traits. In such stories the
same artistic criteria hold. The sustaining of the animal disguise is
still the first requisite; the absence of strong human characters and
the presence of sharply individualized animal characters with a single
dominant human trait seem as important for the social satire couched
in animal terms as for the story whose object is simply laughter at a
human foible; a clear viewpoint again must control the response.
The failure to meet these tests of the successful writer of animal
allegory explains the ineptitudes of so great an allegorist as Spenser
when he tries to tell an animal story.

Mother Hubberds Tale, for all its vivid picture of abuses in
church and court, is not a successful animal satire. The Fox and
the Ape are specious rogues indeed, but we never believe in them as
animals except possibly for the moment of their stealing the Lion's
skin. Many similarities have been shown between Spenser's material
and that of the medieval stories of Reynard, including the basic one
of alliance in trickery of these two animals.[7] But Spenser never
succeeds in giving them the life of their prototypes. Part of his
difficulty in giving his characters reality as animals may come from
his being unable to transmute the images of real men. It seems clear
that the animals stand for actual individuals at Elizabeth's court,
though scholars dispute about the identification of the Ape. The
result of their not becoming convincing animal characters is that the
poem affords none of the pleasure of using the imagination at two
levels, which is the chief reason for being of allegory. When Spenser's
protagonists trick the husbandman into hiring them as shepherd and
dog, they are simply thieves who enjoy stealing and slaying the sheep.
They do eat the flock; but there is no distinction between the eating
done by Ape and Fox, for they are both all the while simply deceitful
men. In the final episode when they come to rule, with the Ape in
the stolen skin of the Lion, we forget altogether that it is a lion's
throne they have usurped and are given almost a lecture on the
abuses of false human courtiers and the pitiful plight of suitors at

court, with the lesson pointed by the contrasting picture of the man who truly loves honor. Spenser is writing here with too much passion of personal disillusion to achieve artistic detachment and the indirection of allegory. Animals are forgotten in lines like these:

> Most miserable man, whom wicked fate
> Hath brought to Court, to sue for had ywist,
> That few haue found, and manie one hath mist;
> Full little knowest thou that hast not tride,
> What hell it is, in suing long to bide:
> To loose good dayes, that might be better spent;
> To wast long nights in pensiue discontent;
> To speed to day, to be put back to morrow;
> To feed on hope, to pine with feare and sorrow;
> To haue thy Princes grace, yet want her Peeres;
> To haue thy asking, yet waite manie yeeres;
> To fret thy soule with crosses and with cares;
> To eate thy heart through comfortlesse dispaires;
> To fawne, to crowche, to waite, to ride, to ronne,
> To spend, to giue, to want, to be vndonne.
> Vnhappie wight, borne to desastrous end,
> That doth his life in so long tendance spend.
>   (ll. 892–908, Variorum ed.)

It is, in fact, startling to return to the story of the sleeping Lion by the awkward device of having Jove send Mercury to awaken him and spur him back to his kingdom to drive out the usurpers. The encounter with the priest whom the Fox and the Ape meet between their tricks as shepherds and as courtiers is a sharply ironic indictment of the worldly practices of churchmen. But the account of the proper way to make a priest's life a soft one is put into the mouth of a real priest, who is all too convincingly human. Consequently, we almost nowhere feel that we are in an animal world; and when Sir Mule or the sheep whose lamb the wolf has killed does appear as an actual animal, we are startled and jarred. *Mother Hubberds Tale* is almost as far from being true animal allegory as is *The Hind and the Panther*. The force of Spenser's satiric feeling and the variety of his poetic power carry us along; but the poem does not succeed as a work of art.

George Orwell, a writer of much less stature than Spenser, has written in *Animal Farm* a more effective social satire than *Mother*

Hubberds Tale. His animals are absolutely real as animals from the first meeting in the big barn to hear Old Major's dream of a world in which the animals are equal and free of their human masters to their frightened approach to the farmhouse window at the end of the book when only those animals who are tall enough can peep in. The horses are always horses who pull loads; the cows are cows who must be milked, however awkwardly, by the pigs, "their trotters being well adapted to this task";[8] the hens are hens who lay eggs and want to keep them; even the bureaucratic pigs remain pigs, hard as they try to be human—which gives its overwhelming force to the dénouement of the story when the terrified subject animals creep back to the window of the farmhouse and look "from pig to man, and from man to pig, and from pig to man again; but already it [is] impossible to say which [is] which" (p. 118).

The point of view is always that of the animals who are being duped. Their plight is deepened for the reader by his being allowed to discover the successive machinations of the pigs only as they are borne in upon the stupider animals. Orwell never forgets and lets us inside the consciousness of Napoleon and Squealer. We simply see the one strutting and lording it over his victims and hear the other giving specious explanations of why the pigs must live in luxury. We see and hear what the subject animals see and hear.

While they are consistently animals, each reveals a predominant human trait. Clover is a "stout motherly mare" from the time when at the opening meeting she makes a protecting wall around the motherless ducklings with her great foreleg, through the time after the purge when the desolate survivors huddle around her, and through her efforts to keep Boxer from overworking and then to rescue him from the knacker, until she leads her fearful fellow creatures up to the farmhouse at the end, to witness the full extent of their betrayal.

Boxer "was not of first-rate intelligence, but he was universally respected for his steadiness of character and tremendous powers of work" (p. 4). His inability to learn the alphabet is linked with his unswerving devotion to his two mottoes: "I will work harder" and "Comrade Napoleon is always right," for there is something stupid in his letting his great strength be used up to serve the interests of the oppressors in the totalitarian state. Yet his loyalty is intensely moving, especially as his strength fails and he still works harder than ever: "Sometimes on the slope leading to the top of the quarry, when he braced his muscles against the weight of some vast boulder, it seemed that nothing kept him on his feet except the will to continue. At such times his lips were seen to form the words, 'I will work harder'; he had no voice left" (p. 98). And when in the knacker's van the drumming of his hoofs grows fainter and dies away, we feel all the force of human goodness traduced so that after the faithful horse has been made into glue and dog meat, there is all the greater sense of outrage at Squealer's fraudulent speech to the Comrades distorting all the circumstances of Boxer's life and death (for which he makes up a sentimental deathbed scene in a beautifully tended hospital instead of the actual slaughter house one) to make the other animals more servile slaves than ever.

The delineation of a single human trait is just as vivid in the other animals: the boar Snowball, the impetuous, inventive leader who is ousted; the other boar Napoleon the dictator, who starts out by taking the milk and apples for the pigs and goes on to the creating of a slave state; Squealer, the pig propagandist, who shifts the commandments to suit the leaders' actions and explains all their oppressions as to the advantage of the comrades; the donkey Benjamin, who is a cynic; Mollie, the pretty white mare who loves ribbons more than principle; and all the others. Even the animals who are not named and appear in groups show up human crowds in single moods. The silly sheep always bleat at the pigs' command, whether their tune is "Four legs good, two legs bad" or "Four legs good, two legs better." The terrible dogs trained as Napoleon's bodyguard are always the ferocious, bloodthirsty instruments of terror. They are the police of the police state.

Since Orwell has succeeded in his underlining of separate human characteristics in his individual animals, his comment on society is convincing. It is because the imaginative scheme of the animal allegory is sustained that the revelation of the ease with which well-meaning citizens can be duped into serving the masters of a totalitarian state achieves its power. Orwell's keeping the point of view consistently that of the helpless animals and letting us make only the discoveries that they make forces us to interpret for ourselves not just the misfortunes of the renamed Manor Farm, but also those of our own world. We are compelled to participate imaginatively. *Animal Farm* is successful social satire because it is successful allegory.

NOTES

[1] *Fables of Aesop and Other Eminent Mythologists: with Morals and Reflexions by Sir Roger L'Estrange* (London, 1692), A$_2$.

[2] Johnson omitted this essay from collected editions of the *Idler*; but it is reprinted at the end of Chalmers's edition. The quotations are from *British Essayists*, ed. A. Chalmers (Boston, 1864), 27, 400–402.

[3] *The Philosophy of Rhetoric* (New York, 1936), p. 100.

[4] Joel Chandler Harris, *Uncle Remus, His Songs and His Sayings* (New York, 1921), pp. 25 and 143.

[5] Joel Chandler Harris, *Nights with Uncle Remus* (Boston, 1911), p. 311. All further quotations from *Uncle Remus* are from this edition.

[6] Quotations are from *The History of Reynard the Fox, translated and printed by William Caxton*, ed. Edward Arber (London, 1880), pp. 96 and 71.

[7] Cf. Edwin Greenlaw, "The Sources of Spenser's 'Mother Hubberd's Tale,'" *Modern Philology, 2* (1905), 411–32.

[8] George Orwell, *Animal Farm* (New York, 1946), p. 22. All quotations are from this edition.

The Mythos of Winter: Irony and Satire

We come now to the mythical patterns of experience, the attempts to give form to the shifting ambiguities and complexities of un-idealized existence. We cannot find these patterns merely in the mimetic or representational aspect of such literature, for that aspect is one of content and not form. As structure, the central principle of ironic myth is best approached as a parody of romance: the application of romantic mythical forms to a more realistic content which fits them in unexpected ways. No one in a romance, Don Quixote protests, ever asks who pays for the hero's accommodation.

The chief distinction between irony and satire is that satire is militant irony: its moral norms are relatively clear, and it assumes standards against which the grotesque and absurd are measured. Sheer invective or name-calling ("flyting") is satire in which there is relatively little irony: on the other hand, whenever a reader is not sure what the author's attitude is or what his own is supposed to be, we have irony with relatively little satire. Fielding's *Jonathan Wild* is satiric irony: certain flat moral judgements made by the narrator (as in the description of Bagshot in chapter twelve) are in accord with the decorum of the work, but would be out of key in, say, *Madame Bovary*. Irony is consistent both with complete realism of content and with the suppression of attitude on the part of the author. Satire demands at least a token fantasy, a content which the reader recognizes as grotesque, and at least an implicit moral standard, the

From *The Anatomy of Criticism*, Princeton, 1957, pp. 223–39. Copyright © by Princeton University Press. Reprinted by permission of the Princeton University Press. This essay should be compared with Frye's earlier version (or draft), "The Nature of Satire," *The University of Toronto Quarterly*, XIV (1944), 75–89.

latter being essential in a militant attitude to experience. Some phenomena, such as the ravages of disease, may be called grotesque, but to make fun of them would not be very effective satire. The satirist has to select his absurdities, and the act of selection is a moral act.

The argument of Swift's *Modest Proposal* has a brain-softening plausibility about it: one is almost led to feel that the narrator is not only reasonable but even humane; yet the "almost" can never drop out of any sane man's reaction, and as long as it remains there the modest proposal will be both fantastic and immoral. When in another passage Swift suddenly says, discussing the poverty of Ireland, "But my Heart is too heavy to continue this Irony longer," he is speaking of satire, which breaks down when its content is too oppressively real to permit the maintaining of the fantastic or hypothetical tone. Hence satire is irony which is structurally close to the comic: the comic struggle of two societies, one normal and the other absurd, is reflected in its double focus of morality and fantasy. Irony with little satire is the non-heroic residue of tragedy, centering on a theme of puzzled defeat.

Two things, then, are essential to satire; one is wit or humor founded on fantasy or a sense of the grotesque or absurd, the other is an object of attack. Attack without humor, or pure denunciation, forms one of the boundaries of satire. It is a very hazy boundary, because invective is one of the most readable forms of literary art, just as panegyric is one of the dullest. It is an established datum of literature that we like hearing people cursed and are bored with hearing them praised, and almost any denunciation, if vigorous enough, is followed by a reader with the kind of pleasure that soon breaks into a smile. To attack anything, writer and audience must agree on its undesirability, which means that the content of a great deal of satire founded on national hatreds, snobbery, prejudice, and personal pique goes out of date very quickly.

But attack in literature can never be a pure expression of merely personal or even social hatred, whatever the motivation for it may be, because the words for expressing hatred, as distinct from enmity, have too limited a range. About the only ones we have are derived from the animal world, but calling a man a swine or a skunk or a woman a bitch affords a severely restricted satisfaction, as most of the unpleasant qualities of the animal are human projections. As Shakespeare's Thersites says of Menelaus, "to what form, but that he is, should wit larded with malice, and malice forced with wit, turn him to? To an ass, were nothing; he is both ass and ox; to an ox, were nothing; he is both ox and ass." For effective attack we must reach some kind of impersonal level, and that commits the attacker if only by implication, to a moral standard. The satirist commonly takes a high moral line. Pope asserts that he is "To Virtue only and her friends a friend," suggesting that that is what he is really being when he is reflecting on the cleanliness of the underwear worn by the lady who had jilted him.

Humor, like attack, is founded on convention. The world of humor is a rigidly stylized world in which generous Scotchmen, obedient wives, beloved mothers-in-law, and professors with presence of mind are not permitted to exist. All humor demands agreement that certain things, such as a picture of a wife beating her husband in a comic strip, are conventionally funny. To introduce a comic strip in which a husband beats his wife would distress the reader, because it would mean learning a new convention. The humor of pure fantasy, the other boundary of satire, belongs to romance, though it is uneasy there, as humor perceives the incongruous, and the conventions of romance are idealized. Most fantasy is pulled back into satire by a powerful undertow often called allegory, which may be described as the implicit reference to experience in the perception of the incongruous. The White Knight in Alice who felt that one should be provided for everything, and therefore put anklets around his horse's feet to guard against the bites of sharks, may pass as pure fantasy. But when he goes on to sing an elaborate parody of Wordsworth we begin to sniff the acrid, pungent smell of satire, and when we take a second look at the White Knight we recognize a character type closely related both to Quixote and to the pedant of comedy.

As in this *mythos* we have the difficulty of two words to contend with, it may be simplest, if the reader is now accustomed to our sequence of six phases, to start with them and describe them in order, instead of abstracting a typical form and discussing it first. The first three are phases of satire, and correspond to the first three or ironic phases of comedy.

The first phase corresponds to the first phase of ironic comedy in which there is no displacement of the humorous society. The sense of absurdity about such a comedy arises as a kind of backfire or recall after the work has been seen or read. Once we have finished with it, deserts of futility open up on all sides, and we have, in spite of the humor, a sense of nightmare and a close proximity to something demonic. Even in very light-hearted comedy we may get a trace of this feeling: if the main theme of *Pride and Prejudice* had been the married life of Collins and Charlotte Lucas, one wonders how long Collins would continue to be funny. Hence it is in decorum for even a satire prevailingly light in tone, such as Pope's second Moral Essay on the characters of women, to rise to a terrifying climax of moral intensity.

The satire typical of this phase may be called the satire of the low norm. It takes for granted a world which is full of anomalies, injustices, follies, and crimes, and yet is permanent and undisplaceable. Its principle is that anyone who wishes to keep his balance in such a world must learn first of all to keep his eyes open and his mouth shut. Counsels of prudence, urging the reader in effect to adopt an *eiron* role, have been prominent in literature from Egyptian times. What is recommended is conventional life at its best: a clairvoyant knowledge of human nature in oneself and others, an avoidance of all illusion and compulsive behavior, a reliance on observation and timing rather than on aggressiveness. This is wisdom, the tried and tested way of life, which does not question the logic of social convention, but merely follows the procedures which in fact do serve to maintain one's balance from one day to the next. The *eiron* of the low norm takes an attitude of flexible pragmatism; he assumes that society will, if given any chance, behave more or less like Caliban's Setebos in Browning's poem, and he conducts himself accordingly. On all doubtful points of behavior convention is his deepest conviction. And however good or bad expertly conventional behavior may be thought to be, it is certainly the most difficult of all forms of behavior to satirize, just as anyone with a new theory of behavior, even if saint or prophet, is the easiest of all people to ridicule as a crank.

Hence the satirist may employ a plain, common-sense, conventional person as a foil for the various *alazons* of society. Such a person may be the author himself or a narrator, and he coresponds to the plain dealer in comedy or the blunt adviser in tragedy. When distinguished from the author, he is often a rustic with pastoral affinities, illustrating the connection of his role with the *agroikos* type in comedy. The kind of American satire that passes as folk humor, exemplified by the Biglow Papers, Mr. Dooley, Artemus Ward, and Will Rogers, makes a good deal of him, and this genre is closely linked with the North American development of the counsel of prudence in Poor

Richard's Almanac and the Sam Slick papers. Other examples are easy enough to find, both where we expect them, as in Crabbe, whose tale *The Patron* also belongs to the counsel-of-prudence genre, and where we might not expect them, as in the Fish-Eater dialogue in Erasmus's *Colloquies*. Chaucer represents himself as a shy, demure, inconspicuous member of his pilgrimage, agreeing politely with everybody ("And I seyde his opinion was good"), and showing to the pilgrims none of the powers of observation that he displays to his reader. We are not surprised therefore to find that one of his "own" tales is in the counsel of prudence tradition.

The most elaborate form of low-norm satire is the encyclopaedic form favored by the Middle Ages, closely allied to preaching, and generally based on the encyclopaedic scheme of the seven deadly sins, a form which survived as late as Elizabethan times in Nashe's *Pierce Penilesse* and Lodge's *Wits Miserie*. Erasmus's *Praise of Folly* belongs to this tradition, in which the link with the corresponding comic phase, the view of an upside-down world dominated by humors and ruling passions, can be clearly seen. When adopted by a preacher, or even an intellectual, the low norm device is part of an implied *a fortiori* argument: if people cannot reach even ordinary common sense, or church porch virtue, there is little point in comparing them with any higher standards.

Where gaiety predominates in such satire, we have an attitude which fundamentally accepts social conventions but stresses tolerance and flexibility within their limits. Close to the conventional norm we find the lovable eccentric, Uncle Toby or Betsey Trotwood who diversifies, without challenging, accepted codes of behavior. Such characters have much of the child about them, and a child's behavior is usually thought of as coming towards an accepted standard instead of moving away from it. Where attack predominates, we have an inconspicuous, unobtrusive *eiron* standard contrasted with the *alazons* or blocking humors who are in charge of society. This situation has for its archetype an ironic counterpart of the romance theme of giant-killing. For society to exist at all there must be a delegation of prestige and influence to organized groups such as the church, the army, the professions and the government, all of which consist of individuals given more than individual power by the institutions to which they belong. If a satirist presents, say, a clergyman as a fool or hypocrite, he is, *qua* satirist, attacking neither a man nor a church. The former has no literary or hypothetical point, and the latter carries him outside the range of satire. He is attacking an evil man protected by his church, and such a man is a gigantic monster: monstrous because not what he should be, gigantic because protected by his position and by the prestige of good clergymen. The cowl might make the monk if it were not for satire.

Milton says, "for a Satyr as it was born out of a Tragedy, so ought to resemble his parentage, to strike high, and adventure dangerously at the most eminent vices among the greatest persons." Apart from the etymology, this needs one qualification: a great vice does not need a great person to represent it. We have mentioned the gigantic size of Sir Epicure Mammon's dream in *The Alchemist*: the whole mystery of the corrupted human will is in it, yet the utter impotence of the dreamer is essential to the satire. Similarly, we miss much of the point of *Jonathan Wild* unless we take the hero seriously as a parody of greatness, or false social standards of valuation. But in general the principle may be accepted for the satirist's antagonists that the larger they come, the easier they fall. In low-norm satire the *alazon* is a Goliath encountered by a tiny David with his sudden and vicious stones, a giant prodded by a cool and observant but almost invisible enemy into a blind, stampeding fury and then polished off at leisure. This situation has run through satire from the stories of Polyphemus and Blunderbore to, in a much more ironic and equivocal context, the Chaplin films. Dryden transforms his victims into fantastic dinosaurs of bulging flesh and peanut brains; he seems genuinely impressed by the "goodly and great" bulk of Og and by the furious energy of the poet Doeg.

The figure of the low-norm *eiron* is irony's substitute for the hero, and when he is removed from satire we can see more clearly that one of the central themes of the *mythos* is the disappearance of the heroic. This is the main reason for the predominance in fictional satire of what may be called the Omphale archetype, the man bullied or dominated by women, which has been prominent in satire all through its history, and embraces a vast area of contemporary humor, both popular and sophisticated. Similarly, when the giant or monster is removed we can see that he is the mythical form of society, the hydra or fama full of tongues, Spenser's blatant beast which is still at large. And while the crank with his new idea is an obvious target for satire, still social convention is mainly fossilized dogma, and the standard appealed to by low-norm satire is a set of conventions largely invented by dead cranks. The strength of the conventional person is not in the conventions but in his common-sense way of handling them. Hence the logic of satire itself drives it on from its first phase of conventional satire on the unconventional to a second phase in which the sources and values of conventions themselves are objects of ridicule. The simplest form of the corresponding second phase of comedy is the comedy of escape, in which a hero runs away to a more congenial society without transforming his own. The satiric counterpart of this is the picaresque novel, the story of the successful rogue who, from Reynard the Fox on, makes conventional society look foolish without setting up any positive standard. The picaresque novel is the social form of what with *Don Quixote* modulates into a more intellectualized satire, the nature of which needs some explanation.

Satire, according to Juvenal's useful if hackneyed formula, has an interest in anything men do. The philosopher, on the other hand, teaches a certain way or method of living; he stresses some things and despises others; what he recommends is carefully selected from the data of human life; he continually passes moral judgements on social behavior. His attitude is dogmatic; that of the satirist pragmatic. Hence satire may often represent the collision between a selection of standards from experience and the feeling that experience is bigger than any set of beliefs about it. The satirist demonstrates the infinite variety of what men do by showing the futility, not only of saying what they ought to do, but even of attempts to systematize or formulate a coherent scheme of what they do. Philosophies of life abstract from life, and an abstraction implies the leaving out of inconvenient data. The satirist brings up these inconvenient data, sometimes in the form of alternative and equally plausible theories, like the Erewhonian treatment of crime and disease or Swift's demonstration of the mechanical operation of spirit.

The central theme in the second or quixotic phase of satire, then, is the setting of ideas and generalizations and theories and dogmas over against the life they are supposed to explain. This theme is presented very clearly in Lucian's dialogue *The Sale of Lives*, in which a series of slave-philosophers pass in review, with all their arguments and guarantees, before a buyer who has to consider living with them. He buys a few, it is true, but as slaves, not as masters or teachers. Lucian's attitude to Greek philosophy is repeated in the attitude of Erasmus and Rabelais to the scholastic, of Swift and Samuel Butler I to Descartes and the Royal Society, of Voltaire to the Leibnitzians, of Peacock to the Romantics, of Samuel Butler II to the Darwinians, of Aldous Huxley to the behaviorists. We notice that low-norm satire often becomes *merely* anti-intellectual, a tendency that crops up in Crabbe (*vide The Learned Boy*) and even in Swift. The influence of low-norm satire in American culture has produced a popular contempt for longhairs and ivory towers, an example of what may be called a fallacy of poetic projection, or taking literary conventions to be facts of life. Anti-intellectual satire proper, however, is based on a sense of the comparative naivete of systematic thought, and should not be limited by such ready-made terms as skeptical or cynical.

Skepticism itself may be or become a dogmatic attitude, a comic humor of doubting plain evidence. Cynicism is a little closer to the satiric norm: Menippus, the founder of the Menippean satire, was a cynic, and cynics are generally associated with the role of intellectual Thersites. Lyly's play *Campaspe*, for instance, presents Plato, Aristotle, and Diogenes, but the first two are bores, and Diogenes, who is not a philosopher at all but an Elizabethan clown of the malcontent type, steals the show. But still cynicism is a philosophy, and one that may produce the strange spiritual pride of the Peregrinus of whom Lucian makes a searching and terrible analysis. In the *Sale of Lives* the cynic and the skeptic are auctioned in their turn, and the latter is the last to be sold, dragged off to have his very skepticism refuted, not by argument but by life. Erasmus and Burton called themselves Democritus Junior, followers of the philosopher who laughed at mankind, but Lucian's buyer considers that Democritus too has overdone his pose. Insofar as the satirist has a "position" of his own, it is the preference of practice to theory, experience to metaphysics. When Lucian goes to consult his master Menippus, he is told the method of wisdom is to do the task that lies to hand, advice repeated in Voltaire's *Candide* and in the instructions given to the unborn in *Erewhon*. Thus philosophical pedantry becomes, as every target of satire eventually does, a form of romanticism or the imposing of over-simplified ideals on experience.

The satiric attitude here is neither philosophical nor anti-philosophical, but an expression of the hypothetical form of art. Satire on ideas is only the special kind of art that defends its own creative detachment. The demand for order in thought produces a supply of intellectual systems: some of these attract and convert artists, but as an equally great poet could defend any other system equally well, no one system can contain the arts as they stand. Hence a systematic reasoner, given the power, would be likely to establish hierarchies in the arts, or censor and expurgate as Plato wished to do to Homer. Satire on systems of reasoning, especially on the social effects of such systems, is art's first line of defence against all such invasions.

In the warfare of science against superstition, the satirists have done famously. Satire itself appears to have begun with the Greek *silloi* which were pro-scientific attacks on superstition. In English literature, Chaucer and Ben Jonson riddled the alchemists with a crossfire of their own jargon; Nashe and Swift hounded astrologers into premature graves; Browning's *Sludge the Medium* annihilated the spiritualists, and a rabble of occultists, numerologists, Pythagoreans, and Rosicrucians lie sprawling in the wake of *Hudibras*. To the scientist it may seem little short of perverse that satire placidly goes on making fun of legitimate astronomers in *The Elephant in the Moon*, of experimental laboratories in *Gulliver's Travels*, of Darwinian and Malthusian cosmology in *Erewhon*, of conditioned reflexes in *Brave New World*, of technological efficiency in *1984*. Charles Fort, one of the few who have continued the tradition of intellectual satire in this century, brings the wheel full circle by mocking the scientists for their very freedom from superstition itself, a rational attitude which, like all rational attitudes, still refuses to examine all the evidence.

Similarly with religion. The satirist may feel with Lucian that the eliminating of superstition would also eliminate religion, or with Erasmus that it would restore health to religion. But whether Zeus exists or not is a question; that men who think him vicious and stupid will insist that he change the weather is a fact, accepted by scoffer and devout alike. Any really devout person would surely welcome a satirist who cauterized hypocrisy and superstition as an ally of true religion. Yet once a hypocrite who sounds exactly like a good man is sufficiently blackened, the good man also may begin to seem a little dingier than he was. Those who would agree even with the theoretical parts of *Holy Willie's Prayer* in Burns look rather like Holy Willies themselves. One feels similarly that while the personal attitudes of Erasmus, Rabelais, Swift, and Voltaire to institutional religion varied a good deal, the effect of their satire varies much less. Satire on religion includes the parody of the sacramental life in English Protestantism that runs from Milton's divorce pamphlets to *The Way of All Flesh*, and the antagonism to Christianity in Nietzsche, Yeats, and D. H. Lawrence based on the conception of Jesus as another kind of romantic idealist.

The narrator in *Erewhon* remarks that while the real religion of

most of the Erewhonians was, whatever they said it was, the acceptance of low-norm conventionality (the goddess Ydgrun), there was
also a small group of "high Ydgrunites" who were the best people he
found in Erewhon. The attitude of these people reminds us rather of
Montaigne: they had the *eiron's* sense of the value of conventions that
had been long established and were now harmless; they had the *eiron's*
distrust of the ability of anyone's reason, including their own, to transform society into a better structure. But they were also intellectually
detached from the conventions they lived with, and were capable of
seeing their anomalies and absurdities as well as their stabilizing conservatism.

The literary form that high Ydgrunism produces in second-phase
satire we may call the *ingenu* form, after Voltaire's dialogue of that
name. Here an outsider to the society, in this case an American Indian,
is the low norm: he has no dogmatic views of his own, but he grants
none of the premises which make the absurdities of society look logical
to those accustomed to them. He is really a pastoral figure, and like
the pastoral, a form congenial to satire, he contrasts a set of simple
standards with the complex rationalizations of society. But we have
just seen that it is precisely the complexity of data in experience which
the satirist insists on and the simple set of standards which he distrusts.
That is why the *ingenu* is an outsider; he comes from another world
which is either unattainable or associated with something else undesirable. Montaigne's cannibals have all the virtues we have not, if we
don't mind being cannibals. More's Utopia is an ideal state except that
to enter it we must give up the idea of Christendom. The Houyhnhnms
live the life of reason and nature better than we, but Gulliver finds
that he is born a Yahoo, and that such a life would be nearer the
capacities of gifted animals than of humans. Whenever the "other
world" appears in satire, it appears as an ironic counterpart to our
own, a reversal of accepted social standards. This form of satire is
represented in Lucian's *Kataplous* and *Charon*, journeys to the other
world in which the eminent in this one are shown doing appropriate
but unaccustomed things, a form incorporated in Rabelais, and in the
medieval *danse macabre*. In the last named the simple equality of
death is set against the complex inequalities of life.

Intellectual satire defends the creative detachment in art, but art
too tends to seek out socially accepted ideas and become in its turn a
social fixation. We have spoken of the idealized art of romance as in
particular the form in which an ascendant class tends to express itself,

and so the rising middle class in medieval Europe naturally turned to mock-romance. Other forms of satire have a similar function, whether so intended or not. The *danse macabre* and the *kataplous* are ironic reversals of the kind of romanticism that we have in the serious vision of the other world. In Dante, for instance, the judgements of the next world usually confirm the standards of this one, and in heaven itself nearly the whole available billeting is marked for officers only. The cultural effect of such satire is not to denigrate romance, but to prevent any group of conventions from dominating the whole of literary experience. Second-phase satire shows literature assuming a special function of analysis, of breaking up the lumber of stereotypes, fossilized beliefs, superstitious terrors, crank theories, pedantic dogmatisms, oppressive fashions, and all other things that impede the free movement (not necessarily, of course, the progress) of society. Such satire is the completion of the logical process known as the *reductio ad absurdum*, which is not designed to hold one in perpetual captivity, but to bring one to the point at which one can escape from an incorrect procedure.

The romantic fixation which revolves around the beauty of perfect form, in art or elsewhere, is also a logical target for satire. The word satire is said to come from *satura*, or hash, and a kind of parody of form seems to run all through its tradition, from the mixture of prose and verse in early satire to the jerky cinematic changes of scene in Rabelais (I am thinking of a somewhat archaic type of cinema). *Tristram Shandy* and *Don Juan* illustrate very clearly the constant tendency to self-parody in satiric rhetoric which prevents even the process of writing itself from becoming an oversimplified convention or ideal. In *Don Juan* we simultaneously read the poem and watch the poet at work writing it: we eavesdrop on his associations, his struggles for rhymes, his tentative and discarded plans, the subjective preferences organizing his choice of details (e.g.: "Her stature tall—I hate a dumpy woman"), his decisions whether to be "serious" or mask himself with humor. All of this and even more is true of *Tristram Shandy*. A deliberate rambling digressiveness, which in *A Tale of a Tub* reaches the point of including a digression in praise of digressions, is endemic in the narrative technique of satire, and so is a calculated bathos or art of sinking in its suspense, such as the quizzical mock-oracular conclusions in Apuleius and Rabelais and in the refusal of Sterne for hundreds of pages even to get his hero born. An extraordinary number of great satires are fragmentary, unfinished, or anonymous. In ironic fiction a good many devices turning on the difficulty of communication, such as having a story presented through an idiot mind, serve the same purpose. Virginia Woolf's *The Waves* is made up of speeches of characters constructed precisely out of what they do *not* say, but what their behavior and attitudes say in spite of them.

This technique of disintegration brings us well into the third phase of satire, the satire of the high norm. Second-phase satire may make a tactical defence of the pragmatic against the dogmatic, but here we must let go even of ordinary common sense as a standard. For common sense too has certain implied dogmas, notably that the data of sense experience are reliable and consistent, and that our customary associations with things form a solid basis for interpreting the present and predicting the future. The satirist cannot explore all the possibilities of his form without seeing what happens if he questions these assumptions. That is why he so often gives to ordinary life a logical and self-consistent shift of perspective. He will show us society suddenly in a telescope as posturing and dignified pygmies, or in a microscope as hideous and reeking giants, or he will change his hero into an ass and show us how humanity looks from an ass's point of view. This type of fantasy breaks down customary associations, reduces sense experience to one of many possible categories, and brings out the tentative, *als ob* basis of all our thinking. Emerson says that such shifts of perspective afford "a low degree of the sublime," but actually they afford something of far greater artistic importance, a high degree of the ridiculous. And, consistently with the general basis of satire as parody-romance, they are usually adaptations of romance themes: the fairyland of little people, the land of giants, the world of enchanted animals, the wonderlands parodied in Lucian's *True History*.

When we fall back from the outworks of faith and reason to the tangible realities of the senses, satire follows us up. A slight shift of perspective, a different tinge in the emotional coloring, and the solid earth becomes an intolerable horror. *Gulliver's Travels* shows us man as a venomous rodent, man as a noisome and clumsy pachyderm, the mind of man as a bear-pit, and the body of man as a compound of filth and ferocity. But Swift is simply following where his satiric genius leads him, and genius seems to have led practically every great satirist to become what the world calls obscene. Social convention means people parading in front of each other, and the preservation of it demands that the dignity of some men and the beauty of some women should be thought of apart from excretion, copulation, and similar embarrassments. Constant reference to these latter brings us down to a bodily democracy paralleling the democracy of death in the *danse macabre*. Swift's affinity with the *danse macabre* tradition is marked in his description of the Struldbrugs, and his *Directions to Servants* and his more unquotable poems are in the tradition of the medieval preachers who painted the repulsiveness of gluttony and lechery. For here as everywhere else in satire there is a moral reference: it is all very well to eat, drink, and be merry, but one cannot always put off dying until tomorrow.

In the riotous chaos of Rabelais, Petronius, and Apuleius satire plunges through to its final victory over common sense. When we have finished with their weirdly logical fantasies of debauch, dream, and delirium we wake up wondering if Paracelsus' suggestion is right that the things seen in delirium are really there, like stars in daytime, and invisible for the same reason. Lucius becomes initiated and slips evasively out of our grasp, whether he lied or told the truth, as St. Augustine says with a touch of exasperation; Rabelais promises us a final oracle and leaves us staring at an empty bottle; Joyce's HCE struggles for pages toward wakening, but just as we seem on the point of grasping something tangible we are swung around to the first page of the book again. The *Satyricon* is a torn fragment from what seems like a history of some monstrous Atlantean race that vanished in the sea, still drunk.

The first phase of satire is dominated by the figure of the giant-killer, but in this rending of the stable universe a giant power rears up in satire itself. When the Philistine giant comes out to battle with the children of light, he naturally expects to find someone his own size ready to meet him, someone who is head and shoulders over every man in Israel. Such a Titan would have to bear down his opponent by sheer weight of words, and hence be a master of that technique of torrential abuse which we call invective. The gigantic figures in Rabelais, the awakened forms of the bound or sleeping giants that meet us in *Finnegans Wake* and the opening of *Gulliver's Travels*, are expressions of a creative exuberance of which the most typical and obvious sign is the verbal tempest, the tremendous outpouring of words in catalogues, abusive epithets and erudite technicalities which since the third chapter of Isaiah (a satire on female ornament) has been a feature, and almost a monopoly, of third-phase satire. Its golden age in English literature was the age of Burton, Nashe, Marston, and Urquhart of Cromarty, the uninhibited translator of Rabelais, who in his spare time was what Nashe would call a "scholastical squitterbook," producing books with such titles as *Trissotetras, Pantochrono-chanon, Exkubalauron* and *Logopandecteison*. Nobody except Joyce has in modern English made much sustained effort to carry on this tradition of verbal exuberance: even Carlyle, from this point of view, is a sad comedown after Burton and Urquhart. In American culture it is represented by the "talk talk" of the folklore boaster, which has some literary congeners in the catalogues of Whitman and *Moby Dick*.

With the fourth phase we move around to the ironic aspect of tragedy, and satire begins to recede. The fall of the tragic hero, especially in Shakespeare, is so delicately balanced emotionally that we almost exaggerate any one element in it merely by calling attention to it. One of these elements is the elegiac aspect in which irony is at a minimum, the sense of gentle and dignified pathos, often symbolized by music, which marks the desertion of Antony by Hercules, the dream of the rejected Queen Catherine in *Henry VIII*, Hamlet's "absent thee from felicity awhile," and Othello's Aleppo speech. One can of course find irony even here, as Mr. Eliot has found it in the last named, but the main emotional weight is surely thrown on the opposite side. Yet we are also aware that Hamlet dies in the middle of a frantically muddled effort at revenge which has taken eight lives instead of one, that Cleopatra fades away with great dignity after a careful search for easy ways to die, that Coriolanus is badly confused by his mother and violently resents being called a boy. Such tragic irony differs from satire in that there is no attempt to make fun of the character, but only to bring out clearly the "all too human," as distinct from the heroic, aspects of the tragedy. King Lear attempts to achieve heroic dignity through his position as a king and father, and finds it instead in his suffering humanity: hence it is in *King Lear* that we find what has been called the "comedy of the grotesque," the ironic parody of the tragic situation, most elaborately developed.

As a phase of irony in its own right, the fourth phase looks at tragedy from below, from the moral and realistic perspective of the state of experience. It stresses the humanity of its heroes, minimizes the sense of ritual inevitability in tragedy, supplies social and psychological explanations for catastrophe, and makes as much as possible of human misery seem, in Thoreau's phrase, "superfluous and evitable." This is the phase of most sincere, explicit realism: it is in general Tolstoy's phase, and also that of a good deal of Hardy and Conrad. One of its central themes is Stein's answer to the problem of the "romantic" Lord Jim in Conrad: "in the destructive element immerse." This remark, without ridiculing Jim, still brings out the quixotic and romantic element in his nature and criticizes it from the point of view of experience. The chapter on watches and chronometers in Melville's *Pierre* takes a similar attitude.

The fifth phase, corresponding to fatalistic or fifth-phase tragedy, is irony in which the main emphasis is on the natural cycle, the steady unbroken turning of the wheel of fate or fortune. It sees experience, in our terms, with the point of epiphany closed up, and its motto is Browning's "there may be heaven; there must be hell." Like the corresponding phase of tragedy, it is less moral and more generalized and metaphysical in its interest, less melioristic and more stoical and resigned. The treatment of Napoleon in *War and Peace* and in *The Dynasts* affords a good contrast between the fourth and fifth phases of irony. The refrain in the Old English *Complaint of Deor*: "Thaes ofereode; thisses swa maeg" (freely translatable as "Other people got things; maybe I can") expresses a stoicism not of the "invictus" type, which maintains a romantic dignity, but rather a sense, found also in the parallel second phase of satire, that the practical and immediate situation is likely to be worthy of more respect than the theoretical explanation of it.

The sixth phase presents human life in terms of largely unrelieved bondage. Its settings feature prisons, madhouses, lynching mobs, and places of execution, and it differs from a pure inferno mainly in the fact that in human experience suffering has an end in death. In our day the chief form of this phase is the nightmare of social tyranny, of which *1984* is perhaps the most familiar. We often find, on this boundary of the *visio malefica*, the use of parody-religious symbols suggesting some form of Satan or Antichrist worship. In Kafka's *In the Penal Colony* a parody of original sin appears in the officer's remark, "Guilt is never to be doubted." In *1984* the parody of religion in the final scenes is more elaborate: there is a parody of the atonement, for instance, when the hero is tortured into urging that the torments be inflicted on the heroine instead. The assumption is made in this story that the lust for sadistic power on the part of the ruling class is strong enough to last indefinitely, which is precisely the assumption one has to make about devils in order to accept the orthodox picture of hell. The "telescreen" device brings into irony the tragic theme of *derkou theama*, the humiliation of being constantly watched by a hostile or derisive eye.

The human figures of this phase are, of course, *desdichado* figures of misery or madness, often parodies of romantic roles. Thus the romantic theme of the helpful servant giant is parodied in *The Hairy Ape* and *Of Mice and Men*, and the romantic presenter or Prospero figure is parodied in the Benjy of *The Sound and the Fury* whose idiot mind contains, without comprehending, the whole action of the novel. Sinister parental figures naturally abound, for this is the world of the ogre and the witch, of Baudelaire's black giantess and Pope's goddess Dullness, who also has much of the parody deity about her ("Light dies before thy uncreating word!"), of the siren with the imprisoning image of shrouding hair, and, of course, of the *femme fatale* or malignant grinning female, "older than the rocks among which she sits," as Pater says of her.

This brings us around again to the point of demonic epiphany, the dark tower and prison of endless pain, the city of dreadful night in the desert, or, with a more erudite irony, the *tour abolie*, the goal of the quest that isn't there. But on the other side of this blasted world of repulsiveness and idiocy, a world without pity and without hope, satire begins again. At the bottom of Dante's hell, which is also the center of the spherical earth, Dante sees Satan standing upright in the circle of ice, and as he cautiously follows Virgil over the hip and thigh of the evil giant, letting himself down by the tufts of hair on his skin, he passes the center and finds himself no longer going down but going up, climbing out on the other side of the world to see the stars again. From this point of view, the devil is no longer upright, but standing on his head, in the same attitude in which he was hurled downward from heaven upon the other side of the earth. Tragedy and tragic irony take us into a hell of narrowing circles and culminate in some such vision of the source of all evil in a personal form. Tragedy can take us no farther; but if we persevere with the *mythos* of irony and satire, we shall pass a dead center, and finally see the gentlemanly Prince of Darkness bottom side up.

ALVIN P. KERNAN

A Theory of Satire

"There was in our time a certain parasite, Golias by name, notorious alike for his intemperance and wantonness . . . a tolerable scholar, but without morals or discipline . . . who did vomit forth against the Pope and the Roman curia a succession of famous pieces, as adroit as they were preposterous, as imprudent as they were impudent."[1] These lines, written in the early thirteenth century by the historian Giraldus Cambrensis, contain a fundamental error: there was no such person as "Golias." There were, however, a number of satiric poems, written in the twelfth and thirteenth centuries by anonymous poets, which were purportedly the work of one Bishop Golias, a sprightly, irreverent, devil-may-care who divided his time between laughing at the clergy and praising the pleasures of the flesh. But Golias himself was the purely poetic creation of those poets called the goliards or *ordo vagorum*, the wandering, witty clerics of the late medieval period, who refused to attach themselves to any benefice or to submit to any strict rule. For them Golias, whose name seems to derive from Latin *gula*, throat and gluttony, became "a kind of eponymous hero,"[2] and under the cover of this *persona* the poets flaunted their own unorthodox wit and wrote their mocking attacks on a world where people like Giraldus took themselves far too seriously.

Giraldus was a historian and he read the goliardic satires as documents, pieces of reporting, making no allowance for their pronounced artistic qualities of obliquity, exaggeration, and irony. The satiric mask of Bishop Golias was for the historian the direct reflection of an actual living person whose discreditable character, revealed by his manner of

From *The Cankered Muse: Satire of the English Renaissance*, New Haven, 1959, pp. 1–36. Reprinted by permission of the Yale University Press. Copyright © 1959 by Yale University Press. Kernan's theory is extended to other works, and in minor respects is modified, in *The Plot of Satire*, New Heaven, 1966.

writing, explained the "preposterous," i.e. historically untrue, nature of his attacks on the church. While Giraldus' particular confusion is evident, his general approaches to satire have tenaciously remained the dominant ones down to our own time. The character who delivers the satiric attack is still identified as the author, the biographical method; and the picture of the world given in satire is taken as an attempt to portray the "actual" world, the historical method. These methods have been applied with varying degrees of sophistication, but even at their best they inevitably lead us to such unanswerable questions as, "Was first-century Rome as completely debased as Juvenal painted it?" or "Did Swift hate mankind as extravagantly as Gulliver hated the Yahoos?" Our attention is thus directed away from the satiric work itself and toward some second object, the personality of the author or the contemporary social scene. In this way satire is denied the independence of artistic status and made a biographical and historical document, while the criticism of satire degenerates into discussion of an author's moral character and the economic and social conditions of his time.

Curiously enough, the authors of satires have encouraged this response to their works, for of all the major literary genres satire has traditionally made most pretense of being realistic. The man who after reading *Gulliver's Travels* tried to find Lilliput on the map may have been a fool, but he was led on by Swift's elaborate apparatus of verisimilitude. Elsewhere the game is not so apparent, and the satirist always assures us most seriously that he alone describes the world as it actually *is*, he deals in "deeds and language such as men do use," he has "stoop'd to truth," his subject is "quidquid agunt homines." He argues that other literary kinds—epic, romance, love poetry—are mere lies which avoid the truth about mankind, and he delights in mocking these genres and parodying them. He emphasizes his own dedication to truth by the use of straightforward language, even slang at times, and fills his work with references to contemporary customs, places, names. He will proudly call attention to the absence from his writing of the usual ornaments of poetry and raise the question, as Horace does in the fourth satire of his first book of *Sermones*, whether on the basis of realism, rough diction, and crude meter satire is even entitled to the name of poetry? Pietro Aretino's boast, which owes a good deal to Horace, is typical of the satirist's proud claim to downrgiht truth without any fancy decoration:

> Caesar and Homer, I have stolen your bays!
> Though not a poet or an emperor;
> My style has been my star, in a manner, for
> I speak the truth, don't deal in lying praise.
> I am Aretino, censor of the ways
> Of the lofty world, prophet-ambassador
> Of truth and smiling virtue.[3]

In short, the satirist makes every effort to repudiate the Muse and to emphasize the down-to-earth quality of himself and his work, but the very vigor of these efforts and their continuous appearance in satire suggest that they are themselves stylistic devices used in a perfectly conventional manner to establish the character and tone traditionally thought appropriate for the satiric genre. Paradoxically, the claim to have no style is itself a trick of style employed by nearly every satirist, and his realistic touches are themselves satiric conventions. In point of fact, the claims to blunt, straightforward, and unskilled honesty made by the satirist are so patently false as to be outrageous, for in practice he is always an extremely clever poetic strategist and manipulator of language who possesses an incredibly copious and colorful vocabulary and an almost limitless arsenal of rhetorical devices. This paradox of the artless artist, innate in satire, has usually been solved either by ignoring all evidences of art and taking the satirist's word for it that he is a truthful, unskilled fellow driven to write by his indignation; or by noting his techniques of exaggeration and dismissing his presentation of himself as a plain man dedicated to truth as a mere pose designed to cover some such sinister intention as blackening the names of his enemies or passing off smut and scandal as truth in order to sell his book. Every major writer of satire has been praised by some critics for his fearless determination to tell the truth about his world and damned by others for a twisted, unstable, prurient liar whose works no careful father should allow his children to open.

This dilemma has been created by the biographical and historical methods of criticism, and to solve it we need to approach satire in the way we do other poetry—as an art; that is, not a direct report of the poet's feelings and the literal incidents which aroused those feelings, but a construct of symbols—situations, scenes, characters, language— put together to express some particular vision of the world. The individual parts must be seen in terms of their function in the total poem and not judged by reference to things outside the poem such as the medical history of the author or the social scene in which he wrote.

There have been in recent years a number of discussions of the art of satire, but these have focused somewhat narrowly on the satirist's use of linguistic devices and his ability to contrive incidental effects. We have been shown that he is a master of irony, caricature, disabling imagery, the unexpected thrust of wit, anticlimax, burlesque, and invective.[4] He seems to be a man with an immense supply of rhetorical tools which he uses in rapid succession to belabor his victims. On the rare occasions when attempts have been made to show that the art of satire extends beyond the manipulation of language, the emphasis has still fallen on isolated effects. Mary Claire Randolph, for example, points out that within formal verse satire we find "miniature dramas, sententious proverbs and quotable maxims, beast fables (often reduced to animal metaphors), brief sermons, sharp diatribes, series of vignettes, swiftly sketched but painstakingly built up satiric 'characters' or portraits, figure-processions, little fictions and apologues, visions, apostrophes and invocations to abstractions. This bewildering array of devices suggests the diverse origins of satire and the appropriateness of its name 'satura,' or 'medley.' "[5] Demonstrations of the satirist's skillful handling of language and management of single effects have made suspect the once popular examination question, "Is Satire Art?" but we are still left with a satirist who is only an artist manqué, a contriver of farragoes rather than articulated wholes.[6]

What is required is a more comprehensive method of describing satire which will not limit our investigations to linguistic analysis or the location of single effects but will instead include all the major elements of composition used in the form. An adequate set of terms will permit us to see individual satires as entities and thus make it possible for us to grasp the relationship of one satire to others, and ultimately to define satire with some exactitude. Historical and biographical critics have focused on what are certainly the two most striking aspects of satire, the picture of the society which is presented as a literal rendering of the *hic et nunc*, and the elusive speaker who is sometimes merely identified as "I" and sometimes given a name. In historical terms the picture of society is identified always as Rome, London, Hollywood, or some other specific place, and in biographical terms the speaker becomes Swift, Juvenal, Fielding, or some other specific author. If, however, we translate the historical and biographical terms into the dramatic terms which they readily suggest, a number of the dilemmas seemingly inherent in satire become comprehensible. Using the terms of drama, the picture of society drawn by the satirist becomes the "scene," and the voice we "hear" becomes the satiric "hero." Since the chief character of satire always lacks so signally the qualities which we associate with heroism, it will be better to refer to him simply as the "satirist," and from this point on when the word "satirist" is used it refers to the chief character—whether named, identified as "I," or the anonymous voice that tells the tale—in a satiric work. The author will be designated by other terms. The adoption of two dramatic terms, scene and satirist, entails the use of a third, "plot," for wherever we have characters in a setting there is always movement, or attempted movement, in some direction.

Satire is, like comedy and tragedy, a very ancient form which appears to have its roots in primitive ritual activities such as formulaic curses and the magical blasting of personal and tribal enemies;[7] and just as we find tragic and comic attitudes outside art, so we find that the attitudes expressed in satire are also felt and expressed by individuals in various extraliterary ways ranging from the sneer to the street-corner tirade. But satire, although critics have always regarded it as a minor form, has long been established as a recognizable literary genre with its own traditions and conventions. The protean nature of satire has interfered with any precise definition of its conventions, but since by general agreement works as surfacely diverse as Jeremiah's bitter denunciation of his sinful people, *Gulliver's Travels*, *The Praise of Folly*, *The Clouds* and *The Threepenny Opera* have been identified as satires, then it would follow that they share some quality which we take to be characteristic of satire. For most of us satire is synonymous with attack, particularly the savage variety, but there are attacks which are not satires—Ahab's bitter descriptions of Moby Dick, for example—and so satire must be a definite kind of attack. That is, there must be specific groupings, roles, tones, patterns, which we implicitly recognize as characteristic of satire, and these I propose to describe in terms of scene, character, and plot.

THE SCENE OF SATIRE

The scene of satire is always disorderly and crowded, packed to the very point of bursting. The deformed faces of depravity, stupidity, greed, venality, ignorance, and maliciousness group closely together for a moment, stare boldly out at us, break up, and another tight knot of figures collects, stroking full stomachs, looking vacantly into space, nervously smiling at the great, proudly displaying jewels and figures, clinking moneybags, slyly fingering new-bought fashions. The scene is equally choked with things: ostentatious buildings and statuary, chariots, sedan-chairs, clothes, books, food, horses, dildoes, luxurious furnishings, gin bottles, wigs. Pick up any major satiric work and open it at random and the immediate effect is one of disorderly profusion. The sheer dirty weight, without reason or conscious purpose, of people and their vulgar possessions threatens to overwhelm the world in Trimalchio's banquet room, the streets of Juvenal's Rome, Langland's "felde ful of folke," Eleanor Rumming's Tavern, Bartholomew Fair, the City as the Dunces set off for Westminster, Don Juan's London streets that "boil over with their scum," and before the Hollywood theater where the vast mob of yokels gathers to see the "movie stars" in Nathanael West's *The Day of the Locust*. Everywhere the satirist turns he finds idiocy, foolishness, depravity, and dirt. "Auriculas asini quis non habet?"[8] (Who is there who has not the ears of an ass?) shouts "Persius," and "Juvenal's" exclamation, "It is difficult *not* to write satire," (difficile est saturam non scribere) expresses the satirist's sense of a world where vice is so omnipresent and so arrant that it cannot be avoided. It is no accident that most satire is set in the city, particularly in the metropolis with a polyglot people.

In satiric painting this quality of dense, turbulent weight is even more immediately striking. The human stupidity and malice concentrated in the faces of Hieronymus Bosch's Dutch burghers crowd in a shapeless, suffocating mass which threatens to overwhelm and obliterate the face of Christ in *The Carrying of the Cross*; and in Bosch's surrealistic pictures such as *The Temptation of Saint Anthony* where human nastiness is given fantastic form, the typical density of the satiric scene finds expression in a vast multitude of small, grotesque monsters who work madly and aimlessly around the praying saint. Hogarth's satiric drawings, e.g. *Gin Lane*, are always crowded with debris and a host of rotting things, human, animal and vegetable. In Reginald Marsh's *Coney Island* vulgarity, vanity, lust, and animality combine to create a writhing mass of flesh and human litter which nearly blots out the sea, the sky, and the sand. In the occasional instances where the literary satirist uses a painting image to heighten the visual impact of his scene, the qualities of density, multiplicity, and disorder are always stressed. Henry Savile, in his "Advice to a Painter to draw the Duke by" begins his instruction on satiric composition by saying,

> Spread a large canvass, Painter, to containe
> The great assembly and the numerous traine,
> Who all in triumph shall about him sitte
> Abhoring wisdome and dispising witt.
>
> (*lines 1–4*)[9]

The chief character in Nathanael West's *The Day of the Locust* is a young painter who is attempting to get on canvas the same horrified and fearful perception of a world gone mad expressed by the book as a whole. The painter's vision is apocalyptic, and his picture, "The Burning of Los Angeles," makes concrete those forces which lie behind all satiric scenes. "Across the top, parallel with the frame, he had drawn the burning city, a great bonfire of architectural styles, ranging from Egyptian to Cape Cod colonial. Through the center, winding from left to right, was a long hill street and down it, spilling into the middle foreground, came the mob carrying baseball bats and torches. For the faces of its members he was using the innumerable sketches he had made of the people who had come to California to die. . . . In the lower foreground, men and women fled wildly before the vanguard of the crusading mob."[10]

The men and women who flee before the mob in "The Burning of Los Angeles," while they are not morally attractive, do represent the only virtues possible in such a world: courage, vitality, intelligence. But their position on the canvas suggests that they are about to be obliterated, and this is typical of the satiric scene. Somewhere in his dense knots of ugly flesh the satiric author or painter usually inserts a hint of an ideal which is either threatened with imminent destruction or is already dead. Humanity, what man is capable of achieving, is reflected in the lovely human faces of Bosch's tortured Christ and his St. Anthony, both about to be destroyed by the monstrosities which surround and press inward on them. Far above and in the distance behind *Gin Lane* rises a church steeple, but the three balls of the pawnbroker, in the form of a cross, dominate the immediate scene of squalor and filth. In Daumier's *Articles Placed in Evidence*, one of a series of satires on the French legal system, only the feet of Christ nailed to the cross show in a picture which hangs behind three bored and stupid judges presiding at a murder trial. Juvenal manages in his satires to refer in a variety of ways to the sturdy independence and moral vigor of the old Romans of the Republic; Celia retains her virtue, somewhat woodenly, in Volpone's palace; Pope can still talk to Arbuthnot; and a copy of Shakespeare still exists and is read by one man in the desert of the *Brave New World*.

Although there is always at least a suggestion of some kind of humane ideal in satire—it may in the blackest type of satire exist only as the unnamed opposite of the idiocy and villainy portrayed—this ideal is never heavily stressed, for in the satirist's vision of the world decency is forever in a precarious position near the edge of extinction, and the world is about to pass into eternal darkness. Consequently, every effort is made to emphasize the destroying ugliness and power of vice. The author of satire always portrays the grotesque and distorted, and concentrates to an obsessive degree on the flesh. Northrop Frye remarks that "genius seems to have led practically every great satirist to become what the world calls obscene,"[11] and it is certainly true that the most unpleasant details appearing in literature are to be found in satire: Juvenal's pathic who tells us in explicit and revolting terms about his relationship with his patron, the descriptions of the excrementary functions of the Yahoos, Trimalchio's purge in *The Satyricon*, Rochester's pictures of the amorous pleasantries of King Charles and his mistresses. The satiric painter cannot be so frank, but he too seems to be fascinated by the flesh, particularly fat and the sagging, graying skin. His subjects if they are young and healthy are always gross and seem to reek of sweat, while if they are old they are either bursting the seams of their clothes or horribly cadaverous. If the satirist is more delicate than in the examples mentioned above, his characters still seem always indecently carnal; man is caught in his animal functions of eating, drinking, lusting, displaying his body, copulating, evacuating, scratching. He is riddled with hideous and deforming diseases, most often venereal: the bone-ache, falling hair, a decayed nose, ulcerous teeth, boils, scurf. Gross, sodden, rotting matter is the substance of the satiric scene and any trace of the beautiful or the spiritual is always in danger of being destroyed by the weight of this mere "stuff."

The faces peering out at us from the crowded satiric scene seldom have normal features but are grotesquely distorted by the vices they mirror. Stupidity, lust, pride, greed, hatred, and envy are revealed in exaggerated facial lineaments, gestures, bodies, and postures. We seem in satire always to be at the extreme: the bore never goes away, but prattles on without end; the flatterer says *any* outrageous thing to the vain man, who believes *all* that is said; the miser wants absolutely *all* the wealth in the world; the fop literally smothers himself under a mass of fantastic clothes; the blockhead can be persuaded to do *anything*; the politician actually sells his mother for advancement. From the "realistic" forms of satire where there is still some degree of resemblance to actual humanity and where man's bestiality, smallness of mind, and mechanistic responses to appetite are suggested by metaphors, it is but a step to more obviously symbolic types of satire where the metaphors are given substantial form. Men *are* fantastic monsters, part rodent and part machine, in Bosch's surrealistic paintings; the ordinary worker *is* a robot in *R.U.R.*; citizens *are* horses and pigs in *Animal Farm*; and humans *are* Lilliputians and Yahoos in *Gulliver's Travels*.

The more "realistic" kinds of satire are always just on the verge of falling over into the overtly symbolic mode, despite the satiric claims to literal truthfulness, and it would be possible to classify satire according to the degree of realism to which it pretends. Working from the point of extreme realism we would begin with satires such as those of Juvenal, or Pope's *Imitations of Horace*, and pass, with the degree of realism progressively diminishing through such works as *The Alchemist, The Adding Machine*, and *The Birds* to beast fables such as "The Nun's Priest's Tale" where literal imitation of the human scene has very nearly disappeared. Criticism has, however, traditionally distinguished, under various names, only two main types of satire: formal verse satire and Menippean satire. The term Menippean originally referred to those satires which were written in a mixture of verse and prose, but it has gradually come to include any satiric work obviously written in the third person or, to put it another way, where the attack is managed under cover of a fable. Dryden—who prefers the alternate term Varronian—cites as examples Petronius' *Satyricon*, some of Lucian's dialogues, *The Golden Ass, The Praise of Folly*, and his own *Absalom and Achitophel*.[12] In the traditional scheme all works short of extreme realism would then be classified as Menippean. Formal verse satire, a loosely defined term at best, has been used to designate those satires written in verse where the author appears to speak in his own person without the use of any continuous narrative, preferring to describe bits and pieces of the world which has stung him into writing. Works falling in our scale at the extreme realistic end would be in the category of formal verse satire: the collections of satires of Juvenal, Hall, Marston, Boileau, Rochester, some of Horace's *Sermones*, Byron's *English Bards and Scotch Reviewers*, and Gay's *Trivia*. While I should prefer to drop the word "verse" from the term formal verse satire to allow the inclusion of works such as Philip Wylie's *Generation of Vipers* which obviously belong in this category, the terms formal and Menippean are useful because as employed today they make a meaningful differentiation of species within the genus satire. But they are confusing if used too rigidly to make something approaching an absolute distinction between two species of satire, for the scene of formal satire, despite the attempts of the author to make it appear a piece of reporting, is as much a selection of significant and interrelated details, a symbolic world, as is the scene of the beast fable where men are transformed into animals living in the forest or the barnyard. The qualities we have isolated as characteristic of the satiric scene, density, disorder, grossness, rot, and a hint of an ideal, are present in both formal and Menippean satire; they are simply made concrete in different terms.

There is, of course, a great deal of variation in the scenes of individual satires: the Rome of Horace is not identical with that of Juvenal, and the Londons of Ben Jonson and Alexander Pope are considerably different. Every author of satire is free to stress the elements of the scene which appear most important to him, but beneath the divergencies of the surface the satiric scene remains fundamentally the same picture of a dense and grotesque world of decaying matter moving without form in response only to physical forces and denying the humane ideal which once molded the crowd into a society and the collection of buildings into a city.

THE SATIRIST

Somewhere in the midst of the satiric scene or standing before it directing our attention to instances of folly and vulgarity and shaping our responses with his language, we usually find a satirist. In some cases he remains completely anonymous, merely a speaking voice who tells us nothing directly of himself, e.g. the narrator in *Nightmare Abbey* or in most satiric novels. In formal satire where the satirist is usually identified as "I," or may even be given the author's name as in "An Epistle to Dr. Arbuthnot," he begins to emerge from the shadows of anonymity, and, while his back is still turned to us, he speaks of himself from time to time, giving us hints of his origins and his character. One step further and the satirist acquires a name—Colin Clout, Pierce Penilesse—and a more complete personality. At this stage it may become fairly obvious that the satirist has an unsavory character himself, and we may begin to wonder if the author is not mocking his own creation while using him to attack others, e.g. Erasmus' use of Folly in *The Praise of Folly*, or Swift's manipulation of the "Modest Proposer" and Lemuel Gulliver.[13] Here too we must place various satirists appearing in plays who are even more unpleasant than the characters they attack: Jonson's Macilente, Shakespeare's Thersites, and Webster's Bosola. Finally, the satirist disappears altogether and we are left with only the fools and the villains who are allowed to expose and punish one another. Examples of this type of satire usually come from the theater (Jonson's *Volpone* or Aristophanes' *The Birds*), although a determined novelist may manage to keep his narration neutral enough to prevent any suggestion of a definite personality existing behind the events of the tale.

We might at this point sharpen our distinction between formal and Menippean satire somewhat and say that in formal satire the satirist is stressed and dominates the scene, while in Menippean satire the scene is stressed and absorbs the satirist, to some degree or altogether. Obviously, in the case of works occupying the middle range (such as *Gulliver's Travels*) the decision as to whether they are formal or Menippean becomes an extremely nice question: is Gulliver to be considered a part of the scene or a satirist describing and defining it? A distinction made on the basis of the extent to which the satirist is featured is useful for describing various subtypes of satire, but, again, it must not be allowed to obscure our perception of the basic unity of satire. The satirist must be regarded as but one poetic device used by the author to express his satiric vision, a device which can be dispensed with or varied to suit his purpose. We can expect, however, that if satire is a true genre then whenever the satirist does appear, whether he remains anonymous, is identified as "I," or is given a name, he will share certain basic characteristics with all other satirists. This basic character will be dictated by his function in the satiric work and established by tradition. The biographical critics of satire have insisted that each satirist is either an exact image of his creator or at least his spokesman, but, ironically enough, their writings tend to confirm the idea of a basic satiric character, for whether they are describing Juvenal, Pope, Byron, Swift or Philip Wylie they seem always to be talking about the same proud, fiery, intolerant, irascible man whom no one would want for a neighbor. There are, of course, considerable differences between the satirists created by different authors at different times, and these will be taken up in more detail shortly, but it should be possible to define in very general terms the essential satirist, those traits, attitudes, passions, which every author of satire brings together, stressing some and repressing others, and gives concrete expresion to in the language, actions, and body of his particular satirist.

Every satirist is something of a Jekyll and Hyde; he has both a public and a private personality. The public personality is the one he exposes to the world, the face which he admits to and, indeed, insists on as a true image of his very nature.[14] The chief features of this personality have already been suggested in the opening pages of this chapter, and we need deal with them only briefly. Very simply, the satirist always presents himself as a blunt, honest man with no nonsense about him. This pose is established in a number of traditional ways. The satirist usually calls attention to his simple style and his preference for plain terms which express plain truth. St. Jerome, who is in fact no amateur in rhetoric, longs for "the ocean of eloquent Cicero" and the "rushing torrents of Demosthenes"[15] to express the absolute depravity of a priest who has used the cave where Christ was born as a place of assignation. When advised to abandon satire and "tell of the feats of Caesar," "Horace" says humbly, "Would that I could, good father, but my strength fails me. Not everyone can paint ranks bristling with lances, or Gauls falling with spear-heads shattered, or wounded Parthian slipping from his horse."[16] Joseph Hall in his *Virgidemiae* tells us that his satires are "but packe-staffe plaine uttring what thing they ment."[17] Professions of this kind are one of the commonplaces of satire, but they need not always be given direct statement. The satirist may suggest that his own style is simple, and therefore truthful, simply by mocking the pretentious styles and pompous jargon of his contemporaries, as Juvenal does in his first satire; or he may employ slang and other idiomatic terms to refer to himself while using the terms of eloquence for his adversaries as Philip Wylie does in the introduction to his *Generation of Vipers*.

The pose of simplicity is frequently reinforced by references to humble but honest origins. The typical medieval satirist assumes the mask of the humble plowman working hard in the fields to support his family, close to Nature and to God. "Pope," in "An Epistle to Dr. Arbuthnot," paints a charming picture of his early years, his retirement from the busy world, his mild acceptance of insults, and his father who "held it for a rule/It was a Sin to call our Neighbour fool," while the "harmless Mother thought no Wife a Whore."[18] Somehow the satirist seems always to come from a world of pastoral innocence and kindness: he is the prophet come down from the hills to the cities of the plain; the gawky farm-boy, shepherd, or plowman come to the big city; or the scholar, nurtured at the university, abroad in the cruel world.

The satirist's moral code, which is too traditional and too straightforward to be called a philosophy, suits his rural background. "Enough for me, if I can uphold the rule our fathers have handed down, and if, so long as you need a guardian, I can keep your health and name from harm,"[19] says "Horace's" father, and the words are a good description of the moral ideals of all satirists. Metaphysics, elaborate ethics, theories of redemption through suffering, these are all beyond the satirist. He views life in social terms and exhorts his audience to return to the ways of their fathers, to live with fortitude, reason, chastity, honor, justice, simplicity, the virtues which make for the good life and the good society. A Christian satirist will usually add repentance and humility before God to the list of pagan virtues, but he too takes these for granted and does not bother with speculations about their ultimate validity.

But mildness and simplicity do not suffice to make a satirist. He must not only shake his head at what he sees, he must attack it, and with vigor, if there is to be any satire. Where other men passively accept the "mortifying sight of slavery, folly and baseness" among which they are "forced to live," or rage inwardly and ineffectively, the satirist responds with that "perfect rage and resentment"[20] of which Swift speaks, and cries out with Juvenal,

> Si natura negat, facit indignatio versum.
> (Though nature says no, indignation forms my verses.)
>   (I, 79)

Or with Pope,

> Ask you what Provocation I have had?
> The strong Antipathy of Good to Bad.[21]

The degree of indignation varies with the man, and the satiric conventions of his time; it ranges from Horace's ironically mild "quid faciam" when faced with the corruption of Rome to the *saeva indignatio* of Juvenal and the violence of Elizabethan satire where, as John Marston puts it, with characteristic exaggeration:

> Unlesse the Destin's adamantine band
> Should tye my teeth, I cannot chuse but bite.[22]

This violent indignation is, of course, somewhat at variance with the pose of the mild, honest man, and the satirist always presents his raging at a wicked world as a compulsion. Things are so bad, vice so arrant, the world so overwhelmingly wicked that even a plain man like the satirist who prefers to live in peace is forced to attack the vice of mankind.

But what his passion forces him to do, his reason assents to, for the satirist views the world pessimistically and sees little hope for reform unless violent methods are used to bring mankind to its senses. His melancholy views on the prospects for the world are best understood by contrast with the situation in tragedy and comedy. Satire shares with comedy the knowledge that fools and foolishness have gotten out of hand, but it lacks the characteristic balance of comedy and the tone of amused tolerance which derive from the underlying certainty in comedy that right reason *is* ultimately the way of the world. Fools in comedy only need to be given enough rope and they will hang themselves, for Nature operates to restore the balance. While watching the fools in their foolishness the comic hero—Philinte, Millamant, Falstaff, or Shaw's St. Joan—can remain relatively detached and good-humored because of the deep conviction that "normality" will reassert itself.

Such consolation is denied the satirist, who typically believes that there is no pattern of reason left in the world. If Nature once operated or society functioned to maintain a reasonable world, the sheer idiocy of mankind has long since thwarted the great plan:

> each Ape,
> That can but spy the shadow of his shape,
> That can no sooner ken what's vertuous,
> But will avoyd it, and be vicious.

> (*The Scourge*, IV, p. 43)

The satirist's despair of man and society, which he builds up with direct statement and catalogues of human depravity, extends to the very operation of the cosmos itself. "With a goose-quill and a bottle of ink," says Aretino, "I mock myself of the universe."[23] The powers divine and human that once kept man virtuous and society healthy seem no longer operative to the satirist, the flow of grace has been stopped by "the slime that from our soules doe flow."[24] If the satirist does not choose merely to relieve his pain by mockery, he regards himself and his satire, all other forces having withdrawn, as the only method of correction left, the last hope of mankind. Swift tells us that "the reason that satire was first introduced into the world" was to control those "whom neither religion, nor natural virtue, nor fear of punishment were able to keep within the bounds of their duty."[25] "Pope" is

> proud to see
> Men, not afraid of God, afraid of me:
> Safe from the Bar, the Pulpit, and the Throne,
> Yet touch'd and sham'd by Ridicule alone.
>
> ("Dialogue II," lines 208-11)

The author of satire may believe, as Pope and Swift clearly did, that God still exists, but when he assumes the mask of the satirist he acts as if God and Nature were withdrawn and he stood alone in the lunatic world to stay its progressive degeneration. For this reason comic detachment and ease are impossible for the satirist. He is convinced that the fate of the world depends solely on him, and this gives rise to the heroic postures he frequently assumes. He becomes the only champion of virtue who dares to speak the truth in a world where the false insolently maintains itself as the real.

Satire shares this darkly serious view of the world with tragedy —thus the resemblance of the satiric and tragic scenes—and both satirist and tragic hero suffer an agonized compulsion to appraise the ills of the world and cure them by naming them. Every tragic hero has pronounced satiric tendencies, but he also has additional dimensions; chief among these are his ability to ponder and to change under pressure. The satirist, however, is not so complex. He sees the world as a battlefield between a definite, clearly understood good, which he represents, and an equally clear-cut evil. No ambiguities, no doubts about himself, no sense of mystery trouble him, and he retains always his monolithic certainty. Since these differences in character control the directions taken by the satiric and tragic plots, they will be discussed more fully later.

This is, very roughly, the public character of the satirist. Now it would be nonsense to argue, as the biographical critic does, that all authors of satire are straightforward, honest, pessimistic, indignant men who dislike ostentatious rhetoric, come from the country, and have simple moral codes. Each of these traditional qualities is a function of satire itself, and not primarily an attribute of the man who writes the satire. The typical satirist we have described is brought into being by the necessities of satire. If the attack on vice is to be effective, the character who delivers it must appear the moral opposite of the world he condemns; he must be fervent, he must be horrified at what he sees, and he must be able to distinguish between vice and virtue without any philosophical shillyshallying about "what is right and what is wrong?" The traditional character of the satirist enables him to perform each of these acts.

If the satirist remained as simple and coherent as his public personality, then his character would give little difficulty. He might appear too uncomplicated to deal with an extremely complicated world, but he would be fully understandable. There is always, however, a darker side to his nature, a private personality which the author may or may not allow his satirist to discuss openly, and this personality is, like the public personality, consequent upon the satirist's functions in satire. As a result of his violent attacks on vice he acquires a number of unpleasant characteristics which make suspect his pose of a simple lover of plain truth. These characteristics are best described as a series of closely related tensions. The most obvious tension results from the satirist's categorical contention that he is showing us the world and man as they actually are. Writers of epic, love poetry, or pastoral are, the satirist assures us, merely writing fiction. Only the satirist truly has for his subject "quidquid agunt homines." The lines from Joseph Hall's *Virgidemiae* (1598) are a typical instance of the satiric boast:

> For in this smoothing age who durst indite,
> Hath made his pen an hyred Parasite,
> To claw the back of him that beastly lives,
> And pranck base men in proud Superlatives.
> . . . .

> Goe daring Muse on with thy thankless taske,
> And do the ugly face of vice unmaske:
> ....
> Truth be thy speed, and Truth thy Patron bee.
>
> (I, Prologue, lines 9–24)

But in no art form is the complexity of human existence so obviously scanted as in satire. The satirist is out to persuade us that vice is both ugly and rampant, and in order to do so he deliberately distorts, excludes, and slants. We never find characters in satire, only caricature: Swift's Yahoos, Juvenal's Romans, Pope's Dunces, Philip Wylie's Moms. The dilemma is inescapable, for the satirist is caught between the conflicting necessities of the claim to truth and the need to make vice appear as ugly and dangerous as possible. Whenever the author of satire allows his satirist to admit his inconsistency, his argument will be that distortion of literal reality is necessary in order to get at the truth. Philip Wylie tells us that he is attempting in *Generation of Vipers* to break through certain ancient dogmatic faiths, and then goes on, "The effort involves a considerable diversion of thought from normal channels and I have twirled a rather elaborate kaleidoscope, to divert it."[26] Wylie's kaleidoscope becomes "squint-eyed sight" in Marston's satirist's attempt to explain his outrageous exaggeration:

> Who would imagine that such squint-eyed sight
> Could strike the world's deformities so right[27]

This distortion of reality in an attempt to make vice as ugly and ridiculous as it truly is always requires a considerable amount of rhetorical skill, but, as we have seen, in order to establish his credibility the satirist must present himself as a plain, outspoken man who calls a spade a spade. In fact he then turns out to be the most cunning of rhetoricians, highly skilled in all the tricks of persuasion. As a result we have the curious spectacle of the most artful of writers pretending, like Chaucer's Franklin to whom "colours of rethoryk been ... queynte," to be rude and artless.

There is an old saying that "he who sups with the devil needs a long enough spoon," and it appears that the satirist has never had a long enough spoon. Inevitably when he dips into the devil's broth in order, he says, to show us how filthy it really is, he gets splattered. In order to attack vice effectively, the satirist must portray it in detail and profusion, and he must explore the nastiest activities of the human animal and dsecribe them in the revolting terms "Pope," for example, uses in the following passage:

> Let Courtly Wits to Wits afford supply,
> As Hog to Hog in huts of *Westphaly;*
> If one, thro' Nature's Bounty or his Lord's,
> Has what the frugal, dirty soil affords,
> From him the next receives it, thick or thin,
> As pure a Mess almost as it came in;
> The blessed Benefit, not there confin'd,
> Drops to the third who nuzzles close behind;
> From tail to mouth, they feed, and they carouse;
> The last, full fairly gives it to the *House.*

> ("Dialogue II," lines 171–80)

The *adversarius* speaks for all of us when he answers, "This filthy Similie, this beastly Line,/Quite turns my Stomach"; and Pope's answer is the standard defense of the satirist, "So does Flatt'ry mine." At times the satirist will go beyond mere prurience and appear pathological in his unending revelations of human nastiness and his paraded disgust with the ordure of the world. Trapped by his need for making sin appear hideous he seems always to be seeking out and thoroughly enjoying the kind of filth which he claims to be attacking. And at the same time that he opens himself to the charge of being a literary Peeping Tom, he also makes it possible to charge him with sensationalism, for the more effectively he builds up catalogues of human vice, the more it will appear that he is merely purveying salacious material to satisfy the meaner appetites of his audience.

The satirist's probity is further compromised by the necessary strength and vigor of his attack on his victims. He denounces them for being intemperate and unreasonable, and the very violence of his denunciations proclaims him equally unreasonable and intemperate. St. Jerome in his satiric letters takes his contemporaries to task for their unchristian behavior, but his own bitter attacks—as he remembers from time to time—violate the fundamental tenet of the Christian religion, charity. Juvenal's satirist adheres to some loose variety of Stoicism, but his fiery indignation stands in direct contrast to the Stoic ideals of passionless calm and stern endurance of misfortune, and he is forced to explain that though Nature, the principle of right reason operating through the universe, forbids his satiric outbursts, indignation insists upon them: "si natura negat, facit indignatio versum." But the satirist's sharp tongue involves him in even more unpleasant contradictions than mere philosophical confusion. He believes that the case of man and society is desperate, and he applies appropriate therapeutic treatments: the whip, the scalpel, the strappado, the emetic, the burning acid.[28] But each of these cruel methods of treatment suggests that the man who uses them exclusively enjoys his work. The more powerfully the satirist swings his scourge—and he usually does so with considerable gusto—the more he will appear to have a marked sadistic tendency.

The necessary straightforwardness of his attacks on vice always opens the satirist to accusations of being proud. As the satirist passes a succession of absolute moral judgments on his fellow men, he inevitably becomes an egoistic monster bursting with his own righteousness and completely devoid of any sympathy for his victims or doubts about his own moral status. "Byron" in *English Bards and Scotch Reviewers* admits that,

> Every Brother Rake will smile to see
> That miracle, a Moralist in me.
>
> (lines 699-700)[29]

"Horace's" adversarius speaks to him about the same question (I.ii. 25-27), "When you look over your own sins, your eyes are rheumy and daubed with ointment; why, when you view the failings of your friends, are you as keen of sight as an eagle?"

All but a few critics[30] of satire have unerringly sought out and concentrated on these weak spots in the satirist's character, his private personality. Thomas Love Peacock, we are told, "showed himself rather obstinately blind to many of the higher aspects of life in general."[31] *Don Juan* consists of "the beastly utterances of a man who had lost all sense of decency,"[32] and William Blackwood was struck with horror by "the vile, heartless, and cold-blooded way in which this fiend [Byron] attempted to degrade every tender and sacred feeling of the human heart."[33] Another critic informs us that John Marston "exhibits an insane delight in raking the cesspits of vice . . . and feels the same pleasure in drawing attention to [evil] . . . that boys experience in chalking up newly-discovered verbiage of obscenity."[34] Speaking of the same author, Thomas Warton pontificates: "The satirist who too freely indulges himself in the display of that licentiousness which he means to proscribe, absolutely defeats his own design. He inflames those passions which he professes to suppress, gratifies the depravations of a prurient curiosity, and seduces innocent minds to an acquaintance with ideas which they might never have known."[35] "Pope," it is argued, "finds himself unable to re-settle the equilibrium in his nervous system until he has taken out his revenge by an extra kicking administered to some old mendicant or vagrant lying in a ditch."[36]

All of the defects of character noted by these critics are unhesitatingly assigned to the authors, and while it is true that some of the greatest satiric authors have not been the most stable of men, the fact seems to have been missed that many of the characteristics confidently attributed to them derive from the very nature of satire itself. Anyone who writes vigorous satire will inevitably appear to share these traits. If, however, we accept the strange, twisted, contradictory satirist as a fictitious character created in order to achieve the satiric end, the exposure of vice and depravity, then we can direct our attention to the ways in which the authors of great satire manipulate their satirists and exploit them in a thoroughly dramatic fashion. Juvenal's stern, impoverished, decayed noble who stamps about the streets of Rome suffering indignities at the hands of the nouveaux riches, and bursting with indignation and sophistic rhetoric; Skelton's crude, rustic, straightforward, unlearned country-man whose simple piety mocks the sophisticated church-men; John Marston's biting, snarling, despairing, contradictory malcontent who noses into all the filth of Elizabethan London and becomes nearly incoherent with rage while denouncing it on the street corners; Swift's bumbling, credulous, prideful Gulliver voyaging from one misunderstood adventure to the next and finally filled with proud disdain for the human animal, the Yahoo—all these are satiric personae.

I have described in the preceding pages a basic satiric persona, and no doubt the reader has by now thought of a number of cases where some of the qualities I have called characteristic are so attenuated that they nearly cease to exist. Savagery, despair, hate, pride, intransigeance, prurience, and sadism may be innate in satire, but Horace, Chaucer, Erasmus, and, to a lesser degree, Ben Jonson, all manage to soften or find out more acceptable variations of these unpleasant traits by avoiding the extreme forms of indignation and the more shocking varieties of vice. They stress the public personality of the satirist. Their kind of satire verges on the comic, and their satirists, without losing their cutting-edge, exude good humor, easy laughter, urbanity. In Johnson's words, they "sport with human follies, not with crimes," and Horace's phrase "ridentem dicere verum" characterizes their method.

On the other hand there is an even larger group of satiric writers who seem to delight in stressing every extravagant attitude and every contradiction in the satiric character. Juvenal, Swift, Pope, Byron, Marston, Rochester, Marvell, all create satirists who lash out with violence, are filled with outrage, and seek out the vilest of men. When Horace goes for a walk he encounters a bore, when Juvenal walks *he* encounters a cast-off pathic. These bitter works are characterized by Juvenal's saeva indignatio, and they seem always to be on the threshold of tragedy. The works of these authors have provided a majority of my examples for the simple reason that such writers, by carrying to the extreme the private personality of the satirist, bring into relief the tendencies of all satire, tendencies which are repressed in the gentler types.

Horace and Juvenal thus provide us with the two extremes of the satirist, and while it seems likely that the personality of the author has some connection with the type of satirist he creates, other factors are more important in molding the satiric figure. The radical characteristics are always necessarily present, but just as each age forges its own typical verse forms or its architectural style, so, allowing for minor differences resulting from the different personalities of the authors involved, each age creates its own satirist who is distinguished from the satirists of the preceding age and the following. Bishop Golias, Piers Plowman, Thersites, the Pope of the *Imitations of Horace* are all related figures, but they are different in many ways, and each is a defining example of the standard satiric character of his age. Changes in satirists seem to come about in conjunction with major shifts in thought, and perhaps the best way of describing this process is to say that the satirist is always an amalgamation of the basic characteristics which develop whenever satire is written and of the ethos of a particular age. It is possible to distinguish a distinctive satiric figure in each of the major periods of our literature, and in later chapters I shall discuss in some detail the medieval satirist and the Renaissance satirist.

THE SATIRIC PLOT

If we take plot to mean, as it ordinarily does, "what happens," or to put it in a more useful way, a series of events which constitute a change, then the most striking quality of satire is the absence of plot. We seem at the conclusion of satire to be always at very nearly the same point where we began. The scenery and the faces may have changed outwardly, but fundamentally we are looking at the same world, and the same fools, and the same satirist we met at the opening of the work. Juvenal begins in his first satire by belaboring a variety of transgressors: the eunuch who has married, the matron who has exposed her breasts and entered the arena, and the former barber who has become one of the richest and most powerful men in Rome; fifteen satires later he is viciously attacking the army, and the brutality with which the soldiers treat civilians. Presumably the eunuch is still married and the barber more prosperous than ever. The scene is still as crowded with fools and villains, and the same forces of luxury, money, and foreign ideas which perverted traditional Roman virtue inside the city have infected the barracks. The satirist is still as indignant, as brave, as skillful, and as certain of himself as ever. His method is still the direct attack despite the fact that in fifteen satires he has not achieved a single result. What is true of formal satire is almost equally true of Menippean varieties, although there usually is more movement when the satire is carried by a fable. Trimalchio is as rich and gross as ever at the end of the description of his banquet; the "Big-enders" and the "Little-enders" come to no recognition of their foolishness in *Gulliver's Travels;* Colin Clout ends his song still complaining about prelates whose ease and power have not been disturbed in the slightest by an attack which Colin knows from the outset will only result in those he is attacking calling him a prating "losel . . . with a wide wesaunt!" Whenever satire does have a plot which eventuates in a change, it is not a true change but simply intensification of the original condition. After a number of adventures Gulliver becomes a more unpleasant kind of simpleton; during the course of *The Dunciad* dullness seeps into every part of London just as the slime from the Fleet ditch pollutes the river; absolutism stamps out the last trace of individualism in *1984*, and the hero is left drinking ersatz gin, crying maudlin tears, and adoring the face of Big Brother on the telescreen.

The normal "plot" of satire would then appear to be a stasis in which the two opposing forces, the satirist on one hand and the fools on the other, are locked in their respective attitudes without any possibility of either dialectical movement or the simple triumph of good over evil. Whatever movement there is, is not plot in the true sense of change but mere intensification of the unpleasant situation with which satire opens. It is here that one of the basic differences between satire and the other major literary genres, tragedy and comedy, becomes evident, for in both the latter kinds the developing plot is very close to being the absolute heart of the form. Perhaps the essence of comedy is that things somehow do "turn out all right." Usually they do so in a rather miraculous, unexpected, and fairly painless manner. An unknown will is discovered, a rich uncle returns from the West Indies, the boy and girl turn out not to be brother and sister after all. The deus ex machina may be anathema in tragedy, but it is a vital part of comedy. In tragedy the progression of events, both psychic and external, leads inevitably to adjustment and change, but for a time it is not unusual for the tragic hero to lock himself in the rigid attitude of the satirist and strive "in his little world of man to out-scorn/The to-and-fro-conflicting wind and rain." Both satirist and tragic hero cry out that they are men "more sinn'd against than sinning," and try to oppose the course of evil with the lash of scorn and vituperation: e.g. Oedipus' attack on superstition and prophecy which he mockingly calls "bird-lore," Hamlet's description of the world as an "unweeded garden," or Lear's magnificent explosions that relieve the unendurable pressure in his heart. But the tragic hero *learns* that evil is too powerful to be opposed in this way, and as he suffers the consequences of his stand he passes on into knowledge that evil is a part of the fabric of the world, not mere depravity or bad manners; and with this recognition he is forced on to see his own involvement in the mixed world and accept the extraordinarily heavy price he must pay to achieve an end which is only dimly perceived.

The tragic plot has been described as a continuing rhythm of "purpose, passion and perception,"[37] in which the tragic hero does something (purpose), is forced to endure the consequences of his act (passion), and then as a result of his suffering comes to a new understanding (perception), which constitutes the basis of a new purpose. The rhythm of satire, however, lacks the crucial act of perception which permits development and forward movement. Instead, the satirist alternates endlessly between his purpose and the passion which it brings on. His characteristic purpose is to cleanse society of its impurities, to heal its sicknesses; and his tools are crude ones: the surgeon's knife, the whip, the purge, the rack, the flood, and the holocaust, all typical metaphors of satire. He employs irony, sarcasm, caricature, and even plain vituperation with great vigor, determined to beat the sots into reason or cut away the infected parts of society; but the job is always too much for him. The massive weight of stupidity, bestiality, greed, and cunning, which is his scene, resists his uttermost efforts, and so he suffers frustration and the agonized sense that evil multiplies faster than it can be corrected or even catalogued. But suffering brings no change in him: his methods, his sense of his own righteousness, and his understanding of evil remain the same. His feelings of futility lead him not to revaluation of his methods and his enemies but to the belief that he simply needs to apply the lash more vigorously, and he doubles his efforts. This constant movement without change forms the basis of satire, and while we may be only half aware of the pattern as we read, it, more than any other element, creates the tone of pessimism inherent in the genre.

English literature contains, of course, a great many poems, plays, and novels with pronounced satiric qualities, which do have a developing plot where movement results in metamorphosis. Ben Jonson's plays usually result in the unmasking and punishment of the fools; Webster's *The Duchess of Malfi* and a number of other Jacobean tragedies are heavily satiric but usually arrive at a much diminished tragic recognition; *Pride and Prejudice* has some of the deftest satire ever written—and one of the finest satirists, Mr. Bennett —but "good sense" and "warm hearts" bring an ending of tolerance and adjustment. Shaw in his plays belabors the English middle class with true satiric delight, but the "life force" works through his satire to bring about comic change in a play like *Man and Superman*, and tragic change, at least for a moment, in *Saint Joan*. Pure satire is far rarer than the mixed kinds in which after a time the satiric stasis is broken and the characters, both satirists and fools, are swept forward into the miraculous transformations of comedy or the cruel dialectic of tragedy.

CONCLUSIONS

Exact definition of any literary genre is perhaps an impossibility, but the terms I have used to describe satire are broad enough to allow for its considerable diversities without permitting the idea of the genre to disappear either in the multitude of different techniques of presentation which have been used to convey satire, or in the mass of shadowy, borderline cases where satire seems inextricably mixed with comedy or tragedy. It would seem that the basic impulse or "sense of life" which lies behind all satire finds concrete expression in a wide variety of ways. In life itself it appears without mediation in the sneer and in the sarcastic remark, or it will be sharpened and organized somewhat in the lampoon, the exposé, and the political cartoon. At this point it passes over into art where it appears in epigrams, "characters," pasquinades, "dictionaries," parodies, and a host of other minor types. But it is in the major satiric works of the literary tradition extending from classical antiquity to the present day, in the pure satires of Horace, Juvenal, Persius, the goliardic poets, Skelton, Marston, Pope, Swift, Byron, that we get the full expression of the satiric sense of life and the development of innate tendencies which are only suggested by the minor examples of the genre. These works exist in a variety of modes extending from the extreme realism of formal satire to the extreme symbolism of the beast fable, and may be presented in poem, play, essay, or novel.

But no matter what the mode of presentation, the elements of satire which I have distinguished remain fairly constant. The scene is always crowded, disorderly, grotesque; the satirist, in those satires where he appears, is always indignant, dedicated to truth, pessimistic, and caught in a series of unpleasant contradictions incumbent on practicing his trade; the plot always takes the pattern of purpose followed by passion, but fails to develop beyond this point. For purposes of discussion I have treated scene, plot, and satirist as distinct from one another, while in any given satire where all are present they interact and reinforce one another to form a composite whole. Take, for example, the well-known tendency of satire to pass rapidly from one subject to another without lingering for very many lines on any single fool or particular piece of foolishness. We can consider this quality, which has earned satire the reputation of being fragmentary, as an attribute of the scene contributing to the effect of a disordered world in which there is a limitless amount of depravity. Or in formal satire, where the scene is described for us by the satirist and has no being in its own right, these rapid transitions reflect the character of the satirist and suggest his sense of urgency, his zeal, and his unwillingness to ponder any situation or investigate it thoroughly. Or we may see this same fragmentary quality as a function of the plot, demonstrating the continuous movement that never brings about change.

The theory of satire offered in this chapter is no doubt rough, and certainly incomplete. Each of the various elements discussed could be developed and refined a great deal by consideration of a larger number of satires than are dealt with here and by more curious examination of scene, satirist, and plot. But the theory I have outlined is a valuable working perspective which permits us to approach satire as literary critics examining a piece of literature made up of symbolic and interacting parts. The testing ground for the theory is English satire of the Renaissance, particularly of that period between approximately 1590 and 1615 when a distinctly nonmedieval type of satire appeared, although the shift in thought which worked the change had been taking place for a good many years before it transformed satire. Before we turn to an examination of this satire we must look briefly at some of the satiric poetry and critical theories with which every Renaissance English author of satire was familiar.

NOTES

1 Giraldus Cambrensis, *Speculum Ecclesiae*, in *Works*, ed. J. S. Brewer (London, 1873), *4*, 291–92. The translation is from Helen Waddell's *The Wandering Scholars* (London, John Constable, 1927), p. 160.

2 G. F. Whicher, *The Goliard Poets* (Norfolk, Conn.: New Directions, 1949), p. 3. The etymology of "Golias" is still a matter of dispute; alternate suggestions are *"guliar,"* to deceive, and "Goliath." See J. M. Manly, "The Familia Goliae," *Modern Philology, 5* (1907), 201–9.

3 *The Works of Aretino*, trans. Samuel Putnam (Chicago: P. Covici, 1926), *2*, 273.

4 See, for example, David Worcester, *The Art of Satire*, Cambridge, Mass., 1940.

5 "The Structural Design of Formal Verse Satire," *Philological Quarterly, 21* (1942), 373.

6 There are a number of recent critical studies, however, in which the coherence of entire satires has been demonstrated. See, for example, Aubrey Williams, *Pope's Dunciad. A Study of Its Meaning*, London, 1955; and W. S. Anderson, "Studies in Book I of Juvenal," *Yale Classical Studies, 15* (1957), 33–90.

7 Inquiry into the magical origins of satire was begun by F. N. Robinson, "Satirists and Enchanters in Early Irish Literature" in

Studies in the History of Religion Presented to Crawford Howell Toy, ed. D. G. Lyon and G. F. Moore (New York, 1912), pp. 95–130. See also Mary Claire Randolph, "Celtic Smiths and Satirists: Partners in Sorcery," *Journal of English Literary History, 8* (1941), 127–59; and R. C. Elliott, "The Satirist and Society," *ELH, 21* (1954), 237–48.

8 Persius, Satire I, 121. All translations of Persius and Juvenal are from *Juvenal and Persius*, ed. and trans. G. G. Ramsay, Loeb Classical Library, London, 1930.

9 Printed in *The Poems and Letters of Andrew Marvell*, ed. H. H. Margoliouth (Oxford Univ. Press, 1927), *1*, 197. The "advice to a painter" became a popular satiric technique in the late 17th century. For a good example see Andrew Marvell's "The Last Instructions to a Painter," where he prescribes such a vast number of scenes, objects, and persons that the compositional techniques of even a painter such as Bosch would be strained to include them all in a single canvas.

10 (New York, New Directions, 1950), pp. 165–66.

11 *Anatomy of Criticism* (Princeton Univ. Press, 1957), p. 235.

12 "A Discourse Concerning the Original and Progress of Satire," in *Essays of John Dryden*, ed. W. P. Ker (Oxford Univ. Press, 1925), 2, 66–67.

13 For a discussion of Swift's creation and handling of his satirists see Martin Price, *Swift's Rhetorical Art*. Yale Studies in English, *123* (New Haven, 1953), pp. 57–102.

14 The manner in which Pope employs this "public personality" in his satires is discussed by Maynard Mack, "The Muse of Satire," *Yale Review 41* (1951–52), 80–92; who points out that in creating this type of persona the satiric author is following Aristotle's advice to the rhetorician to establish with his audience a character which will lend credence to what he has to say.

15 "Calling a Lecherous Priest to Repent," in *The Satirical Letters of St. Jerome*, trans. Paul Carroll (Chicago: Gateway, 1956), p. 115.

16 *Sermones*, II. i. 12–15. All translations of Horace are from *Horace, Satires, Epistles and Ars Poetica*, ed. and trans. H. R. Fairclough, Loeb Classical Library, London, 1926.

17 III, Prologue, 4. All citations of *Virgidemiae* in my text are to *The Collected Poems of Joseph Hall*, ed. Arnold Davenport, Liverpool Univ. Press, 1949.

18 Lines 382–84. All citations of Pope in my text are to the

Twickenham Edition of the Poems of Alexander Pope, Vol. *4, Imitations of Horace*, ed. John Butt, London: Methuen, 1939.

[19] *Sermones*, I. iv. 116–19.

[20] These quotations are from a passage in Swift's letter to Pope, June 1, 1728, in *The Correspondence of Jonathan Swift*, ed. F. E. Ball (London: G. Bell, 1910–14), *4*, 34.

[21] "Epilogue to the Satires, Dialogue, II," pp. 197–98. Hereafter referred to as "Dialogue II."

[22] *The Scourge of Villanie* (1598–99), Satire VIII, p. 82. Hereafter referred to as *The Scourge*. All citations of *The Scourge* are to the facsimile edition of G. B. Harrison, Bodley Head Quartos, *13*, London, 1925. Since the lines are unnumbered, references are given to satire and page numbers.

[23] *Works, 1*, 17.

[24] *The Scourge*, VII, p. 76.

[25] "The Examiner," No. 39, in *The Prose Works of Jonathan Swift*, ed. Temple Scott (London: G. Bell, 1902), *9*, 253.

[26] (New York, Rinehart, 1942), p. xiv.

[27] *The Metamorphosis of Pigmalions Image And Certaine Satyres*, (1958), Satire II, lines 37–38. Hereafter cited as *Pigmalion*. All citations of *Pigmalion* in my text are to *The Works of John Marston*, ed. A. H. Bullen (Boston: John Nimmo, 1887), Vol. *3*.

[28] The traditional use of this type of imagery in satire is discussed by Mary Claire Randolph, "The Medical Concept in English Renaissance Satiric Theory: Its Possible Relationships and Implications," *Studies in Philology, 38* (1941), 125–57.

[29] *Works*, ed. E. H. Coleridge (London, J. Murray, 1905), Vol *I*.

[30] Marynard Mack, "The Muse of Satire," and John Holloway, "The Well-Filled Dish: An Analysis of Swift's Satire," *Hudson Review, 9* (1956), 20–37, call attention to the division that exists between the author of satire and the personality he assumes in order to perform his critical function.

[31] George Saintsbury, *English Prose*. ed. Henry Craik (New York, 1896), *5*, 286.

[32] Harriet Beecher Stowe, *Lady Byron Vindicated* (Boston, 1870), p. 62.

[33] From a letter quoted by F. H. C. Oliphant in *William Blackwood and His Sons* (New York, 1897), *1*, 381.

[34] J. Le Gay Brereton, *Writings on Elizabethan Drama* (Melbourne Univ. Press, 1948), p. 43.

[35] *The History of English Poetry* (London, 1778–81), sec. 65.

[36] Thomas DeQuincey, "Lord Carlisle on Pope" in *The Collected Writings of Thomas DeQuincey*, ed. David Masson (Edinburgh, 1890), *11*, 126–27.

[37] The terms Francis Fergusson's and form the basis of his discussion of drama in *The Idea of a Theater*, Princeton Univ. Press, 1949.

ROBERT C. ELLIOTT

The Satirist Satirized:
Timon of Athens

The great misanthropes of literature—Timon, Alceste, Gulliver of the last voyage—are mighty railers at man, but it is a question whether they belong strictly to the type discussed in the previous section. The affiliations are obvious, the differences more difficult to specify. The misanthropes move in a different world from that of Thersites, Bricriu, and the rest, outside the peculiar ambiance of courts and heroes and ritualistic behavior. Their diatribes are likely to be directed at Man rather than at individual men, and they have no special license. Actually, there is no reason that a misanthrope, generally speaking, need rail at all. One of the first references to Timon of Athens—that of the hero of Phrynicus' comedy *The Misanthrope* (415 B.C.)—implies that Timon was silent: "I live like Timon. I have no wife, no servant, I am irritable and hard to get on with. I never laugh, I never talk, and my opinions are all my own."[1] But over the centuries, as the Timon story takes on its unique form, the convention develops that the misanthrope shall be frantically voluble in expressing his hatred of man. Whether he is a true "railer" or not, the fact is that he rails superbly.

Timon of Athens, Timon the Misanthrope, seems to have been an actual person who lived in the fifth century B.C. References to him in Greek Old and Middle Comedy establish that his singular fame rested on his reputation as a hater of man and the gods. As Plutarch says, the comedians "mocked him, calling him a vyper, and malicious man unto mankind, to shunne all other mens companies...."[2]

From *The Power of Satire: Magic, Ritual, Art*, Princeton, 1960, pp. 141–67. Copyright © 1960 by Princeton University Press. Reprinted by permission of the publisher.

Plutarch's account of Timon in the life of Mark Antony is one of two classical sources chiefly responsible for the proliferation of the legend. It is brief, "factual," contains a number of essential elements of the story. According to Plutarch, Timon's misanthropy resulted from "the unthankefulnes of those he had done good unto, and whom he tooke to be his frendes...." Timon would suffer only one companion, the "bolde and insolent" Alcibiades, whom he made much of because, as Timon said, "one day he shall do great mischiefe unto the Athenians." Plutarch tells two anecdotes involving Timon's bitter jokes and then says matter of factly that he died in the city of Hales (there is no mention of how he died) and was buried near the sea. He records two epitaphs, one allegedly written by the misanthrope himself, the other by the poet Callimachus. Elsewhere, in the life of Alcibiades, Plutarch elaborates the story of the relationship between Timon and the brilliant soldier (*Lives*, II, 107–8). In this account Alcibiades has just received new honor as the result of an eloquent oration. Timon, breaking his custom, went straight to Alcibiades, took him by the hand and said: "O, thou dost well my sonne, I can thee thancke, that thou goest on, and climest up still: for if ever thou be in authoritie, woe be unto those that followe thee, for they are utterly undone."

I go into this detail because Shakespeare, in his treatment of the Timon legend, used Plutarch freely. In just what way he used Lucian's *Timon, or the Misanthrope*, the second major source of the story, is not entirely clear. Lucian's dialogue did not exist in English in Shakespeare's lifetime, although there were Italian and French translations. Further, Lucian was certainly the source of an anonymous Elizabethan academic play, *Timon*, which probably antedates Shakespeare's version and which he may or may not have known. In any event, Shakespeare's *Timon* contains material that appears in Lucian but not in Plutarch, and material that appears in the anonymous *Timon* and in neither of the classical sources. It seems reasonable to suppose that Shakespeare knew Lucian's version of the story either directly or through an intermediate source.[3]

Lucian's dialogue, the earliest literary treatment of the Timon story we have, makes Timon a comic figure. To be sure, he is unmistakably the misanthrope; he rails at men and gods with remarkable abandon, but the violent diatribes are consistently undercut by Lucian's wit and by comments of other characters in the work. While we sympathize with Timon in his denunciations of the parasites who haunt him, we are never allowed to identify with him completely. We see him always from the angle of vision given by comedy.

The dialogue opens with a long, mocking diatribe against Zeus uttered by the impoverished Timon, now so low in fortune that he is dressed in filthy skins and earns a living as a ditchdigger: You! he shouts, you who are supposed to be so powerful, where is your vaunted thunderbolt now? "You neither hear perjurers nor see wrong-doers; you are short-sighted and purblind to all that goes on and have grown as hard of hearing as a man in his dotage." When will you punish all the wickedness in the world? Come, you marvellous ruler, take my case: "After raising so many Athenians to high station and making them rich when they were wretchedly poor before and helping all who were in want, nay more, pouring out my wealth in floods to benefit my friends, now that I have become poor thereby I am no longer recognized or even looked at by the men who formerly cringed and kowtowed and hung upon my nod."[4] Timon's statement of his case elicits sympathy until we overhear Hermes, a voice of reason throughout the dialogue, explaining Timon's situation to Zeus: "Well, you might say that he was ruined by kind-heartedness and philanthropy and compassion on all those who were in want; but in reality it was senselessness and folly and lack of discrimination in regard to his friends. He did not perceive that he was showing kindness to ravens and wolves, and while so many birds of prey were tearing his liver, the unhappy man thought they were his friends... But when they had thoroughly stripped his bones and gnawed them clean... they went away and left him like a dry tree with severed roots..." (p. 335). Nevertheless, Zeus remembers fondly Timon's former sacrifices to him and orders Hermes to escort Riches and Treasure down to the unfortunate man who is causing the commotion on earth. Timon greets them with snarls of rage: "I hate all alike, both gods and men.... I should be content if I could bring sorrow to the whole world, young and old...."

"Don't say that, my friend," says Hermes reasonably, "they do not all deserve sorrow."

Timon threatens to break Riches' head with his pick, for he blames all his own misfortunes on him. But Riches rather plaintively observes: "It is I who brought you everything that is delightful,—honour, precedence, civic crowns, and every form of luxury; and you were admired and puffed and courted, thanks to me. On the other hand, if you have suffered any cruel treatment at the hands of the toadies, I am not to blame; rather have I myself been wronged by you because you so basely put me at the mercy of soundrels who praised you and bewitched you and intrigued against me in every way" (p. 369). Bowing to the power of the gods, Timon is finally constrained to accept Treasure. He digs and lo! there is gold. The discovery, which he welcomes with comic alacrity, is the occasion for Timon's most extended outburst of man-hatred. He resolves to "associate with no one, recognize no one and scorn everyone. Friends, guests, comrades and Altars of Mercy shall be matter for boundless mockery." His favorite name shall be the Misanthrope and the character traits he will cultivate are "testiness, acerbity, rudeness, wrathfulness and inhumanity. If I see anyone perishing in a fire and begging to have it put out, I am to put it out with pitch and oil; and if anyone is being swept off his feet by the river in winter and stretches out his hands, begging me to take hold, I am to push him in headforemost . . ." (pp. 373–75).

It is an impressive paean to hatred. But even this cannot be taken very seriously, for Timon's manner of expression insulates the statement of hatred from connection with the real world. Framing the utterance is a rhetorical flourish of Timon's own devising: although he is quite alone he pretends to be addressing a body of lawmakers. "Be it resolved and enacted into law," he begins, "to be binding for the rest of my life, that I shall associate with no one, recognize no one and scorn everyone." And after he has sworn to push drowning persons in deeper, the extraordinary outburst ends: "Moved by Timon, son of Echecratides, of Collytus; motion submitted to the assembly by the aforesaid Timon" (p. 375). The device is one of make-believe, removing the passage from the context of day-to-day reality. It requires us to discount the literal significance of what are, after all, appalling sentiments. Timon is not allowed to escape from the comic frame.

In the last scene of the dialogue Timon abandons railing in favor of swinging his pick and hurling stones at the swarm of parasites who gather at the whiff of gold. His one sustained speech (pp. 387–89) is not misanthropy but a deft satirical character of Thrasycles in the best Theophrastian manner. At the end our sympathies are with Timon as he drives off his tormenters.

This is excellent comedy; and, as so often in Lucian, it makes its point fairly explicitly. We are asked to recognize that wholesale prodigality is as foolish as extreme miserliness. (I have praise, says

Riches "only for those who . . . observe moderation . . . neither holding
hands off altogether nor throwing me away outright" [pp. 343–45]).
We understand that generosity is admirable, but that Timon was a
fool in his failure to discriminate between the worthy and the
unworthy, between true friends and jackals. And finally, as Hermes
puts it (p. 365), it is reasonable for Timon to hate those who have
treated him horribly. But beyond this, the whole weight of the
dialogue demonstrates that Timon's indiscriminate rage and hatred
make for comical folly. The railer, like Thersites and like Senchán
in the Irish tale, is mocked.

  The point of view of Shakespeare's *Timon* is far less easy to
stipulate. For every interpretation, a dozen counter-readings are
possible and have been advanced; yet it, too, falls, I believe, roughly
within the same pattern.[5]
  The editors of the First Folio (the only source of our text)
included *Timon of Athens* among the tragedies, probably as a last-
minute substitution for *Troilus and Cressida*; and most critics have
considered it as a tragedy. Professor Sisson's comment in his recent
edition of *Timon* is characteristic. The play, he says, is a "powerful
and tragic study of character." Shakespeare "made Timon himself a
noble, generous idealist, whose misanthropy is one with his high-
mindedness, who, like Hamlet, is a true prince among men." Timon
has been compared in various contexts to Lear, Othello, Macbeth,
Coriolanus; his fall has been said to equal theirs in tragic grandeur.
The most extreme presentation of this tragic Timon (and one of the
most brilliant) is that of G. Wilson Knight, whose "prince-hearted,
love-crucified" misanthrope is famous.[6]
  These interpretations are based directly on the text of the play
and particularly on the first scene or two. "In no play of Shakespeare
is the opening more significant," says Mr. Knight, and unquestionably
the early scenes are laced with eloquent testimony to Timon's noble
(and potentially tragic) character. The Poet, the Painter, the Jeweller, the Merchant, the Lords, various followers—all ring changes
on the same tune:

> The noblest mind he carries
> That ever govern'd man

says the First Lord (I, i, 291–92); and only Apemantus dissents.

If we put ourselves, as Mr. Knight and others seem to do, in Timon's position—see everything through his eyes, hear everything through his ears—we will then accept at face value every such speech and every such character. In this cloudless world exact correspondence will hold between word and concept; language will once again be performing its ancient creative function: what it states, by virtue of being stated, is. Here is no room for ambiguity, irony, misapprehension, doubt—to say nothing of deliberate deceit. In the world Timon creates for himself, as in the world of Gulliver's Houyhnhnms, to say the thing which is not is inconceivable. But unlike Timon, we cannot remain part of such a world, being uncomfortably aware of the perplexing possibilities in language and behavior. Unlike Mr. Knight, we are reluctant to accept the Poet, the Painter, the Jeweller, and the Merchant as pure representatives of art, wealth, and trade (as he puts it), as the symbols of progress, civilization, and happiness. We listen to their language and note its ambiguities; we are aware of discordant effects beneath the opulent surface of the dialogue. We hear Apemantus. Even without the evidence of later scenes, this should be enough to show us the falseness of Timon's court, a falseness by which Timon is tainted and to which he contributes.

Our problem is to decide what, in the ways appropriate to literature, the play *Timon of Athens* means; this may be reduced, in effect, to the problem of identifying Timon: who is he? what is he? If Timon is indeed "prince-hearted, love-crucified," we will be forced to consider his self-exile, his man-hatred, his suicide (or willed death, or however one interprets it) as tragic, and to conceive the play in tragic terms. If, on the other hand, we think of Timon as a "naked gull," as one of the characters speaks of him, our conception will be quite different. The only evidence is language on the printed page: what the words say the characters say—and our uncertain sense that beyond, behind, between the interstices of words lies a truth: the truth of the play, which the language of the characters sometimes catches whole and pure, but sometimes obscures.

In criticizing a play we are hypothetically directing it; at least we are making a sketch for a production. Our interpretation will be the image of the production as we see it in our "mind's eye." Theoretically, we will see the production whole; our reading of any particular line will have behind it the weight of the entire five acts of the play. In this respect we are god-like in comparison to the characters: we know how things come out; they do not. Our interpretation of events in Act I will differ from theirs. Furthermore, as critics we have faith that a great dramatist will have made his play so that in the end will be the beginning; and in the beginning, the end.

It seems necessary to restate some of these platitudes because of the curious way critics have approached the opening scenes of *Timon*, as though those scenes had no connection with what comes later, as though a character in Act V is somehow discontinuous with the same character in Act I. In Act V, Scene i, the Poet and the Painter whose words had opened the play reappear, magnetically drawn to Timon's cave by the rumor that he is again "full of gold." They have a brief colloquy (overheard by Timon) in which they make totally explicit the shameless hypocrisy of their natures:

> POET. Then this breaking of his has been but a try for his friends?
>
> PAINT. Nothing else. You shall see him a palm in Athens again, and flourish with the highest. Therefore 'tis not amiss we tender our loves to him in this suppos'd distress of his. It will show honestly in us. . . .
>
> POET. What have you now to present unto him?
>
> PAINT. Nothing at this time but my visitation. Only I will promise him an excellent piece.
>
> POET. I must serve him so too. . . .
>
> PAINT. Good as the best. Promising is the very air o' th' time. . . . To promise is most courtly and fashionable; performance is a kind of will or testament which argues a great sickness in his judgment that makes it. . . .
>
> POET. I am thinking what I shall say I have provided for him. It must be a personating of himself; a satire against the softness of prosperity, with a discovery of the infinite flatteries that follow youth and opulency.
>
> TIM. [aside] Must thou needs stand for a villain in thine own work? Wilt thou whip thine own faults in other men?

Now, unless Shakespeare has taken monstrous liberties with characterization, the essential elements of these cardboard characters should have appeared in the opening scene of the play.[7] They do in fact appear. There is no open confession of villainy. But consider the hints for a sensitive director in the first lines. The Poet and the

Painter greet each other; the Poet asks if there is anything new in
the world, anything not matched by "manifold record." "See," he
cries, pointing to the Jeweller, the Merchant, the Mercer—to all,
including himself and the Painter, who throng at Timon's door:
"See,"

> Magic of bounty, all these spirits thy power
> Hath conjur'd to attend!

The implication is that bounty's magic is an old one whose conjuring
power is well attested in manifold record. The tone is ironic. It is
important in fixing the range of our attitudes toward what follows.
"I know the Merchant," continues the Poet, intending perhaps simple
identification but implying also that he knows his character, sees his
motives in dancing attendance. The Merchant and the Jeweller
exchange praise of Timon:

> A most incomparable man; breath'd, as it were,
> To an untirable and continuate goodness,

says the Merchant. "I have a jewel here—" responds his companion,
firmly encompassing the praise with avidity of personal gain. As
early as line 15 the Poet introduces a theme to which he continually
reverts—that of hypocritical praising:

> 'When we for recompense have prais'd the vile,
> It stains the glory in that happy verse
> Which aptly sings the good.'

Later he speaks of "glib and slipp'ry creatures," the "glass-fac'd
flatter," those who fill Timon's lobby with tendance,

> Rain sacrificial whisperings in his ear,
> Make sacred even his stirrup, and through him
> Drink the free air. (I, i, 81–83)

These are the hangers-on against whom he will warn Timon in his
poetic allegory of the hill of Fortune. The Poet's tactics are among
the oldest in the annals of rascality; he attacks in others the vice he
bears in himself. The passage already cited from Act v, which
hammers home his crucial point, is full commentary.

Timon's entrance reveals him in his most characteristic stance:
distributing largesse, buying love, like Lear, at so much per talent.
He rescues Ventidius from creditors:

> I am not of that feather to shake off
> My friend when he most needs me (I, i, 100–101)

—the tone of complacency jars. He endows his servant Lucilius so
that he may marry the daughter of a very thrifty Athenian:

> To build his fortune I will strain a little,
> For 'tis a bond in men.

He promises money to Poet, Painter, and Jeweller, and affably bears
their commendation. The scene closes with a brief dialogue between
two Lords, sometimes cited by critics as establishing beyond cavil
Timon's essential nobility:

> 1. LORD.   Come, shall we in
>   And taste Lord Timon's bounty? He outgoes
>   The very heart of kindness.
> 2. LORD.   He pours it out. Plutus, the god of gold,
>   Is but his steward. No meed but he repays
>   Sevenfold above itself. No gift to him
>   But breeds the giver a return exceeding
>   All use of quittance.
> 1. LORD.   The noblest mind he carries
>   That ever govern'd man.
> 2. LORD.   Long may he live
>   In fortunes!

Unquestionably the words of the first Lord are a superb tribute;
in a different context they would certify to Timon's towering virtues.
But the second Lord's comments act so powerfully as a gloss on the
simple attribution of virtue that the gloss assimilates the text.
Throughout the first part of the play this grotesque metamorphosis
operates consistently: nobility *becomes* the disgorgement of gold. The
Lords who use the language of virtue so perversely are native to the
world which flourishes around Timon; they are flat figures, have no
characters, and because they are alone on the stage, they have no
motive to flatter. Their tone is one of heightened adulation and

wonder, like the tone of the Poet and the Painter as they praise extravagantly each other's works. Except for Apemantus, this is the only tone heard at Timon's court. Everyone talks alike. It is a disease, brought on by a superfluity of gold, and it is presented as a disease. No Jacobean audience could have missed the point: the deliberately trite hill of Fortune allegory of the Poet; the insistent emphasis on prodigality; the fawning and flattering and the reiterated hope that good fortune will last (the fortune-equals-money equation constantly present)—all this could presage nothing but disaster.

The one exception to the pervasive tone is important. Apemantus' corrosive words cut cleanly through the treacle of adulation to the rottenness beneath. This cynic, this "churlish philosopher," is a perfect type of the railer-fool. He hates everyone, is "ever angry," as Timon says. His grotesque wit converts all experience into ugliness —but reveals much truth thereby. His license to rail is absolute:

> TIMON.   Look who comes here.
>   Will you be chid?
> JEWELLER. We'll bear, with your lordship.
> MERCHANT. He'll spare none. (I, i, 175–77)

Apemantus' railing is, in one sense, a performance, a kind of game; various characters egg him on, feed him lines, to see the clown perform ("... here comes the fool with Apemantus. Let's ha' some sport with 'em" [II, ii, 47]); but, in another sense, his railing peels off layer after layer of fraudulence, as it cuts its way to the core of things. Outrageous as Apemantus is, bitter, cynical, snarling, his view of the reality at Timon's court is healthy by comparison with what prevails. Thou liest, he says to the Poet, because "in thy last work ... thou hast feign'd him [Timon] a worthy fellow."

> POET. That's not feign'd; he is so.
> APEMANTUS. Yes, he is worthy of thee, and to pay thee for
> thy labour. He that loves to be flattered is worthy o' th' flatterer.
> (I, i, 228–33)

Apemantus has an eye for the thing itself and, like other malcontents who brood on degeneration, the moral bias of the idealist manqué. Appalled at the ceremoniousness he sees about him—a ceremoniousness divorced from the moral order which might give it meaning— he bursts out:

> That there should be small love amongst these sweet knaves,
> And all this courtesy! The strain of man's bred out
> Into baboon and monkey. (I, i, 258–60)

Even for him there had once been a true strain of man. But it is easy to exaggerate: Apemantus can carry little moral authority; his hatred is as general and indiscriminate as Timon's easy love, and his chief function here is to set counter-currents working.

The second scene continues and elaborates themes already established. Timon's generosity reaches fabulous heights as he dispenses money, jewels, horses, and hospitality in boundless profusion. The more he gives, the more he is praised, although one may occasionally detect a faint note of irony (I, ii, 21). The munificence of Timon so far has been almost mechanical; that is, it has not been related to an inner life, but in this scene we see something more of what moves him. He refuses on principle Ventidius' offer to repay the recently-provided money:

> there's none
> Can truly say he gives, if he receives. (I, ii, 10)

In practice, Timon insists on maintaining the one-way flow of friendship. In theory, as he shows a few lines later, he is willing to entertain contradictory possibilities: "O you gods, think I, what need we have any friends if we should ne'er have need of 'em? . . . We are born to do benefits; and what better or properer can we call our own than the riches of our friends? O, what a precious comfort 'tis to have so many like brothers commanding one another's fortunes!" The sentiment in more austere circumstances would be noble; here, as must be apparent to the audience, it is fatuous. "Why, I have often wish'd myself poorer, that I might come nearer to you," cries Timon and weeps at the joy he envisions in such a possibility. "I promise you, my lord, you mov'd me much," says the third Lord. "Much!" says Apemantus.

In the course of the scene, Flavius, the faithful servant (who along with Apemantus recognizes the falseness of the friends [I, ii, 209–10]), indicates that the great flow of Timon's generosity comes out of an empty coffer. His master has been inaccessible to warning, is still ignorant that the fabulous estate has been dissipated in the "flow of riot" (II, ii, 3). The irony of the munificence is sharpened:

> Methinks I could deal kingdoms to my friends
> And ne'er be weary,

cries Timon, emphasizing strongly his removal from reality; and warnings, ironic and direct, come thick but are unheeded.

Thus by the end of the first Act an image of Timon in prosperity has been firmly established. He is a man so victimized by the excess of a good quality, generosity, so blinded by his indiscriminate love of all humanity, that he is incapable of seeing the reality about him. His hallucinatory vision metamorphoses flatterers into friends and sycophants into brothers. Material wealth, in Timon's view, is inexhaustibly magical, the act of dispensing it enough to convert evil into good. Timon plays god in these scenes, but his love lacks humility, and his "worshipers" basely serve their own ends.[8] The many references to Timon's nobility must be discounted by our awareness of who utters them and why, and Timon himself must seem more gullible than heroic. The audience waits for the inevitable crash, and, knowing it well-deserved, waits, I should think, without much sympathy for the man whom Apemantus calls, at the best, an "honest fool."

This, our earliest impression of Timon, is most important; but it is qualified—or, more accurately, in the curious way of this play, it is contradicted—by later evidence which tends to build Timon's character in retrospect. In Act III, Scene ii, after Timon has been denied by his friends, a Stranger, over-hearing, speaks:

> For mine own part,
> I never tasted Timon in my life,
> Nor came any of his bounties over me
> To mark me for his friend; yet I protest,
> For his right noble mind, illustrious virtue,
> And honourable carriage,
> Had his necessity made use of me,
> I would have put my wealth into donation....

One might question why, if his admiration is sincere, he does not proffer aid of his own accord; but then one understands that the Stranger too has been tainted by the corruption of the times:

> I perceive,
> Men must learn now with pity to dispense;
> For policy sits above conscience.

Timon's servants are remarkably steadfast: "Yet do our hearts wear
Timon's livery" (IV, ii, 17); and Flavius, after his early irritation
with his blind master, consistently gives him a good character:

> Poor honest lord, brought low by his own heart,
> Undone by goodness! (IV, ii, 37–38)

The special quality here is that of loyal, uncritical devotion, revealing
rather more of Flavius than of Timon.[9] Finally, the last words of
the play, Alcibiades' elegiac utterance, must be put into the balance;
Alcibiades speaks of Timon's grave hard by the sea:

> ...rich conceit
> Taught thee to make vast Neptune weep for aye
> On thy low grave, on faults forgiven. Dead
> Is noble Timon, of whose memory
> Hereafter more.

It is difficult to know what to make of Alcibiades. The Emperor Hadrian's remark in the fictional *Memoirs* by Marguerite
Yourcenar is apt: "Alcibiades had seduced everyone and everything,
even History herself. . . ."[10] Shakespeare's characterization may in part
be an example. In Plutarch's *Life* Shakespeare found a portrait of a
man dazzlingly brilliant but fatally unstable. Plutarch has high praise
for Alcibiades' eloquence, his wit and courage, his talents in general;
but he is consistently severe on Alcibiades' dishonesty, his licentiousness, his chameleon-like qualities: "the unconstancie of his life, and
waywardnes of his nature and conditions."[11] Alcibiades is even spoken
of as having been corrupted by money (II, 192). It is worth quoting
again Plutarch's version of an encounter between Alcibiades and
Timon. The misanthrope took the brilliant young orator by the hand
and said: "O, thou dost well my sonne, I can thee thancke, that
thou goest on, and climest up still: for if ever thou be in authoritie,
woe be unto those that followe thee, for they are utterly undone."
Plutarch continues: "When they had heard these wordes, those that
stoode by fell a laughing: other reviled Timon, other againe marked
well his wordes and thought of them many a time after . . ." (II, 108).
This is the portrait with which Shakespeare presumably worked.
Clearly he altered it in important respects. At the end of the play, at
least, Alcibiades seems closer to Fortinbras than to Plutarch's character. Still, he is a contradictory Fortinbras: noble and war-like,

surely, and steadfast in defense of his friend, but extraordinarily bloodthirsty as his first words (beyond those of formal greeting) show. Timon has remarked: "You had rather be at a breakfast of enemies than a dinner of friends." Alcibiades answers: "So they were bleeding new, my lord, there's no meat like 'em" (I, ii, 78–81), thus partaking of the cannibal theme, the imagery of which is pervasive in the play. He is prompted to war against Athens by the unfeeling harshness of the corrupt Senators, yet is pleased to be able to strike at his native city in a cause he thinks worthy his spleen and fury. The most discreditable blot on Alcibiades, however, is that with no qualms he enjoys the company of two of Shakespeare's foulest women, the whores Phrynia and Timandra. "Thy lips rot off!" is Phrynia's first utterance; and after Timon has urged them (in a monstrous tirade) to "Be strong in whore" so that they will infect the entire race, the women raise their aprons at his bidding and call for more counsel with more gold: "Believe't that we'll do anything for gold" (IV, iii, 63–167). Alcibiades departs in their company for Athens, that "coward and lascivious town," he calls it (v, iv, 1), lashing in others the vice that consumes him. I may have pushed this dubious matter further than it warrants—nothing could be more statesmanlike, we must recognize, than Alcibiades' final speech—but the unresolved character of the man is puzzling, and it is a question whether we are justified in taking without reservation the "noble Timon" of his obituary.[12]

In any event, the Stranger, the servants, Flavius, and Alcibiades —all relatively disinterested witnesses—testify to the nobility of Timon's character. An odd feature of this evidence is that it comes late in the play, is strangely abstract compared to the concreteness of early impressions, and contradicts rather than modifies the image we have of Timon from the first Act. A general disposition for good in him we can recognize at that point, the disposition vitiated, however, by his lack of humility and the failure of his intelligence. As we observe Timon's acts, listen to his voice, and overhear those who smother him with flattery, it is impossible to think of this man, so willfully unaware of the evil to which he contributes, as truly noble.

Timon's abrupt plunge into misanthropy is psychologically and dramatically sound. He is a man of excess; from his cave he repeats the excesses of his court, substituting hate for love, but dealing out gold as lavishly as before. The most powerful commentary on his early imbalance is the extreme to which his disillusionment brings him. Dr. Johnson speaks of Timon's "malignant dignity" as he utters his hatred. He has that quality, but not consistently. After the transition scene of the mock banquet comes the first great rolling curse, an invocation of the anarchy against which the willed order of Ulysses' speech in *Troilus* is arrayed:

> Matrons, turn incontinent!
> Obedience fail in children! Slaves and fools,
> Pluck the grave wrinkled Senate from the bench
> And minister in their steads! To general filths
> Convert o' th' instant, green virginity!
> Do't in your parents' eyes! Bankrupts, hold fast!
> Rather than render back, out with your knives
> And cut your trusters' throats! Bound servants, steal!
> Large-handed robbers your grave masters are
> And pill by law. Maid, to thy master's bed!
> Thy mistress o' th' brothel. Son of sixteen,
> Pluck the lin'd crutch from thy old limping sire;
> With it beat out his brains! Piety and fear,
> Religion to the gods, peace, justice, truth,
> Domestic awe, night-rest and neighborhood,
> Instruction, manners, mysteries and trades,
> Degrees, observances, customs and laws,
> Decline to your confounding contraries
> And let confusion live! (iv, i, 3–21)

The long list of imperatives ends, almost as an afterthought, with an invocation to the gods—"you good gods all"—to confound the Athenians and allow Timon's hate to grow.

There is dignity here, if only in the grandeur of the demonic conception and in the attempted resuscitation of atavistic powers. Curse follows on curse as Timon fixes the range of his misanthropy; his hate is as all-embracing and indiscriminate as was his love:

> All's obliquy;
> There's nothing level in our cursed natures
> But direct villainy. Therefore be abhorr'd
> All feasts, societies, and throngs of men!
> His semblable, yea, himself, Timon disdains.
> Destruction fang mankind! (iv, iii, 18–23)

A procession of visitors to his cave feeds his rage. Alcibiades is exhorted to universal slaughter in Athens: Spare not old age, mothers, virgins, Timon urges; the dimpled babe: "mince it sans remorse."

The soldier is then cursed himself. The harlots are dipped in the most spectacular horrors of their trade in language brutal beyond belief; but they emerge untouched, their sensibilities assuaged by gold. Apemantus, the bandits, Flavius, the Senators—all are subjected to a flood of vituperation that must finally seem mad in its excess. But by the end the dignity has gone and Timon is an object of derision.

The crucial scene is that between him and Apemantus, between the new misanthrope and the old railer, who seems jealous of his prerogative. Apemantus' insight into Timon's condition is as sharp after the fall from prosperity as it has been before:

> Men report
> Thou dost affect my manners and dost use them
> . . . .
> This is in thee a nature but infected,
> A poor unmanly melancholy sprung
> From change of fortune. (IV, iii, 198–204)

(Earlier, Alcibiades had explained to "sweet Timandra" that Timon's wits are drowned; later the first Bandit reports that "The mere want of gold and the falling-from of his friends drove him into this melancholy" [IV, iii, 401–3].) "Shame not these woods," says Apemantus, "By putting on the cunning of a carper." My willing misery, he argues, brings more content and is more worthy than your enforced misery. Timon debates with Apemantus the question of which one has the best title to hate men: he who had the world as his confectionary, or he who was born a rogue. For a moment Apemantus seems softened by the power of Timon's claims; he offers him food. But Timon will not soften reciprocally—he will no more accept food now than earlier he would accept repayment of money—and he wishes for poison to sauce his fellow's dishes.[13] Apemantus' comment is to the point: "The middle of humanity thou never knewest, but the extremity of both ends."

The dialectic of man-hatred continues, developing a curious self-congratulatory air. Apemantus would turn the world over to the beasts and would become one himself. Timon is at such ingenious pains to explain what a beastly ambition this is that Apemantus seems delighted: the pupil is surpassing the master. The mutual self-indulgence is unmistakable. But as Apemantus prepares to leave, the tone shifts significantly.

TIM. I had rather be a beggar's dog than Apemantus.

APEM. Thou art the cap of all the fools alive.

TIM. Would thou wert clean enough to spit upon!

APEM. A plague on thee! Thou art too bad to curse.

TIM. All villains that do stand by thee are pure.

APEM. There is no leprosy but what thou speak'st.

TIM. If I name thee.
    I'll beat thee—but I should infect my hands.

APEM. I would my tongue could rot them off!

TIM. Away, thou issue of a mangy dog!
    Choler does kill me that thou art alive;
    I swoond to see thee.

APEM.   Would thou wouldst burst!

TIM.   Away,
    Thou tedious rogue! I am sorry I shall lose
    A stone by thee. [*Throws a stone at him.*]

APEM.   Beast!

TIM.   Slave!

APEM.   Toad!

TIM.   Rogue, rogue, rogue!

The form, the content, the tone of this are familiar. It is a conventional wit-combat in invective, much like that described by Horace in the "Journey to Brundisium": the contest in scurrility between Sarmentus and Messius at which Horace and Maecenas and Virgil laughed.[14] The rapid tempo, the give and take of abusive epithet, the element of contest as one tries to outdo the other, the total lack of dignity—these are characteristics of stichomythia, of a flyting, a performance. The participants are for the moment buffoons, *scurrae*; they would not be greatly out of their element in a drum-match among the Eskimos. After the grandiose intemperance of language in this Act, the final inarticulate sputters ("Beast!" "Slave!" "Toad!" "Rogue, rogue, rogue!") and the throwing of the stone can only be grotesquely comic. The scene is past rage and into the ridiculous. There is a clear sense in which Apemantus' characterization of Timon, "A madman so long, now a fool," is precise.

The episode colors indelibly the rest of the play; for, while the lost dignity is reasserted, the curses sound a different tone. What moral authority Timon brought into misanthropy he has forfeited by making himself an object of ridicule. Still, he maintains his bitter course to the end. Although he can ask forgiveness for his "general and exceptless rashness" and recognize that one honest man ("Mistake me not—but one!") exists, his advice to Flavius is of a piece with his rigidly undiscriminating temper:

> Hate all, curse all, show charity to none,
> But let the famish'd flesh slide from the bone
> Ere thou relieve the beggar. (IV, iii, 534–36)

Lear's disillusionment brings insight: "They told me I was everything. 'Tis a lie—I am not ague-proof" (IV, vi, 107). Timon's does not; he is incapable of breaking out of the circle of hatred he has drawn about himself. There are flashes of self-recognition, as when he says he is worthy only of the venal Senators who come for his aid, and they worthy of him (almost the words of Apemantus in I, i, when he said that Timon was worthy of the flatterer, and the flatterer of him). But his last utterance issues from passionate pride:

> Sun, hide thy beams! Timon hath done his reign. (v, i, 226)

Mr. J. C. Maxwell speaks of the "intangible and mysterious consummation" which is Timon's end, and it is true that a new tone in his utterance leads one to think in lyrical terms: ". . . say to Athens," he tells the Senators,—

> Timon hath made his everlasting mansion
> Upon the beached verge of the salt flood,
> Who once a day with his embossed froth,
> The turbulent surge shall cover. Thither come
> And let my gravestone be your oracle. (v, i, 217–22)

But the grandeur of the rhetoric belies the sentiment, and the consummation is flawed. The oracle is Timon's grotesque epitaph:

> Here lies a wretched corse, of wretched soul bereft.
> Seek not my name. A plague consume you wicked caitiffs left!
> Here lie I, Timon, who alive all living men did hate.
> Pass by, and curse thy fill; but pass, and stay not here thy gait.[15]

Timon's last words from out the nothingness he coveted are a snarl.

They are not, however, the last words about him. These, as we have seen, come from Alcibiades, who before the walls of Athens speaks of "noble Timon" and of "faults forgiven." Alcibiades' march on the city has been halted and his bloody purpose blunted by the arguments of certain Senators. Critics have neglected these arguments, mistakenly, I think, for they seem to me to constitute a choral commentary on the theme of the play. The Senators plead for the concreteness of individual moral responsibility as opposed to the abstraction of mass guilt. They ask for rational discrimination between those who deserve punishment and those who do not:

> We were not all unkind, nor all deserve
> The common stroke of war. (v, iv, 21–22)

(We recall Hermes in the *Timon* of 1500 years earlier: when the misanthrope wanted to bring sorrow to the whole world, Hermes quietly spoke, "Don't say that, my friend, they do not all deserve sorrow.") Some of the guilty have already paid, we learn; the Senators responsible for Alcibiades' banishment have died of shame —a remarkable touch! But, "All have not offended," argues a senator:

> Like a shepherd,
> Approach the fold and cull th' infected forth,
> But kill not all together.

The Senators plead, in short, for precisely the virtues that Timon lacked; for Timon was never, from beginning to end, able to discriminate between the healthy and the infected.

Whatever our misgivings about Alcibiades, he speaks at this moment as one aware of heroic responsibilities; he accedes to the Senators' plea: the guilty will be "set out" from the innocent, and only they shall fall.

> Bring me into your city,
> And I will use the olive, with my sword,
> Make war breed peace, make peace stint war, make each
> Prescribe to other, as each other's leech.

Alcibiades' tone helps create a sense of reasserted sanity. The money-madness which has corrupted Athens has been purged in Timon's wild excesses. The fabric of Athenian society is being rewoven.

Although *Timon of Athens* ends in a manner appropriate to tragedy, Professor Campbell's denomination of it as a tragical satire is just; the play is entangled in the most complicated ways with problems of satirical theory and practice. A Jacobean audience, for example, would have associated both Timon and Apemantus with satirists; or, at least, they would have recognized in the misanthropic utterances a tone that had become conventional for satirists of the period. Renaissance usage having to do with satire was no more strict than our own. For Puttenham, *Piers Ploughman* was a "Satyr" and its author "a malcontent of that time," whom Puttenham places in the tradition of Lucilius, Juvenal, and Persius, characterizing them all by their "rough and bitter speaches, and their inuectiues." Skelton also was a "sharpe Satirist, but with more rayling and scoffery then became a Poet Lawreat"; he was, in fact, says Puttenham, a buffoon.[16]

Throughout the period the over-riding influence of Juvenal sanctioned the satirist in the most extravagant flights of invective and general intemperance of language. Marston is an excellent example. In one of his formal satires, after a noxious description of sexual perversion in London, he gropes for authority. Shall I, he asks,

> Halter my hate, and cease to curse and ban
> Such brutish filth?

Shall I, he continues to question over seventy-five perfervid lines, be silent in the face of such enormities? The answer:

> No, gloomy Juvenal,
> Though to thy fortunes I disastrous fall.[17]

As for style, like Juvenal he will violate convention, hurl his invective at the top of his bent:

> O how on tip-toes proudly mounts my muse!
> Stalking a loftier gait than satires use.
> Methinks some sacred rage warms all my veins,
> Making my sprite mount up to higher strains

> Than well beseems a rough-tongu'd satire's
>   part.... (*Scourge*, IX, 5–9)

Almost without question Marston patterned the lines after Juvenal's similar declamation at the end of his Sixth Satire.[18] Invective and vituperation were the stock-in-trade of the satirists of the 1590's (Marston was a "rugged Timon," according to Bullen); and their subjects—lust, hypocrisy, miserliness, usury, greed—covered an astonishing range of man's vice as well as his folly. True, they rarely attack man as such, as Timon does; but when Timon inveighs against lust and gold and hypocrisy, his voice, though grander than theirs, is well within their key.

Timon even adopts as an occasional tactic the satirists' mocking, bitter humor. In Act V, Scene i, the Senators plead with him to intervene against Alcibiades' savage approach to the city. Timon answers:

> If Alcibiades kill my countrymen,
> Let Alcibiades know this of Timon,
> That Timon cares not. But if he sack fair Athens
> And take our goodly aged men by th' beards,
> Giving our holy virgins to the stain
> Of contumelious, beastly, mad-brain'd war,
> Then let him know (and tell him Timon speaks it
> In pity of our aged and our youth)
> I cannot choose but tell him that I care not....

His rhetoric is palpably designed to tantalize the Senators, to raise their hopes and keep them up, delicately balanced, through several lines of verbiage—then to bring them crashing down in a derisive anti-climax. Precisely the same technique is employed in the bitter joke about the tree which immediately follows: the tree will cure all afflictions, says Timon, and Athenians high and low are welcome to hang themselves from it. These are tricks of the snarling satirist.

Now, what of Apemantus? Like Carlo Buffone, Malevole, Thersites, and others, he is a buffoon, a scurrilous railer and detractor; the only question is whether in Shakespeare's day a railer could be considered a satirist. To be sure, there is considerable frowning on buffoonery in the period. Puttenham feels that Skelton's scurrilities assort ill with his Laureateship, although he does call Skelton a satirist. The formal satirists themselves attack cynics and railers and detractors.

> Who cannot rail?—what dog but dare to bark
> 'Gainst Phoebe's brightness in the silent dark?
> . . . .
> Vain envious detractor from the good,
> What cynic spirit rageth in thy blood?

asks Marston contemptuously, and the same attitudes are echoed by various contemporaries.[19] Such evidence leads Professor Campbell to say that the formal satirists distinguish "true satire from raillery [railing?] and mere detraction. . . . The cynic's spirit, they knew, was a metempsychosis of a snarling dog and utterly unsuited to satire."[20] But the satirists had many moods. They often arrogate to themselves the license (particularly in obscenity of expression) which in literature and legend had been the privilege of the railer; and for some moods nothing seemed more appropriate than the snarl of a dog. Marston frequently refers to himself as a barking or a sharp-fang'd satirist;[21] he boasts of his "respectless rude satiric hand," swears to "rail upon/This fusty world."[22] He writes a "Cynic Satire" (*Scourge*, VII) in which the interlocutor, tired of the Cynic's detraction, says he will stop "thy currish, barking chops (l. 102)." But the interlocutor is an *ingénu*, a butt; the Cynic is the satirist and is thus identified throughout (ll. 50, 92). *T. M. Gent's Micro-cynicon: Sixe Snarling Satyres* (1599) snarls more fiercely than it bites; but it is apparent from this and other works that in the 1590's the posture was conventional. In *Timon of Athens*, "dog" is the epithet most frequently applied to Apemantus. His *is* the role that is projected by many young satirists of the period. If it would be naïve to identify unequivocally the poets with the surly *personae* they adopt,[23] it is impossible to ignore the fact that satire is, in part, at least, precisely the kind of thing that Apemantus utters. His fine, edged speech on flatterers (IV, iii, 205ff.) has clear counterparts in Donne, Marston, and others; and his cynical comments may be matched many times over in the formal satires of Shakespeare's contemporaries.

To identify both Timon and Apemantus as satirists is by no means, of course, to imply that they are identical. Occasionally, it is true, they speak alike, particularly when Timon is being least himself. In the buffoon scene examined above, their rhetoric is indistinguishable. Again, when Phrynia spits at Timon: "Thy lips rot off!" his response is worthy Apemantus:

> I will not kiss thee; then the rot returns
> To thine own lips again. (IV, iii, 64–65)

But by and large the resemblance is smothered beneath the weight of difference. It is enough to reiterate that Apemantus has all the characteristics of the railer, a type we have examined. We have also seen in earlier chapters the prototypes of Timon. After his fall from prosperity Timon's language takes on the incantatory tone of a prophet. He tries to preempt the full power of the archaic curse, calling on the gods, the heavens, the earth—and, as it were, the demonic power within himself—to confound the hated creature man. It is as though Timon were reenacting an ancient role, attempting to change the world through the power of language. He is a magician manqué, a primitive satirist ages out of his time. Part of his frustration, part of his ultimate humiliation, is the fact that magic is no longer viable. The Irish poet Laidcenn satirized and cursed the men of Leinster "so that neither grass nor corn grew with them, nor a leaf, to the end of a year." Timon calls upon the sun to "draw from the earth/Rotten humidity" and infect the air. He commands the earth: "Dry up thmy marrows, vines, and plough-torn leas," commands it to go great with tigers, to teem with new monsters. But Timon's words break on the cold substantiality of a world from which magic has vanished, and the only monster he can conjure up is man.[24] Still, the awful words affect us; in obscure ways we are moved by Timon's efforts to manipulate atavistic powers. Even in our revulsion we are attracted, as was Yeats:

> Myself must I remake
> Till I am Timon and Lear
> Or that William Blake
> Who beat upon the wall
> Till Truth obeyed his call.[25]

If Apemantus is a satirist-railer in the tradition of Thersites, Timon is a satirist-curser in the tradition of Aithirne and others of his kind. The distinction is pointed up in the play by their debate and made a question of class. Apemantus was "bred a dog," as Timon says, and never knew Fortune's tender clasps:

> Why shouldst thou hate men?
> They never flatter'd thee. . . .
> If thou wilt curse, thy father (that poor rag)
> Must be thy subject, who in spite put stuff
> To some she-beggar and compounded thee
> Poor rogue hereditary. (IV, iii, 269–74)

Apemantus, in short, is the poor man's misanthrope. Timon, who had the world as his confectionary,

> The mouths, the tongues, the eyes, and hearts of men
> At duty. . . .

is entitled to curse until the heavens crack; but his words, unlike those of Lear, which find an echo in nature, seem mere madness to his auditors.

The words cannot, however, be dismissed easily. The denunciation of man has a hideous kind of cogency. It is so powerfully stated that many critics have been led to identify Timon's words with Shakespeare's psyche, to speak of black periods in the dramatist's life and of mental breakdowns. This seems unnecessary. The full horror is there, of course, its statement about man ineradicable. That in one sense it is Shakespeare's statement is clearly true. But in the full literary sense the Timon view of man is qualified, contradicted, by the structure of the play. There is, in fine, a third satirist: Shakespeare himself. Again we have the ancient complication: the created character, hurling curses and invective, using language as a magical instrument, functioning in effect as a primitive satirist—he being satirized, in the sophisticated sense of the term, by his creator. Timon's indiscriminate love and his indiscriminate hate are shown dramatically to be folly. The denunciation of man is frightfully powerful and it stands; but Shakespeare sharply undercuts its effect by pulling Timon down from heights of vatic eloquence to the mud, where he plays the buffoon with Apemantus.

The play can hardly be said to argue *for* anything, except by implication. It argues most clearly against excess: the excess, first, of Timon's "love," with its lack of humility, its flaccid refusal to discriminate, its abstractness; then against the excess of his liberality, which perverts into destructive fully a disposition originally virtuous; finally, against the excess of his hate. It argues against the abstraction that would hold all Athenians (all men) worthy and against that which would hold them all vicious. To say that the play argues implicitly for moderation, for rational discrimination in judging the ways of men, while at the same time it takes full cognizance of the dreadful power of the extreme, is to sound almost trivial; for the virtues of moderation are not in great demand in the twentieth century, dominated as it is by the *exigence d'absolu*. Yet such is the burden of the

satirist-satirized theme as it appears in Lucian and in Shakespeare's
Timon.

NOTES

[1] Cited in Ernest Hunter Wright, *The Authorship of Timon of
Athens* (New York, 1910), p. 8.

[2] *Plutarch's Lives*, Englished by Sir Thomas North, Introd.
George Wyndham, The Tudor Translations (London, 1896),
VI, 73.

[3] See E. K. Chambers, *William Shakespeare: A Study of Facts
and Problems* (Oxford, 1930), I, 483–84; George Lyman Kittredge, ed., *The Complete Works of Shakespeare* (Boston, 1936),
pp. 1045–46. All quotations from Shakespeare are from this
edition.

[4] *Lucian*, trans. Harmon, II, 327–31.

[5] Professor Oscar J. Campbell has urged something like this interpretation of the play against the majority of critics. My reading differs from his, however, in a number of ways. See his
Shakespeare's Satire (New York, 1943), pp. 168–97.

[6] C. J. Sisson in his edition of Shakespeare, *Complete Works*
(London, 1954), p. 910; Knight's interpretation is advanced at
length in *The Wheel of Fire* (Oxford, 1930), pp. 227–62, although the quoted phrase comes from *The Shakespearian Tempest* (London, 1953), p. 206.

[7] The deplorable state of the text raises problems. Most scholars
today accept E. K. Chambers' hypothesis that the entire play is
Shakespeare's but that it was left unfinished. This at least allows
us to consider the play as one thing, even if flawed, and does
away with the gambit which dismisses contradictory or awkward passages by reference to an assumed interpolation by an
unknown hand. The Poet and Painter scene in Act v has been
so dismissed; see, e.g., Kenneth Muir, "In Defence of Timon's
Poet," *Essays in Criticism*, III (1953), pp. 120–21.

[8] A Senator, one of Timon's creditors, professes to love and
honor him but makes his actual contempt explicit:

> Still in motion
> Of raging waste? It cannot hold; it will not.
> If I want gold, steal but a beggar's dog
> And give it Timon—why, the dog coins gold. (II, i, 3–6)

⁹ The same quality appears in Laches, the servant of the anonymous Elizabethan *Timon* which Shakespeare may or may not have known. (There is no comparable character in Plutarch or Lucian.) In that play Timon is introduced as a monster of foolish pride, wallowing in adulation. When Laches remonstrates about his prodigality, Timon threatens to cut out his tongue and turns him out of doors. But Laches remains uncritically faithful. See *Timon*, ed. Rev. Alexander Dyce (London, for The Shakespeare Society, 1842).

¹⁰ *Memoirs of Hadrian*, trans. Grace Frick (New York, 1955), p. 166.

¹¹ *Lives*, trans. North, II, 108.

¹² J. C. Maxwell in his perceptive " 'Timon of Athens,' " *Scrutiny*, xv (1947–48), p. 206, n. 16, expresses puzzlement at the appearance of Phrynia and Timandra with Alcibiades. "I should be reluctant to regard it as intended to indicate that the claims of Alcibiades . . . to regenerate Athens are to be taken cynically." See also the Introduction to his ed. of *Timon* (Cambridge, 1957). I have profited from both essays.

¹³ William Empson points to the reversal of roles here. In his first speech in the play, Apemantus has said he will not be gentle until Timon becomes a dog (the common Renaissance epithet for "cynic,") and the knaves honest. The knaves are "honest" only in that they have revealed their villainy; but Timon snarls like a cynic and Apemantus offers charity. See *The Structure of Complex Words* (London, 1951), pp. 177–78.

¹⁴ *Satires*, I, 5, ll. 51–69.

¹⁵ Shakespeare here joins the contradictory epitaphs recorded in North's Plutarch: the one said to be by Timon himself, the other by Callimachus.

¹⁶ *The Arte of English Poesie*, ed. Willcock and Walker, p. 62.

¹⁷ Satire III, ll. 126–27, 195–96, *The Scourge of Villainy in Works*, ed. Bullen, III, 322–25.

¹⁸ See Chap. III above and cf. Joseph Hall, Prologue, *Virgidemiarum*, ll. 19–23.

> *Goe daring Muse on with thy thankless taske,*
> *And do the vgly face of vice vnmaske:*
> *And if thou canst not thine high flight remit,*
> *So as it mought a lowly Satyre fit,*
> *Let lowly Satyres rise aloft to thee. . . .*

Collected Poems, ed. A. Davenport (Liverpool, 1949), p. 11.

19 Satire IV, ll. 9–10, 25–26 in *Works*, III, 280–81.

20 *Comicall Satyre*, p. 67. See above, Chap. I, 3, n. 9, where both Greek and Irish satirists are associated with wrathful dogs.

21 See "The Author in praise of his precedent Poem [Pygmalion]," l. 46; *The Scourge of Villainy*, Sat. II, l. 8; Sat. IV, l. 4 (Works, III, 262, 312, 362).

22 Scourge, Sat. VIII, 48; Sat. II, 12–13 (*Works*, III, 355, 312).

23 The authors sometimes make the distinction explicit. T. M. Gent. writes "His Defiance to Envy" (in imitation of Hall) as a preface to *Micro-cynicon*. The last couplet of the "Defiance" reads:

> I, but the author's mouth, bid three avaunt!
> He more defies thy hate, thy hunt, thy haunt.

Here "I" is the *persona*, "He" the poet himself. See Middleton, *Works*, ed. Bullen, VIII, 114.

24 For the power of Laidcenn and other Irish satirists, see Chap. I, 3, above. The references to *Timon* are from IV, iii, 1–3, 189–93.

25 "An Acre of Grass," *Collected Poems* (New York, 1957), p. 299.

EDWARD W. ROSENHEIM, JR.

The Satiric Spectrum

We have spoken of the "moments" in which we recognize satire
within a particular work. To speak in this fashion implies an initial
fact about our experience with satire, namely that it *can* be a matter
of moments, of brief, transitory significance within literary products
whose total nature, though generally affected by whatever satire they
contain, is of itself by no means satiric. This fact, in turn, points to
the resolution of a preliminary question. Must satire be considered
as an "element," an ingredient which subserves goals describable only
in other, broader terms? Are we, that is, confined to speaking about
satiric "touches" or passages or satiric "coloring" in works which, in
their entirety, must be described as comedies or arguments or allegories? Or is satire, on the contrary, a genuine literary form, possessing,
like the literary species established by Aristotle, its own "peculiar
power" or (in terms other than those of the *Poetics*) some hallmark
of its own—in structure, substance, style, or motive—which allows us
to classify the work in its entirety as "a satire"? The answer again lies,
I think, in our experience with satire. It is simply that satire may be
either of these things.

There are works which we think of as essentially satiric, and
the recognition that we have described informs our entire reaction to
them and must be sustained throughout. On the other hand, there
are the "moments" in other works—the passing remarks, brief scenes,
single passages—which we stamp as satiric before passing on to other
elements to which we respond in very different ways. Between the
satire which is incorporated in a work of another species such as
comedy and that which is sufficiently dominant so that the work itself
is largely satiric, there is a difference which is one of degree. If the

From *Swift and the Satirist's Art*, Chicago, 1963, pp. 10–34. Reprinted
by permission of the University of Chicago Press.

total work demands from us that frame of mind peculiarly required by satire—sets us to asking certain kinds of questions and seeking certain kinds of satisfaction—then we are in the presence of writing which is predominantly, though seldom exclusively, satiric. If, on the contrary, the satiric elements are quantitatively subordinate in the work (and hence as a rule qualitatively subordinate in our response to it), we must seek elsewhere to explain the kind of total literary product with which we are dealing.

This question and its answer seem self-evident. They must be understood at the outset, however, for, in the first place, they indicate that we shall not be advancing what is ordinarily regarded as a theory of literary "form"; we shall, that is, be discussing a species of writing but not necessarily a species of complete written work. If satire, moreover, is found in a quality or group of qualities which may subserve or dominate, augment or order the work as a whole, we must be alert for the non-satiric as well as the satiric constituents of the writings we are considering. Thus, when confronted with a particular writing by Swift, we cannot be misled by either its reputation as "satire" or its authentic satiric qualities, notable though they may be, into the assumption that it is entirely or even predominantly "a satire." And this fact imposes upon us the obligation to determine, with respect to every significant part of the work, the presence or absence of satire. It reveals the possibility that satire may be juxtaposed to, or proceed concurrently with, other kinds of writing and the likelihood that these other kinds will be precisely those which, because of their frequent identification with satire, must be distinguished from it. It should be added, however, that this view relieves us of the burden under which certain analysts of satire have at times labored unnecessarily, namely the explication of all parts of a work in order to show their contribution to a purely satiric end. If a book accomplishes ends other than those of satire, we must be aware of these accomplishments; we must, furthermore, not confuse these other accomplishments, whatever their nature or importance, with those of satire itself.

To return to the sources of our common feeling that we are in the presence of satire, there is one general quality which, although it has been given various names, seems most readily and widely recognized. This is the quality which, although the term may seem rather loose, we shall describe as *attack*. For in one way or another, satire seems always to treat an object of some kind in an unfavorable way.

To speak of "unfavorable" treatment is inexact, yet the difficulty is that a more limited definition ("criticism," "ridicule," or "exposure," for instance) will not do justice to the full range of writing which merits description as satire.

It is evident that a considerable number of satiric works strive for goals which are substantially the same as those of polemic rhetoric, and to such works the term "attack" seems readily applicable. Here the classic rhetorical categories can be illuminating: satire may truly "expose" evils or infirmities hitherto unrecognized by its audience; it may elicit blame, employing any of countless intellectual or emotional strategies, for individuals, groups, institutions, or ideas; it may urge its audience to future action, in some measure hostile, against the object under attack. And these rhetorical modes may be combined in various proportions to achieve various persuasive ends. Thus the traditional categories of rhetoric—forensic, epideictic, and deliberative—may often be imposed upon satire, although always in their "negative" aspect; i.e., the forensic exposure of past folly or evil, the epideictic incitement to blame rather than praise, and the deliberative exhortation to hostile action.

Many generalizations about satire imply that its characteristic effect is inevitably persuasive. Of this sort are the assertions, often advanced apologetically by satirists themselves, concerning the moral power of the art. And it is quite true that the concept of satire as a kind of uniquely effective rhetorical weapon is entirely just in many cases—including some of Swift's most notable writings.

At the same time, there are many works which we are prepared to regard as satiric but which, if we are to be candid, do not seem to "persuade" us, in any reasonable sense of the term. In such works, the object under satiric treatment emerges, to be sure, in an unfavorable light, but it is a light which is accepted a priori by the audience. No new judgment is invited; no course of action is urged; no novel information is produced. The audience, rather, is asked chiefly to rejoice in the heaping of opprobrium, ridicule, or fancied punishment upon an object of whose culpability they are *already* thoroughly convinced.

If the reader considers, for example, poems such as Dryden's *Mac Flecknoe* or Pope's *Dunciad*, he should see how difficult it is to assign any genuinely rhetorical function to these works, even though they are traditionally discussed and acclaimed as satiric productions. In *Mac Flecknoe*, Shadwell's dulness is entirely taken for granted.

The apt humor of his accession to the throne vacated by Flecknoe, with all of its attendant devices, is effective only if one *assumes* from the beginning that Shadwell is an inferior poet, worthy of comparison to Heywood, Shirley, Ogleby, and his own Sir Formal. Neither the plot nor the details of diction, however ingenious they may be, are directed to altering our opinion, providing new grounds for scorn, or presenting any systematic argument against the historical Shadwell. The character of the protagonist is assumed to be familiar to the reader, whose part is solely to delight in the just abuse of an accepted figure of fun. The same may be said of virtually the entire *dramatis personae* of *The Dunciad*. Indeed, it may be precisely because we are required, from the outset, uncritically to accept far too much about the deficiencies of these hapless scribblers that *The Dunciad* is viewed with distaste by certain modern critics.[1] Pope's dunces are "punished," violently and often wittily, but it is the exceptional passage in the poem which truly exposes or even exploits their actual sins. If we delight in the treatment they receive, it is chiefly because we are prepared to believe, for reasons largely unrelated to what Pope actually says in the poem, that the treatment is deserved. Over the centuries, it is true the historical figures of Theobald and Cibber have suffered (in the former case at least most unjustly) because Pope singled out as monarchs of dulness, but this is not attributable to any demonstration on Pope's part. He has "persuaded" posterity, if at all, only by erecting an impressive monument to his own hostility. And, indeed, with the passing of time we lose most of our awareness of the historical figures against whom satire of this order is directed. The Shadwell of Dryden's verses and the Cibber of Pope's have become, for the common reader, little more than characters of fiction, whose relationship to their historical counterparts is now scarcely more significant than that of Falstaff to the misty figure of John Oldcastle.

There appears, then, to be a kind of satire which does not truly seek to be "persuasive" and to which a term like "punitive" may be more aptly applied. We should be at no loss to discover specimens of this kind of satiric procedure. It crops up repeatedly in various forms of popular entertainment in our own day—most commonly, perhaps, in the performances of those comedians who specialize in what is "good for a laugh" and, by ringing changes on the same well-established foibles of public men and institutions, produce a kind of humorous satire of derision. It is not difficult, if we are honest in considering our own responses, to distinguish between the most plainly representative works of persuasive and of punitive satire. Clearly there is a difference between, for example, the occurrences in *The Dunciad*, Book II (which its chain of ribald indignities which might have been inflicted upon any victims whom the reader was willing to accept as suitably culpable) and the bill of particulars which supports the critical assaults in Pope's *Peri Bathous*. In the former instance, most of us are amused without being induced at any point in the course of our reading to change our opinions of anything. In the latter case, Pope provides us with a special kind of proof—fragmentary, to be sure, and distorted as is proper to satire—which, for all its playfulness, reveals the authentic presence and badness of the writing which he calls bathetic.

But like most of the distinctions which will be suggested in this essay, that between persuasive and punitive satire is not always easy to make, and many instances can be cited, in satiric passages and entire satiric works, in which the reader may purport to find *both* persuasive and punitive effects. To take, as an example, a famous passage from Swift, it has always been agreed that Gulliver's account of the rope-dancing agility of Flimnap, the Lilliputian Treasurer in *Gulliver's Travels*, is a satiric thrust against Sir Robert Walpole. Now from one point of view, the passage does not seem calculated to alter opinions about the historical Walpole: one assumes that, for an audience already convinced that the Lord Treasurer was a slippery opportunist, the rope-dancing appeared only as an appropriately debasing image—and thus a kind of artistic castigation—for vices firmly recognized by readers before the book was ever opened. On the other hand, it may be argued that the rope-dancing episode sheds new light on a questionable faculty of Walpole's—one which might previously have passed muster as facile statesmanship but is now revealed only as a kind of low agility, subject to the caprice of fortune and the king's mistresses. To call Walpole a "rope-dancer" becomes, in the latter case, no mere epithet but an apt epitome, capable of disclosing to readers in a novel way the questionable character of the gifts on which the man's eminence chiefly rests. In this instance, therefore, we seem to be confronted with a "borderline" situation—with an effect which may be described either as punitive or persuasive, depending upon several variables, of which the most important is the previous knowledge and attitude of the reader.

What should be seen, however, is that if we truly seek to judge the satirist's art, our assumptions as to its persuasive or punitive character may lead to very different conclusions. And if we are unwilling to commit ourselves to the view that writing like the rope-dancing passage is exclusively one or the other, we should be prepared to see that the satirist achieves at least two very different things, according to the approach which we select. For the distinction between persuasive and punitive discourages a quest for rhetorical accomplishment in works which, while genuinely and often superlatively satiric, do not necessarily seek to persuade us of anything. If, for example, there is satiric brilliance in *The Rape of the Lock*, it does not lie (despite Pope's jocularly didactic claims in the introductory epistle) in the power of the poem to implant conviction in the reader's mind. The converse is equally true: the work which seeks seriously to persuade, expose, or exhort may often conspicuously lack the pleasurable characteristics—and notably the humor—of the more purely punitive kinds of satire. American readers probably derived very little amusement from George Orwell's *1984*; it seems safe to say, however, that many of them received new, disturbing opinions from that book. And when a work is less plainly a specimen of the punitive or the persuasive, the distinction remains equally important to acknowledge. *The Battle of the Books* has often been seen as a highly effective satiric weapon, employed in the cause of the Ancients against the Moderns and constituting an authentic development in that famous controversy. For some readers, however (and the present writer is among them), it is chiefly a humorous, immensely ingenious exploitation of convictions, long held by those sympathetic to the Ancient cause, concerning the personalities, issues, and occurrences of the affair. The two approaches, each quite defensible, have very different consequences for the judgment of Swift's satiric achievement, since, for example, they would regard in two very different lights Swift's obvious failure to join issue with Bentley and Wotton on the substantive, scholarly points which had been made in defense of "modernity."

Although this distinction calls for commitment to the view that a satiric work or passage be regarded as either punitive or persuasive, it would be wrong to regard these categories as inviolable compartments into which, because of some intrinsic quality, all satire can be firmly thrust. It may prove more useful to regard these kinds of satire as areas in what a contemporary scholar has called—although with a somewhat different intent from mine—the "satiric spectrum."[2] If we say that one portion (let us call it the lower half) of this spectrum is occupied by persuasive satire, then, in turn, at the lowest point in this area would be that work which is most plainly and exclusively persuasive. To works which can be placed at such a point, the modes of analysis appropriate to rhetoric should be profitably applicable, and the work may well be judged ultimately by the degree to which it achieves one or another of the traditional rhetorical ends. Questions of humor, of imaginative artistry, or of absolute intellectual merit would, in such instances, be relevant only in their relationship to the more basic question of persuasive effect.

The remaining, "upper," half of the spectrum in such a scheme will represent punitive satire, and at its extreme upper limit will be located the kind of work which, with no discernible attempt at persuasion, seeks to delight the reader by the indignities to which a pre-established victim or dupe is exposed. From this kind of satire the categories of rhetoric are remote, for we are here confronted with imaginative artifice, and our delight determines the measure of the artist's success.

Midway between the areas of the persuasive and the punitive, we may place the intangible line which separates the two, and near it, on one side or the other, will lie writing which, like the passage we noted from *Gulliver's Travels,* may be legitimately described in terms appropriate to either area. The possibility of employing either approach to such writing should make clear what is characteristic of the entire view of satire which is here suggested. The problem is not to determine conclusively whether a given piece of literature *is* unqualifiedly punitive or persuasive; it is to recognize that, though in many instances elements of both are present, we need to ask the most profitable and relevant questions and hence to assume, at least temporarily, that one effect or the other is paramount.

The device of the satiric spectrum can thus be employed to suggest the scope and the broadest divisions of what is meant by the satiric attack. Obviously, however, I have not yet offered a definition of satire which will distinguish it from other literary kinds. It will be noted, for example, that as yet nothing has been said to distinguish between persuasive satire and rhetoric itself. If, we may ask, the satirist's effect can in many instances be described in the traditional terms of rhetorical analysis, in what respects, if any, does what we call persuasive satire differ from ordinary polemic rhetoric?

In answering this query, we encounter the first of two qualities which, for our purposes, set apart the satiric from the non-satiric and apply, although in greatly varying degrees, to the entire satiric spectrum. For all satire involves, to some extent, *a departure from literal truth* and, in place of literal truth, a reliance upon what may be called a *satiric fiction*. The true rhetorician is assumed to proceed in a literal manner. His evidence is presumably susceptible of objective scrutiny; his emotional appeals are taken to rise from and be directed to authentic emotions; his logic should withstand the rigors of logical examination. The satirist, on the other hand, depends, to the extent that his procedure is actually satiric, upon a *recognized* departure from truth and upon the ability of his audience to assert, "What you say cannot be taken literally, but I am aware of the true meaning which, in your non-literal fashion, you seek to convey."

To be sure, the rhetorician himself often fails in his obligations to truth. Hyperbole, distortion, and suppression are all devices which are familiar to us, largely because of their rhetorical employment. But if such devices really succeed, it is because the rhetorician "brings off" his falsehood and rhetorically successful precisely because the audience has accepted fiction for truth. If, on the other hand, the audience detects falsehood in the rhetoric which purports to be true, the attempted deception is plainly a failure. And if the rhetorician departs at any point from literal truth into a deliberate fiction which he intends the audience to recognize for what it is, if this fiction is a means for conveying or augmenting his literal argument, and if that argument involves an "attack" as we have been using the term, then the rhetoric assumes, however transiently and transparently, the character of satire!

As the central, indispensable element in the satirist's "method," the satiric fiction can assume an infinite number of forms. It may appear as a slight but patent exaggeration, a brisk derisive metaphor, a manifest sarcasm—constituting, it may well be, the kind of "wit" which for most of us marks the satiric "touches" imbedded in writing whose general nature is not satiric at all. At the opposite extreme, the term "fiction" applies equally well to book-length narrative structures which are fictional in every detail. Although not always recognized as such, the satiric fiction has been the subject of considerable critical discussion and of various attempts at classification, professing to impose categories upon what have been variously described as "devices," "situations," and "stages" of satire itself.[3] The discussion of "high" and "low" satire recognizes, implicitly at least, a fictional construction which either directly debases or mockingly elevates the non-fictional object which is its counterpart in the world of reality.[4] Once the satiric fiction is isolated, it is entirely possible, if one wishes, to impose upon it virtually any kind of classification. For, in the construction of the fiction, the satirist is a literary artist at whose disposal lies the entire range of imaginative creations.

The earnest classification of possible satiric fictions, however, seems to be of limited usefulness, particularly when one is confronted by a writer like Swift, who moves without warning and with incredible nimbleness among fictions of enormously varied kinds and degrees. Such classifications do little to aid us in meeting the fundamental question of determining, in any satiric writing, what precisely *is* fictional and the nature of the truth, or alleged truth, which the fiction has been constructed to convey or exploit. Once the fiction has been thus identified, it may, of course, be analyzed, classified, and compared with other fictions, and it is obvious that, from such examination, useful generalizations concerning the habits of the satirist may often be formed.

Generalizations concerning the satiric fiction, however, can be misleading, especially when they are either too broad or too narrow to do justice to the *particular* fiction in a specific satiric work. An example of this sort of danger can be seen in the overworked term, "irony."[5] A very general definition of the word is offered by Worcester, who suggests that irony is, as much as anything, "a grand artistic lie."[6] Professor Bullitt, while recognizing the range of meanings which have been applied to the term, asserts that its "very essence ... whether considered as a rhetorical trope (along with synecdoche, metonymy, and hyperbole) or as a whole way of life, is *dissimulation*: the ironist appears to say or to be one thing while making it apparent to his audience that he means or is something quite different."[7] But what has thus been described as a "lie" or "dissimulation" appears to be nothing other than the "fiction" which, we have argued, is to some extent the mark of all satire; and to seize, for example, upon a debasing allegory—which plainly says one thing but means another— as "ironic" would be to obscure rather than to illuminate the distinction between kinds of satiric fiction, presumably sought by the introduction of such a term as "irony." At the other extreme, the meaning of irony is often confined to "inversion," a term which, on analysis, means no more than simple sarcasm or the statement of a position so antithetical to the truth that authentic meaning can be attained by pure negative inference. This narrow definition is grossly inadequate

as an explanation of many, if not most of the false positions deliberately assumed by such a satirist as Swift. If, like some critics, we are
tempted, for example, to assume that the *persona* who serves as Swift's
satiric spokesman represents the opposite of the author's actual position, a moment's reflection should reveal the strange consequences of
such an approach. For if *A Modest Proposal* is an "ironic" argument
in this sense, then it appears that Swift has written the tract to prove
that Irish babies should not be eaten; or, again, we should be forced
to infer, from this position, that the famous *Argument* is truly intended
to advocate the abolition of Christianity!

"Irony," as a term applied to situations in which a "speaker"
professes a position which is patently not his own, is doubtless an
innocuous term. At the same time, except in those instances in which
it describes a patently sarcastic, "inversional" situation, the use of the
term does little to disclose the precise nature of the fictional posture,
the degree to which it departs from the satirist's authentic position,
or the nature of the authentic position itself. And discoveries of this
character are, inevitably, unique with respect to any single piece of
satiric writing. The familiar practice of describing as "ironic" whatever pose or invention or obliquity makes more salient the truth
from which it appears to depart serves, indeed, to enforce our view
that a manifest fiction is an indispensable element of satire, but it
does little or nothing to indicate the manner in which such a fiction
appears.

Despite the difficulty of imposing classifications upon the huge
range of fictional procedures open to the satirist, it is possible to note
certain broad distinctions among the methods which he may undertake. To generalize upon our common experience with satiric works,
it would appear that their fictional components may be seen as
distortions, analogies, or "pure" *fabrications.*

These general terms, like others I have introduced, may be useful
in reminding us of the several fundamentally different kinds of
achievements attributable to the satirist and in discouraging confusion or unprofitable comparison between widely disparate sorts of
satire. Excessive reliance upon them for analytic purposes, however,
is imprudent, for a writer like Swift can employ these distinct procedures in close conjunction—and even concurrently. These terms,
moreover, must not be regarded as descriptive of satiric "devices,"
since beneath each of these rubrics are subsumed almost infinite possibilities for the actual conduct of the satiric attack.

We may call "distortion," for example, any kind of description, assertion, or argument in which an authentic state of affairs or a sincerely held conviction undergoes palpable alteration. Thus it will be seen that the term can apply to all modes of partial and unflattering selection: a degrading synecdoche, relentless emphasis upon infirmities alone, disregard for natural contexts and associations, suppression of mitigating facts, and the like. It can apply, too, to the very different form of attack involved in "mock elevation," of which sarcastic praise and overstatement provide familiar examples. What seems common, however, to all forms of distortion is that an authentic position or state of affairs, no matter how fragmented, warped, elaborated, or partially concealed, is ultimately discernible by our taking into account the character and purpose of the distortion. And thus, when the satirist's method is distortion, his reader's method is that of "restoration," of grasping the literal meaning which is, as it were, the inception of the satiric procedure.

The analogical fiction, on the other hand, provides us with some kind of independent construction—narrative, character, description, or argument—which ordinarily possesses an autonomous capacity to interest us yet relies, for its proper satiric effect, upon our recognition of salient resemblances between the fictional artifice and the truth. Distortion is, in a sense, frequently involved in the satiric analogy—a living person or institution may appear, for instance, in a new, palpably debased identity—but in other instances, notably in some satiric allegory, the fictional "transformation" is not in itself degrading, and we are required to draw, from the narration of events for example, the inferences which provide fundamental satiric meaning. In either case, the satirist has not merely manipulated the truth but has engaged in a novel creation, and the reader's task is not only to restore a distorted truth to its proper proportions but to find correspondences and draw inferences.

In the "pure" satiric fabrication, we are in the presence of a myth, recognizable neither as analogy nor as mere distortion, but acceptable, presumably, because we are convinced that there is something apt about the humiliation or degradation which, entirely fictitiously, the satiric victim undergoes. When such a fabrication, inhabited by authentic figures, exposes its victims to abuses that do not appear appropriate or, at the least, intrinsically amusing, it will represent little more than a piece of bad-tempered wishful thinking. And the greater the role played by fabrication alone—that is, the greater the departure from the facts and issues of reality—the less persuasive the attack is likely to be. Pure satiric fabrications are, to turn Marianne Moore's phrase to our own use, "imaginary gardens with real toads in them." And the imagined indignities to which real toads or rogues or fools are exposed may provide us with a good deal of satisfaction but very little in the way of enlightenment or conviction.

But, however we may choose to classify or describe the satiric fiction, what is important is that we recognize it *as* fiction. The case of *Defoe's Shortest Way with the Dissenters,* in which Defoe's mocking assumption of a fiercely militant Anglican position was not immediately noted and hence failed entirely to produce the intended effect, is only one dramatic example of the unrecognized fiction. As we shall point out later in greater detail, even such a widely admired work as Swift's *Argument against Abolishing Christianity* has been misinterpreted in some quarters because of a failure to identify the satiric fiction from which Swift's entire attack proceeds. In fact, every commonplace instance in which sarcasm "misfires" plainly represents a failure to recognize the fiction which, in this simple form of abuse as in the most elaborate artifice, is the central element by which the direct expression of hostility or criticism is transformed.

The presence of a satiric fiction, then, distinguishes the kind of satire which we have assigned to the "lower," persuasive range of the satiric spectrum from the art which is purely rhetorical. At the very bottom of this area there lie those works or parts of works whose reliance upon the satiric fiction is minimal and whose essential procedure is by the literal methods of true polemic. Such writings or speeches may rely fleetingly upon an obvious figure or analogy, upon a manifestly false or distorted characterization, and so on; to that extent alone, they partake of the nature of satire. But in the absence of some kind of manifest fiction, as we have defined the term, the attack lies beyond the satiric spectrum altogether. Thus, in our scheme, the lower limits of that spectrum coincide with the boundary of true polemic rhetoric.

When we consider the punitive kind of satire, which we have assigned to the upper portion of the spectrum, a new distinction is called for. We have already noted that the presence of the satiric fiction is necessary to both persuasive and punitive satire. But if the persuasive quality disappears—if, that is, we are exposed in punitive satire to neither argument nor exhortation, however obliquely couched, but to the abuse of a victim of whose culpability we are already properly convinced—we appear to be dealing with something very like comedy. Among most traditional attempts to define the comic, there is wide agreement that comedy represents humiliation, discomfort, frustration, or some similarly defined experience on the part of agents who fail in some way to adhere to normally expected standards of conduct.[8] The comic victim, that is, ordinarily tends to be duped or discountenanced, to undergo some form of distress which pleases us pretty much to the degree that it seems just and relevant to his character, as previously established. Seen in such general terms, the comic formula seems entirely applicable to what we have described as punitive satire. It reveals what occurs to the protagonists of both *Mac Flecknoe* and *Volpone*, to the dunces of Pope as well as to the enchanted innocents of *A Midsummer Night's Dream*.

The relationship of comedy and satire almost inevitably receives attention in discussions of the satirist's art—and often, as well, in systematic treatments of the comic. Interest in this relationship stems, it can be supposed, from nothing more complicated than our tendency to discover what is laughable in many satires or, conversely, to suspect that many of the things we ordinarily laugh at have their satiric aspects. Students of this relationship have rarely gone so far as to equate the two species, yet have, for the most part, remained fairly indifferent to the need for a distinction between them. We can discover passages which tacitly assume that satire is a class or an ingredient of comedy, that the comic is a category or a tool of satire, and hence that "satiric comedy" or "comic satire" are terms which can be legitimately employed, presumably in the description of writings which make us laugh and do something else as well.[9] Here, however, it is urged that the presence of satire elicits special awarenesses, invites particular questions, and accomplishes particular effects, and it follows that these must, in some way, be distinguished from those we regard as comic. Moreover, most of us would agree that some comedy is clearly without satiric impact, however we may define the latter, and—a previously made point in which any student of Swift should concur—satire of a persuasive kind can affect us in ways which are very far from comic.

The distinction which we are seeking—that between punitive satire and comedy—requires a further general description of satire, one which, once more, applies in some measure to all writing which falls within the limits of the satiric spectrum. All satire is not only an attack; it is an attack upon *discernible, historically authentic par-*

ticulars. The "dupes" or victims of punitive satire are not mere fictions. They, or the objects which they represent, must be, or have been, plainly existent in the world of reality; they must, that is, possess genuine historic identity. The reader must be capable of pointing to the world of reality, past or present, and identifying the individual or group, institution, custom, belief, or idea which is under attack by the satirist. *Mac Flecknoe* acquires its satiric dimension not only by the punishment which its "hero" undergoes but also by the fact that a historical Shadwell lived and can be identified with the dullard protagonist of Dryden's poem. And, indeed, when—as I have suggested sometimes happens—the historical identity of a satiric victim pales or disappears with time, the satiric quality of the work diminishes accordingly and its continued survival comes to depend upon facts, whether accidental or artistic, which are extrinsic to its original satiric character.

I have said that persuasive satire moves toward rhetoric as the fictional quality becomes subordinate to literal polemic and that, when the fiction is no longer apparent and operative, the bottom limit of the satiric spectrum is crossed. In an analogous fashion, as the tie to the historic particular becomes less important, punitive satire 'ascends" in the satiric spectrum until it ceases to be satiric in any way. Just as "truth" dominates and destroys the fictional in those persuasive works which tend to lose their satiric quality, so the fictional element tends to dominate literal significance in those punitive writings which approach the upper limit of the satiric spectrum. At that limit lies the region of the genuine comic, of plots and speeches and poses which may resemble in their structure and language those of many satires but which, in the absence of reference to the authentic and the particular, make no claim to satiric effect.

Punitive satire is distinguished from the comic by the presence of *both* the historically authentic and the historically particular; in the absence of either, the satiric quality disappears. In other words, the satiric is lost when the object of attack is entirely imaginary (or "false" with respect to historical reality) or when, as a phenomenon so persistently recurrent and widespread as to be regarded as "universal," it cannot, without further qualification, be assigned specific historical identity. The first condition is easy enough to understand. Falstaff, Tony Lumpkin, and Donald Duck are, for all their appealing "humanity," manifest fabrications, composites of qualities which, though each may be very familiar to us, are here joined in synthetic combination. It is sometimes said that each of these figures inhabits his own "world" of fantasy; if true, this suggests how very far from satiric is the appeal which they have for us. If, in their presence, our world and our preoccupations tend to slip away from us for the time, then, in a frame of mind which is almost the antithesis of that invited by satire, we rejoice in our escape from the issues and problems and "significance" of ordinary existence.

But aside from these rare and, in a sense, "unlikely" creations, most comic characters may be said to have a crucial correspondence with reality and to derive verisimilitude from our worldly familiarity with the most important qualities they display. The moralistic critic of comedy, moreover, often insists that it is precisely because basic human weaknesses and the dilemmas to which they lead are represented by the comic artist that his work deserves our serious attention. If, therefore, the great majority of comedies can be said to expose very real and familiar human frailties, why are they not, for this reason, satiric? And if this is true, is there not, at the least, a satiric element in most of the literature which moves us to laughter?

To these questions, the answer appears to be that between sheer comedy and those satires which produce laughter by the employment of comic formulas the difference is one of *particularity* in the object of attack. It is true that the most common sort of comic dupe is the character who, we suggest as we look around at our neighbors, might well have been Smith or Jones or Robinson. This is, indeed, an appropriate reaction, for the credibility and interest of such figures depend heavily upon their conforming to our own knowledge of human nature. But in such statements, the "might have been" is of central importance. In satire, the victim *is* Smith, Jones, or Robinson —or, if not, belongs to a particular group or embraces a particular view which can be isolated, for the purpose of receiving our unflattering attention, from the rest of the world about us.

Of the several assertions which are here made about satire, it is likely that this insistence upon the particularity of the satiric object will prove most controversial. Traditionally, satire has more often than not been discussed as though its principal function were to oppose vice and folly, if not in the abstract, then at least in terms sufficiently general to admit wide and profitable application to common human problems. Satirists themselves (Swift among them, at times) have tended to insist that their assaults are prompted not by limited and specific aversions but by a hatred of evil, however and in whomever manifested. This is a position with which it is easy to sympathize; a serious writer cannot be expected to relish the role of a mere controversialist. It is similarly understandable that audiences conspire in this lofty view of the satiric mission, since most of us find gratification in the belief that our entertainment can provide us with "insights" into profound questions of human conduct.

Insistence upon the particularity of satire raises, moreover, a further formidable difficulty in the fact that "particular" is itself an elusive and relative term. Distinctions are, again, quite clear if one cites extremes. Thus, sin and folly—or such aspects of them as avarice, cruelty, or imprudence—are subject to no temporal or geographic restrictions, and an attack upon them, rather than upon the authentic, particular individuals in whom they may be embodied, can be readily discerned. At the opposite extreme, we should have little difficulty in sensing how the overt identification of, let us say, a specific living person with the dupe or villain of a literary performance is a signal of satiric intent.

The difficulty again lies in a middle region, in determining whether phenomena of major historical magnitude—intellectual abstractions, beliefs held by millions, institutions embracing similar millions, or pervasive habits of behavior—are objects of satiric attack. Is religion or man's religious instinct a "particular" object? Is organized religion, in all its forms? Is Protestantism—or Puritanism? If an attack upon foppishness as a general human foible is not satiric, what shall we say about an attack upon *women's* preoccupation with fashion—or upon a vogue for sword-knots or Ivy League trousers? How "particular" is the concept of democracy, or the conviction that it is a noble concept? Does the degree to which a work may be regarded as satiric increase in direct proportion to the particularity of the object which it assails? Or is it possible that strictures against womankind, American women, American "career" women, and American female psychiatrists may all be conducted in equally satiric fashion?

I have already said that the object of satiric attack must have an authentic historical identity. In effect, such an object may be vast or small, abstract or concrete, yet it must yield meaningfully to historical predications and descriptions and should do so without the need for further refinement and specification. In effect, then, the "particularity" with which we are concerned is found in any phenomenon whose temporal or geographic confinement permits the kind of description which is characteristic of the historian. A doctrine is a phenomenon about which it is generally possible to make many firm historical propositions; a human trait, in its abstract or universal aspects, is not. It is difficult to make any meaningful historical assertion about all of womankind; it is, on the other hand, perfectly possible to speak in conventional historical terms of modern American women—and hence to satirize them. To the extent, of course, that what is originally generic and not historically specified becomes manifested within particulars which permit historical identification, it will yield to satiric attack. Thus the "spirit" of faction and controversy is, doubtless, always with us and, in this timeless aspect, not an appropriate target for the satirist; when, however, it becomes, in the eyes of Swift, a positive social and political force, operating within a clear historical context to produce certain specific consequences, it is an object for satiric attention.

From the standpoint of the satirist himself, the particularity of the satiric object is a matter of selectivity. Whether he is viewed as a controversialist, moralist, or mere tease, the satirist must be successful in his choice of opponent or victim, and he must accordingly seek a target which is identifiable and vulnerable. In truth, the satire which, in Swift's famous words, "is a sort of Glass, wherein Beholders do generally discover every body's Face but their Own" is ineffectual, if it is satire at all. The victims of true satire must "suffer," whether through their own injured awareness of assault or in the ridicule or hostility which the satirist produces in the minds of others. The ultimate wellspring of the satiric spirit is perhaps benign, and sin itself, rather than the sinner, may be the true object of the satirist's wrath. But the essence of the satiric procedure is attack, and the attack launched impartially against everyone is no attack at all.

In the distinction between the satiric and the comic, as in that between satire and rhetoric, since it is difficult, of course, to draw absolute divisions, it is prudent to speak rather of tendencies toward one or the other of the species. Yet the difference between satire and comedy becomes the more crucial when we are confronted by works which may lay claim to being either. In Molière's *Tartuffe*, for example, we are shown the machinations and the ultimate discomfiture of the hypocrite. Now, as a stereotype of the sanctimonious dissembler, known to all ages and nations, Tartuffe remains a comic character, with a didactic capacity to "make clear" in Molière's own phrase, "the distinction between your hypocrite and your man of true devotion."[10] But Tartuffe may also readily be taken to represent a highly particular, historically authentic manifestation of religious hypocrisy; and so he was taken by Molière's enemies. These, insisting in effect that the play was satiric rather than purely comic, read it as an attack upon the power and practices of the French Jesuits under Louis XIV. The repressions, banning, deletions, and revisions which form the history of *Tartuffe* in print and on the stage may well be said to revolve about the presence or absence of *satire* within the work.[11] For the crux of the controversy lies in the question as to whether the evils Molière is assailing are limited and historically identifiable or timeless and universal.

An example of this kind suggests anew the extent to which the identity of a satiric victim must be established if we are to speak about true satiric achievement. When, either by calculation or inadvertence, the historically authentic object of attack is obscure, the satiric impact of the work is plainly weakened—although often we properly find our chief satisfaction in other literary qualities it possesses. There are works of fiction which provide us with a delight that is little affected by our belated recognition of individualized attacks which may accompany their purely inventive elements. Students who have long admired such novels as *Bleak House* or Huxley's *Point Counter Point* may, at some time, discover that Harold Skimpole, in the former, represents the hapless Leigh Hunt or that many of the characters of the latter were drawn by Huxley with specific contemporaries in mind. In such instances, a satiric element is established and a satiric "reading" is possible; yet these characters, compounded as they are of familiar follies and infirmities, continue to delight as essentially fictional dupes and villains, and analysis of the novels as predominantly satiric does scant justice to their stature as products of the creative imagination.

Not all critical or hostile literary treatment of universal phenomena is, of course, comic or entertaining. It is clearly possible to deal, through the use of some kind of fiction, with problems that are grave, generic, and recurrent. Here the sources of the author's uneasiness, skepticism, or hostility transcend time and place and are rooted in the changeless facts of the human condition. Such works are distinguishable from satire by their ultimate effect, which is basically didactic—and, in fact, philosophic. For they consider, albeit unfavorably, the timeless nature of man and his world.

Plato, for example, is largely critical and even destructive, and he employs obliquities, understatements, and myths, which can all be regarded as satiric fictions. We do not generally regard his dialogues as satire (although to the degree that they attack such historical particulars as the Sophists or Athenian leadership, they *are* satiric), because the errors of thought to which they are addressed are generic and timeless—because they become the objects of an attention which, however unfavorable, is essentially philosophic. Indeed, to consider universal propositions, in whatever light, is not mere "attack," but, if it is to be effective, philosophic inquiry. A true "satire against mankind"—on the assumption that it transcends particular men or groups of men yet strives to speak the truth—would lie beyond our definition of satire. If it were frivolously or insincerely conceived, of course, it would become, if not philosophy *manqué*, then some species of imaginative writing in which a fictional pose dominated rather than subserved the truth. If, more significantly, it sought to provide us with authentic and meaningful propositions about man and the universe, such propositions, however hostile, would be those of philosophy itself.

This is, perhaps, the moment for summary. It has been urged that the principal achievement of satiric writing may always be described as, in some measure, "attack," this attack being directed either to persuading us to look or act unfavorably toward the satiric victim or to pleasing us by the representation in a degrading manner of an object which, we already assume, deserves such treatment. I have further asserted that the attack in satire proceeds by the use of a "recognizable fiction," a departure in some way or other from a literal truth of which the audience must be in possession. Finally, it has been argued that the objects attacked by either persuasive or punitive satire must constitute historically authentic particulars, recognized as such by the audience. To gather these observations into a single sentence, we may say that *satire consists of an attack by means of a manifest fiction upon discernible historic particulars.*

In describing this view of satire, I have employed the figure of a "spectrum" to suggest that satire begins, on one hand, at a point where traditional polemic rhetoric discards literal argument in favor of manifest fiction; that within the area of attack by the use of fiction we find works whose purpose is to persuade as well as those which seek only to deride objects which are plainly culpable; that at the limit of satire which lies farthest from rhetoric we approach comedy, in which objects of attack or ridicule are either without meaningful historic reality or so general as to prevent our finding in them any significant particulars.

It must be pointed out once more that this conception of satire does not have as its object a classificatory system of absolute validity or a "key" to secrets which have hitherto eluded readers of satire. Still less does it offer criteria of excellence which will enable critical readers to tell good satire from bad. We are here concerned with modes of inquiry, with questions that may be profitably asked in our reading of works we are prepared to call satiric. The "responsibilities" implicit in such modes of inquiry are, in the last analysis, suggestions as to the kinds of questions which will make our use of the term "satire" most meaningful and increase our awareness of the special achievements of the satiric artist.

In the actual scrutiny of allegedly satiric works, therefore, we must, in the first place, determine the possibility of viewing the total work as satiric and, in the absence of such a possibility, identify as precisely as possible the nature and magnitude of its non-satiric as well as its satiric elements. It seems difficult, moreover, to advance any useful assertions about whatever satire the work contains without establishing the precise object or objects which are under satiric attack. This discovery inevitably requires a recognition of the method by which the attack proceeds, and, since the satirist's method crucially depends upon a fiction of some kind, the location and description of the satiric fiction are equally necessary. Fuurther, since we have indicated that the satiric attack may be of two basically different sorts, we should, as a preliminary to any judgment of the satirist's art, consider how his antagonist is treated. In an awareness that the pleasure afforded by punitive satire differs sharply from our response to persuasive procedures, that is, we must consider the satirist's means in terms appropriate to the end he appears to be seeking. Finally, we must remain alert to the fact that whatever distinctions we make also imply relationships; for example, that the non-satiric elements— comic, rhetorical, etc.—may justify, enforce, or heavily depend upon the satiric, or that the discrete objects of attack we isolate may bear a significant relationship to each other.

No laws, of course, require the satiric writer to adhere to satire throughout, to maintain a single mode of satiric assault, to limit in any special way the objects of his attention, or to strive for the kind of "unity" which many other species of literature lead us to expect. In the case of a writer like Swift particularly, the reader must proceed in an awareness that a single paragraph—or a single sentence—may contain abrupt changes in method, and even in purpose. The unpredictable flexibility of such an artist will inevitably elude narrow analytical procedures. If it appears that certain questions may be usefully regarded as paramount, there is still no limit upon the sources to be consulted in answering them.

Thus it is often impossible to establish, through inspection of the text alone, the precise objects of the satirist's attack or the essential truth by which the identification of the satiric fiction proceeds. The popular distinction between "criticism" and "historical scholarship," the insistence that rigorously "autotelic" analyses of texts are necessary preliminaries to judgment, tend to break down in the presence of genuine satire. We have stressed the indispensable relationship between satire and historic fact. Whatever can disclose relevant historic fact is accordingly a legitimate—and usually an indispensable—source for the student of satire. The search within the canon of the author, through the contemporary materials which may prove germane, and into more remote sources which have conceivable bearing upon the satirist's intention is, of course, a formidable task with results that are rarely definitive. In such searches, however, the student may find one principle of considerable value.

This principle is simply that the satirist presumably writes to be understood. His attack is designed to persuade or delight. In consequence, the objects of his attacks must be discernible to his audience; the fiction which he constructs must be recognizable as fiction; the true position which he wishes, however obliquely, to convey must emerge clearly if his satire is to be successful. These facts are heartening, for they imply that men, documents, ideas, and events which were obscure for the satirist's original audience are far less likely to be importantly reflected in the work than those which the audience found clear, familiar, and immediate. As a result, our search for the satiric object may ordinarily proceed on the assumption that what must be recaptured was once intelligible and interesting to an audience not very different from ourselves. Even here, of course, the task may be difficult, perhaps impossible, yet the maxim that satire which has once been successful must, at the same time, have been intelligible may lend order and economy to our extra-textual researches.

One of the persistent questions raised about satire concerns its power of survival—the capacity of a satiric work to engage our interest long after the issues to which it is addressed have lost all claim upon our attention. Admittedly, the principles I have proposed do not seem very helpful in answering this question. By discouraging the view that satire is addressed to general and timeless problems, we have destroyed a traditional explanation of the satirist's lasting appeal. If we insist that Swift's chief target is the Royal Society rather than vanity in general, Walpole rather than man's venal tendencies, Puritan Enthusiasm rather than the vice of affectation, the task of recapturing and sharing the conviction and delight of Swift's original readers seems difficult.

In subsequent essays, I shall offer some views about the lasting appeal of Swift's writing and shall even, in certain instances, suggest that the appeal may well have changed over the centuries. Here, however, I shall initially urge that we lay the groundwork for an understanding of his art by becoming vicarious members of his original audience. Hume's prescription for the appreciation of rhetoric applies very well to the understanding of satire. We must, that is, suspend what Hume calls our "prejudices," those habits and attitudes which would keep us forever and inelastically our twentieth-century selves. As preacher, jester, or poet, Swift may have written for "Prince Posterity." As satirist, he wrote for those to whom his assaults on men, ideas, and institutions had immediacy of meaning and effect. The artist whose audience is particularized, whose mission is limited by historical circumstances, and whose motives are of the same genuine but ephemeral sort which most of us share most of the time is probably harder to understand and admire than is the writer whose "message" is transparently intended for posterity. But he is none the less an artist, for all that. If we are prepared to understand, if not necessarily to admire him, let us begin on his own terms. As for the admiration—wit, imagination, and verbal artistry can compel it on grounds quite other than the merit of the goals they are employed to serve. If we understand what Swift is doing, it is likely that we can sense the intrinsic power of his gifts to make themselves felt in any cause and any context.

NOTES

[1] See in particular Gilbert Highet, "The Dunciad," *Modern Language Review*, XXXVI (July, 1941), 320–43. Professor Highet's hostile re-examination of the poem proceeds upon sever-

al grounds, none of which explicitly stresses the particular interpretation I have suggested. But, in his strictures against Pope's "subject" and in his assertion that "Pope has made his enemies into criminals" (p. 321), Highet in effect reveals his unwillingness to accept Pope's original, unsupported assumption that the punishment he will mete out fits the crimes of his victims.

2 Arthur Melville Clark, "The Art of Satire and the Satiric Spectrum," in *Studies in Literary Modes* (Edinburgh and London, 1946), pp. 31–49. Although the views expressed in this study coincide with those of Clark in certain particulars—notably the "occasional" quality of satire, its essential hostility, and, to some extent, the relation of satire and humor—his definition of the satiric spectrum is not the same as mine nor does he employ this figure for the purpose it serves here.

3 Thus, for example, since Worcester attempts "to construct a simple rhetoric of satire" (*The Art of Satire*, p. 9), it is natural that the various kinds of satiric procedure he considers be viewed as "devices" of an essentially persuasive sort. A. M. Clark's "spectrum" on the other hand is composed of "stages" which mark the satirist's progress from the benignity of the humorist to the mirthless malignity of invective (pp. 45–49). In both these instances, the categories of satire established could be—although they are not—distinguished from each other in terms of the nature and purpose of the satiric fiction. To the best of my knowledge, the only study which deliberately sets out, albeit in terms of a rather limited problem, explicitly to classify satiric writings in terms of the fictions they employ is Ricardo Quintana's "Situational Satire: A Commentary on the Method of Swift," *University of Toronto Quarterly*, XVII (1948), 130–36. Although Quintana's discussion is very brief, he clearly recognizes the crucial importance of the satiric fiction and is able, moreover, to show that differences in kind among fictions (or, as he calls them, "situations") account for basic differences in kinds of satire.

4 The "high-low" gambit is manifestly susceptible of many mutations. The difficulties this approach involves can be seen even when it is applied to the very limited area of satire on literary works (conventionally described as "parody," "burlesque," and the like). Richmond P. Bond's *English Burlesque Poetry, 1700–75* (Cambridge, Mass., 1932) works within the two simple variables of "form" and "content" yet emerges with a series of terms which are highly complex and extremely difficult (at best) to apply in analyzing individual works of "literary" satire.

5 The range of uses to which, historically, the word has been put is made elaborately evident in Norman Knox's *The Word "Irony" and Its Context, 1500–1755* (Durham, North Carolina, 1961). Although this careful study establishes the limits of the very ample variety of meanings which the term assumed during the period under discussion, it confirms one's doubts as to the utility of the concept of irony for analytical purposes. It is also interesting to note that the simple notion of "inversion" (praise-by-blame or blame-by-praise) dominates the historic employment of the term.

6 Worcester, *The Art of Satire*, p. 80.

7 Bullitt, *Jonathan Swift and the Anatomy of Satire*, pp. 49–50. Both Bullitt and Norman Knox rely considerably on G. G. Sedgewick, *Of Irony Especially in Drama* (Toronto, 1948), whose emphasis on the Socratic origins of the concept of irony serves to expand rather than confine the range of its meanings.

8 Aristotle's famous observation that comedy involves a form of painless suffering on the part of men worse than ourselves (*Poetics*, 1448*a* and 1449*a*) subsumes—or is at least compatible with—the most familiar attempts to define comedy in later times with a few such benign exceptions as Meredith. Thus, for example, Bergson's view of the comic as the "mechanical encrusted upon the living" derives essentially from the notion of man's inability to perform, physically, morally, and socially as man should (see Henri Bergson, *Laughter: An Essay on the Meaning of the Comic*, trans. Cloudesley Brereton and Fred Rothwell [London, 1911], esp. pp. 1–66). The ultimate moral function assigned to comedy by Bergson (and by such frankly moralistic arguments as those of Molière and Fielding) rests, as does the more sophisticated functional account of Freud (*Wit and Its Relation to the Unconscious*, trans. A. A. Brill [New York, 1917]), upon the exposure or discovery of human qualities in some measure shameful.

9 Bullitt's treatment of "exposure by ridicule," for example, discusses seventeenth- and eighteenth-century notions of the ridiculous, of contempt, of the "comic attitude" and of satire without, it seems to me, making clear how the satiric exploitation of the ridiculous differs from that of comedy. He points out, however, that the "defense and justification of satire urged by Swift and supported by a sizable number of the writers and critics of his day is ... an appeal to the moral usefulness of this minor genre" (*Jonathan Swift and the Anatomy of Satire*, p. 37).

[10] The quotation is from Molière's preface to the first edition of the play. I have used the translation of Curtiss Hidden Page (New York, 1908), p. 8.

[11] For a history of the vicissitudes of *Tartuffe* during the lifetime of Molière, see Henri d'Almeras, *Le Tartuffe de Molière* (Amiens, 1928).

SHELDON SACKS

From: Toward a Grammar of the Types of Fiction

Let us assume tentatively that satires are works which ridicule particular men, the institutions of men, traits presumed to be in all men, or any combination of the three.[1] But they do not do this incidentally; all their parts are designed to this end and, indeed, can only be understood *as* parts of a whole to the extent that they contribute to such ridicule. In other words, this is the principle that actually informs the work. Unless all the elements of a work make such a contribution, we will temporarily refuse to classify it as a coherent satire. If we assume also that *Gulliver's Travels* is a coherent satire, then all the elements of fiction it contains—the traits ascribed to the created characters, the actions portrayed, the point of view from which the tale is told—will have been selected, whether consciously or intuitively, to maximize the ridicule of some combination of the three objects of satire. If this is true, there are some obvious consequences to our description of the form. One consequence is that none of the fictional creations in *Gulliver's Travels* can ever themselves be satirized; since all three objects of satire are extant only *outside* the fictional world created in the book, any ridicule which attaches to Gulliver, the Houyhnhnms, or the Lilliputians, or disgust which attaches to the Yahoos, can be understood, in relation to the whole work, only as an attempt to facilitate the ability of the fictional creations to ridicule the objects, of whatever sort. Similarly, any virtues which attach to the fictional creations within the book can be understood only as traits

From *Fiction and the Shape of Belief: A Study of Henry Fielding with Glances at Swift, Johnson and Richardson*, Berkeley and Los Angeles, 1964, pp. 7–15. Reprinted by permission of The Regents of the University of California.

which enable Swift to maximize the ridicule directed at the external world.

Let us assume also that there is another class of prose fiction, of which *Rasselas* is a perfect example, which we will call "apologues." The informing principle of all such works is that each is organized as a fictional example of the truth of a formulable statement or closely related set of such statements. Again, since we are interested in establishing classes of literary creations—in this case, classes of works of prose fiction differentiated according to variant principles of coherence—all the parts of any apologue, including all the techniques of prose fiction, can be understood as parts of the whole only to the extent that they contribute to the effectiveness with which the fiction illustrates the truth of the statement.[2]

It should be immediately evident that the form of satire and the form of apologue, as they have been defined, can in no sense overlap; even though some episodes of the works may contain similar elements, as *parts* of *Gulliver's Travels* or *Rasselas* they will not have the same relationship to the whole work in which they appear.

If Swift had wished to attack gluttony, he might very well have included an episode in which skinny men are represented as virtuous and wise while fat men are shown to be foolish and wicked. This would in no sense indicate that Swift admired skinny men, since, if gluttony is an object of satire, all fictional elements, including the virtue attaching to skinny men, must be subordinated to an effective attack on gluttony. It is barely conceivable that Swift did admire skinny men, but nothing in the work tells us this. To interpret the preferential depiction of skinny men as, in its own right, an exemplary portrait, a fictional example of the truth of the statement that skinny men are admirable, is to forget that *Gulliver's Travels* is a satire.[3] It is to treat *Gulliver's Travels as if* it were organized like *Rasselas*.

To take a less trivial but more complicated example, if *Gulliver's Travels* is organized as a satire in the sense defined above, then, no matter how many virtues are ascribed by Swift to the Houyhnhnms, it is unreasonable to interpret his rational horses as portraits of Swift's ideal of rationality or, for that matter, of any other ideal. Knowing Swift's religious beliefs, we should certainly make at least a working assumption that he is attacking what an advocate of his brand of Christianity could be expected to deplore in mankind; but the virtues of such fictional creations as the Houyhnhnms have not been selected with a view—intuitive or otherwise—toward creating a fictional example of a virtuous society. The virtues ascribed to the Houyhnhnms have been chosen according to how well they facilitate the ridicule of certain of the traits, manners, and institutions of men. If this is indeed so, when we discover striking discrepancies between virtues ascribed to the Houyhnhnms and what Swift would probably have considered virtues in an ideal society, we have no justification for a *prima* facie case that the Houyhnhnms themselves are *objects* of satire or even of ridicule. Not only is it true that the fictional creations in *Gulliver's Travels* cannot themselves be "satirized," but, if the work is organized as satire, we would expect to find that some of the virtues ascribed to his fictional creations are virtues Swift would wish for in an ideal society and others are not. It is obvious, for example, that the approbation of the Brobdingnag rules that no "law of that country must exceed" twenty-two words and that "to write a commentary upon any law is a capital crime" provide excellent platforms from which to hurl appropriate ridicule at the obscurantist deficiencies of English law. But one can hardly entertain the notion that Swift at his most misanthropic would literally approve an English government which tried to hang a man because he had written a commentary on the law.[4] And yet it would be patently fallacious to infer from this observation that Swift is "satirizing" or even ridiculing the Brobdingnagian rules. He is doing only what we would expect him to do if he were satirizing English law and lawyers: ascribing those virtues to his fictional creations which will facilitate the ridicule of what he finds reprehensible in the external object of satire. Swift is hardly a nudist because the Houyhnhnms don't wear clothes and Gulliver finds it impossible to explain to his "master" "why nature should teach us to conceal what nature had given."[5]

The reverse of the coin is apposite also. In *Rasselas*, ridicule is leveled against the pretentious inventor of the flying machine. And a very strong argument has been advanced that Johnson was familiar with John Wilkins' *Mathematical Magic* and drew heavily on parts of it in the "Dissertation on Flying."[6] Had a similar incident appeared in *Gulliver's Travels*, with many elements derived directly from Wilkins, we should not be able to rest content even with the observation that Swift was ridiculing the experiments of the "new science." If the elements taken from John Wilkins were obvious enough to identify the *Mathematical Magic* to knowledgeable contemporaries Swift, a failure to recognize the ridicule of Wilkins would be a failure to comprehend one of the particular objects of the satire and there-fore its full force. We can learn a great deal about Johnson's methods of composition from the discovery of the connection between his and Wilkins' work; we can see how Johnson wrestled with his material, how he altered, selected, modified his source to create an episode which contributes greatly to the fictional exploitation of the organizing theme of Rasselas. But interesting as a study of Wilkins as one of Johnson's sources may be, the complete lack of this informa-tion could modify our understanding of *Rasselas* only to the extent that ignorance of the fact that the character of Brett Ashley was suggested to Hemingway by a lady whom F. Scott Fitzgerald disliked would alter our view of *The Sun Also Rises*; Brett Ashley's role in the novel is defined without reference to the little-known lady, and the role of Johnson's would-be Daedalus is defined in the apologue without reference to Wilkins.

To sum up, no part of a coherent apologue can be organized as satire and no part of a coherent satire can be organized as apologue, except in works which contain digressions—i.e., in works in which the informing principle is temporarily in abeyance or ceases permanently to function.[7] Apologue and satire are mutually exclusive forms when considered from the point of view of their informing principles. The task that any episode must perform in the one differs radically from that which any episode must perform in the other.

But since the capacity of men to make inferences from any sample of language is almost infinite, if we ask irrelevant questions about *Gulliver's Travels* or *Rasselas* we will find some sort of answers. If we start to find the organizing themes of *Gulliver's Travels* we will find them as surely as we find them in *Rasselas*. But if we do so—still assuming that *Gulliver's Travels* is organized in the manner described—our answers will be valid only on the supposition that it is an apologue. Such answers dangerously distort our view of its form if it is not organized as apologue. Only by considering it a satire may we legitimately ask how Swift might have embodied his beliefs, opinions, prejudices, in it. Take, for example, a deceptively simple question which, I believe, underlies much of the recent controversy about the fourth book of *Gulliver's Travels*: Are the Houyhnhnms represented as Swift's ethical ideal for humanity or are they satirized? No question is more susceptible of producing equally persuasive but contradictory answers; it depends upon a dichotomy which obscures the task of both critical enquiry and historical research. If the inform-

ing principle of *Gulliver's Travels* is something like the one we have
assumed, the only relevant answer to the question must be *neither*.
The Houyhnhnms cannot be a representation of Swift's ethical ideal,
since all parts of the work, including the virtues ascribed to the
rational horses, have been selected to facilitate ridicule of the external
objects of the satire, not to create fictional examples of ethical truths.[8]
They cannot themselves be "satirized," since one of the conditions of
such a work is that the objects of satire are external. It is possible
that they are represented as ridiculous in part, but, if so, such ridicule
must be obvious enough to maximize the attack on one of the external
objects; if the ridicule is so evanescent that we may argue about its
very existence, it is unlikely to be present in a satire.[9] In any event,
however convincingly we argue that a theologian of Swift's time,
persuasion, personality, would consider the graceless world of Houy-
hnhnmland unchristian or otherwise undesirable, the information has
no bearing on whether the Houyhnhnms are meant to be ridiculous.
Such discrepancy is precisely what one would expect to find in a
work organized to ridicule external objects.

The term "satire" is used not only to discriminate among
literary forms, but in a far more general sense even when it is applied
to literary works. When we speak of "elements of satire" in a literary
work we normally refer either to elements ridiculed within the work
which have some sort of an identifiable counterpart external to the
created fictional world, or simply to elements ridiculed within the
work without consideration of an external counterpart. In the first
sense we may justifiably call the episode in *Rasselas* which deals with
the Stoic who loses his daughter "satiric," since the character is
ridiculed and the brand of Stoicism he professes is an identifiable
philosophic position maintained in eighteenth-century England. In
the second sense we may say that Imlac is satirized when, in a fit of
enthusiasm, he defines a poet's qualifications in impossibly grandiose
terms. Or, to turn from apologue to an as yet undefined form, it is
in the first sense that we can call Jane Austen's Sir Walter Eliot,
with all his displayed and unwarranted pride of birth, an element of
satire in *Persuasion*, but in the second sense that the incessantly
chattering Miss Bates is satirical in *Emma*. But the two uses easily
overlap: we have all, I suspect, known people who define their own
professions in grandiose terms, and chattering women are always with
us. Any writer of fiction with a moderate share of human antipathies is
likely to ridicule some character, action, or social attitude in his work,

and a critic would have to be very limited indeed who could not discover in the external world a counterpart to the object of ridicule in the fictional world.

It is only mild hyperbole to assert that any fiction writer of prominence who exhibits social awareness may look forward with assurance to an article, thesis, or book purporting to describe the elements of satire in his work. If we are aware that the term "satire" is being used in a flexible sense, such critiques may prove illuminating. But from the moment that we confuse the everyday use of the term with its use in discriminating a literary type according to an informing principle, chaos results. At the moment we claim that Johnson embodied one of his beliefs in *Rasselas* as a satire on Stoicism, or that Jane Austen embodied hers in *Persuasion* as a satire on pride of birth, we have advanced halfway to irretrievable confusion. The ridicule attached to Miss Bates, for example, is not included in *Emma* to facilitate a scornful attack on chattering women: the ridicule not only has its own role to play as part of a work whose informing principle is different from that of satire, but, in addition, an examination of the principle of selection of elements may show us that the ridicule attached to Miss Bates' inconsequential volubility achieves an end opposed to that of satire. That is, in fact, the situation in *Emma*, when the annoying chatter of Miss Bates leads the heroine gratuitously to mock her at the Box Hill outing. This, the most obviously culpable social act performed by Emma, leads to her verbal castigation by the "hero" and to her own recognition of the unworthiness of her action. Throughout the early stages of the novel, Jane Austen has represented Miss Bates' aimless conversation at sufficient length to justify Emma's irritation, but has been careful to include just enough indications of the character's good nature and freedom from malice so that we are shocked at Emma's callous act. The partial justification for her irritation is one of the elements that leads us to desire the heroine's reformation rather than her serious punishment. If we can infer anything at all from such a state of affairs about Jane Austen's attitude toward chattering women outside the fictional world she created, it is surely that they merit tolerance, not ridicule.

Oddly enough, the confusion of the two uses of the term "satire" has unfortunate consequences not merely for an enquiry into how novelists' beliefs are embodied in their novels, but also for our more general critical concerns: if we interpret part of a work organized by another principle as if it were part of a satire, we cannot discuss the artistic choices which have, in fact, made the work effective, though we may well have experienced aesthetic pleasure only because of their inclusion. If we interpret the portrait of Miss Bates as if it were part of a satire, it is all too easy to describe those stylistic elements which delightfully ridicule that voluble lady. But it is unlikely that we will recognize the adeptness with which Jane Austen has revealed, with exquisitely appropriate understatement, Miss Bates' essential good nature and freedom from malice, so that, when Emma errs, the extent of her culpability is precisely defined. Any conscious recognition we may have of the virtuous traits revealed in Miss Bates' meanderings might well be interpreted as a flaw in a satire to the extent that it prevents maximizing the ridicule of the external object —in this case the chattering woman.

An inability to explain the artistic virtues that have made us feel that a work is excellent is a probable consequence of considering parts of works which are not satires as if they were, even when no serious distortion of a wirter's beliefs results.[10]

Possibly, interpreting Johnson's ridicule of the Stoic in *Rasselas* as a satire on Stoicism would not lead to a distortion of his attitude toward that philosophic school. But, leaving aside the many subtly rendered elements in the relevant episode, Johnson's choice of the death of the Stoic's daughter as the instrument to reveal the inadequacy of Stoicism in preventing human misery would alone mark him as an inept satirist, had he inded been writing satire. To select as an instrument for such a revelation an event which, if anything does, justifies passionate misery is perfectly comprehensible in a work which demonstrates by fictional example that human activity—including conscious commitment to a philosophy—can never prevent earthly unhappiness. The very choice of the episode, as well as its masterful portrayal, testifies to the excellence of the apologue, though the merest novice could show Johnson that, if he wished to facilitate ridicule of Stoicism as an external object of satire, he could hardly have made a worse choice. The more trivial the cause that motivates the Stoic's despair, the greater the possibilities for ridiculing Stoicism. As a matter of fact, Johnson's selection—perfect as it is for *Rasselas* —must have presented him with some difficult artistic problems. The death of the Stoic's daughter and his consequent misery had to be represented with at least enough plausibility to make the episode a convincing fictional example. And yet, had Johnson invested the

Stoic with one grain more of individuality or had he removed a single mocking reference to the countenanced blackmail by the Stoic's servants, Rasselas' dispassionate reaction to the death of an admired teacher's only child must certainly have branded him as a character worthy of condemnation, despite the revealed discrepancy between Stoical pretensions and human practices. Without a single remark to indicate compassion for the intense suffering expressed by the Stoic, Rasselas, whose humanity admittedly "would not suffer him to insult misery with reproof,"[11] does refrain after a while from argument with the mourner. But his sole reaction to the misery of the former Stoic is to understand "the emptiness of rhetorical sound, and the inefficacy of polished periods and studied sentences."[12] Surely this is a rationalistic monster who must either be punished severely for insensibility to human suffering or undergo strenuous reformation. But this callous recognition of "the emptiness of rhetorical sound" actually constitutes the desired "reformation" in Rasselas: comprehension of Imlac's warnings that teachers of morality "discourse like angels, but they live like men."[13] The truth of the matter is, of course, that Rasselas is no monster, but rather the main character in an apologue. Johnson's fiction, from beginning to end, has been organized so that it prevents the reader from even considering the possibility that Rasselas' reaction to misery was unfeeling. Each episode is represented so that interest in what will happen to any characters, or to the altering relationships among a group of characters, has been deftly subordinated to consideration of the thematic statement which dictated their inclusion in the first place. If we become more interested in Rasselas' emotional reaction to the Stoic's misery than we are in his recognition of the futility of achieving earthly happiness by the acquisition of "invulnerable patience,"[14] the apologue has failed: all elements of the fiction have not been subordinated to the creation of an example of the truth of a formulable statement. The episode, no matter how interesting in itself, would obscure the theme it is to help exemplify. It would not, in such a case, be a coherent part of a work informed by still a third principle.

NOTES

[1] Though I am sure that Professor E. W. Rosenheim would disagree with many of my remarks in this chapter, my notions

about satire derive in part from his extremely suggestive doctoral
dissertation, *Swift's Satire in a Tale of a Tub* (University of
Chicago, 1953).

2 For the moment it is useful to insist that all elements of any
one work must share the defined similarity to the whole if we
are to regard it as coherent. This notion is considerably modified
in this chapter and in chapter five.

3 It is important to note that the organizing principle of a satire
is not the same as that of a negative apologue—i.e., of a work
organized as the fictional example of a negative statement.

4 Swift is notorious for his virulent dislike of lawyers. But one
of the signs of satire is that when we interpret elements which
appropriately ridicule an external object as if they were the
author's positive suggestions about how to deal with the objects
he dislikes, the satirist will inevitably appear a fool or a monster.
Swift, of course, was neither.

5 Jonathan Swift, *Gulliver's Travels*, ed. Arthur E. Case (New
York: The Ronald Press Co., 1938), p. 256.

6Gwin J. Kolb, "Johnson's 'Dissertation on Flying' and John
Wilkins' *Mathematical Magic*," MP, XLVII (1949), 24–31.
For many of my subsequent remarks about *Rasselas* I am heavily
indebted to Kolb's published works about Johnson, particularly
to "The Structure of *Rasselas*," *PMLA*, LXVI (1951), 698–717.

7 The problem of what constitutes a digression in an otherwise
coherent work is intricate and, to myself, fascinating, both because of the insight into artistic coherence afforded by investigating the problem and because of the subtlety with which eighteenth-century novelists have been able to employ digressions to
achieve special effects. (For a detailed discussion see chap. five.)
A perfectly coherent literary work may, of course, be a bad one,
and a work containing many digressions may be a very good
one. Indeed, some of the more interesting works of English
fiction, both before and during the eighteenth century, do not
depend for their effects upon a strong principle of coherence at
all. (For a brief discussion of a work of this sort see my remarks
on *Moll Flanders* in chap. six.)

8 It is simple enough to imagine a work constructed so that it
represents in its initial stages a completely virtuous world and
demonstrates in the last part, with many particular references,
how the writer's age falls short of ethical perfection. But such a
work, though it very well might ridicule, would be coherent not

as satire but as apologue: a fictional example illustrating the truth that men do not live up to the ideal.

[9] The ways in which Swift employs ridicule are sometimes incredibly subtle, but that subtlety itself depends on almost a blatant assurance of the presence of ridicule where it is intended. After the first four or five chapters of *Gulliver's Travels*, it would have been difficult for Swift to include an episode which did not ridicule an external object.

[10] We may expect similar results from a confusion of any of the three types of prose fiction discussed in this chapter.

[11] *Samuel Johnson: Rasselas, Poems, and Selected Prose*, ed. Bertrand T. Bronson (New York, Rinehart and Co., 1958), pp. 546–47.

[12] *Ibid.*, p. 547.

[13] *Ibid.*, p. 546.

[14] *Ibid.*, p. 545.

RONALD PAULSON

The Fictions of Satire

THE CENTRAL SYMBOL OF VIOLENCE

What we remember from a satire is neither character nor plot per se, but a fantastic image, or a series of them. At the center of almost every satire there is an image which, if effective, the reader cannot easily forget: the copulation of an ass and a woman (Apuleius' *Metamorphoses*), a fanatic leaping into a bonfire (Lucian's *Death of Peregrine*), the drowning of half the populace of Paris in a flood of urine (Rabelais' *Gargantua*), the sawing off of a man's head (Waugh's *Decline and Fall*). In the field of cannibalism alone there are such incidents as the projected cooking and eating of children (Swift's *Modest Proposal*), the eating of a pet spaniel and a tutor (Byron's *Don Juan*), and the eating of a fiancée (Waugh's *Black Mischief*). In Juvenal's Satire XV Egyptians devour an enemy soldier, and in Petronius' *Satyricon* the heirs of Eumolpus must eat his body before they can share his suppositious estate. At the center of Nathanael West's *A Cool Million* is the dismemberment of the hero and the repeated rape of the heroine, and in *Gulliver's Travels* there is the threat of blinding or mastication.

Such a scene is, of course, in one sense a poetic strategy. The satirist uses cannibalism as a metaphor for aggression. But poetry is incidental result rather than intention; more to the point, these scenes represent the characteristic fictions through which the satirist conveys his subject matter: the corruption of an ideal and the behavior of fools, knaves, dupes, and the like.

(1) *Corruption.* The corruption or degeneration of the normative or ideal is conveyed by a static image, usually related to the

From *The Fictions of Satire*, Baltimore, 1967, pp. 9–31. Reprinted by permission of the Johns Hopkins University Press.

Theophrastan "character." Behind the copulation of beast and bestial woman is the normal relationship between man and woman. The woman in Juvenal's Satire VI who has become a gladiator is juxtaposed with the feminine ideal; the rakehell is measured against the statues of his heroic ancestors (Satire VIII); or the pretender to social status against the proper social values (Horace's Satire I.9). In Pope's *Dunciad* unreason and wretched writing ("Dulness") are simply placed alongside the great literary works of the past.

(2) *Consequences.* But while the corruption of an ideal is almost always at least implicit, it only rarely appears as the sole subject of the satire. The basic polarity of an ideal (usually in the past) and a degenerate present provides a useful frame for the argument of a satire; but the only comment it has to offer is, "Alas, what a falling away!" A merely static contrast cannot demonstrate other areas of satiric subject matter—folly and knavery on the part of the degenerate. In order to portray these subjects the satirist must present (or at least imply) an act of some kind, for example, the copulation of ass and woman, which is shown to be the consequence of the woman's lust.

Satire characteristically judges by consequences rather than by causes or motives, which are too slippery; the final standard is an objective one like success or failure. (The satirist is, in fact, fond of showing up the subjective standard of motive or intention by the concrete fact of its consequence.) The satirist who wishes to convey his indictment by a fictive rather than a discursive structure must (if his indictment is very severe) employ a physical encounter which ends in violence. The scenes noted above are all shockingly violent concatenations of action and consequence; they are, in effect, symbolic actions that convey the central meaning of the satire. Peregrine's self-immolation proves his self-consuming folly, as the eating of children, spaniel, tutor, and fiancée demonstrate the eaters' cannibalistic viciousness.

Punishment is the most extreme, and at the same time most common, consequence in satire. The satirist can show the consequences of folly in the punishment of the guilty (Peregrine burned), or he can show the guilty in the process of punishing, or persecuting, the innocent (the savage treatment of the hero and heroine in *A Cool Million*). The latter paradoxical situation is obviously the more popular one with a satirist: its attack is less direct and less optimistic than the straightforward administration of justice. The punishment of the innocent, however, while producing a striking momentary effect and an appropriate atmosphere, tells us nothing about the victim and relatively little about the punisher. Punishment of people with varying degrees of guilt can permit elaborate analysis and exposition of the public as well as the private aspects of a character.

In Apuleius' *Metamorphoses*, Lucius is punished for his spiritual and physical lusts by being turned into a symbol of lust, an ass, and thereafter frequently threatened with gelding. What follows for him is, in fact, one long punishment. But the same befalls the subsidiary characters: the robber Lamachus puts his hand through a keyhole in order to lift the bar inside. The owner of the house nails the housebreaker's hand to the inside of the door (a suggestion of crucifixion, the punishment for robbers) ; in order to make their escape the robbers cut off Lamachus' arm at the elbow (the offending member is removed). Elsewhere Thelyphron loses his ears and nose as a consequence of his excessive self-confidence. The evil boy who has tormented Lucius is eaten by a bear, a murderous slave is crucified, a murderous woman is condemned to copulation with an ass, the eunuch priests are carted off to jail, the robbers are rolled off a cliff, and the wicked sisters of Psyche are plunged to their deaths. The adulterous husband, whose wife takes revenge by throwing herself and her child into a well, is eaten by ants (as by the lusts that drove him to adultery). If we may judge by Apuleius, the satirist seldom bothers to punish the totally innocent, and the first feeling of persecution is quickly followed by its opposite, a suspicion of justice.

The implications of the device of punishing the guilty are clarified by a survey of its sources. A satire is said to "pillory" or "lacerate" or "blister" the person it attacks. The convention of punishing a knave within the satiric fiction was probably first based on the belief that by a pre-enactment of his wishes the satirist could somehow coerce nature into making the fiction real; in this sense, punishment is a vestige of satire's origin in ritual and magic. Certainly one source is the primitive satirist's curse which enumerates the poxes and floggings he wishes to see descend upon his enemy. The satirist who wants to materialize the curse (and perhaps recall some of its vigor) must describe a physical chastisement of the villain. The ancient satirist Archilochus asks that his enemy be shipwrecked: "Shivering with cold, covered with filth washed up by the sea, with chattering teeth like a dog, may he lie helplessly on his face at the edge of the strand amidst the breakers—this 'tis my wish to see him suffer, who has trodden his oaths under foot, him who was once my friend."[1] Helplessness and isolation are not an arbitrary revenge; they describe the character of the turncoat who has cut himself off from human loyalties.

The curse itself derives from the idea that external appearance should correspond to inner reality, a diseased body to a diseased soul, and so (some satirist must have inferred) the marks of punishment will suggest the quality of the soul within that merits such punishment. A pox is both a painful punishment for transgression and an externalization of an internal corruption. As in the case of Lucius, punishment adjusts the false appearance until it does correspond to the inner reality. It fastens on the delicate spot, exaggerating it, inverting it, or in some way distorting it.

These punishments represent very literally a rhetorical stance transformed or objectified into an image of evil. By contrast, the commonest of literary punishments, in which the culprit is simply roasted in hell fire or whipped unmercifully or submerged in excrement, is more an objectification of the satirist's disgust than of the evil man's sin. When Ezra Pound (*Cantos* XIV and XV) describes his usurers covered with filth, he is attempting to make us share his own feelings about them by giving us an objective correlative which presumably excites in us similar feelings. The result is that the image lacks cognitive particularity. As too often happens, the punishment is decorative and tells us very little about the person or crime punished.

In all of these instances, however, the satirist has attempted to convey a truth about his sinners which is not apparent on perusal in ordinary circumstances. Only in hell—or in the agony of punishment—is it possible to see that they *are* (spiritually) splitting open with their excess, or that their sin is actually consuming them, not they it. Even Pound's newspaper and banking barons appear in the "last squalor, utter decrepitude" in hell because that is their reality —the reality their money and power prevent us from seeing. The poetic justice of these punishments is irrelevant to the satiric effect; but their symbolic appropriateness describes an inner state that cannot be exposed simply by showing the knave in action tormenting the innocent.

Carried far enough, the image of punishment leads to the belief that the manner of one's dying defines the man; or, as Kenneth Burke has noticed, we say not that a man is "by nature a criminal"

but that "he will end on the gallows."[2] In the picaresque satire *La
Picara Justina* (1605), the heroine gives us accounts of the violent
deaths of her many ancestors, each symbolic of the ancestor's crime.
For example, her gluttonous mother stole steaks and puddings; when
she was finally caught, "for fear of a discovery, [she] cramm'd in half
a yard of *Pudding*, which being thrust down too hastily, stop'd up
the Passage, so that there was no moving forwards or backwards, nor
could she Speak or Breathe." The merchant interrogated her, "but
she could return no answer; and the best of it was, that a long piece
of *Pudding* hung out at her Mouth, so that she look'd like a *Bear* in
Heraldry, Arm'd and Langued."[3] In her suffering and death she
creates the satiric image (almost an escutcheon) that sums up her
essential character. Punishment and death are terminal actions that
round off tidily the vicious actions they conclude. They obviate
potentialities and establish a fixed, complete portrait. Justina's mother
brings about her own end, demonstrating neatly that, as with a glutton
whose gluttony only increases his appetite, the crime is its own
punishment.

Punishment thus conveys a definite admonition: this is the
consequence of your foolish act, this is the effect of X's evil act; or,
beware! this is what you could look like or what X does in fact look
like. There is also, of course, a strong element of the therapeutic in
punishment: besides the lash and the strappado, the purge and the
scalpel define the distemper as they remove it.[4] But if satire is
essentially a study of evil, we can interpret punishment of the guilty
as a way to present the psychological reality of the vice, its ethos;
while punishment of the innocent presents the objective effects of
the vice. One is concerned primarily with the criminal, the other
with the crime (and sometimes with the suffering of the innocent,
which may lead out of satire into sentimentalism).

In many satires, we may note in passing, the punishment is also
objectified in the satirist's image of himself as a surgeon or public
executioner—with the effect of drawing the reader's attention away
from both persuasion and presentation to the interesting image of
the performer and his operations.

(3) *Distance*. A determining factor in the effect of the satiric
symbol is the distance maintained between the reader (and the
author) and the satiric fiction that is being presented. At one extreme
is an ironic, oblique presentation, about which the reader, as a
member of an elite, feels rather superior. If in some sense he is the

ordinary, lethargic backslider, he is distinct from the evil tendencies the satirist presents. The satirist's irony, which goes over the head of the guilty party, is understood by the intelligent and morally-aware reader. The other satiric approach, in effect, rubs the reader's nose in the dirt of which it is trying to make him aware. If forces him by intimate sensuous contact to suffer such revulsion that he will see a truth he has overlooked, change his ways, or campaign against the evil in question. In Gulliver's fourth voyage there are the filthy Yahoos, and in Juvenal's famous portrait of Messalina (Satire VI) we smell and feel the sheets, see her feverish body and its gestures.

The satiric scene, however, is ordinarily carefully distanced from the reader. Imagine the death of Prendergast in *Decline and Fall* full of blood and Prendergast's agony: as opposed to Waugh's account, held at arm's length by the secondhand source who is inserting the information into the verse form of a hymn being sung at chapel. One is reminded of the difference between the cartoon submitted to *The New Yorker* which showed one fencer slashing off the other's head with blood spattered everywhere, and the printed drawing (the caption, "Touché") by James Thurber, executed with the very minimum of detail. Sensuous detail is almost entirely absent, and the act is kept as abstract as possible while remaining suggestive. Swift's babies are hypothetical and unparticularized; their fate is particularized in the extreme (fricasseed, put in ragout, made into gloves for ladies) but applied to abstractions.

The discrepancy created by ironic understatement, as has often been remarked, may make the horror greater; but the distancing, or the remove at which we witness the act, also keeps us from losing ourselves in the horror. The butchery of Prendergast or of babies, we are reminded, is not itself the main point of the image, merely a metaphorical notation for the real one. Whereas, as the sensuous immediacy of the action increases, the image becomes more a thing for its own sake in which the reader is immersed. The satirist, in short, demands decisions of his reader, not mere feelings; wishes to arouse his energy to action, not purge it in vicarious experience.

The detachment demanded by satire, however, is different from that we feel when we witness a farce, for example an animated cartoon of the cat and mouse, Tom and Jerry. The satiric image has to be taken seriously in a way altogether different from its cousin, the farcical image of Jerry squashing Tom's head between millstones. Or better, take the example of Titania kissing Bottom the tailor (transformed into an ass) in *A Midsummer Night's Dream.* Here the reader is so detached from the characters that the comedy is, as Meredith would say, very pure. To be satire there would have to be (among other things) a great deal of impurity—the reader would have to grimace when the lovely, deluded queen kissed the hairy mouth. The satiric image lacks the complete abstraction of the comic: a certain disgust, a certain physical involvement of the reader is always necessary. One way this seriousness of involvement is maintained is by the basic causality that is stressed in satire's world: when a head is sawed off, the man dies; but also by introducing enough physical details to be suggestive without breaking the abstraction of the idea. Waugh does imbed in the hymn two details about Prendergast, his screams and their duration: "Poor Prendy 'ollored fit to kill/For nearly 'alf an hour." The balance is a delicate one between contemplation and arousal.

(4) *Corrective.* As its ritual origin shows, the satiric fiction is a throwback that has not yet completely transformed sexual orgy into the more genteel comic resolution of romantic marriage. The leather phalli are still in view, and the conflict presented between the forces of fertility and of barrenness is much less veiled—and also much more obviously a conflict, with the author clearly on the side of fertility. If punishment (as curse) is one aspect of its action, copulating, eating, and defecating are others. In Aristophanes' plays the phallic costume constantly reminds the spectator of the norm behind the play, of the characters' shared humanity, of their true and basic motives and desires beneath fashion and hypocrisy. Thus in *Lysistrata* Aristophanes shows the women's refusal to sleep with their husbands (the frustrated phalli much in evidence) as an analogue to the barrenness caused by the war—spiritual as well as material. Sexuality is Juvenal's most basic symbol for life and human relationships, all of which spiral down toward sexual perversion. Horace uses sexual passion to represent all kinds of excess in his Satire I.2, and many satirists from Rabelais to Rochester make sexuality a microcosm of their world. Juvenal's (or Petronius') attack on the sterility of perversion suggests that his satire still carries a vestige of the fertility ritual. Copulation is one of the most basic, natural, unavoidable acts of men, offering a universality that few other examples can have; it reminds us, when we become proud, of our ties with the animal. The eating and excreting of food, even more basic acts, are the other favorite symbols of the satirist. Both

love-making and eating make the gratuitous, romantic, or perverse easily apparent.

Animal functions contribute still another important characteristic of satiric violence: the sense of release, which is the motive force behind Aristophanes' plays. Aristophanes' action is presented as a fantastic explosion of energy, only in the most general sense sexual. In the midst of a long, hopeless war one citizen makes a private peace with Sparta and sets up his own small, independent, and prosperous state within Athens; another travels up to Olympus on the back of a dung beetle to secure the goddess Peace; two other citizens, disgusted with the present state of affairs in Athens, found a city of birds between earth and heaven and intercept the burnt offerings to the gods. Aristophanes' action may be a parody of the miraculous or magical event at the center of romances; in a more important sense it derives from the mythos of the fertility ritual, showing a hero trying to bring the moribund society of the present—made so by continued war or political stagnation—back to life. The plot consists of a revolutionary plan that is acted upon to solve the insoluble problem faced by the Athenians.

When the violent importation of one situation into an alien one is related to moral values it becomes universe-changing, order-disrupting, attitude-mixing, a reversal of values; and if the emphasis is on the disruption as a corrective and the thing disrupted as wrong, the result is revolutionary satire. The effect is to shatter the world of custom and convention, to break open the coffin in which Athens has immured itself.

But this is to see the revolutionary plan in too simple a way. At best it is a fantastic if not ridiculous plan, which by its madness shows up the situation against which it reacts. It says: Things are so impossibly terrible that this, fantastic as it is, is the only answer. The "plan" is not a serious proposal but a ridiculous alternative that indirectly illuminates the nature of the problem. The facts that the hero is unheroic and buffoonish—a parody of epic and romance heroes—and that his antagonist is only an alazon are also part of the comically hopeless situation as Aristophanes dramatizes it. The heroes of Marathon are now old and decrepit, eager for the status quo, the government is dominated by fools, and the duty of resuscitation is left to the most ordinary citizen.

There is also, we should notice, a sense in which Aristophanes' most revolutionary satire is in fact conservative. The analogy of ancient fertility ritual is useful to explain the conservatism that underlies even revolutionary satire, as a self-justification if not a pose. The old god or king died or was killed in ritual combat, but the new god who defeated or replaced him was not new in the sense of *different*. He was the same man restored to his youth, and the new killed and replaced the old simply because age had hardened his arteries, softened his brain, slowed him to a walk, and induced impotence. In terms of Frye's mythical categories, the new, true society is always a return to an older society (usually visualized as a Golden Age in the past), whose place has been usurped by an intermediate, aging, and false society. Depending on the emphasis—whether it is on the nonconformity and deviation of the false society from old norms, or on its rigidifying of the old ways—the satire can be conservative or revolutionary, its aim to attack release or to use it as a foil to stultification.

The Aristophanic exuberance can serve two antithetical purposes in satire. The more common use is to interpret the outburst of energy as the chaos of uncontrol, of vicious individualism. The emphasis on eating, defecating, and making love, which in Aristophanes is almost a comic ideal in itself, in the Roman satirists—particularly in Juvenal—becomes the multiplicity of disorder, sinking from gluttony to cannibalism, from unrestrained to perverted lusts. These satirists see the world as a simple, stable social order with forces at work trying to undermine or overthrow a beautiful status quo—or perhaps the overthrow has already taken place and the satirist looks back with nostalgia to the time of order. The result is less an imitation of exuberance than of overripeness, rottenness, a sinister often horrible quality. This quality is altogether lacking in the work of the satirist who sees the world as per se a place of complexity and disorder. His satire is offensive, clownish, seeking the new which may open unsuspected possibilities for individual fulfillment and shading off into comedy. A satirist who believes that his society is stuffy, overordered, and convention-ridden employs revolutionary satire, and a satirist who sees his society as chaotic, individualistic, and novelty-seeking tries to rein it by using a defensive satire.

Thus to the demonstration of folly and knavery, can be added a further function of the violent symbol of action and consequences: to serve as a corrective. Looking again at some of those violent actions with which this section began, we can classify them according to their intention. Basil Seal's eating of his fiancée in *Black Mischief* is evil, its purpose being to reveal in a dramatic image the truth about Basil, that he is indeed a cannibal (the same is true of the heirs of Eumolpus and the English and Irish landowners in the *Modest Proposal*). On the other hand, Gargantua's drowning of half the population of Paris in a flood of urine, however fatal to the Parisians, is good because Paris has become moribund, dry, and parched. The sawing off of Prendergast's head, while not in itself good, does serve to point up Prendergast's withdrawal from all human commitments by having him sawed on for half an hour by the most committed of men, a homicidal maniac. The act also, of course, reflects back on the prison warden with his narrowly progressive penal theories. The dismemberment of the protagonist of *A Cool Million* is largely a commentary on the vicious society, but partly also on the naïve protagonist himself.

The dual use of the violent image points to the conclusion that it is essentially equivocal and is exploited as such. Being a rhetorical form, satire invariably engages in casuistry and inconsistency —often at the expense of the coherence of its fiction. The significant characteristic of the satiric symbol is its flexibility; it can be used in more than one way at the same time and to catch as many different —often contradictory—facets of falsity or evil as possible. Its absence of consistency is a complement of its flexibility; it is operative less as a device of verisimilitude than as a device to "catch the conscience of the king."[5]

The evil represented, then, is either an excessively disordered or an excessively ordered society, with its opposite used as a foil or, sometimes, as a complement (both of them wrong). The contrast can extend to illusion and reality, affectation and plain-speaking, rebellion and complaisance—any set of extremes between which the satirist takes one or neither side. These extremes are the areas imitated by the satirist. They are ordinarily represented, however, with one doing something to the other, or to itself. The action, reaction, or interaction is finally the object represented.

RELATIONSHIP: THE FOOL AND THE KNAVE

The consequence of an action in satire can be either the effect it has on other people, or the repercussions it brings upon oneself. In either case the fictions used by satire are essentially relationships between people. Plots may be borrowed, but certain relationships—

between the bad, the foolish, the good—are indigenous to satire. Even the static emblematic image of punishment usually involves the punisher as well as the punished. Without a situation in which one man exploits or injures another, knavery cannot be demonstrated; and to demonstrate folly he must himself be discomfited. A knave is only finally a knave by virtue of his impingement on the lives of others; a fool's actions are not foolish unless they are ineffectual or bring down upon him unpleasant consequences. The satirist even goes so far as to suggest that the knave is less a knave when his villainy fails or backfires, or when he is punished; these consequences may turn his knavery into folly.

It is possible for a fool to appear alone in a satire: a single glutton, his health worn away, his character undermined, his money gone, can exemplify folly. But a knave can never appear without a victim in sight. There must be a dupe, or a fool, or an innocent for him to prey upon, otherwise he becomes himself a fool expending his energy on air. An Iago can be evil in soliloquy because tragedy looks at the inner life as an independent world. But a satiric Iago, without an Othello, would be a fool spinning bootless plots. In his sixth satire Juvenal writes primarily about women, not about marriage, but he can define their evil only in terms of marriage or some similar relationship. In the central part of the satire, where the women are without an object of aggression, he exposes only their folly: here they are drunken Venuses unable to control themselves, the prey of eastern superstitions, oracles, and charlatans. But once their husbands and stepsons, slaves and neighbors, are back in the picture, their folly again turns to cruelty and destructiveness, progressing from infidelity toward murder.

The distinction between Horatian and Juvenalian satire is largely one of focus on fool or knave: Horace focuses on the fathers who are hated, while Juvenal focuses on the sons who kill their fathers. The fictions they employ are therefore basically different, and since most subsequent satire derives from one or the other, they should be clearly distinguished.

Horace gives his attention almost exclusively to fools. There is no real knave in his world because one of his assumptions is that deviant behavior brings its own punishment, that those who give the appearance of being knaves are in fact fools. Punishment, the most frequent consequence of action in his satires, turns crime into folly, apparent knaves into fools. Anyone (says Horace) is a fool who fails to see his own best course of action, who mistakes a false for a real good. Accordingly, Horace shows the miser the unpleasantness that results from burying one's money in the ground and spending sleepless nights worrying about it, when, in spite of all his care, the money that has been hoarded will be run through in no time by his heir (Satire I.1). When the miser drives his son away, it is he and not the son who suffers; he is an exploiter not of others but of himself. The adulterer Satire I.2 is not wicked, only foolish, and his foolishness is proved by his fate at the hands of irate husbands and loyal servants.

Even such a monster as the witch Canidia is shown to be a fool rather than a knave. In Epode V she buries an innocent boy up to his neck and starves him to death (food is placed just beyond his lips), her aim being to transfer his longing to the man who has not returned her love. Although she destroys the boy, we are given ample evidence that she will not get her man; her witchcraft has not worked in the past and will not work now. The boy's curses point to an ironic similarity between the hopeless passivity of his position and that of his tormentor's. Though immediately destructive, and in that sense evil, Canidia is in the long run ineffectual, as she was earlier in Satire I.8 when Priapus routed her and dispelled all her factitious incantations by a single vulgar and natural gesture. Even the worst knaves, Horace shows, finally turn out to be fools. The detection of folly at the heart of apparent knavery, as much as the light carefree tone, explains the difference between the satire of Horace and Juvenal. As Plato phrased it, "ignorance in the powerful is hateful and horrible, because hurtful to others both in reality and in fiction, but powerless ignorance may be reckoned, and in truth is, ridiculous."[6]

In Satire I.9 Horace presents the basic situation of his kind of satire: a bore pursues and unmercifully bothers the speaker ("Horace"), trying to break into the charmed circle of Maecenas, Virgil, Horace, and their friends. The outsider only succeeds in making a fool of himself, and solid Roman society shakes its head in disapproval. The bore seeks social status, Canidia seeks love, and Nasidienus (in II.8) tries to give a fashionable dinner; while the insider, who understands the nature of society, affection, and hospitality, points out wherein the upstarts fall short. The outsider is outside because he is a fool, and will remain so until he adjusts to the proper standards of conduct.

The ridiculing of an outsider from the security of a conservative, order-conscious society is one of the most pervasive conventions of satire. Horace, however, characteristically extends his satire to one insider, himself. The actual subject of Satire I.9 turns out to be as much the discomfiture of "Horace" as the aggression of the bore who annoys him. Otherwise there would be no reason for Horace's inclusion of the vignette concerning the friend who refuses to extricate him from his comic dilemma. Horace too, unable to adjust to this threat from outside, is something of a fool; he is satirizing himself— and all people who cannot cope with bores—as well as the bore. Horace's satire is essentially self-oriented, and in the satires that Eduard Fraenkel and other Horatian scholars consider most characteristic (those that lead to the *epistolae*) he identifies himself with the subject, his "I" with the admonitory "you." He finds the folly in himself and uses himself as an example of the universal folly: "If I am foolish, and admit it, perhaps you had better examine your own conduct." He claims to walk about the streets of Rome questioning his own actions and motives, seeking self-improvement. The fools he observes are important only insofar as their folly illuminates his problems.

For Juvenal evil is a potent and destructive force, and it lacks the comic element that accompanies impotence. He is much more concerned with the effect of aggressive behavior than with its repercussions on the foolish agent. The story of the patron who sends away his dependents, gorges himself on a huge banquet alone, and has a stroke in his bath afterward (Satire I), is an exceptional situation in Juvenal. In his later satires, as he adjusts himself to the benevolence of the Emperor Hadrian, he does deal (though by no means frequently) with retribution for the wicked. In Satire XIII punishment is shown to be an inevitable accompaniment of crime, whether it is imposed by a judge or by the criminal himself. But most often—in those satires which we think of as characteristic—Juvenal is concerned with a relationship between two people, and with the effect of one person on another. One is the evil man who, unlike Horace's harried characters, is unfazed as he pursues his merry, wicked way; the other is either a fool or an innocent.

To understand Juvenal's kind of satire it is necessary to relate his use of the fool-knave relationship to his use of the static contrast of an ideal and its corruption. Discussing Juvenal's rhetorical structure, W. S. Anderson has shown that his satire ordinarily moves from a statement of a paradox (Rome no longer Roman, or sexual perverts with pious faces) to the splitting of the paradox into polar opposites of good and evil (Roman values versus the corrupted city, or piety versus perversion).[7] The truth of the paradox lies in the fact that the society of the present does not repudiate the old forms but rather conceals its own perversion behind them, paying virtue the compliment of hypocrisy. Juvenal begins with amazement or fierce indignation at the paradoxical situation he sees before him, and then shows why it is paradoxical by separating the ideal from the corruption of the ideal. As Anderson suggests, Juvenal's practice is the reverse of Horace's typical method, which is dialectical: Horace begins with a thesis (wild spending), follows with an antithesis (stinginess), then resolves his extremes with a compromise (the ideal of moderate spending). Moderation is not ordinarily a Juvenalian ideal. He opposes black to white instead of settling for Horace's intermediate shade. Roman values, and the past in which they were effective, are Juvenal's positive pole; the foreigner-infested present, with its mercenary values, is his negative pole. All that lies between must gravitate to one pole or the other.

My description might suggest that Juvenal's satires are simpler than Horace's; they are not. In order to see their complexity and originality we must regard them as fictional rather than rhetorical structures. Juvenal only displays the positive pole from time to time as a sort of obbligato; he achieves his complexity not in his contrast of good with evil but in his portrayal of the various aspects of evil contained in the negative pole.

The series of metonymies Juvenal uses to represent un-Roman Rome consists of social relationships between husband and wife, father and child, friend and friend, emperor and adviser, patron and dependent—all of which serve Juvenal as paradigms for the degeneracy he attacks. Each relationship at one time had been an ideal, involving reciprocal respect, duty, and responsibility, and each had once been associated with the traditional coherence and solidarity of Roman society. In Satire III the failure of the relationship between the patron and his dependent is generalized to the failure of all relationships, climaxing in the case of the man who is beaten up by rowdies or crushed into nothingness beneath a load of marble. The breakdown extends to crumbling or burning buildings and (for Codrus) sheer starvation.

The relationship Juvenal uses most tellingly is the typically Roman one between a patron and the poet or scholar who is his de-

pendent (or client). The ideal behind the patron-dependent relationship stood ready to hand for Juvenal in the satire of Horace, where
the solidarity of the Maecenas circle—the ideal relationship between
the patron and his dependent—served as the norm by which the deviant behavior of bores, misfits, and other outsiders was measured.
In the satire of Juvenal the situation of Roman society has become
reversed: the satirist, the upholder of standards, is himself outside
society as it now exists. The forces of chaos and vice are in control,
and so they exclude the deviant satirist, the maintainer of old values.

In the patron-dependent relationship, then, the good dependent, who upholds the old social standards, is simply driven out. There
is no room for him. In Satire I, where the patron and his dependent
are introduced to embody Juvenal's attack on avarice, the old relationship has deteriorated to the point that money is all that holds the two
parties together and financial support is merely a dole. In Satire III
the old dependent is thrown out of the patron's house and his place
is taken by the pliant foreigner or the "foreign" Roman. He therefore
becomes the positive ideal of the satire, and the negative pole becomes
both the corrupt patron and the corruptible dependent who has filled
the gap.

Juvenal's fiction enables him to portray two kinds of satiric subject matter at once: the folly of one party and the knavery of the
other (with a third, the degeneration of the ideal relationship, implicit
in the background). The dependent who accepts the false values of
his corrupt patron is a fool (as is proved by the brutal treatment he
receives for his trouble), and the patron who imposes them, exploiting
his dependent, is a knave. Satire V demonstrates the reciprocal quality
of the guilt Juvenal exposes. The speaker is addressing a poor dependent, Trebius, who has accepted the corrupt values of his patron,
and for whom the *summum bonum* is now a good meal. Trebius
deserves the humiliations he receives from his patron, for he has
allowed wealth to enslave him; and Juvenal points relentlessly to the
consequences—the stinking eel from the sewers of Rome and the
undrinkable wine, as opposed to the exquisite repast served to the
host. But the satire also catches the patron. If Trebius has sacrificed
his self-respect and his freedom, Virro has set himself up for a
tyrannous exploiter of his fellow Romans. The standards of Trebius
and Virro are precisely the same, the only difference being that Virro
has the money. In a digression Juvenal remarks that if only Trebius

happened to become rich the tables would be turned—then Virro would be *his* dependent. Both members of the relationship must adhere to the perversion to make it flourish in its full degeneracy. Without a toadying dependent the corrupt patron would cease to exist.

Satire IX picks up Virro again and offers a savage parody or *reductio ad absurdum* of the patron-dependent relationship in the association of the homosexual with his pathic. Again the dependent, Naevolus, is essentially the fool in the relationship: he is not strictly speaking a homosexual himself (as we gather from his relations with Virro's wife) but allows himself to fall in with Virro's desires simply for the money involved, just as Trebius did in Satire V. Like Trebius he is mistreated and discarded in favor of more alluring rivals. But Virro, too, is something of a fool. In a sense Naevolus is exploiting his unnatural desires, both by taking his money and by doing Virro's sexual duty to his wife (all Virro's children are in fact Naevolus'). Virro is driven by perverted lust, Naevolus by avarice—and so they interact as fool and knave, knave and fool.

The fool has become more specifically a dupe in Satire III ("Rome"), in which the ideal is the true Roman Umbricius, who is fleeing from an un-Roman Rome to the provinces, where there may still be something of the genuine Roman values left. Opposite Umbricius is a squalid alliance between the present money-mad Romans and the foreigners who are exploiting them. Like the dependents in Satires V and IX, these Romans, because they accept the false values of the foreigners, are fools rather than innocent victims; here they are used as dupes by the foreigners who wish to advance themselves socially to the position of "true" Romans.

Even in those Horatian satires of Juvenal's later years that focus on the bitter consequences of folly, the fool's behavior is used as a reflector of knavery. To wish for wealth or power, he says in Satire X ("The Vanity of Human Wishes"), is folly: look at the consequences to yourself. In Horace's satire a consequence would be to grow fatter and fatter, or perhaps to become a tyrant and therefore be hated by one's sons. In Juvenal what begins as the repercussions of folly ends as the effects of a knave's evil. The man who foolishly wishes for riches can expect to be murdered by scheming relatives or wiped out (his fortune confiscated) by an envious king; the mother who wishes for a beautiful daughter can expect to see her raped. While admonishing fools, the satire also attacks the knaves who batten on human follies. Juvenal's emphasis is on the folly (and this emphasis distinguishes Satire X from his earlier satires), but the evil is always present—the fool is never without his knave.

The first conclusion to be drawn from the satires of Horace and Juvenal is that a satiric relationship tends to diffuse guilt. Horace too is a fool in his satires; in Juvenal's the guilt extends to the persecuted fool as well as to the knave. Satire populates the world not with knaves and innocents but with knaves *and* fools or other knaves, one reason being, of course, that normative people have no prominent place in satire. Here, however, we must make a crucial distinction between the satiric scene and the character who observes and frames it. Horace's speaker is morally a part of the scene, but Juvenal's is separate and personally unstained by contact with bores. The role of the satirist himself is as different in their satires as is the composition of the scene he observes.

Like all subsequent satirists, both claim that their satire is the result of circumstances beyond their control. The satirist does not want to write satire, but he must. The fiction invented to convey this impression relies, like the rest of the satire, on consequences and relationships. The Juvenalian persona says that his satire is literally forced out of him by knavish surroundings or by a knave's behavior. Faced with such evil, "difficile est saturam non scribere."

Horace, we have seen, writes primarily because of what he is himself. Satire is simply an expression of his turn of mind, a consequence of his own character. At its most Juvenalian, it follows from Horace's Venusian ancestors, who guarded the Roman border against barbarians, as Horace does figuratively now. But most of the time he claims his satire as a weapon of personal defense, not, like Juvenal's, a sacred weapon. In neither case does the satirist have any control over his writing, but Horace's satire is in a sense a lack of control over himself, almost an eccentricity, and so is ridiculous. It must be apologized for because it is an excessive reaction, not consonant with the moderation Horace advocates, and not necessary for ideal men like Maecenas.

Juvenal keeps himself rigorously separate from the folly and the knavery he portrays. He purposely reduces the character of his persona to an abstractness far beyond Horace's: he is merely a bundle of old Roman virtues, including significantly the military, which offers an explanation for his outbursts of indignation. Roman discipline appears in the alternative periods of control—sometimes arrived at by a change of tone, sometimes by a simple splitting of his persona, in the militant spirit of "Juvenal" and the more controlled performance of Umbricius (Satire III). This abstractness sets aside the Juvenalian persona as a point of view and an ideal and little more.

Horace uses his persona as the central fact of his satire, making of him a complex figure of Everyman rather than an ideal; this Everyman addresses himself to other ordinary citizens in order to share his self-knowledge. His satire is aimed at the reader, who is the object of his attack, and it advises him of his follies. Juvenal ordinarily addresses himself to those few like himself who are weathering the storm, but never to the fools or knaves. His attack is therefore aimed at someone other than the reader (at *les autres*), and if any advice is involved it is advice to the reader to *écrasez l'infâme*. He has thrown up his hands in despair over the reformation of the evil (a rhetorical pose, of course, and an effective one), and he can only warn the good to keep away.

In the works of Horace and Juvenal we can distinguish two modes of satire. One we can call admonitory and subjective, the other presentational and objective. Horatian satire is most interested in outlining a practicable code of conduct. Through the opposite extremes of examples to be avoided the Horatian dialectic at length points the way to just how one *should* act in certain circumstances, and leads indirectly to spiritual autobiography or to ethical essays like those of Montaigne. The Juvenalian gives only the sketchiest advice as to a way of conduct: the ideal of the past offers little but a signpost from which the reader can take his bearings in the labyrinth of Juvenal's fictional embodiment of evil. What we remember is the presentation of the masculine wife and her effeminate husband, the homosexual and his pathic, the city with a Clytemnestra in every street and houses toppling on unwary pedestrians—in short, the complex and fantastic world that results when evil is dominant *and* regarded by an isolated, agitated, good man.

This "good man," insofar as the reader is made to associate with him, is a rhetorical device, parallel to Horace's "you." Although Horace and Juvenal are usually (with justice) regarded as extremes of detachment and involvement, there is a sense in which both immerse their readers. Horace—to borrow an image used earlier—rubs his reader's nose in his own dirt; Juvenal rubs his reader's nose in someone else's. With Horace the reader's experience is to feel complicity in the guilt; with Juvenal it is to feel repugnance at the evil. Satire always strives toward one or the other of these experiences: oneness with, or separateness from, the evil; complicity and guilt, or outrage; action directed toward oneself, or toward others; punishment of the guilty, or persecution of the innocent. Ultimately, as representation, they amount to the imitation of the foolish or evil man experiencing himself, or of the morally sensitive man experiencing folly or evil.

To the extent that it materializes the 'you" and "I" of his satire, Horace's admonitory stance can become a representation of man's lower potentials as he recognizes them and struggles upward or slides downward. Rhetorically, Horace makes the reader identify to some extent with the deviant (though remaining distinct enough to judge him); as representation, he involves the "I" and the "you" with each other, combining subject and object. The result can be either self-discovery or self-revelation.

The other—Juvenalian—kind of satire is less closely allied to the essay than to the epic or tragedy, even to the lyric, or to other presentational as opposed to argumentative (or persuasive) arts. While it operates from a moral viewpoint, and so is informed by indignation, its main purpose is to present and explore the nature of evil as it plays upon a poet's sensibility: two movements which appear sometimes separately and sometimes together.[8] As the people on the satirist's side dwindle and he is left alone, and the enemy becomes bigger, more terrible, and more powerful, the satire moves to another area, indicated by Plato, where the situation is no longer comic at all, and yet it is satiric. When the deluded fool has the power to enforce his illusion on others the situation is no longer ridiculous, but it may still be satiric. Juvenal believed this to be a transition from comic to tragic satire. To the commonsensical Horatian satirist, however, it might seem to be a movement in the direction of melodrama. In the practice of some Juvenalian imitators it became a movement away from the satiric object toward the isolated and suffering satirist-observer, and so toward sentimentalism.

NOTES

[1] The quotation is from the Strassburg Fragment (97A), trans. G. L. Hendrickson, "Archilochus and the Victims of his Iam-

bics," *American Journal of Philology*, XLVI (1925), 115. Satiric punishment is also perhaps related to the "elaborate ritual of the defeat of winter known to folklorists as 'carrying out Death'" (Frye, *Anatomy of Criticism*, p. 183); and to God's punishment of sinners, which carries a sanction that no civil punishment could (see, e.g., *Isaiah* 3:16–17; 28:14–22).

2 "The Imagery of Killing," *Hudson Review*, I (1948), 162.

3 Francisco de Ubeda, *La Picara Justina* (1605), in *The Spanish Libertines*, trans. Capt. John Stevens (London, 1709), p. 20.

4 Mary Claire Randolph has discussed this subject in "The Medical Concept in English Renaissance Satiric Theory: Its Possible Relationship and Implications," *Studies in Philology*, XXXVIII (1941), 125–57.

5 It might even be argued, with Sheldon Sacks, that if we accept the idea that every part of a satire ideally contributes to the generic aim of ridicule, there can be no expression of an ideal as such. Ideals are present only to set off the evil, and tell us nothing of the satirist's positive values. See Sacks' *Fiction and the Shape of Belief* (Berkeley and Los Angeles: University of California Press, 1965), pp. 8–9.

6 *Philebus* 49, in *The Dialogues of Plato*, trans. B. Jowett (New York: Random House, 1937), II, 384.

7 "Studies in Book I of Juvenal," *Yale Classical Studies*, XV (1957), 89.

8 Edward Rosenheim (*Swift and the Satirist's Art* [Chicago, Ill.: University of Chicago Press, 1963], p. 15), divides satiric purpose into two types, persuasive and punitive; the latter does not attempt to urge the reader to any action but merely displays the vice and analyzes it. It is misleading, however, to call this punitive, with all of its connotations of chastisement. "Presentational" seems to me a more useful term, although a fictive punishment is sometimes a part of this presentation.

PATRICIA MEYER SPACKS

Some Reflections on Satire

Is satire a genre at all? Attempts to define or describe it as one frequently founder; descriptions which seem plausible in theoretical isolation turn out to be useless in dealing with actual satiric documents. And satire often occurs in strange combination with other literary modes: Edward Albee's *American Dream* gleefully satirizes the American bourgeoisie only to shift toward the end to sentimentality about the causes of our corruption. *Alice in Wonderland* satirizes some Victorian pieties but indulges in others. Evelyn Waugh describes Hollywood burial customs in *Life* magazine with no satiric exaggeration (there are photographs to prove it); he describes them in almost exactly the same terms in *The Loved One*. Satire or realism?

Efforts to isolate the nature of satire have fallen historically into two general categories, emphasizing either purpose or technique. The classical view, which persisted through the eighteenth century, stressed the central importance of satire's moral intent. John Dryden, in his *Discourse Concerning Satire* (1693), accepts a definition by Heinsius: "Satire is a kind of poetry, without a series of action, invented for the purging of our minds; in which human vices, ignorance and errors, and all things besides, which are produced from them in every man, are severely reprehended."[1] Of Horace, Dryden remarks that his satiric purpose was "to correct the vices and the follies of his time, and to give the rules of a happy and virtuous life" (II, 125). He soon makes clear that the positive aspect of satire—its providing of rules for virtue—seems to him as important as the negative. "The poet is bound . . . to give his reader some one precept of moral virtue, and to caution him against some one particular vice or folly" (II, 146). Even in Juvenal's *Sixth Satire*, Dryden argues, "which seems only an

From *Genre*, I (1968), 13–20. Reprinted by permission of the author and the editors of *Genre*.

arraignment of the whole sex of womankind, there is a latent admonition to avoid ill women, by shewing how very few who are
virtuous and good are to be found amongst them" (p. 146). His
logic may be dubious, but his sense of satire's moral function is vivid.
Finally he maintains that "satire is undoubtedly a species" of heroic
poetry (p. 149) : it has, at its best, the dignity of epic.

But the nineteenth century brought Byronic satire, which glori-
fied the individual and implied no program of reform. And twentieth-
century definitions, abandoning the idea of satire's necessary moral
purpose, try to locate its special techniques. Alvin Kernan in two
book-length studies—*The Cankered Muse* (1959) and *The Plot of
Satire* (1965)—has tried to isolate the characteristic satiric scene, plot,
and character. Edward Rosenheim modifies the modern stress on technique by insisting that satire can be identified partly by its concern
with historic particulars: if we find no such particulars, a work is not
satire. His definition of satire is, "an attack by means of a manifest
fiction upon discernible historic particulars."[2] This position forces him
to find new designations for such works as the fourth book of *Gulliver's
Travels*, a book which contains satiric elements but is not, he argues,
satire: it is philosophic myth, "a mythical statement of a profound
and terrible belief about the human condition" (p. 101). Rosenheim's
definition shares with Dryden's only the insistence on attack as a
vital element in satire; for Dryden's concern with purpose it sub-
stitutes awareness of technique ("manifest fiction") and of context.

Gilbert Highet's exhaustive discussion of satiric tradition suggests a number of elements by which we can recognize satire: they
range from the author's explicit statement of satiric intent to a special
vocabulary and set of literary devices traditionally associated with such
intent.[3] The purpose of satire, in his view, is to combine jest and
earnest, "to tell the truth laughing." The best satire contains the
minimum of convention, a maximum of reality: satire constantly approaches truth-telling, but truth-telling formed and limited by special
techniques.

Perhaps the most influential modern theorist about satire is
Northrop Frye, on whose definition Professor Rosenheim relies. His
description of satire is—or seems to be—simple and lucid; it reveals
the change that has taken place since Dryden's time. Only two elements are essential to satire, Professor Frye writes: "one is wit or
humor founded on fantasy or a sense of the grotesque or absurd, the
other is an object of attack."[4] Like Kernan, Rosenheim and Highet,

Frye dismisses moral purpose as a necessary component. He points out, however, that the moral norms of satire "are relatively clear, and it assumes standards against which the grotesque and absurd are measured" (p. 223). These standards need not be stated or embodied in the work, but they dominate it none the less: the author's moral awareness becomes a component of his technique.

These sketchily summarized positions may stand as representative of the modern critical view of satire. They reflect the shift in satiric practice from the eighteenth century to our own time: Pope's satires almost always contain some figure who embodies the author's moral norms and reminds us of his moral purpose; twentieth-century satire rarely includes such figures. Its "positive" characters are often naifs, protected by their innocence from the evils of the world; but innocence is not a state one can strive toward. We are conscious of passion in the satire of our own time, less aware of moral purpose. We *are* likely to be aware of special techniques which we recognize as satiric. Indeed, the modern critical descriptions of satire suggest the possibility that satire is indeed not a genre (as Dryden thought it to be) but a literary procedure, not a kind of writing but a way of writing. As a procedure it can, of course, be used in combination with other procedures. Historical circumstances may justify it, but they do not identify it. It is a means to special ends, justified by those ends, oriented always toward them.

The ends are not necessarily moral: Dryden's vision is not an adequate description of modern practice. The best account of satiric intent has been supplied by a theorist who did not propose to describe satiric effects at all. Bertolt Brecht's account of the purposes of his "epic theatre" is suggestive about the purposes of satire. In the conventional "dramatic" theatre, Brecht writes, "the stage embodies a sequence of events, involves the spectator in an action and uses up his energy, his will to action." In the epic theatre, "the stage narrates the sequence, makes [the spectator] an observer but awakes his energy." This theatre "demands decisions" of the spectator instead of allowing him feelings. It uses arguments rather than suggestion to affect the audience, and it shows man as "an object of investigation, alterable and altering," not man as a known quantity.[5] In his "Short Organum for the Theatre," Brecht wrote, "We need a type of theatre which not only releases the feelings, insights, and impulses possible within the particular historical field of human relations in which the action takes place, but employs and encourages those thoughts and feelings which help transform the field itself."[6]

The theatre Brecht imagined—and which he partially realized —strives for alienation rather than empathy in its spectators. Its aim, as the quotations above suggest, was to cause action to take place in the real world, to "transform the field itself." The audience deprived of emotional fulfillment or catharsis in the theater gains energy and impulse to change the society there depicted, to recognize the causes of its discontent, to take action against them. "Poetry makes nothing happen," wrote W. H. Auden, but Brecht dreamed of a literary art, and a theatrical enactment of it, that would in fact cause action. A similar dream is shared, I believe, by the satirist.

This is not to say that satire does make things happen in the world, only that its purposes are to some extent extra-literary, that its intent is to achieve on and through its readers some effect beyond immediate emotional impact, beyond insight, beyond the personal. Robert C. Elliott's stimulating study of satire's traditional relation to myth, magic, and ritual,[7] reminds us of the possibility that satire originated in the immediate desire to achieve psychic, military or social dominance. Satire has traditionally had a public function, and its public orientation remains. Although the satirist may arraign God and the universe (Brecht does this himself in *The Good Woman of Setzuan*), he usually seems to believe—at least to hope—that change is possible. Personal change, in his view, leads to social change; he insists that bad men make bad societies. He shows us ourselves and our world; he demands that we improve both. And he creates a kind of emotion which moves us toward the desire to change.

This kind of emotion, I would argue, is one of the most important distinguishing marks of satire: perhaps a more dependable guide than any characteristic pattern of plot, scene or character or any special technique. If it is less readily identifiable than the historical particulars that Professor Rosenheim demands, it is also less limiting. It accounts for some peculiarities of satiric effect, and it may help to clarify value judgments about satire.

What, exactly, *is* the satiric emotion? The only critic I know of who has considered this problem is Gilbert Highet, who suggests that the satiric emotion combines amusement and contempt in varying proportions. "Hatred which is not simply shocked revulsion but is based on a moral judgment, together with a degree of amusement which may range anywhere between a sour grin at the incongruity of the human condition and a delighted roar of laughter at the exposure of an absurd fraud—such are, in varying proportions, the effects of satire. When they are absent from a piece of fiction, it is not satirical."[8] This description does not seem adequate, however, to the works of Swift: amusement is hardly a component of one's response to *A Modest Proposal*, and contempt is not an adequate description of what one actually feels. There are amusing moments in the fourth book of *Gulliver*, but its most powerful sections evoke neither amusement nor contempt. It is difficult to see, moreover, why these particular emotions, alone or in combination, should create any impulse toward action. Amusement is its own fulfillment; contempt, directed toward others, is satisfying in itself, with its implication of the scorner's superiority; directed toward the self, it produces despair.

If satire sometimes generates self-satisfaction and complacency (when we can clearly identify its victims as other than ourselves), a more important satiric response is, I would suggest, uneasiness—the kind of uneasiness Brecht wished to induce in his audiences by refusing them the security and satisfaction of emotional release in the theater. In satire, as in the Brechtian theater, one is not allowed to identify with the characters; one does not *wish* to identify with them. The satiric plot, as Professor Kernan has demonstrated, does not provide the satisfaction of completion. The reader is left insecure, unanchored; if positive standards have been by implication reasserted, they have been shown as seriously threatened by reality. To resolve the insecurity, the revealed tension between *is* and *ought*, the reader must take—or plan, imagine, speculate about—action. The satirist does not give him any view of the universe which leads to exalted tragic or resigned comic acceptance. He depicts a universe full of unresolved problems. In the best satire he is likely to create level upon level of uneasiness; as our insight increases, we see ever more sharply our own involvement in tangles which it is our responsibility to unravel. In the most powerful satire, too, uneasiness plays constantly against complacency: we identify the victims as others and feel our superiority, only to find ourselves trapped a moment later, impaled by the scorn we have comfortably leveled against the rest of the world.

It has often been suggested that satire is not really possible in the twentieth century: either everything is satire or nothing is. Read a Sears Roebuck ad: "Newest U.S. M-16 Rifle Assault Weapon

System. Complete set $4.88. Dash through the underbrush, toss cap-exploding grenade and trigger off cap-firing M-16 rifle. 30-inch rifle field strips to form 3 other weapons for sniping, covering fire or close combat. Caps store in clip, scope removes. When you can, sip water from canteen. You wear a jungle bush hat, dog tags, soft 9½-inch knife in leg sheath. Plastic and metal." In the context of a catalogue full of toys, this hardly gives us a pause: it describes a common artifact of our time. Isolated, taken out of context, it seems an attack on our corrupt values, an attack which works by grotesque exaggeration: satire. The difference between the two kinds of understanding of the same paragraph is a difference in emotional response. If we read the advertisement with no response other than a judgment of the toy's entertainment value, it has no satiric effect; it we respond with an uneasiness which leads immediately to social criticism, it seems satiric.

Obviously, we never really take the Sears Roebuck ad as satire because we are aware of the commercial intent which forms it. An advertisement is not a literary phenomenon and we do not judge it as one. But there is a serious point here. The language of the blurb, like the procedures of Forest Lawn Cemetery, could be put without further heightening into a satiric context; it would then generate satiric uneasiness; it would become in effect satire.

The importance of the psychic disturbance satire creates is of course clearest and most significant in works of satiric intent. Jonathan Swift's *Modest Proposal for Preventing the Children of Ireland from being a Burden to their Parents or Country* demonstrates how effective a satiric device is the generation and complex maneuvering of the reader's uneasiness. Swift works, here as in his other satiric writing, by exploiting various degrees of awareness in his readers. One's responses to the *Modest Proposal* are likely to proceed by an orderly heightening and deepening of emotion. First the speaker presents himself as a rational, practical man. He invites our participation in his concern for Ireland, the concern of a man aware of economic realities but full of feeling as well: the first words of the piece are, "It is a melancholly Object . . ." We assume (I am trying to recapture the initial reponse to the essay: obviously a second or third reading contaminates the opening paragraphs with our knowledge of what is to come)—we assume that we are intended to identify with the speaker in his intent to make "these Children sound and useful Members of the Commonwealth,"[9] that the satiric target will be elsewhere. No uneasiness so far: everything seems set up to encourage our complacency at our ability to grasp social problems in larger and more meaningful terms than mere sentimentality.

We are not long allowed to remain in our state of self-satisfaction. The point at which we become suspicious of the speaker depends on the degree of our sensitivity. Is it at the end of the second paragraph, where his motivation seems connected with his desire to see his "Statue set up for a Preserver of the Nation"? Or in the fourth paragraph, where he refers to "a Child, *just dropt from its Dam*"? By the time we reach paragraph six, where the modest proposer treats stealing as an economic solution with no apparent awareness of any moral question associated with it, we are almost certain to have become nervous; the next paragraph, with its consideration of boys and girls as salable commodities, is positively disturbing. The suggestion that children be sold for food occurs shortly thereafter, making further identification with the speaker finally untenable.

For a moment, then, we are turned adrift. As our skepticism about the speaker's values increases, we must question our own values, which have earlier seemed to coincide with his. The speaker, we begin to feel, is the object of satire; and we, as readers, are implicated. But the resultant uneasiness soon yields to a new kind of complacency. At least now we realize more than the speaker does; we can judge him with the superiority of moralists, recognize and condemn his moral impoverishment, shudder at the barbarity which Swift's diction constantly calls to our attention.

But we are not yet secure. The next series of disturbing suggestions concerns the state of affairs the proposer's suggestions are designed to correct. First the speaker claims that cruelty "hath always been with me the strongest Objection against any Project, how well soever intended" (p. 113). Apparently he does not find his own proposal cruel. Why not? Perhaps we answer that he lacks self-knowledge, he does not realize what he is suggesting. But he goes on to describe the people, "*dying*, and *rotting*, by *Cold* and *Famine*, and *Filth*, and *Vermin*" (p. 114); to suggest that his proposal will have the advantage that "Men would become as *fond* of their Wives, during the Time of their Pregnancy, as they are now of their *Mares* in Foal, their *Cows* in Calf, or *Sows* when they are ready to farrow; nor offer to beat or kick them, (as is too *frequent* a Practice) for fear of a Miscarriage" (p. 115); to reveal that at present the poorer tenants own nothing, "their Corn and Cattle being already seized, and *Money a Thing Unknown*" (p. 115). We begin to suspect what we only feel fully at the end of the essay: that the true horror is in the state of affairs that produces the proposal, not in the proposal itself, which comes to seem more and more dreadfully plausible. Is this cannibalism not, after all, quite rational; is it not, indeed, almost inevitable under the circumstances the projector so graphically and specifically describes? "I desire the Reader will observe," he writes, "that I calculate my Remedy *for this one individual Kingdom of Ireland, and for no other that ever was, is, or, I think, ever can be upon Earth*" (p. 116). He has looked coolly at the facts of the situation; sheer rationality has led him to his solution. Centuries of traditional morality forbid us to take it seriously; still we become aware of its compelling logic. Since we cannot accept the logic we recognize, we face a new dilemma, a more radical source of uneasiness: rationality itself is being called into question. If rational thinking leads to barbarity, must we reject our commitment to it? Does our contempt for the speaker involve us in contempt for clear-headedness? Is our regard for morality mere sentimentality, and misguided sentimentality at that?

Once more, Swift rescues us: we do not have to remain in our uneasiness, we climb to a new level of security and shift from satiric uneasiness (we are implicated, we can't even understand quite how, we don't know how to get out) to satiric superiority with the list of solutions which the proposer declares to be impossible because the Irish people will not put them into practice. These solutions supply a refreshing note of sanity (they are solutions which Swift straightforwardly recommended elsewhere). We grasp at them eagerly, and note that they combine economic awareness with moral sensitivity. Shopkeepers are to have "*a Spirit of Honesty, Industry, and Skill*" (p. 116); at present they treat their customers unfairly. Absentees should be taxed, local production utilized, pride, vanity and idleness cured: throughout the long list, economic solutions merge with moral ones. We realize now that the proposer possesses rationality but not reason in the eighteenth-century definition, which makes reason a moral as well as a rational faculty (cf. the fourth book of *Gullivers Travels*). We have new grounds for feeling superior to the projector who fails by Swift's clear standards, with which we now gratefully align ourselves. But Swift is not yet through with us.

A residue of uneasiness remains after the list of positive proposals because of the speaker's firm assurance that there is unlikely ever to be "some hearty and sincere Attempt to put *them in Practice*" (p. 117). The standard of true reason is tempting, we cling to the assurance it provides, but perhaps it is irrelevant to the immediate situation. The nature of that situation suddenly becomes more vivid, in the next to the last paragraph of the essay. The projector seems to recognize the possibility of objections to his proposal, but he challenges anyone to find a counter-proposal "equally innocent, cheap, easy, and effectual." Anyone who offers another solution, he points out, must consider two points:

> First, as Things now stand, how they will be able to find Food and Raiment, for a Hundred Thousand useless Mouths and Backs? And *Secondly*, There being a round Million of Creatures in human Figure, throughout this Kingdom; whose whole Subsistence, put into a common Stock, would leave them in Debt two Millions of Pounds *Sterling*; adding those, who are Beggars by Profession, to the Bulk of Farmers, Cottagers and Labourers, with their Wives and Children, who are Beggars in Effect; I desire those Politicians, who dislike my Overture, and may perhaps be so bold to attempt an Answer, that they will first ask the Parents of these Mortals, Whether they would not at this Day think it a great Happiness to have been sold for Food at a Year old, in the Manner I prescribe; and thereby have avoided such a perpetual Scene of Misfortunes, as they have since gone through; by the *Oppression of Landlords*; the Impossibility of paying Rent, without Money or Trade; the Want of common Sustenance, with neither House nor Cloaths, to cover them from the Inclemencies of the Weather; and the most inevitable Prospect of intailing the like, or greater Miseries upon their Breed for ever. (pp. 117–18)

This paragraph introduces no important new facts. With great economy and point, it reviews data previously presented, and it suggests—almost enforces—the cataclysmic shift of perspective hinted earlier. Through most of the essay we have felt secure in our superiority to the projector. If we waver briefly in our assurance about the grounds of our superiority, we proceed to the conviction that by the highest standards we can judge him and find him wanting. Now, though, his calm rationality suggests that he might with equal validity judge us and find us wanting. The people he describes would think it a happiness to be sold for food, to avoid the horrors of the life they live. The proposal that they be so sold is barbarous; the situation that might lead the victims to welcome it is worse. Most people, of course, accept the starvation, helplessness, hopelessness of masses of others with perfect equanimity. The modest proposer has offered an intolerable solution to an intolerable situation. We judge his solution inhuman, and condemn him for suggesting it. But if the situation is worse than the solution, if it is even equally bad, surely the people who accept it as the given state of affairs, who coolly evaluate solutions and reject proposals and proposers alike without themselves doing anything to alleviate the problem—surely such people must be condemned. And who are they? The piece becomes an indictment of the people of Ireland, who do nothing about their plight, and of the people of England, who do nothing either; and, like so much of Swift's work, it reaches out beyond its time and place to indict the twentieth-century reader who accepts as inevitable man's inhumanity to man, who rests secure in his reason and morality without involving himself in the horror of social inequity. Swift's positive standards include humanity as well as reason. If we take his essay seriously, allow ourselves to be affected by it, we are left in a state of profound uneasiness, recognizing our involvement in the evil to which we have earlier felt superior.

It is dangerous to try to specify what a reader's reaction will be to any work of art. There are readers and readers; there are even readers who remain unaffected by Swift's manipulations, who read *A Tale of a Tub* without questioning their own sanity or the standards by which they judge sanity, read the fourth book of *Gulliver* without wondering about their own self-satisfactions. One can only try to specify the effects the work of art seems to demand; and the most important effect demanded by the *Modest Proposal* is profound disturbance, achieved by the development of various levels of uneasiness and complacency.

There is no critical disagreement about the fundamental satiric intent of the *Modest Proposal;* but the idea of uneasiness as a crucial satiric emotion is also useful in leading us to recognize satiric effects where the intent is less clear. A case in point is *Joseph Andrews,* which originated, we are told, in a desire to burlesque the assumptions of *Pamela* but unquestionably turned into more than burlesque. What, exactly, it turned into remains a vexed question. Most critics feel that it is comedy with touches of satire; I would argue that the satiric effect is more complex than is commonly supposed.

It is easy to make a case for this novel as comic—fundamentally sympathetic toward its characters, causing us to love life rather than to criticize it. Fielding's positive values are apparent: honesty, integrity, simplicity, charity. By these values Joseph and Parson Adams are successful throughout. They are frequently ridiculous by ordinary social standards, but if we judge by such superficial standards we only demonstrate our own corruption. Their simplicity makes them seem foolish in a sophisticated and corrupt world, but their dignity survives, as in the episode where Adams is mauled by dogs and mocked by men, yet remains at all points the clear moral superior of his tormentors. Fielding recognizes the imperfectibility of human nature; he gives his characters flaws, causes them to demonstrate their weaknesses, but he loves their humanity. He responds to the comedy of pretension; as he says himself, his main concern here is "affectation" in all its forms. But although Beau Didapper or Parson Trulliber may suffer the full force of satiric condemnation, the enveloping tone of the novel is benign; human affairs work out at the end in a way which suggests that the universe itself is benign; like classic comedies, the novel ends with a marriage.

This description does not, however, account for the complicated feelings which the novel is likely to generate in its readers. In the first chapter of Book III, Fielding remarks, "I describe not men, but manners; not an individual, but a species."[10] As an example he uses the lawyer in the stage coach who argues for an act of charity on the grounds of self-interest. Such men, Fielding says, have always existed. This lawyer should not be taken as a portrait of any specific living person: it would do him "little honour to imagine he endeavours to mimic some little obscure fellow, because he happens to resemble him in one particular feature, or perhaps in his profession; whereas his appearance in the world is calculated for much more general and noble purposes; not to expose one pitiful wretch to the small and contemptible circle of his acquaintance; but to hold the glass to thousands in their closets, that they may contemplate their deformity, and endeavour to reduce it, and thus by suffering private mortification may avoid public shame. This places the boundary between, and distinguishes the satirist from the libeller: for the former privately corrects the fault for the benefit of the person, like a parent; the latter publicly exposes the person himself, as an example to others, like an executioner" (p. 159).

The distinction Fielding here makes between the private effect of satire and the public one of libel resembles that between uneasiness, the response to recognition of one's own flaws ("private mortification"), and complacency, the response to the evil of others. In fact, the characterization of the lawyer in the coach would seem more likely to produce the second response. It belongs to a group of characterizations in the novel which have been generally recognized as satiric in their broad strokes of caricature and their systematic presentation of social types. Such characterizations, although they are acute in their social observation, do not examine individual springs of action. Sometimes a sentence suffices to reveal a man. The famous coach scene provides abundant examples. First the postilion suggests that there is a "dead man" groaning in the ditch:

> "Go on, sirrah," says the coachman; "we are confounded late, and have no time to look after dead men." A lady, who heard what the postilion said, and likewise heard the groan, called eagerly to the coachman to stop and see what was the matter. Upon which he bid the postilion alight, and look into the ditch. He did so, and returned, "That there was a man sitting upright as naked as ever he was born."—"O J-sus!" cried the lady; "a naked man! Dear coachman, drive on and leave him." Upon this the gentlemen got out of the coach; and Joseph begged them to have mercy upon him; for that he had been robbed, and almost beaten to death. "Robbed!" cries an old gentleman: "let us make all the haste imaginable, or we shall be robbed too"— (p. 42)

The lawyer then points out that they might be in legal jeopardy if they fled after noticing the man's existence; they should rescue him for fear of what a jury might find. The lady remarks that "she had rather stay in that place to all eternity than ride with a naked man." The coachman wants to know who will pay a shilling for Joseph's carriage; the lawyer threatens him with an indictment for murder if he refuses to carry the young man; the old gentleman decides that "the naked man would afford him frequent opportunities of showing his wit to the lady," and the various arguments of self-interest finally combine to effect Joseph's rescue.

Fielding feels no need for direct authorial comment on these bits of action and dialogue; they are self-sufficiently revealing, their meaning depending on their conjunction as well as on the facts of each individual case. Only the lady seems controlled by that principle of affectation which Fielding has declared to be his central issue; the others, confronted with the Biblical situation of a naked man in a ditch, reveal without disguise their limited and selfish concerns; the satiric bite and focus are inescapable.

When Joseph begins to function in relation to this group, he is their clear moral superior, though the satirist's eye turns on him, too. "Joseph was now advancing to the coach, where, seeing the lady, who held the sticks of her fan before her eyes, he absolutely refused, miserable as he was, to enter, unless he was furnished with sufficient covering to prevent giving the least offence to decency. So perfectly modest was this young man; such mighty effects had the spotless example of the amiable Pamela, and the excellent sermons of Mr. Adams, wrought upon him" (p. 43). The riders in the coach act and speak by their conceptions of their social roles. The coach-man worries about his fees and his schedule, the lady about her modesty, the lawyer thinks only of his profession. The old gentleman considers himself first as a man of wealth, later as a man of wit. Joseph, in contrast, governs himself by moral rather than social principles. He is manifestly less corrupt than his social superiors; he thinks about others rather than only about himself (although one may speculate that his ultimate concern is with his own "self-image"); yet he is hardly less ridiculous than the lady whose modesty he fears to offend. Perfect modesty is a virtue, by Fielding's standards and even by ours. Yet to place its value before that of life itself seems misguided, and Fielding's invocation of "the spotless example of the amiable Pamela" at this point suggests his ironic awareness of the fact.

In another context such an episode might be taken as sheer comedy rather than satire, an amusing perception of the common weakness of mortals with no serious intent of criticism. But in this novel it functions as one of many episodes of the same kind, and the total structure makes a satiric network which involves the reader, forces him to self-examination in the privacy of his closet, however different he may be in all obvious respects from Joseph and Parson Adams at one extreme, from Beau Didapper at the other. Over and over *Joseph Andrews* calls our attention to people's deep conviction of their own rightness. Much of the comedy of the early scenes comes from the tension between Lady Booby's unshakable self-confidence ("Have you the assurance to pretend, that when a lady demeans herself to throw aside the rules of decency, in order to honour you with the highest favour in her power, your virtue should resist her inclination?" p. 32) and Joseph's equally unshakable confidence in the importance of his own virtue ("I can't see why her having no virtue should be a reason against my having any." p. 32). The narrowest and pettiest of mortals believe that the laws by which they govern themselves are immutable principles: Parson Trulliber, Beau Didapper, Lawyer Scout, the practical jokers who set upon Adams and attack Fanny's virtue. Parson Adams, most large-spirited of men, has a similar conviction: so he alienates the generous host of the inn by stubbornly opposing theory to fact, insisting that "a skilful physiognomist will rarely be deceived" (p. 155) in the face of his own deception by the owner of a kindly face. So he preaches fortitude under distress, but is quite unable to practise it. Joseph refusing Lady Booby or refusing to ride in the coach is similarly governed by theory rather than awareness of actuality. The difference between the "good" and the "bad" characters is that in the knaves, bad theory produces bad practice; when Joseph and Adams fill the satiric role of fools, it is because their good theories are inadequate to their complex experience. The good theory that men should be chaste makes Joseph insensitive, tactless and priggish in speech, but he refuses Lady Booby's advances; the related theory that modesty is vital makes him act foolishly in placing feminine sensibilities before survival. The good theory that Christians should be patient in distress makes Parson Adams talk rather than act when Fanny's virtue is endangered; it helps him not at all in his own brief bereavement. But foolish or wise, practical or impractical, vicious or virtuous, every character in the novel retains an unalterable belief in the justice of his own principles, perceptions and actions. Lady Booby finds in herself a conflict of principles, her belief in the importance of rank and wealth clashing with her belief in her right to self-indulgence, but she really questions neither, although she pays lip-service to "virtue."

Lady Booby's talk of virtue ("How much more exquisite is the pleasure resulting from the reflection of virtue and prudence than the faint relish of what flows from vice and folly! Whither did I suffer this improper, this mad passion to hurry me, only by neglecting to summon the aids of reason to my assistance?" pp. 282-83) exemplifies another theme and technique of the novel, closely related to its moral considerations. Fielding repeatedly calls attention to his own language or to that of his characters to dramatize the gap which may exist between language and substance, form and content. Lady

Booby prating of virtue is thinking of lust; she adopts the language of the heroine of a sentimental novel or tragedy to disguise even to herself her true feelings and concerns. The dichotomy between tone and substance is yet more conspicuous in the mock-heroic sections where Fielding treats mundane affairs in epic vein; at the opposite extreme, he offers a commonplace explanation of his practice of dividing his work into books and chapters: "it becomes an author generally to divide a book, as it does a butcher to join his meat, for such assistance is of great help to both the reader and the carver" (p. 75). Sometimes the two techniques co-exist: an elaborate satiric panegyric to Vanity precedes a down-to-earth disclaimer: "I know thou wilt think that, whilst I abuse thee, I court thee, and that thy love hath inspired me to write this sarcastical panegyric on thee; but thou art deceived: I value thee not of a farthing; nor will it give me any pain if thou shouldst prevail on the reader to censure this digression as arrant nonsense; for know, to thy confusion, that I have introduced thee for no other purpose than to lengthen out a short chapter; and so I return to my history" (p. 57). The effect is constantly to violate expectation—a comic effect but, in this case, a satiric one as well. If, as I believe, the satiric center of the novel is the human tendency to be sure of oneself in exactly the situations where one should doubt, Fielding's repeated demonstration that language is not a safe guide to meaning—but that men (and women) treat it as though they could impose meaning at will on their experience—participates in the satiric statement. "The question is, which is to be master," as Humpty Dumpty remarked in another satiric work centrally concerned with language. On one level, Lawyer Scout manipulates language to make the law conform to the desires of his patroness; Lady Booby uses language to conceal reality; Mrs. Slipslop in her Malapropisms dramatizes the arbitrariness of linguistic impositions. On another level, the novelist himself plays with linguistic modes to demonstrate the lack of necessary relation between form and content. On a more profound level still, the reader finds himself involved in the problem of certainty. Like the characters, he wants to be sure of meanings; unlike them, he has had his attention called to the gulfs beneath his feet. The cavalier fashion in which comedy resolves its problems, creating infinite complications, unraveling them with scant regard to probability, becomes itself part of the satiric meaning. In a universe full of arbitrary events, where the most pious theory is inadequate to the demands of experience, where can sureness be found? Fielding's answer, of course, is that one can be sure of the value of virtue in action. Honesty, integrity, simplicity, charity, the positive values of this satire, provide the only security as they are exemplified in practice. But the human need to locate sureness in theory finds no answer in Fielding's universe. And one's uneasiness at being forced to recognize this fact, and to recognize one's own participation in the fruitless human attempt to assert more certainty than exists, is the satiric response.

It is not an intense or agonized response; uneasiness can be a gentle, almost a subliminal, emotion. Inasmuch as Fielding's satire involves Joseph and Parson Adams and finally the reader, it is gentle satire, close to the line of comedy. (Contrast the relative satiric intensity of the presentation of Mrs. Tow-wouse or Lawyer Scout.) But gentle satire is still satire, and mild uneasiness still uneasiness, as Pope pointed out in a letter concerned with *The Rape of the Lock*, most gentle of satires: "This whimsical piece of work, as I have now brought it up to my first design, is at once the most a satire, and the most inoffensive, of anything of mine. People who would rather it were let alone laugh at it, and seem heartily merry, at the same time that they are uneasy. 'Tis a sort of writing very like tickling."[11]

Pope here suggests his awareness that uneasiness is the natural response to satire and that it can co-exist with responses very different in kind, and he hints that the co-existence of contradictory emotions in a reader may be an index of literary quality. The faint uneasiness created by *The Rape of the Lock* and the intense moral disturbance generated by *A Modest Proposal* indicate the polar possibilities of satiric response. On the other hand, a work that evokes no real uneasiness in the reader is in effect not a satire at all. It may at one time have been one: a case in point is Dryden's *Mac Flecknoe*, which satiric theorists unaccountably tend to group with Pope's *Dunciad*. The two poems seem to me dramatically different. The *Dunciad*, like Dante's *Inferno* (a work which also has its moments of satiric intensity), impales and immortalizes the poet's personal enemies by giving them more than personal significance. Like Sporus, Atossa, Balaam in Pope's shorter satires, Bentley and Theobald and Cibber, even such minor characters as James Ralph, become emblematic of moral and intellectual failings which have existed in all times and places. Any twentieth-century reader of intellectual pretensions— surely any reader who has ever thought of himself as a critic—can hardly avoid feeling disturbed at the possibility, the probability, that he participates in the sins here so conclusively damned. One reads

Mac Flecknoe with a kind of innocent joy. If it was ever true satire, if Shadwell ever seemed to exemplify faults beyond himself, it has become with the passage of time mere lampoon. Lampoon, to be sure, of the highest order: Dryden's wit, verve, inventiveness display his own superiority to the poetaster he mocks, demonstrate in action the value of true poetic power. The positive values of the poem survive; its target has shrunk. Although *Mac Flecknoe* may achieve a moral effect on its readers through its embodiment of its positive values, it works entirely through the response of complacency (we are not, thank God, such as Shadwell) without creating any real disturbance.

Or a work existing in a satiric borderland (the borders, as Northrop Frye has illustrated, are comedy and tragedy) may be satire for some readers, not for others. *Alice in Wonderland* seems to some adults an entertaining fantasy with Freudian overtones. Others find it a satiric attack on the values, assumptions and procedures of the adult world which reveals the hypocrisy, arbitrariness and cruelty of that world through the eyes of a child. Alice's curious versions of the poems she has been taught frequently embody the true as opposed to the professed values of the world in which she is growing up. The adult reader perceptive of satiric nuance finds himself implicated, sees himself as almost one of the mythical creatures surrounding Alice. He may be more disturbed than Lewis Carroll could have intended by the fact that the positive standards of the satire are contained in the idea of childish innocence, a state which can only be yearned for and regretted, never re-achieved. In its romantic image of the child (this despite the fact that it demonstrates awareness of the child's potentiality for cruelty, unfairness, thoughtlessness) *Alice in Wonderland* seems a typical nineteenth-century product; yet in its satiric implications it foreshadows the despair characteristic of twentieth-century satire, which exposes a corrupt world, demonstrates the power of intelligence in understanding the evil which surrounds us, but offers no hope of significant change.

Some twentieth-century satire attempts too easy a way. Barbara Garson's *Mac Bird* has been hailed in some quarters as brilliant contemporary satire. The response it evokes, it seems to me, is complacency without uneasiness: in other words, it lacks the perceptual complexity of true satire. Certainly it begins with a clever, if rather collegiate, idea, the notion that light can be shed on our current political corruption by placing it in a Shakespearean context. The implementation of the idea does not equal the conception. The author seems out of control of her material, unable even to manipulate the plot so that it says what she wants to say. (She has published several disclaimers of any serious intent to suggest that President Johnson was involved in the assassination of President Kennedy.) Her ear for verse rhythms is crude, her sense of humor obvious; the play contains no real surprises and achieves no authority. Those who admire it tend to be those who share the political convictions from which it derives. They find it a satisfying attack on the enemy. In no way are they involved or judged or questioned by the action or the language; if the play causes in them uneasiness about the state of the nation, this is not the satiric kind of uneasiness. Mrs. Garson's effort is likely to generate only self-satisfaction in its admirers. For those who do not share the play's political stance it seems tasteless or irrelevant or both. It enforces no new awareness; it asserts, rather than engineers assent. In order to evoke uneasiness, satire must be convincing, or at least compelling. This kind of pseudo-satire—it is really burlesque or travesty—convinces only those who are convinced already. It lacks the genuine satiric tickle.

Mac Bird is by no means representative of twentieth-century satiric acievement; I have discussed it only because its critical reception suggests some questions about the response to satire. More interesting directions for satire emerge in the political allegories of Huxley and Orwell; the social commentary of early Waugh, early Kingsley Amis, late Anthony Burgess; the verse of W.H. Auden and Robert Lowell (whose recent version of Juvenal's *Vanity of Human Wishes* exemplifies vital differences between classical and modern conceptions of satire's function); the science fiction of Kurt Vonnegut, Jr.; the songs of Tom Lehrer, the skits of Mike Nichols and Elaine May, of Flanders and Swann. All these works appeal to a limited audience, if only because none but limited groups now hold standards in common. All involve their audiences in a special tension of perception, encourage complacent superiority only to shatter it, tease the onlooker until he does not know whether he feels pleasure or pain. Such has always been the special achievement of satire.

NOTES

[1] John Dryden, *Of Dramatic Poesy and Other Critical Essays*, ed. George Watson, II (London, 1962), 143.

[2] Edward W. Rosenheim, Jr., *Swift and the Satirist's Art* (Chicago, 1963), p. 31.

3 Gilbert Highest, *The Anatomy of Satire* (Princeton, 1962), pp. 14–23.

4 Northrop Frye, *Anatomy of Criticism* (Princeton, 1957), p. 224.

5 Quoted in Eric Bentley, *The Playwright as Thinker* (New York, 1957), p. 215.

6 Bertolt Brecht, "A Short Organum for the Theatre" (1948), tr. John Willett, in *Playwrights on Playwriting*, ed. Toby Cole (New York, 1960), pp. 85–86.

7 *The Power of Satire: Magic, Ritual, Art* (Princeton, 1960).

8 *Anatomy of Satire*, p. 150.

9 *The Prose Works of Jonathan Swift*, ed. Herbert Davis, Vol. XII: *Irish Tracts, 1728–1733* (Oxford, 1955), p. 109. Succeeding page references to the *Modest Proposal* are to this text.

10 Henry Fielding, *Joseph Andrews and Pamela*, ed. Martin C. Battestin (Boston, 1961), p. 159. Succeeding page references to *Joseph Andrews* are to this text.

11 Letter to Mrs. or Miss Marriot, 28 February [1713/14], *The Correspondence of Alexander Pope*, ed. George Sherburn, I (Oxford, 1956), 211.